Cloud Computing Patterns

Christoph Fehling • Frank Leymann •
Ralph Retter • Walter Schupeck •
Peter Arbitter

Cloud Computing Patterns

Fundamentals to Design, Build, and Manage Cloud Applications

 Springer

Christoph Fehling
University of Stuttgart
Stuttgart
Germany

Frank Leymann
University of Stuttgart
Stuttgart
Germany

Ralph Retter
T-Systems International GmbH
Frankfurt
Germany

Walter Schupeck
Daimler AG
Stuttgart
Germany

Peter Arbitter
Microsoft Deutschland GmbH
Unterschleißheim
Germany

Additional material to this book can be downloaded from http://extra.springer.com.

ISBN 978-3-7091-1953-2   ISBN 978-3-7091-1568-8 (eBook)
DOI 10.1007/978-3-7091-1568-8
Springer Wien Heidelberg New York Dordrecht London

Printed on acid-free paper

Springer is part of Springer Science+Business Media (www.springer.com)

To Carina and my parents, Elisabeth and Horst.   Thank you for your love and support.
— Christoph

To the woman of my dreams!
– Frank

To Anni and Emil.
– Ralph

To my grandsons Leonardo and Max Viktor.
– Walter

To Annika, Paulina, Nils, and my lovely wife Martina.
– Peter

Foreword by Gregor Hohpe

Over the recent years, you may have observed a strategy, dare I say "pattern," for software engineering books: take a popular buzzword and append the word "patterns" to suggest that this particular title contains a substantial treatment of the subject matter and is organized as a collection of easy to digest chapters, which promise to provide solutions to recurring problems. For the pattern community, this is a definite sign of success, and not one that is due to large marketing budgets but rather many successful titles that deliver on this very promise. A recent search on the "world's largest bookstore" in the category "Books – Software Development" yielded no less than 499 titles containing the word "patterns." How does one pick out the gems from such a vast collection of solutions to recurring problems?

First, good patterns books present a coherent pattern language, not just a collection of patterns, in line with Christopher Alexander's seminal title *A Pattern Language*. Structuring a pile of patterns into a sequence of chapters is laudable but does not make a language. Rather, a pattern language covers a specific domain and usually offers multiple patterns for common design challenges and offers a clear road map through the patterns.

Many influential software patterns books have also adopted a strong visual language. I may be biased because *Enterprise Integration Patterns* was one of the first titles to expand the notion of a pattern *sketch* to a visually coherent iconic language, but because software architecture and specifically software patterns aim to communicate complex design ideas in an easy-to-grasp way, a visual language is a strong asset.

Almost all significant software patterns books are not simply the result of the authors' deep insight or determination but have been a true community effort. For example, the Pattern Languages of Programming (PLoP) conference, which has been running since 1994, has been the birthplace of many great patterns books. While it is certainly not a requirement for pattern authors to workshop their papers at PLoP, the claim that patterns are harvested rather than invented points to the importance of community participation. This also means that good patterns books don't usually pop out of nowhere but are the pinnacle of a lengthy process of stepwise refinement based on community feedback.

Last but not least, most successful patterns books strike a delicate balance between academic rigor and real-world applications. The academic world brings depth of thinking and a clear structure, while the industry contributes the required validation and real-world examples.

If you are wondering why the foreword to *Cloud Computing Patterns* muses about the pattern movement as a whole, I invite you to revisit after reading this title. I hope you will agree that I was in fact describing the essential properties of *cloud computing patterns*! I have not much left to say but congratulate the authors on the successful delivery of a relevant, well-structured, and community-validated software patterns title. Because I am sure I won't have to convince you that cloud computing is one of the most relevant software engineering topics of the last decade.

– Gregor Hohpe, coauthor of *Enterprise Integration Patterns* (Hohpe, G., Woolf B.: Enterprise Integration Patterns: Designing, Building, and Deploying Messaging Solutions. Addison-Wesley. http://www.eaipatterns.com/ (2003)).

Gregor Hohpe

Foreword by Robert Hanmer

The forecast for computing is full of clouds. The computer press and the public media are abuzz with "cloud-this" and "cloud-that," but what does it all mean? In many industries, service providers are looking to the cloud to help simplify their hardware management and increase their flexibility and adaptability to change and to provide new and innovative services, but much of what's written about clouds is about the nuts and bolts and offerings of specific cloud providers. The big picture of how to build useful and robust applications to support business needs on top of clouds is missing. Specific case studies are useful, but they can be limiting because they also are tied to specifics. What's needed is a resource to understand the ins and outs of clouds and how they can be used from a top-down perspective. This book is that resource.

I first met the authors at the 2011 Pattern Languages of Programming Conference in Portland, OR, USA. They submitted a paper to the conference that was about early work that ultimately led to this book. Because a paper about clouds was timely, it was one of the most popular papers at the conference. Everyone wanted to learn more about clouds, and all were intrigued by the range of cloud solutions studied to understand the patterns.

Patterns in the style of Christopher Alexander and the *Design Patterns* book [2] (aka the Gang of Four - GOF patterns) are based on real-life experiences and proven practices, not unproven theories. The successes, failures, and "aha's" of real-life solutions were captured in these patterns which were mined from projects across several industries. The authors aren't trying to sell clouds and they aren't just patting themselves on the back because they've built something nice with clouds. They explain clouds based on what they've seen work in practice. The topics range from the basics of on-demand self-service, broad network access, pay per use, and rapid elasticity to complex topics like structuring multi-tier applications and how to best handle issues like fault tolerance and performance.

Patterns explain not just what a cloud is or what you must do to effectively use a cloud but also explain the trade-offs involved in using the cloud. The patterns tie the cloud definitions back to the NIST Definitions of Cloud Computing [3] to thoroughly cover the topic. I agree with the authors that the pattern form is a good way to explain clouds, because patterns explain the design decisions and trade-offs you must be aware of to build an effective cloud solution. The authors' experiences help you to know why things are the way they are as well as highlight how to work around or benefit from that rationale.

You'll find seven chapters in this book. Each chapter contains many patterns, which describe a solution to a problem with an explanation of why that solution is the right one. The chapters build from the basic fundamentals of the NIST definition of a cloud all the way to cloud application shapes and sizes. In between, the authors cover the basics of the different kinds of cloud offerings that you'll find and the basics of designing your solution's cloud architecture and how to manage your cloud. The last chapter talks about problems and pitfalls to avoid, for example, the mismatch between the requirements imposed from the bottom up by the cloud providers and the requirements pressing downward from the business analysts.

I especially like the author's treatment of non-functional requirements. They don't ignore the issue of fault tolerance and robustness which would give you a view of only the sunniest days ahead. This book points out that the rapid elasticity of the cloud is not a guarantee of high reliability by itself but that further design principles like elasticity and resiliency management are needed to ensure that the application achieves the required level of reliability and availability.

I think that this book will help us all better utilize the cloud. And it's a good example of using patterns to explain a complex topic. The scope of computing-related patterns is expanded from the range of technical domains like fault-tolerant software and small memory systems to enterprise applications and then all the way towards structuring complete business processes and environments like we see here with cloud computing.

Cloud-this and cloud-that are explained in this book, which will help you prepare for whatever the cloudy future of computing delivers.

– Robert S. Hanmer, author of *Patterns for Fault Tolerant Software* (Hanmer, R.: Patterns for Fault Tolerant Software. Wiley, Chichester (2007)).

Robert Hanmer

Preface

Which is the right cloud computing provider for my company?
How do I use the cloud computing products of a certain provider and how do they compare to the products I already have in place? We use an infrastructure as a service platform already. What is different now?
How does cloud computing impact existing applications if they are moved to the cloud?
How can I use cloud computing to reduce provisioning and setup times, so my users can access servers more quickly?

During the past years of our collaborative research and consulting on cloud computing, we often encountered these questions or very similar ones. Often, these questions were driven by the need to rapidly produce results in big enterprise cloud initiatives that were founded with the ambitious goals to reduce the cost of IT tremendously and make provisioning of IT resources faster. We also encountered a general trend that cloud computing initiatives are often driven *bottom-up*, starting with infrastructure automation activities. These initiatives, therefore, tend to focus on the IT infrastructure and how to change its setup, deployment, and management and leave application architecture standards for the enterprise untouched. Results are company-internal infrastructure-as-a-service offerings that can provision virtual servers in a fast and efficient manner via a self-service portal. In this book, we describe how cloud computing changed IT infrastructure provisioning and management as well, but mainly we focus on the following questions:

How does cloud computing change the architecture of applications using it efficiently? How can I use cloud infrastructure and platform offerings to efficiently and rapidly design, build, and manage applications to support the changing needs of my business?

Many products found in the cloud computing market display similar functionality that customers may use to build their cloud applications. The discussions of IT architects and developers are often hindered by different product names, provider-specific terminologies, the different distributions of common functionality among products, as well as the fact that some products are merely *cloud-washed*, and thus their name is extended with the term "cloud" to make them more attractive. In our research, we, therefore, analyzed cloud products as well as applications built using different cloud vendors and cloud computing technologies. The goal of this analysis has been to extract common behavior and common components of cloud products as well as the common architecture principles involved to build cloud applications. The result is the book you hold in your hands.

The reason for abstracting from existing cloud providers and cloud applications is to capture provider-independent and sustainable knowledge abstracted from concrete products. This abstract description covers how to build cloud applications, how different cloud products behave, and when to choose a particular form of a cloud offering given a concrete usage scenario.

What You Will Learn and What This Book Is About and Not About

In this book, we build upon our experiences and approach cloud computing principles with a *top-down* mind-set. The goal of this book is not to show you the benefits of cloud infrastructure automation technology over traditional data centers but to show you how cloud principles can be supported on the business and application layers. This book should give you nuggets of advice in the form of patterns that allow you to better understand how you can support cloud properties on the application level and how to select appropriate cloud infrastructure and platform offerings to make your life easier. Furthermore, this book gives IT architects and developers a common vocabulary when discussing about cloud products and architectures of custom cloud applications without focusing on a concrete cloud provider.

During our consulting and research experiences, we often missed the abstraction of cloud definitions from concrete provider offerings and vendor products. Thus, we chose to use a pattern-based approach to describe cloud offerings vendor neutrally in our technical report (Fehling, C., Leymann, F., Mietzner, R., Schupeck, W.: A collection of patterns for cloud types, cloud service models, and cloud-based application architectures. Technical report, University of Stuttgart) in 2011. As this approach proved very popular wherever we presented and discussed it, we decided to revise and extend this approach and the resulting pattern catalogue into what you will find in this book. In order to not lose track with reality, we describe the essential properties of a pattern and then add concrete providers and vendor offerings where we are aware of them in "known uses" sections of the pattern. These sections are by no means exhaustive; they should give you an initial idea on providers and vendors offering a product that exhibits the properties described in the pattern.

If you take this book as a catalogue of patterns that will help you to design, build, and manage *cloud-native* applications as well as select suitable cloud infrastructure and platform offerings, it will provide you with the most value. We wish you as much motivation and satisfaction reading about and applying the patterns in the book as we had collecting and presenting them at various conferences and events. For further information, please also refer to:

http://www.cloudcomputingpatterns.org   Christoph Fehling
Germany   Frank Leymann
                                                         Ralph Retter
                                                         Walter Schupeck
                                                         Peter Arbitter

Trademarks

The use of general descriptive names, registered names, trademarks, service marks, etc. in this publication does not imply, even in the absence of a specific statement, that such names are exempt from the relevant protective laws and regulations and, therefore, free for general use. While the advice and information in this book are believed to be true and accurate at the date of publication, neither the authors nor the editors nor the publisher can accept any legal responsibility for any errors or omissions that may be made. The publisher makes no warranty, expressed or implied, with respect to the material contained herein.

The authors have tried to identify all trademarks mentioned in this book; however, some may have been missed. Thus, all other names mentioned in this book may be trademarks or registered trademarks of other companies. The authors acknowledge all of these that have not been included in the following list. The following trademarks or registered trademarks are the property of the following organizations:

MongoDB is Registered Trademark of 10gen, Inc.

Acronis is Registered Trademark of Acronis International GmbH.

Akamai is Trademark of Akamai Technologies.

Amazon CloudFront, Amazon CloudWatch, Amazon EC2, Amazon Elastic Beanstalk, Amazon Elastic Compute Cloud, Amazon RDS, Amazon Relational Database, Amazon S3, Amazon Simple Queue Service, Amazon Simple Storage Service, Amazon SimpleDB, Amazon SQS, Amazon Web Services, AWS, AWS Import/Export, CloudFront, EC2, SimpleDB, SQS are Trademarks or Registered Trademarks of Amazon Web Services LLC.

OS X is Registered Trademark of Apple Inc.

Xen is Registered Trademark of Citrix Systems, Inc.

SFPark is Registered Trademark of City and County of San Francisco.

CloudBees is Registered Trademark of CloudBees Inc.

CloudFlare is Registered Trademark of CloudFlare Inc.

Crashplan is Trademark of Code 42 Software.

Cordys is Trademark of Cordys B.V.

DMTF is Trademark of Distributed Management Task Force, Inc.

Dropbox is Trademark or Registered Trademark of Dropbox Inc.

Gladinet is Trademark or Registered Trademark of Gladinet Inc.

Google App Engine and Google Web Toolkit are Trademarks of Google Inc.

DB2, IBM SmartCloud, MQSeries, System Z, Websphere are Trademarks or Registered Trademarks of International Business Machines Corporation (IBM).

IEEE is Trademark of IEEE.

Jclouds is Trademark of Jclouds, Inc.

Linux is Registered Trademark of Linus Torvalds.

Hyper-V, Office 365, SQL Azure, SQL Server, Windows, Windows Azure, Active Server Pages (ASP.net), Microsoft are Trademarks or Registered Trademarks of Microsoft Corporation.

Metasonic is Trademark or Registered Trademark of Metasonic AG.

NOAA is Registered Trademark of National Oceanic and Atmospheric Administration.

OASIS is Trademark of the OASIS consortium.

OpenNebula is Trademark of OpenNebula Project.

OpenStack is Registered Trademark of OpenStack Foundation.

Java, MySQL, Oracle, VirtualBox are Trademarks or Registered Trademarks of Oracle Corporation.

Python is Registered Trademark of Python Software Foundation (PSF).

Rackspace is Registered Trademark of Rackspace US, Inc.

JBoss is Registered Trademark of Red Hat, Inc.

RightScale is Registered Trademark of RightScale, Inc.

RunMyProcess is Trademark of RunMyProcess SAS.

Force is Registered Trademark of salesforce.com.

Salesforce is Registered Trademark of salesforce.com.

SAP is Registered Trademark of SAP AG.

Scalr is Registered Trademark of Scalr Inc.

Storsimple is Trademark or Registered Trademark of Storsimple Inc.

Apache CouchDB, Apache, Apache ActiveMQ, Apache Camel, Apache CouchDB, Apache Hadoop, Apache Libcloud, Apache Tomcat, Libcloud, Apache Cassandra, Apache ODE are Trademarks or Registered Trademarks of The Apache Software Foundation.

PHP is Registered Trademark of The PHP Group.

CloudFoundry, vCenter, vCenter Converter, Vmware are Trademarks or Registered Trademarks of VMware, Inc.

WSO2 is Registered Trademark of WSO2, Inc.

Acknowledgments

This book would not have been possible without the support of many persons with whom we discussed architectural styles, the individual cloud computing patterns, and cloud computing in general. Even though these discussions may not have been related to the writing of this book directly, they were essential to our understanding of cloud computing, architectural patterns, their creation, and their use.

For a first feedback to our research results, we would like to thank all participants of the writers' workshop held at the 2011 Conference on Pattern Languages of Programs (PLoP). Ernst Oberortner provided excellent feedback on our first patterns and Ralph E. Johnson was a great workshop leader and teacher. Their feedback helped us to present the first book draft at the 2012 Chili Conference on Pattern Languages of Programs (ChiliPLoP), where the book was discussed in detail. Especially, we would like to thank Richard P. Gabriel, Joseph W. Yoder, and Anthony Kwiatkowski for the detailed discussions. For continuous reviews of this book during its writing and significant help, we would also like to thank

Olaf Zimmermann

Robert Hanmer

This book was not only influenced by persons who helped us write and improve it but also by our colleagues and friends with whom we enjoyed doing research in the area of cloud computing. We would like to thank David Schumm, Daniel Schleicher, Oliver Kopp, Tammo van Lessen, Tolga Dalman, Thilo Ewald, and Jochen Rütschlin for the time we worked together. Finally, this book was not only influenced by our work but also by our personal life. We would like to thank our families and friends for supporting us during this time and patiently enduring "book-writing moods," especially Carina Traut, Sven Tschersich, and Anni Retter as well as little Emil.

Contents

1 Introduction 1
1.1 Essential Cloud Computing Properties 3
1.2 Essential Cloud Application Properties 5
1.3 Use of Patterns for Cloud Computing 7
1.4 Pattern Format Used in This Book 9
1.5 Overview of This Book 11
1.6 How to Read This Book 13

2 Cloud Computing Fundamentals 21
2.1 Overview of Fundamental Cloud Computing Patterns 22
2.2 Application Workloads 23
    2.2.1 Static Workload 26
    2.2.2 Periodic Workload 29
    2.2.3 Once-in-a-Lifetime Workload 33
    2.2.4 Unpredictable Workload 36
    2.2.5 Continuously Changing Workload 40
2.3 Cloud Service Models 42
    2.3.1 Infrastructure as a Service (IaaS) 45
    2.3.2 Platform as a Service (PaaS) 49
    2.3.3 Software as a Service (SaaS) 55
2.4 Cloud Deployment Models 60
    2.4.1 Public Cloud 62
    2.4.2 Private Cloud 66
    2.4.3 Community Cloud 71
    2.4.4 Hybrid Cloud 75

3 Cloud Offering Patterns 79
3.1 Overview of Cloud Offering Patterns 80
3.2 Impact of Cloud Computing Properties on Offering Behavior 81
3.3 Cloud Environments 86
    3.3.1 Elastic Infrastructure 87
    3.3.2 Elastic Platform 91
    3.3.3 Node-Based Availability 95
    3.3.4 Environment-Based Availability 98

3.4   Processing Offerings 100
      3.4.1   Hypervisor 101
      3.4.2   Execution Environment 104
      3.4.3   Map Reduce 106
3.5   Storage Offerings 109
      3.5.1   Block Storage 110
      3.5.2   Blob Storage 112
      3.5.3   Relational Database 115
      3.5.4   Key-Value Storage 119
      3.5.5   Strict Consistency 123
      3.5.6   Eventual Consistency 126
3.6   Communication Offerings 131
      3.6.1   Virtual Networking 132
      3.6.2   Message-Oriented Middleware 136
      3.6.3   Exactly-Once Delivery 141
      3.6.4   At-Least-Once Delivery 144
      3.6.5   Transaction-Based Delivery 146
      3.6.6   Timeout-Based Delivery 149

4 Cloud Application Architecture Patterns 151
   4.1   Overview of Cloud Application Architecture Patterns 152
   4.2   Fundamental Cloud Architectures 155
         4.2.1   Loose Coupling 156
         4.2.2   Distributed Application 160
   4.3   Cloud Application Components 166
         4.3.1   Stateful Component 168
         4.3.2   Stateless Component 171
         4.3.3   User Interface Component 175
         4.3.4   Processing Component 180
         4.3.5   Batch Processing Component 185
         4.3.6   Data Access Component 188
         4.3.7   Data Abstractor 194
         4.3.8   Idempotent Processor 197
         4.3.9   Transaction-Based Processor 201
         4.3.10 Timeout-Based Message Processor 204
         4.3.11 Multi-Component Image 206
   4.4   Multi-Tenancy 208
         4.4.1   Shared Component 210
         4.4.2   Tenant-Isolated Component 214
         4.4.3   Dedicated Component 218
   4.5   Cloud Integration 221
         4.5.1   Restricted Data Access Component 222
         4.5.2   Message Mover 225
         4.5.3   Application Component Proxy 228

        4.5.4   Compliant Data Replication   231

        4.5.5   Integration Provider   234

5   Cloud Application Management Patterns   239

   5.1   Overview of Application Management Patterns   240

   5.2   Management Components   242

        5.2.1   Provider Adapter   243

        5.2.2   Managed Configuration   247

        5.2.3   Elasticity Manager   250

        5.2.4   Elastic Load Balancer   254

        5.2.5   Elastic Queue   257

        5.2.6   Watchdog   260

   5.3   Management Processes   264

        5.3.1   Elasticity Management Process   267

        5.3.2   Feature Flag Management Process   271

        5.3.3   Update Transition Process   275

        5.3.4   Standby Pooling Process   279

        5.3.5   Resiliency Management Process   283

6   Composite Cloud Application Patterns   287

   6.1   Overview of Cloud Application Patterns   288

   6.2   Native Cloud Applications   289

        6.2.1   Two-Tier Cloud Application   290

        6.2.2   Three-Tier Cloud Application   294

        6.2.3   Content Distribution Network   300

   6.3   Hybrid Cloud Applications   303

        6.3.1   Hybrid User Interface   304

        6.3.2   Hybrid Processing   308

        6.3.3   Hybrid Data   311

        6.3.4   Hybrid Backup   314

        6.3.5   Hybrid Backend   317

        6.3.6   Hybrid Application Functions   320

        6.3.7   Hybrid Multimedia Web Application   323

        6.3.8   Hybrid Development Environment   326

7   Impact of Cloud Computing Properties   331

   7.1   Cloud Computing Properties on Levels of the Application Stack . . .   332

        7.1.1   Downwards-Propagation of Requirements   334

        7.1.2   Upwards-Propagation of Properties   335

        7.1.3   Meet-in-the-Middle for Cloud Properties

                and Requirements   335

   7.2   Impact of Core Cloud Properties   336

        7.2.1   Pay-Per-Use   336

        7.2.2   Rapid Elasticity   337

        7.2.3   Homogenization   340

        7.2.4   Resource Sharing/Multi-Tenancy   342

7.3   Impact of Other Common Cloud Offering Properties   345
        7.3.1   Environment-Based Availability   346
        7.3.2   Eventual Consistency   349
        7.3.3   At-Least-Once Messaging   351

References   353

Index   363

List of Figures

Fig. 1.1 Mapping of chapters to a cloud reference application 12
Fig. 2.1 Pattern map of cloud computing fundamentals 21
Fig. 2.2 Exemplary resource provisioning 24
Fig. 2.3 Exemplary static workload 27
Fig. 2.4 Exemplary periodic workload 30
Fig. 2.5 Exemplary once-in-a-lifetime workload 34
Fig. 2.6 Exemplary unpredictable workload 37
Fig. 2.7 Exemplary continuously changing workload 41
Fig. 2.8 Application stack and associated cloud service models 43
Fig. 2.9 Infrastructure as a service in the application stack 46
Fig. 2.10 Platform as a service in the application stack 50
Fig. 2.11 Software as a service in the application stack 56
Fig. 2.12 Level of elasticity and pay-per-use of different cloud deployment
          types 61
Fig. 2.13 Public cloud 63
Fig. 2.14 Private cloud, outsourced private cloud, and virtual private
          cloud 67
Fig. 2.15 Community cloud, outsourced community cloud, and virtual
          community cloud 72
Fig. 2.16 Hybrid cloud in the cloud scope 76
Fig. 3.1 Pattern map of cloud offerings 79
Fig. 3.2 Eventual consistency scenario 84
Fig. 3.3 Components of an elastic infrastructure 88
Fig. 3.4 Components of an elastic platform 92
Fig. 3.5 Exemplary node-based availability 96
Fig. 3.6 Exemplary environment-based availability assurances 99
Fig. 3.7 Hypervisor types using virtualization and para-virtualization 102
Fig. 3.8 Execution environment in an application stack 105
Fig. 3.9 Elastic map reduce using key-value storage 107
Fig. 3.10 Images of a block storage being mapped to virtual drives 111
Fig. 3.11 Blob storage accessed via HTTP 113
Fig. 3.12 Exemplary relational storage 116
Fig. 3.13 Exemplary read operation on a key-value storage 120
Fig. 3.14 Exemplary strict consistent replicas 124

Fig. 3.15   Exemplary eventual consistent replicas 127
Fig. 3.16   Self-service interface for configuration of virtual networking 133
Fig. 3.17   Exemplary VLAN setup 134
Fig. 3.18   Firewall setup for an example application 134
Fig. 3.19   VPN from a corporate network to an IaaS provider 135
Fig. 3.20   Message-oriented middleware and related patterns 137
Fig. 3.21   Message filter used to guarantee exactly-once delivery 142
Fig. 3.22   Communication between a sender and a receiver to ensure
             at-least-once delivery 145
Fig. 3.23   Operations of the transactional reception of a message 147
Fig. 3.24   Operations of timeout-based reception of a message 150
Fig. 4.1   Map of the cloud application architecture patterns 151
Fig. 4.2   Realization of loose coupling through an intermediary 158
Fig. 4.3   Exemplary decomposition into three tiers 162
Fig. 4.4   Process-based decomposition 162
Fig. 4.5   Pipes-and-filters-based decomposition 162
Fig. 4.6   Stateful application components 169
Fig. 4.7   Stateless application components 172
Fig. 4.8   User interface components in a common setup 176
Fig. 4.9   Integration of different portlets into a portal 177
Fig. 4.10   Processing component in a standard setup 181
Fig. 4.11   Exemplary pipes-and-filters video processing application 182
Fig. 4.12   Exemplary process-based video processing application 183
Fig. 4.13   Batch processing component in a standard setup 186
Fig. 4.14   Data access components integrating stateful components and
             storage offerings residing in two clouds 189
Fig. 4.15   Data access component interface and data structure 191
Fig. 4.16   Exemplary data abstractions 195
Fig. 4.17   Idempotent component for messaging (*left*) and storage
             offerings (*right*) 199
Fig. 4.18   Operations of the transactional processing of a message (*left*)
             and data (*right*) 202
Fig. 4.19   Operations of the timeout-based processing of a message 205
Fig. 4.20   Two application components managed as one multi-component
             image 207
Fig. 4.21   Clients accessing a shared component 211
Fig. 4.22   Clients accessing a tenant-isolated component 216
Fig. 4.23   Table-based tenant isolation (*left*) and row-based tenant
             isolation (*right*) 216
Fig. 4.24   Clients accessing dedicated components 219
Fig. 4.25   A data access component and a restricted data access component
             providing data to a secure and an insecure environment 223
Fig. 4.26   Message mover integrating queues of two environments 226
Fig. 4.27   Application component proxy bridging two environments 229

Fig. 4.28   Compliant data replication between a secure cloud and an
            insecure cloud 232
Fig. 4.29   Integration provider integrating two private environments 235
Fig. 5.1   Map of the cloud application management patterns 239
Fig. 5.2   Abstract management architecture 241
Fig. 5.3   Exemplary provider adapter component accessed
            synchronously 244
Fig. 5.4   Exemplary provider adapter component accessed
            asynchronously 245
Fig. 5.5   Polling (*left*) and pushing (*right*) of managed configurations 248
Fig. 5.6   Elasticity manager interacting with an elastic platform or
            elastic infrastructure 251
Fig. 5.7   Elastic load balancer interacting with an elastic platform or
            elastic infrastructure 255
Fig. 5.8   Elastic queue interacting with an elastic platform or an elastic
            infrastructure 259
Fig. 5.9   Watchdog supervising application components hosted on IaaS
            and PaaS 261
Fig. 5.10   Elasticity management flow 268
Fig. 5.11   Feature flags management process 273
Fig. 5.12   Update transition process for application components accessed
            through load balancers and queues 277
Fig. 5.13   Decommissioning executed by the standby pooling process
            and interacting components 280
Fig. 5.14   Provisioning executed by the standby pooling process and
            interacting components 281
Fig. 5.15   Resiliency process handled by the watchdog 285
Fig. 6.1   Map of composite patterns for cloud computing 287
Fig. 6.2   Exemplary architecture of a two-tier cloud application 291
Fig. 6.3   Exemplary architecture of a three-tier cloud application 295
Fig. 6.4   Content distribution from a storage offering to two cloud
            environments 301
Fig. 6.5   Hybrid user interface in an elastic cloud and a static
            data center 305
Fig. 6.6   Hybrid processing in a static data center and an elastic cloud 309
Fig. 6.7   Hybrid data residing in a static and an elastic environment 312
Fig. 6.8   Hybrid backup using an elastic cloud to archive data 315
Fig. 6.9   Hybrid backend using a static data center and an elastic cloud ... 318
Fig. 6.10   Hybrid UI, processing, and data deployment 321
Fig. 6.11   Hybrid multimedia web application residing in an elastic cloud
            and a static data center 324
Fig. 6.12   Hybrid development environment and its integration with a
            production environment 327
Fig. 7.1   Propagation of requirements in the application stack 333

Fig. 7.2   Workloads and elasticity requirements 337
Fig. 7.3   Elasticity on different levels of the stack 338
Fig. 7.4   Resource sharing/multi-tenancy on different levels in the stack 343
Fig. 7.5   Mitigation of environment-based availability on higher levels
           of the application stack 346

Introduction

Cloud computing is the logical evolution of Information Technology (IT) in a world that is becoming more and more based on the division of work. From small family-owned stores to big corporations the trend to outsource IT is prevalent. Cloud computing brings principles that are long established in other industries to the IT. Take the transportation industry as an example. If you want to use a car you can get this functionality in a wide range of service models. From your own car that you buy and are responsible for, to cars sourced from a company-internal pool, to a rental car from one of the rent-a-car agencies, from car-sharing models, to taxis the functionality is essentially the same – a car enabling fast self-paced driving from A to B. The differentiating factor of these mobility providers is their business model to deliver functionality and the level of guaranteed quality of service. Cloud computing brings a new choice to the service models in which IT is delivered. Cloud computing is the IT equivalent of the rent-a-car model. The promise of cloud computing is to consume IT resources (be it infrastructure, middleware platforms, software, or whole business processes) when you need them in the quantity you need them *at a certain time*. While this IT delivery model is not new from a technical perspective, the fundamental change is the business model that you only pay for IT resources *when you actually use them*. Similar to the car industry this can be game-changing and can save you lots of money, speed up your time-to-market, and make your business and IT more flexible. In other cases, where you cannot embrace this business model fully, it can be complicated and more expensive than just buying the respective IT resources and maintaining them yourself.

Another evolution that cloud computing is often compared to is the industrialization of electricity, when businesses started to rely on large centralized power plants and distribution networks rather than generating their own electricity. Today, such decentralized generation of electricity is mostly used for backup purposes. However, what makes cloud computing very different from renting a car or the consumption of electricity is data. As cloud computing stores data on the provider

---

All figures published with kind permission of © The Authors 2014. See list of figures.

C. Fehling et al., *Cloud Computing Patterns*,
DOI 10.1007/978-3-7091-1568-8_1, © Springer-Verlag Wien 2014

side, concerns regarding privacy, security, and trust in the provider are raised. This property of cloud computing allows jet another analogy to a long established business model: banks. Storing our data away from a private data center in an intangible cloud environment is similar to trusting your money to banks. And probably, the first banks faced similar trust issues and skepticism as cloud providers do today. But this perception will likely shift or do you know anybody still storing large amounts of cash in mattresses or dry walls?

We are not aiming at creating yet another cloud computing definition or a definition of associated technologies in this book. Instead we focus on the basic properties of cloud computing, help you understand them, and guide their use in your IT infrastructure and applications. Thus, this book gives you a toolbox that you can employ and customize based on your role in the cloud business domain. It will help you solve a wide range of tasks that we have come across in various consulting engagements, while building cloud offerings, in research projects, while working on standards in the cloud field, as well as during the usage of cloud offerings in various applications. We make this toolbox available using the means of a *pattern language* interconnecting a set of *cloud computing patterns*. A cloud pattern is a small human readable document of a well-defined format describing a good solution to a cloud-related problem. We researched and captured such patterns describing different types of clouds, the offerings they provide, and how to build applications with them. Through the interconnections between patterns, a reader is guided from pattern to pattern to find applicable solutions to problems when using cloud computing. As this book is, therefore, not a list of concrete cloud offerings and their properties, but rather a list of nuggets of advice on how to cope with the generic properties of cloud offerings, we believe that a pattern language is the right format as is leaves the reader a certain freedom about the order in which to read the book (see Sect. 1.6 for some possible reading orders). We distilled the essential patterns that you should be aware of in the following situations:

- Evaluation of cloud offerings.
- Building applications on top of cloud offerings.
- Building custom cloud offerings.
- Evaluation of application landscapes for *cloud-readiness.*

The goal of this book is that after reading it in full or in parts, that you are enabled to acknowledge the benefits of cloud computing but also to decide when cloud principles do not provide any benefits in a situation you may be in. After you have read this book you will be able to compare cloud offerings on an architecture level and you will be sure what their impact is on your applications and your application landscape. You will be able to consider cloud-readiness in the architecture design of applications – thus, you will have a very good idea what it means to build applications that embrace cloud principles and make use of them extensively. You will also have the necessary mental toolbox to build and architect *cloud-native* applications. Throughout the book, you will find two kinds of text boxes with additional information:

Side Notes shortly summarize important information about the current chapter that should be remembered. Think of them as the *nuggets of advice* to take with you from reading this book.

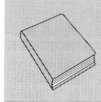 ***Further Reading*** text boxes are used to point to other books and related work that describe a covered topic in greater detail. Think of them as a starting point to find *more detailed information* on subjects that we do not cover completely.

In the remainder of this introduction, we will cover the essential cloud computing properties, give an introduction to patterns and describe the used pattern format. We further give an overview of the cloud computing patterns using a sample cloud application and cover several user stories on how to read this book.

1.1 Essential Cloud Computing Properties

In the following, we consider *IT resources* that support a company's data processing needs. These resources can be, for example, a server, a middleware platform, or a complete software application. A cloud offering provides such IT resources *as a Service* accessible over a network and displays the essential cloud computing properties described in this section. These offered IT resources experience a certain *workload* that is the impact of user requests to a cloud offering resulting in processing load, communication traffic, or data to be stored. In scope of clouds, we also use the term *cloud resource* to refer to IT resources hosted in a cloud environment

Since the business model to offer IT resources over a network has been well established, the boundaries between cloud computing and other computing paradigms are often blurred. Especially, the large numbers of existing products, which suddenly have the term "cloud" added to their name, sometimes called "cloud washing" [6], lead to confusion. And there are many long-established technical and non-technical concepts that have been integrated in cloud computing offerings [3]. However, it is the combination of these concepts that makes cloud computing special and introduces several new properties found in cloud services.

For the following discussions it is important to note that we explicitly talk about properties of cloud offerings provided *as a Service*. As a result there are at least two roles involved: The *cloud provider* offering the service and the *cloud customer* consuming the service. Thus, the cloud customer buys a service with a well-defined contract from the cloud provider. The customer and the provider can be different legal entities or parts of the same legal entity, i.e., an IT department providing IT resources to local business units. To understand the implications that the outsourcing of cloud services has, the understanding of their fundamental properties is essential.

Among all attempts to define this set of cloud properties, the NIST Definition of Cloud Computing [3] has been most accepted and will also be employed as a basic definition of cloud computing in this book. The NIST definition introduces five fundamental properties that characterize a cloud offering: *on-demand self-service, broad network access, measured service (pay-per-use), resource pooling and rapid elasticity.* These are described in more detail in the following:

On-demand self-service: customers may reserve and release IT resources independently exactly as needed. Throughout the remainder of this book, we will use the terms "provision" and "decommission" for these activities, respectively. This functionality may be provided through graphical or command line user interfaces to be used by humans or as application programming interfaces (API) to be used by applications in an automated fashion.

Broad network access: IT resources are made available over a high-speed network. The general availability of such powerful networks is essential for the integration of distributed IT resources in applications, because data access times become less dependent on the physical location where data is stored.

Measured service (pay-per-use): the use of IT resources for storage, processing, or data exchange is measured to ensure transparency for both the cloud customer and the cloud provider. Commonly, this metering is used to enable pay-per-use pricing models, thus, customers of cloud offerings only pay for the service when they use it and only for the intensity in which they use it. Long-term upfront investments in IT resources are reduced and transformed to operational expenses. Cloud computing is, therefore, said to enable the shift of capital expenditures (CAPEX) in IT to operational expenditures (OPEX), which can be increased or decreased more flexibly depending on the growth of a business. The benefit of measured service and the enabled pay-per-use pricing models for the customer is quite obvious as no more investments in non-used or under-utilized IT resources is necessary. To make the business case for the provider, the provider must deal with the fact that resources can be returned by customers when they do not need them. However, these resources can then be assigned to other customers or applications when they need it. As the measured service property often manifest in pay-per-use billing, these terms can often be used interchangeably, even though the fact that a service is measured does not impose any pricing model on the provider.

Resource pooling: to deal with the demand for pay-per-use, cloud providers offer IT resources using a large IT resource pool that is shared by multiple customers. To be able to assign resources of the resource pool dynamically to customers, it is required that the resource pool supports elasticity, i.e., customers can rapidly grow or shrink the share of the resource pool assigned to them. The assignment of IT resources to customers can be done manually by the customer via the self-service interface or programmatically through an application programming interface (API). Also, the cloud provider can automatically detect underutilized IT resources or increased demand of customers and assigns IT resources accordingly. Depending on the *cloud deployment model* used (see Sect. 2.4), customers of a cloud can be multiple companies but can also be various internal project teams or departments of the same company. In this scope, a customer is often referred to as a *tenant* that has multiple users working for it.

The sharing of a set of resources between multiple customers has a very important side-effect on the cloud environment: *homogenization* of IT resources is enforced as customers cannot use very specific resources any longer but have to rely on commoditized resources offered by the provider. Therefore, the differentiating factors of hardware and software platforms vanish, homogenizing the runtime environment found in the cloud of one provider. This homogenization is very important for the cloud provider as heterogeneity of an IT landscape increases IT management complexity [7] and, thus, is a major cost driver for IT departments [8].

Rapid elasticity: multi-tenant or tenant-aware IT resource pools used to provide cloud offerings enable providers to exploit *economies of scale*. Economies of scale in the scope of cloud computing means that providers offer a (shared) cloud offering to a very large number of customers to reduce the costs for individual customers. By sharing IT resources between customers the utilization of provided IT resources in consequence of customer accesses – we call this *workload* – can be handled using all IT resources in the pool. The different workload requirements of customers are, therefore, leveled since higher-demand of one customer may be handled by resources that another customer does not require at that moment. Through the size of their offerings, cloud providers may allow customers to provision and decommission IT resources flexibly in very short time frames. This enables customers to adjust the actual number of provisioned IT resources tightly to the currently experienced workload of a business process, an application, or platform. However, this capability, just as the ability to scale elastically, has to be supported by hosted applications. In addition to being able to distribute workload among independent resources, an *elastic* application has to be able to free resources flexibly, if they become underutilized.

Individually, these cloud properties may be known already and are often available in different well-established products and services, for example, server hosting solutions or public Web applications. It is the combination of these concepts and techniques in addition to a significant improvement of Internet connectivity and data transfer speed that distinguishes cloud computing from existing products and services and that justifies calling cloud computing a "new big thing". When we use the term *cloud properties* in the following chapters of this book we explicitly refer to the above mentioned five fundamental cloud properties: *broad network access, on-demand self-service, measured service (pay-per-use), resource pooling* and *rapid elasticity*.

1.2 Essential Cloud Application Properties

With respect to the cloud computing properties covered in the previous section, a number of application properties can be derived enabling a cloud-native application to benefit from a cloud environment. These cloud-native applications are built on top of IT resources provided by cloud offerings. Just like other cloud offerings, they experience a certain workload due to user requests that have to be processed, result in communication traffic, and generate data that has to be stored. Cloud-native applications have to exploit the properties of cloud offerings to handle this workload in an efficient manner, which is achieved by ensuring the following cloud application properties. The best practices captured in this book are, therefore, design guidelines to ensure the following properties of IDEAL cloud-native applications:

Isolated state, Distribution, Elasticity, Automated management, Loose coupling (to ease comprehensibility we do not use this order in the following definition).

Distribution: by nature, cloud environments are large, possibly globally distributed environments that consist of many IT resources (see the resource pooling cloud property). Therefore, cloud applications have to be decomposed into separate application components that can be distributed among resources in this environment.

Elasticity: cloud applications should by *scaled out* instead of being *scaled up*, thus, to address increasing workload the number of resources assigned to a customer or an application is increased, not the capabilities of individual resources. Therefore, in a scaling-out approach, also called *horizontal scaling* the number of independent IT resources, such as servers, is increased if an application requires more processing power, storage etc. The application, therefore, has to be designed to run on multiple independent resources. In contrast to horizontal scaling, *vertical scaling* (also called *scaling up*) refers to the approach of increasing the performance of an application by increasing the capabilities of the IT resources on which it runs without changing their number. While a vertical scaling approach can also be used in the cloud, it is limited by the capabilities of individual IT resources offered by a cloud provider.

In addition to being horizontally scalable, cloud applications also need to be elastic. Scalability refers to the ability of the application to increase its performance when additional IT resources are added and often does not consider the removal of these resources. Elasticity specifically focusses on both the dynamic addition and removal of IT resources and demands that the application can add and free IT resources to adjust its performance quickly if the workload changes. This ability is essential to exploit the *pay-per-use* cloud property.

Isolated state: a concept that is closely related to elasticity is to design large portions of a cloud application to be *stateless*, thus, isolating state in small portions of the application. The notion of *statelessness* commonly refers to *session state* – the state of a client's interaction handled by a Web application. We extend this notion to also incorporate *application state* – the data handled by the application. Session state and application state may severely impact a cloud applications ability to be scaled out either through custom developed management functionality or automatically by the cloud provider. An IT resource that does not hold application state can be added and removed more easily as no state information has to be synchronized to newly provisioned resources or extracted from removed ones. Cloud providers, therefore, often restrict where application state may be handled in automatically scaled applications.

Side Note: with the term *stateless*, we subsume the properties of an applications component not to store *session state* or *application state*. The *stateful component* (168) pattern and *stateless component* (171) pattern discuss this notion of state in greater detail, how it may be handled, and how management functionality discussed in Chap. 5 is affected by it.

Automated management: due to the elasticity of a cloud application, resources are constantly added and removed during runtime. These tasks should be automated by monitoring system load and interacting with management interfaces of cloud providers to provision or decommission resources. Many cloud providers do not assure an availability of individual IT resources, such as particular virtual servers, but only for the offering as a whole, i.e., the ability to start new virtual servers. This behavior increases the need for automated management to ensure that a cloud application is failure resistant.

Loose coupling: as the number of IT resources on which a cloud application relies constantly changes, the dependencies between application components should be minimized. This eases provisioning and decommissioning tasks and also reduces the impact of failing application components. Loose coupling is a well-established concept in distributed applications. This makes related technologies, such as Web services comprising a Service Oriented Architecture (SOA) [9–11] and asynchronous messaging [1] equally usable and relevant for cloud applications.

1.3   Use of Patterns for Cloud Computing

The concept of patterns used in this book originated from the area of real architecture. Alexander [12, 13] gathered architectural knowledge and best practices regarding building structures in a pattern format. This knowledge was obtained from years of practical experience. A pattern according to Alexander is structured text that follows a well-defined format and captures nuggets of advice on how to deal with recurring problems in a specific domain. It advises the architect on how to create building architectures, defines the important design decisions, and covers limitations to consider. Patterns can be very generic documents, but may also include concrete measurements and plans. Their application to a certain problem is, however, always a manual task that is performed by the architect. Therefore, each application of a pattern will result in a differently looking building, but all applications of the pattern will share a common set of desired properties. In building architecture, pattern-based descriptions of best practices and design decisions proved especially useful, because many desirable properties of houses, public environments, cities, streets, etc. are not formally measurable. They are perceived by humans and, thus, cannot be computed or predicted in a formal way. Therefore, best practices and well-perceived architectural styles capture a lot of implicit knowledge how people using and living in buildings perceive their structure, functionality, and general feel. Especially, the indifferent emotion that buildings trigger, such as awe, comfort, coziness, power, cleanness, etc. are hard to measure or explain and are also referred to as the *quality without a name* or the *inner beauty of a building* [12]. How certain objectives can be realized in architecture is, thus, found only through practical experience, which is then captured by patterns. For example, there are patterns describing how lighting in a room should be realized so that people feel comfortable and positive. There are patterns describing how eating tables should be sized so that people can move around the table freely, get seated comfortably, find enough room for plates and food, while still being able to communicate and talk during meals without feeling too distant from people seated across the table. While the properties of the table are easy to enforce once concrete distances and sizes are specified, they are extremely hard to determine theoretically or by pure computation using a building's blueprint. Therefore, architects capture their knowledge gathered from existing buildings and feedback they received from users in patterns describing well-perceived building design. In this scope, each pattern describes one architectural solution for an architectural problem, for example, for the above mentioned eating area. It does so in an abstract format that allows the implementation in various ways. Architectural patterns, thus, capture the essential properties required for the successful design of a certain building area or function while leaving large degrees of freedom to architects. Multiple patterns are connected and interrelated resulting in a *pattern language*. This concept of links between patterns is used to point to related patterns. For example, an architect reviewing patterns describing different roof types can be pointed to patterns describing different solutions for windows in these roofs and may be advised that some window solutions, thus, the patterns describing them cannot be combined with a certain roof pattern. For example, a *flat rooftop* cannot be combined with windows that have to be mounted vertically. Also, a pattern language uses these links to guide an architect through the design of buildings, streets, cities, etc. by describing the order in which patterns have to be considered. For example, the size of the ground on which a building is created may limit the general architecture patterns that should be selected first. After this, the number of floors can be considered, the above mentioned roofing style etc. [13].

In a similar way, the pattern-based approach has been used in IT architecture to capture best practices how applications and systems of applications should be designed. Examples are patterns for general application architectures [14], object oriented programming [2], enterprise applications [15], message-based application integration [1], or for fault-tolerant software [4]. Again, these patterns are abstract and independent of used programming language or runtime infrastructure to form *timeless knowledge* that can be applied in various IT environments. In the domain of IT architecture, the gathered knowledge is not necessarily obtained from application users. There are user interface design patterns [16] and some will be discussed in this book as well, but the desirable properties in IT architecture are also manageability, flexibility to make changes, and, especially, the cloud computing properties and cloud application properties introduced in Sects. 1.1 and 1.2. The properties of IT architecture become apparent over time while an application is productively used, evolves to meet new requirements, has to cope with failures, or has to be updated to newer versions. During this lifecycle of an application, architects can, therefore, reflect on the IT architecture to determine whether it was well designed to meet such challenges. These best practices obtained from existing applications and documented knowledge of other IT architects has been captured in this book to describe the IT domain of cloud computing applications. As patterns are abstract solution blueprints they are ideal to document cloud-specific properties of cloud offerings as well as good practices on how to deal with these properties in a programming language-neutral and technology-neutral fashion. Thus, the pattern format allows us to be very specific in sketching solutions and describing cloud properties while still being generic enough so that patterns remain applicable across different cloud providers, different technologies, and different products. This very specific, yet technology neutral understanding of the properties of clouds and their impact is key to be able to make use of cloud offerings and to develop applications on top of them.

In this book we, therefore, introduce a pattern language – the *cloud pattern language* to describe the cloud-specific properties of cloud offerings as well as to give advice on how to solve the most common challenges when using cloud offerings to build custom applications.

Side Note: patterns are structured text describing abstract problem-solution pairs.
The patterns in this book describe *abstract solutions to recurring problems* in the domain of cloud computing to capture *timeless knowledge* that is *independent of concrete providers*, products, programming languages etc.

The cloud computing patterns have been gained from existing applications and products to describe architectural styles, basic runtime modules, and cloud application components. They share a *common format* and are *self-contained* in subsections of this book. The patterns are *connected*, refine other patterns, are used in a similar scope, are used exclusively etc., thus, building a pattern language.

1.4   Pattern Format Used in This Book

The cloud computing patterns are covered in separate sections of this book each structured according to the same pattern format. While the NIST cloud properties are described fairly generic and do not cover specific properties of different cloud service models and cloud deployment models, we want to describe these properties in more detail. For this detailed description we use a pattern format. This well-defined pattern format is used to ease the understanding of the patterns [17] and to enable an easier access to readers. Patterns are interconnected with cross-references in their sections to point to patterns describing the environment in which a pattern can be applied, patterns that are likely to be used together, patterns that are alternatives etc. In addition to these inline references, we introduce each pattern chapter with a pattern map. The pattern map contains the patterns of a chapter and depicts a suggested order in which patterns may be considered as an alternative to the default sequential reading order of each chapter. This map enables you to leave out patterns relevant only in scope of other patterns, which you may have already identified as inapplicable in your usage scenario. The individual patterns are then structured as follows:

Pattern Name

The name is used to identify each pattern. If a pattern name is mentioned outside of the pattern description, pattern names are in italics followed by the page number on which the pattern is described, for example, *public cloud* (62).

> *Intent*: at the beginning of each pattern, its purpose and goal is shortly stated, to describe what the solution represented by the pattern contains.

| | *Driving Question*: *this question captures the problem that is answered by the pattern. Stating this question at the beginning allows readers to identify if the pattern fits the problem they have in a concrete use case.* |
| Icon | |

Icon: each pattern has a graphical representation and all icons of the patterns in this book are of the same size. They are intended to be used in architectural diagrams modeling a cloud application and in sketches given in the solution section of patterns.

Context

This section describes the environment and forces leading to the problem solved by the pattern. It also may describe why naïve solutions can be unsuccessful or suboptimal. Other patterns may be referenced here. Especially, we use the pattern format to describe *cloud deployment models*, *cloud service models*, and *cloud offerings*, even though these patterns are not implemented by developers. Instead, they describe how cloud environments and the contained offerings behave and when they should be selected to be used in applications. These patterns, therefore, often form the context in which other patterns implemented by developers can be applied to create custom cloud applications on top of cloud offerings.

Solution

The solution section briefly states how the pattern solves the problem raised by the driving question. It is kept brief, because readers shall be enabled to quickly read the intent, question, and solution sections to get an idea what the pattern is doing in detail. The solution section is commonly closed with a sketch depicting the architecture of the solution.

Result

In this section, the solution is elaborated in greater detail. The architecture proposed by the sketch is described and the behavior of the application after implementation of the pattern is discussed. New challenges that may arise after a pattern has been applied may also be included here, together with references to other patterns addressing these new challenges.

Variations

Often, patterns can be applied in slightly different forms. If the differences of these variations are not significant enough to justify their description in a separate pattern, they are covered in the variations section.

Related Patterns

Several patterns are often applied together as they are solving related problems, but the application of one pattern may also exclude other patterns from being applicable. These interrelations of patterns are described in this section. It, therefore, forms the structure of the cloud pattern language and guides readers through the set of patterns.

Known Uses

Existing applications implementing a pattern, products offering a pattern or supporting its implementation, are covered here exemplarily.

1.5   Overview of This Book

The cloud pattern language is structured according to a *sample cloud application* that is depicted in the center of Fig. 1.1. This application is accessed by a *user group* through a *load balancer*. This load balancer distributes user accesses among a *presentation tier* that is scaled-out, thus, more processing power can be added to this tier by adding more instances of application components. The presentation tier accesses a *business logic tier* asynchronously through a *message queue*. The business logic tier provides the application functionality and operates on data stored in a *separate data tier*. The business logic tier is also scaled out by adding more application component instances. A *management component* depicted on the right of Fig. 1.1 handles the operations for elastic scalability, resiliency to cope with component failures etc. The complete application is deployed on a *cloud environment* that provides *processing offerings* on which application components are hosted, *communication offerings* used to exchange information between tiers, and *storage offerings* used to store data of the application. The chapters of this book can be mapped to the entities of this reference

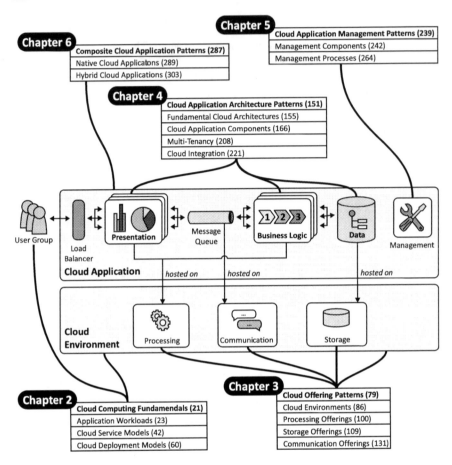

Fig. 1.1 Mapping of chapters to a cloud reference application

application, meaning that the patterns contained in these sections describe the behavior of the mapped entity or describe the best practices how these entities may designed and created. In Fig. 1.1 the book chapters and subsections are mapped to the sample cloud application. A more detailed mapping of the individual patterns contained in each chapter to the cloud reference application can be found in the preface of this book.

Chapter 2 covers the **cloud computing fundamentals**. It gives an overview of different *application workloads* created by the user group that have to be handled by the cloud application. Regarding the cloud runtime environment, it covers the basic style how IT resources are offered according to different *cloud service models* and the properties of different hosting options for clouds, i.e., the *cloud deployment models*. Therefore, this chapter covers the style how cloud providers offer

IT resources to a level of detail that has to be understood by customers in order to build applications on top of provided clouds.

Chapter 3 covers **cloud offering patterns** describing the functional behavior of provider-supplied *cloud environments* and the contained offerings for *processing, communication* and *storage*. These patterns do not describe in detail how such offerings are implemented, but cover their properties, functions, and when to choose a certain offering. Therefore, these patterns are not implemented by cloud application developers but guide them to select the suitable cloud offerings for their custom applications.

Chapter 4 describes **cloud application architecture patterns** that use the cloud offering patterns as a runtime environment to build custom cloud applications. These patterns cover the fundamental *architectural styles of cloud applications* and how to design *application components* of the cloud reference application. Furthermore, it is also covered how application components can support *multi-tenancy*, thus, how they can be used by multiple isolated customers. *Cloud integration patterns* close this chapter by describing special application component that can be used to interconnect applications deployed among different cloud environments.

Chapter 5 focuses on the **cloud application management** functionality required by the sample cloud application. We cover how *management components* may be integrated with other application components. These management components execute *management processes* to enable cloud application properties, such as the automated management of elasticity or resiliency. Updating the application to a new version and graceful failing in case cloud resources cannot be obtained quickly enough are additional challenges addressed in this chapter.

Chapter 6 deals with **composite patterns** to describe how combinations of patterns covered in other chapters can be used in specific application scenarios. Especially, it covers the sample cloud application and its different variations in the form of *native-cloud application* patterns. The possible distribution of the application components comprising the cloud reference application among different cloud environments is then covered by *hybrid cloud application patterns.*

Chapter 7 takes a properties-based approach to summarize how some of the cloud properties introduced in Sect. 1.1 propagate upwards and downwards through application landscapes and application stacks. We describe how cloud-specific properties can be mitigated or enforced at different layers of the stack by employing different patterns and, thus, emphasize the connection between patterns and cloud properties.

1.6 How to Read This Book...

Chances are – now that you are reading this section – that you have read the other parts of the introduction – if not then in any case you should do this first as it introduces the book and the patterns as a whole. Then, the relevance of further parts of this book can be different depending on whether you are a software architect, developer, software project manager or general manager, whether you are acting as a cloud application provider or as a customer of a cloud offering.

Therefore, we collected a set of user stories that we consider typical for readers of this book. These user stories can be thought of an additional structuring of the cloud pattern language extending the structuring introduced by the sample cloud application in Sect. 1.5. The user stories listed below give an order in which different readers may consider the cloud computing patterns and, thus, help you to make the most efficient use of the book. Each user story gives you the necessary hints on what is of high priority to read in your situation and which chapters you might skip. If you do not want to stick to a user story, you can read the book sequentially. Chapters go from general considerations about cloud applications and the cloud environment to concepts how to build and manage such applications and, finally, to a set of application usage scenarios.

Customer of Cloud Offerings

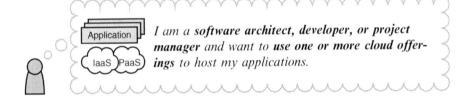

*I am a **software architect, developer, or project manager** and want to **use one or more cloud offerings** to host my applications.*

You have been assigned the task of building an application that shall make use of a cloud offering. This is motivated by the need to reduce time-to-market and costs of your applications or to increase their flexibility to react to changing requirements during runtime. Chances are high that you already know which concrete cloud offering you were tasked to use. Then, it is of fundamental importance to understand the **specific properties** of this cloud offering to design and **build your application accordingly** and, thus, to meet your application's specific requirements. If you just intend to use a cloud offering but do not know which particular one or if you should use cloud computing at all, it is still important to understand the specific properties of cloud offerings. It will help you to select the right one for your usage scenario.

To understand these specific properties of cloud offerings you should be familiar with the cloud computing fundamentals described in Chap. 2 (*Cloud Computing Fundamentals*). In particular, you should be aware of the kinds of workloads your application may incur. Section 2.2 (*Application Workloads*) on Page 23 will help you to determine that. Then, you should understand how the cloud provider offers IT resources. You should have an idea about the service model (**-aaS*) and cloud deployment type – *public cloud* (62), *private cloud* (66), *community cloud* (71), or *hybrid cloud* (75) – of the offerings in question. Section 2.3 (*Cloud Service Models*) on Page 42 and

Sect. 2.4 (*Cloud Deployment Models*) on Page 60 describe these two categories in the necessary level of detail so that you understand how it impacts your architecture.

Chapter 3 (*Cloud Offerings*) you can read very selectively depending of the kind of offering you would like to use. Section 3.3 (*Cloud Environments*) on Page 86 introduces different hosting environments offered by clouds. If you want to make use of a cloud offering virtual servers (such as Amazon EC2 [18], Rackspace [19], or VMware vCloud [20]) read the *elastic infrastructure* (87) pattern. If you wish to use a provider-supplied application hosting environment, such as the Google App Engine [21], read the *elastic platform* (91) pattern. These patterns also point to patterns for processing offerings, communication offerings, and storage offerings provided by these cloud environments. In either environment, you should understand whether a provider assures *node-based availability* (95) or *environment-based availability* (98) as this severely impacts the application architecture that you should aim for. If you want to make use of cloud storage offerings or communication offerings, such as messaging, read Sect. 3.5 (*Cloud Storage Offerings*) on Page 109 and Sect. 3.6 (*Cloud Communication Offerings*) on Page 131. In particular you should know whether your storage offering offers *eventual consistency* (126) or *strict consistency* (123) and whether your messaging offering guarantees *at-least-once delivery* (144) or *exactly-once delivery* (141). These properties also have severe impact on your application. Having understood the basic principles of the cloud offering(s) in question you can now read Chap. 4 (*Cloud Application Architectures*) fully to understand how to make **use of cloud properties** such as elasticity and pay-per-use in your application.

After reading these sections you will be aware of issues to consider when selecting a cloud offering as basis for your application. Additionally, you will have learned that building an application, which makes use of cloud properties on lower layers, requires the adoption of some paradigms such as horizontal scaling instead of vertical scaling to fully embrace the chances the cloud offers you.

Provider of a Software as a Service Application

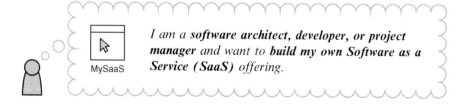

*I am a **software architect, developer, or project manager** and want to **build my own Software as a Service (SaaS)** offering.*

MySaaS

You will need to understand what it means to develop an application that is provided as a cloud offering itself, thus, to understand the **specific properties** of this cloud service model.

You should be familiar with the cloud computing fundamentals introduced in Chap. 2 (*Cloud Computing Fundamentals*). Especially, you should have a clear understanding of the **specific properties** of *Software as a Service – SaaS* (55) and should decide which cloud deployment type you application uses *public cloud* (62), *private cloud* (66), *community cloud* (71), or *hybrid cloud* (75) as described in Sect. 2.4 (*Cloud Deployment Models*). If you want to base your offering on *Infrastructure as a Service (IaaS)* (45) or *Platform as a Service (PaaS)* (49) you also act as a customer of cloud offerings. Therefore, you should read the chapters described in the previous user story as well. Furthermore, it is of high importance to get a concept on what you need to do to **provide the cloud properties** introduced in Sect. 1.1. Therefore, Chap. 6 (*Composite Cloud Application Patterns*) is what you should read next to understand which composite application scenarios are relevant for your offering. Afterwards, deep-dive into the application architecture patterns in Chap. 4 (*Cloud Application Architecture Patterns*) used to build the relevant composite applications. In a selective fashion, you can work through Chap. 5 (*Cloud Application Management Patterns*) to understand cloud-specific management that your SaaS application may implement. Especially, patterns on elasticity in this chapter will guide you to make your offering elastic.

After reading these chapters you will know how to build application components comprising a *SaaS* application. Also, you will have gained an overview of properties to consider when selecting cloud providers. You will also have a concept of how to deal with the cloud-specific management tasks.

Provider of a Infrastructure or Platform Cloud Offering

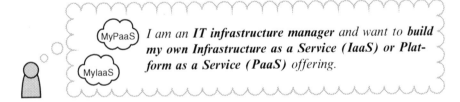

In this case you should read Chap. 2 (*Cloud Computing Fundamentals*) and Chap. 3 (*Cloud Offering Patterns*). However, it is important to note that this book will not tell you specifically how to build an *Infrastructure as a Service – IaaS* (45) or *Platform as a Service – PaaS* (49) cloud, i.e., it will not give you advice on how to design your datacenter or how to design a cloud environment using a particular type of middleware as a basis. Nevertheless, you will learn about the cloud properties that customers expect from your *IaaS* (45) or *PaaS* (49) cloud. Therefore, you can design your offering accordingly to support those properties. It may also make sense browse through Chap. 4 (*Cloud Application Architecture Patterns*) and Chap. 5 (*Cloud Application Management Patterns*) to understand what customers of your offering will have to consider when building their application architectures and what kind of interfaces they will require to scale them elastically. Also, the management processes covered in Chap. 5 (*Cloud Application Management Patterns*) can be provider-supplied, thus, you may implement and provide them to customers using your cloud offering. In this scope, you will make assumptions about the managed application components that your customers will deploy. You may use the patterns covered in Chap. 4 (*Cloud Application Architecture Patterns*) to express such assumptions regarding the patterns that you expect your customer to implement. For example, your management process handling elastic scaling may require customer-developed application components to implement the *stateless component* (171) pattern.

Further Reading: in case you are interested in physical data center architectures, the following references may also be of interest. Bauer and Adams [22] cover availability and security for cloud data center infrastructures. Allspaw [23] describes capacity planning for multiple scenarios. Barroso and Hölzle [24] provide advice on the physical setup of large scale data centers.

Enterprise Architect

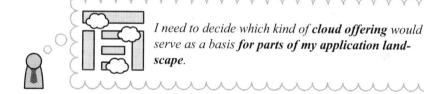

*I need to decide which kind of **cloud offering** would serve as a basis **for parts of my application landscape.***

Given your tight schedule and the amount of applications to consider, you should focus on the **general cloud properties**. Thus, Chap. 2 (*Cloud Computing Fundamentals*) is the right one for you to read first. It gives you an idea on how the workload patterns of your applications determine what type of clouds you should use. You will also understand the differences between the cloud service models (Sect. 2.3 on Page 42) and cloud deployment models (Sect. 2.4 on Page 60). Having inhaled these core concepts you should directly move to Chap. 7 (*Impact of Cloud Properties*). Here you will find the necessary information on how to **make use of cloud properties** of various levels on the application stack and how the selection of the cloud deployment model impacts which applications can share resources with each other. Occasionally you will need to dive in into one of the patterns of Chap. 3 (*Cloud Offering Patterns*), Chap. 4 (*Cloud Application Architecture Patterns*), and Chap. 5 (*Cloud Application Management Patterns*) to get additional background information for the decision.

After reading the mentioned chapters you will have understood the basic properties that cloud offerings display and what you have to consider selecting a cloud offering. The most important aspect that you will have learned is that you will only incur fundamental savings above those for consolidation and homogenization of IT infrastructure, if applications fully embrace the cloud properties *elasticity* and *pay-per-use*. Most existing applications are likely not built for this, thus, they would have to be re-architected before they become *cloud-native*.

Technology Evaluator and Consultant

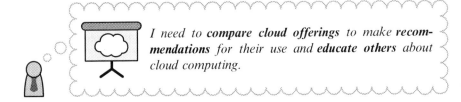

*I need to **compare cloud offerings** to make **recommendations** for their use and **educate others** about cloud computing.*

Given the broad market of cloud computing products and services as well as the number of products in use at one of your clients, technology consulting often starts with a categorization of existing solutions and possible alternatives. Chap. 3 (*Cloud Offering Patterns*) describes how offerings found in the cloud behave and when to select them. These patterns may, therefore, be used for an abstract categorization of products and offerings. Chap. 6 (*Composite Cloud Application Patterns*) covers cloud-native applications and their concrete deployments to different cloud environments. These patterns may be refined to match the concrete use cases of a company. Especially, the *two-tier cloud application* (290) pattern and *three-tier cloud application* (294) pattern may be refined to consider the concrete products and services used by a company.

After reading these chapters, you can, therefore, refine the content of this book to concrete development guidelines for a company. Chap. 2 (*Cloud Computing Fundamentals*) may then be consulted to determine application requirements regarding experienced workload and hosting environments in order to express requirements when the development guidelines should be followed.

Chief Information Officer (CIO)

*I need to understand the **impact of cloud computing
on my business** regarding **security** and **compliance**
to laws and regulations, as well as on **costs**.*

This book will not cover the laws and regulations relevant to cloud computing or give a detailed cost-evaluation when cloud computing is profitable. However, Chap. 2 may support you during these tasks by describing the style how cloud resources are offered according to different *cloud services models* and their possible impact on IT costs. Also, the *cloud deployment models* covered in this chapter describe how cloud environments are shared by different user groups significantly affecting security and privacy properties. If you are interested in a feasibility analysis regarding the move of concrete applications to the cloud, you should read about *application workloads* (Sect. 2.2 on Page 23) and *fundamental cloud architectures* (Sect. 4.2 on Page 155). These will help you to determine whether the workload experienced by an application is suitable for the cloud and the degree to which its architecture would have to be adjusted, respectively.

After you have read these sections, you will have an idea what changed in the cloud that may have an impact on laws and regulations your company has in place. Also, you will be able to review applications' suitability for the cloud and, thus, determine whether a migration is economically feasible or not.

Student

*I want to **educate myself** about cloud computing and
am **on a tight schedule**.*

In this case you should read Chap. 2 (*Cloud Computing Fundamentals*) in full and browse through Chap. 4 (*Cloud Application Architecture Patterns*), Chap. 5 (*Cloud Application Management*), and Chap. 6 (*Composite Cloud Application Patterns*) as well as the full Chap. 7 (*Impact of Cloud Properties*).

After you have read these chapters you will have gained the basic knowledge to be able to dig deeper. These chapters contain the basis of cloud computing and the basic understanding of this book.

 Further Reading: the content of this book extends existing publications of the authors. In [5], we presented a first collection of cloud computing patterns. The use of these patterns for cloud application management has been covered in [25]. A summary of patterns in this catalog has been presented at the Pattern Languages of Programs Conference (PLoP) 2011 [26]. A detailed overview on the research process we followed to identify these patterns has been presented at the IEEE International Conference on Cloud Computing (CLOUD) 2012 [27]. For this book, existing patterns were extended significantly and new ones have been added. For up-to-date information please also refer to our website:
http://www.cloudcomputingpatterns.org

Cloud Computing Fundamentals

2

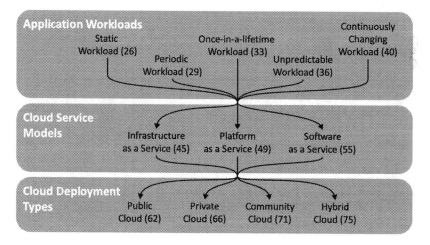

Fig. 2.1 Pattern map of cloud computing fundamentals

In this chapter, we introduce the fundamentals required for the understanding of the following chapters. As stated in the introduction, the cloud computing properties – access via network, on-demand self-service, measured service (pay-per-use), resource pooling and rapid elasticity – fundamentally change how IT resources are provided and used. It is important to understand why cloud offerings have these properties, how these properties are delivered on different levels of a typical application stack and under which conditions an application benefits from them. We begin by examining application workloads (Sect. 2.2) and show how they influence the decision for the adoption of cloud offerings. Especially, we discuss how applications experiencing different types of workloads can benefit from the cloud computing properties covered in Chap. 1. As in that previous chapter, we use

C. Fehling et al., *Cloud Computing Patterns*,
DOI 10.1007/978-3-7091-1568-8_2, © Springer-Verlag Wien 2014

the NIST cloud definition [3] and emphasis on those aspects that are important to understand the following chapters.

Having motivated the need for cloud offerings to handle different workloads we introduce common cloud service models (Sect. 2.3) that describe different styles to offer IT resources on different levels of an application stack. We cover the layers of this application stack and their function in an application. Furthermore, we discuss how the corresponding service models *Infrastructure as a Service*, *Platform as a Service* and *Software as a Service* enable the cloud computing properties. In the last section of this chapter, we introduce the cloud deployment models (Sect. 2.4) and describe how they differ regarding the sharing of IT resources, reaction to varying application workloads, economies of scale, and costs. These properties significantly affect cloud adoption in companies influenced by the concern that outsourcing parts of an application stack and sharing IT resources with other companies can negatively impact privacy and security of data and processes.

 Side Note: the patterns in this chapter differ from other patterns in this book. They are not implemented by developers, but characterize the context in which other patterns are applicable. We used the pattern format to correlate them with other patterns in a uniform way and use their icons to characterize cloud environments and application requirements in Chap. 7.

2.1 Overview of Fundamental Cloud Computing Patterns

As seen in Fig. 2.1, the map of patterns covered in this chapter for application workloads, cloud deployment types, and cloud service models are strong interconnected. While this is not the case for most of the other patterns in this book, these fundamental patterns form the basis for the understanding of the remaining patterns and should always be considered completely when designing cloud applications.

Patterns for application workloads (Sect. 2.2) describe different user behavior resulting in changing utilization of IT resources hosting an application. This workload can be measured in the form of user requests, processing load on servers, network traffic, amount of data stored etc. In detail, we cover *static workload* (26) that only changes minimally over time, *periodic workload* (29) that has recurring peaks, *once-in-a-lifetime workload* (33) that has a peak once, *unpredictable workload* (36) that changes frequently and randomly, and *continuously changing workload* (40) that grows or shrinks over time.

Once the workload experienced by an application can be described and categorized, it is important to understand the cloud service model (Sect. 2.3) used by a cloud provider. It affects the pricing model of providers and, therefore, how workload should be measured and evaluated in applications. We cover the three

NIST cloud service models [3] in a pattern format. *Infrastructure as a Service (IaaS)* (45) describes how servers are offered by cloud providers. *Platform as a Service (PaaS)* (49) covers cloud offerings providing complete execution environment for a specific type of applications, i.e., those developed in a certain programming language. *Software as a Service (SaaS)* (55) describes how complete applications can be offered to customers.

Cloud service models and cloud deployment models are two viewpoints on the cloud provider: cloud service models describe the style how IT resources are offered. Cloud deployment models describe the cloud environments hosting these IT resources, especially, regarding the group of customers they are made available to. Therefore, a combination of cloud service model and cloud deployment type characterizes the environment of a cloud provider. For each of the cloud deployment model patterns we describe the combinations with cloud service model patterns in the related patterns section and discuss the usage scenarios for each combination. The covered cloud deployment models are as follows: A *public cloud* (62) is generally available to everyone. A *private cloud* (66) is hosted exclusively for one company. A *community cloud* (71) is a cloud environment between these two extremes and is made accessible only to a certain group of companies or individuals that trust each other and often wish to collaborate. Finally, *hybrid clouds* (75) provide means to interconnect clouds of the other deployment models to distribute applications among various hosting environments.

2.2 Application Workloads

We use the term workload to refer to the utilization of IT resources on which an application is hosted. Workload is the consequence of users accessing the application or jobs that need to be handled automatically. Workload becomes imminent in different forms, depending on the type of IT resource for which it is measured: servers may experience processing load, storage offerings may be assigned larger or smaller amounts of data to store or may have to handle queries on that data. Communication IT resources, such as networking hardware or messaging systems may experience different data or message traffic. In scope of the abstract workload patterns, we merely assume this utilization to be measurable in some form. These measurements form the basis to increase or decrease the number of IT resources assigned to an application during elastic scaling, one of the cloud application properties introduced in Sect. 1.2 on Page 5.

From a customer perspective the desire to only pay for the IT resources that are actually used is common across many outsourcing domains – whether they are IT or not. A non-IT example of this desire is an airplane ticket – the customer of the transport capability only pays for the exact flights he or she takes and does not need to buy a plane upfront, train the pilots and deal with the maintenance of the plane afterwards just to take a flight. The requirement to reduce up-front capital expenditures (CAPEX) and move costs to operational expenditures (OPEX) that grow and shrink with the actual consumption of a service has led to the adoption of

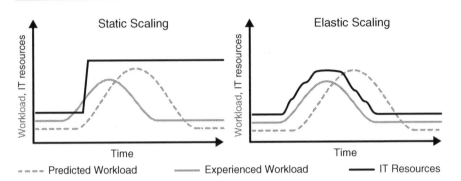

Fig. 2.2 Exemplary resource provisioning

pay-per-use as one of the fundamental properties of cloud offerings. As customers desire to pay for used resources only, providers must employ the principle of rapid elasticity to elastically grow or shrink the resources assigned to a customer based on that customer's demand. Therefore, at least two of the essential cloud properties – pay-per-use and rapid elasticity – result from the demand to cope with non-static application workloads. Varia [28] discusses the total cost of ownership in detail for handling different workloads .

In the following we examine some common utilizations of IT resources over time. This *workload* is the result of user requests to an application or cloud offering resulting in processing load, communication traffic, or data to be stored. The workload patterns discussed in this section cover different types of workloads we found in literature an observed in applications. For each of these workload patterns, we discuss how they can be handled efficiently in a cloud environment.

Figure 2.2 shows a general problem that arises in scope of workload changes to which a scaled-out application has to react by changing resources numbers. Whenever workload is predicted as shown by the *predicted workload* curve, it may be experienced slightly different, as shown in the *experienced workload* curve. In this example, a predicted peak in workload started a little earlier than expected and resource numbers have to be adjusted accordingly.

In case of static scaling, where physical servers are provisioned, the time it takes to order, setup and start them may not be reactive enough to handle the faulty prediction. Therefore, the necessary resources become available too late resulting in an "*underprovisioned*" application. To cope with the inflexibility of such resources, they have to be provisioned for the predicted peak-load right from the beginning and are hard to decommission once the workload decreases. This results in an "*overprovisioned*" application after the peak. This over- and underprovisioning has a direct impact on the properties of the hosted applications. An underprovisioned application usually cannot provide the desired user experience, as performance is reduced and, for example, reactiveness of the application decreases. Overprovisioning has a lesser impact on the user of the application, but leads to higher costs as resources are provisioned but remain unused.

Elastic scaling depicted on the right of Fig. 2.2 can provision and decommission resources much more flexibly and, thus, is not as dependent on workload predictions. Once the increase is detected, new resources are provisioned in small intervals and this provisioning is stopped even though the predicted workload peak has not been reached. Therefore, elastic scaling allows a much tighter alignment of IT resource numbers to experienced workloads, but has to be respected by the application architecture. In consequence, when an application is deployed in the cloud and experiences some of the workload patterns covered in this section – it has to be built in a way underlying IT resources can be added and removed. Now, we discuss the workload patterns, how they benefit from cloud properties, and point to entry points in the following chapters where the necessary application architectures enabling these benefits are covered.

2.2.1   Static Workload

IT resources with an equal utilization over time experience static workload.

 How can an equal utilization be characterized and how can applications experiencing this workload benefit from cloud computing?

Context

Static workloads are characterized by a more-or-less flat utilization profile over time within certain boundaries. This means that there is normally no explicit necessity to add or remove processing power, memory or bandwidth for change in workload reasons. When provisioning for such a workflow the necessary IT resources can be provisioned for this static load plus a certain overprovisioning rate to deal with the minimal variances in the workload. There is a relatively low cost overhead for this minimal overprovisioning.

Solution

An application experiencing *static workload* is less likely to benefit from an elastic cloud that offers a pay-per-use billing, because the number of required resources is constant. The elasticity of a cloud environment is not required to handle *static workload*, but applications may still benefit from shorter IT resource provisioning times in case of resource failures or during maintenance. Homogenization of these resources, an effect of the cloud computing property *resource pooling* introduced on Page 4 in Sect. 1.1 also reduces the complexity of the runtime environment and may enable applications to be developed and deployed more quickly.

   Figure 2.3 depicts an exemplary *static workload* handled using static scaling (left) and elastic scaling (right). Both provisioning approaches have the same amount of overprovisioned resources in case the experienced workload is lower than the predicted workload. In scope of elastic scaling, small adjustments may be made if the experienced workload comes close to utilizing the IT resources completely. However, the benefits of such dynamic adjustments are very limited as *static workload* does not change at all or only very little over time.

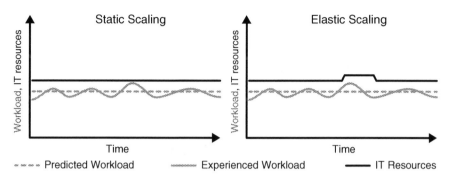

Fig. 2.3 Exemplary static workload

Result

An elastic cloud may be beneficial even for *static workloads*, because elasticity does not only provide costs savings. As clouds can provision new resources very quickly, often, within minutes, elasticity also simplifies provisioning and decommissioning tasks that are necessary for other reasons, for example, to address resource failures or for maintenance purposes. In case resources fail or need to be taken down for maintenance, an elastic cloud would, therefore, enable the rapidly provisioning of new resources to continue normal operation. Moving *static workloads* to a cloud offering can also be beneficial because of the IT resource homogenization. As the provider of the cloud offering can exploit economies of scale, the use of a standardized cloud offering might be cheaper than a build-your-own solution even when the workload transferred to the cloud offering is static.

In conclusion, the cost benefits of a cloud offering might be limited or non-existent in case of *static workload*. Costs may even increase. However, in certain cases the effects of homogenization of IT resources and elasticity in failure cases may still provide the necessary benefits to use a cloud.

Related Patterns
- *Infrastructure as a Service (IaaS)* (45): this cloud service model describes how (virtual) resources, such as servers, may be provided by a cloud. An application experiencing *static workload*, requires a fixed number of such servers, but may still benefit from such an environment if the provider supplies ready-to-use server configurations. Also, a server failure may be easier to cope with using provider-supplied management functionality.
- *Platform as a Service (PaaS)* (49): according to this cloud service model, the provider offers an environment to which custom developed applications are deployed directly. This alleviates the application developer from maintaining the hosting infrastructure required by the application. Elastic scaling of hosted application can also be handled by the provider transparently to the customer,

however, this is not the main benefit for applications experiencing static workload.

- *Software as a Service (SaaS)* (55): if complete applications experiencing static workload are obtained from a cloud environment, customers commonly pay on a per-user basis and benefit from provider-supplied infrastructure management.
- *Cloud deployment types* (Sect. 2.4): these patterns should be considered during the selection of a cloud provider to ensure that the application's requirements regarding security, privacy, and trust are met.
- *Elastic infrastructure* (87) and *elastic platform* (91): these patterns describe the how cloud offerings providing the runtime for the application behave, what interfaces they provide and which application artifacts have to be provided by developers. The interfaces are what an application experiencing static workload would interact with to provision replacements for failing resources as mentioned above.
- *Watchdog* (260): this pattern describes how applications may be monitored for failures. How to react to them automatically is further covered by the *resiliency management process* (283) that is executed by a *watchdog*.
- *Update transition process* (275): this pattern describes how the elasticity of a cloud may be used to switch between application versions. As this necessity is independent of the workload experienced by an application, is it also useful for applications experiencing *static workload*.

Known Uses

Static workload is experienced by many applications that do not fully utilize a single (virtual) server. Examples are private Websites or Websites of small and medium sized enterprises. Many small applications used internally by companies, are used continuously by a smaller user group, i.e., a documentation wiki used by one department or development group and, therefore, also experience *static workload*. Such small applications often cannot benefit from elasticity as it is impossible to shut them down them down during non-utilization, because their implementation was not designed for it. Also, these applications may be used periodically throughout a day hindering their shutdown as well.

2.2.2 Periodic Workload

> IT resources with a peaking utilization at reoccurring time intervals experience periodic workload.

 How can a periodically peaking utilization over time be characterized and how can applications experiencing this workload benefit from cloud computing?

Context

In our real-lives periodic tasks and routines are very common. For example, monthly paychecks, monthly telephone bills, yearly car checkups, weekly status-reports, or the daily use of public transport during rush-hour, all these tasks and routines occur in well-defined intervals. They are also characterized by the fact that a lot of people perform them at the same intervals. As a lot of the business processes supporting these tasks and routines are supported by IT systems today, there is a lot of periodic utilization that occurs on these supporting IT systems.

The problem with periodic tasks and static scaling of IT resources is that there must be enough IT resources to handle the utilization peaks while during the non-peak times these resources are unused. This *overprovisioning* results in a low average utilization of the allocated IT resources.

Solution

From a customer perspective the cost-saving potential in scope of *periodic workload* is to use a provider with a pay-per-use pricing model allowing the decommissioning of resources during non-peak times. This has the effect that the customer does not pay for the resources during these times. Cloud providers enable this elastic use by offering IT resources to a large group of customers that displays versatile workload behavior, a strategy that leads to the resource pooling property of clouds described on Page 4 in Sect. 1.1. Therefore, IT resources not needed by one customer are used by different customers resulting in a leveled overall utilization of the cloud offering.

Figure 2.4 shows the handling of *periodic workload* using static scaling (left) and elastic scaling (right). Static scaling always provisions IT resources for the predicted peak load regardless of the experienced workload. Elastic scaling enables the monitoring of the experienced workload. If this workload increases, new IT

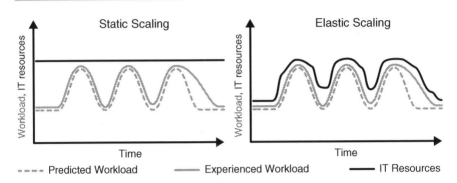

Fig. 2.4 Exemplary periodic workload

resources are provisioned dynamically. This makes the approach also less dependent on workload prediction. If the experienced workload deviates from predictions
as is the case for the last peak in Fig. 2.4, monitoring detects this abnormality and
resources are provisioned or, in this case, decommissioned accordingly.

Result

The benefits for customers result from unneeded resources being decommissioned
during non-peak times and, thus, these resources not generating costs during these
times. While the pay-per-use pricing model enables the customer to pay for used
resources only, the provider still has to provision static resources to host the
offering. To solve this discrepancy, the provider uses the resource-pooling cloud
computing property described on Page 4 in Sect. 1.1. The resources not used by one
customer can now be assigned to another customer. Thus, the business case for the
provider is based on the fact that multiple customers of the cloud offering have
workload patterns that complement each other in a way that the combined workload
is more-or-less *static workload* (26) on the provider side. In a *public cloud* (62)
offering, this static combined workload is achieved by making the cloud offering
generic enough and let very diverse customers use the cloud offering. In a *private
cloud* (66) the setting must be carefully evaluated so that multiple users, which can
be different applications, departments or local-business units, have a combined
workload that is somewhat static.

   Some cloud providers, furthermore, motivate a static long term use of their
offerings. For example, Amazon offers virtual servers of its Elastic Compute Cloud
(EC2) [18] at lower prices if they are provisioned for longer time periods, an option
called reserved instances [29]. Under such conditions, application developers
should consider provisioning some IT resources required by their custom
applications in a static fashion even when obtaining them from an elastic cloud.
Therefore, customers may face similar challenges as the cloud provider who has to
provision static resources for the peak-load of his or her offering. Due to the above

mentioned static pricing models of some *public clouds* (62), the same considerations can also lead to cost reductions when using *public clouds*.

Related Patterns
- *Infrastructure as a Service (IaaS)* (45): clouds of this service model provide (virtualized) servers on demand. To handle *periodic workload*, servers can, therefore, be provisioned and decommissioned as needed. The integration of these servers into an application has to be enabled by the application architecture as covered by the patterns discussed in Chap. 4.
- *Platform as a Service (PaaS)* (49): this cloud service model provides a hosting environment for custom applications that are deployed directly to it. Application management, i.e., to handle scaling or failure resiliency can be offered by the provider as well. Therefore, IT resource provisioning and decommissioning during the peaks of *periodic workload* may be handled transparently to the customer. However, provider-supplied management functionality often has to be configured, for example, regarding the intensity at which resources are provisioned when a workload increase is monitored. These configurations should be evaluated carefully in scope of *periodic workload* to ensure that provisioning and decommissioning offered by the provider is reactive enough for the concrete application scenario.
- *Software as a Service (SaaS)* (55): complete applications offered as a service are commonly billed per user. Pricing models can be, for example, on a per-month basis. This can hinder the effective use of such clouds in scope of *periodic workload* if the periodic peaks occur too frequently. For example, if a *SaaS* application is billed per user and month, peaks that are monthly or more frequent hinder efficient use of the offering.
- *Public cloud* (62), and *community cloud* (71): *periodic workloads* are good candidates to be outsourced to a cloud as they benefit from elasticity and pay-per-use pricing. This elasticity in most likely to be supported by *public clouds* and *community clouds*.
- *Private cloud* (66): one important aspect of *periodic workload* is that is often predictable. As the peaks are not unforeseen, the provider can plan with these peaks and try to find suitable other workloads with peaks that level-out the low-utilization times of customers. Thus, *periodic workloads* are good candidates for a resource-restricted *private cloud* where a provider can level out different users with *periodic workloads*.
- *Elasticity manager* (250), *elastic load balancer* (254), and *elastic queue* (257): to determine when to provision or decommission resources, the workload experienced by an application has to be monitored. These three patterns describe how additional management functionality can be integrated with the remainder of an application. They can be implemented best, if the application follows certain architectural styles that we cover in Chap. 4.

Known Use

One of the services provided by T-Systems to the T-City Friedrichshafen [30] is an online kindergarten signup application, where parents may sign up their children for kindergarten places available throughout the city. This sign up is only open twice per year, which is why the workload experienced by the application follows the *periodic workload* pattern.

2.2.3 Once-in-a-Lifetime Workload

IT resources with an equal utilization over time disturbed by a strong peak occurring only once experience once-in-a-lifetime workload.

 How can equal utilization with a one-time peak be characterized and how can applications experiencing this workload benefit from cloud computing?

Context

As a special case of *periodic workload* (29), the peaks of periodic utilization can occur only once in a very long timeframe. Often, this peak is known in advance as it correlates to a certain event or task. Even though this means that the challenge to acquire the needed resources does not arise frequently, it can be even more severe. The discrepancy between the regularly required number of IT resources and those required during the rare peak is commonly greater than for *periodic workloads* (29). This discrepancy makes long term investments in IT resources to handle this one-time peak very inefficient. However, due to the severe difference between the regularly required IT resources and those required for the one-time peak, the demand can often not be handled at all without increasing IT resources.

Solution

The elasticity of a cloud is used to obtain IT resources necessary to handle the *once-in-a-lifetime workload* flexibly. The provisioning and decommissioning of IT resources as well as their use and integration in an existing application can often be realized as a manual task performed by humans, because it is performed very rarely at a known point in time.

In Fig. 2.5, an exemplary *once-in-a-lifetime workload* is depicted. Characteristic for this type of workload is the large difference between the IT resources required during the peak and those required otherwise. As for *periodic workload* (29), static scaling provisions IT resources for the predicted workload peak. If this prediction is wrong and the experienced workload is higher, as is the case in Fig. 2.5, additional resources often cannot be provisioned quickly enough affecting the performance of the application and possibly the user experience. On the right side of Fig. 2.5, the same workload is handled using elastic scaling. As IT resources are provisioned manually for the one-time peak the IT resource curve shows sudden increases and

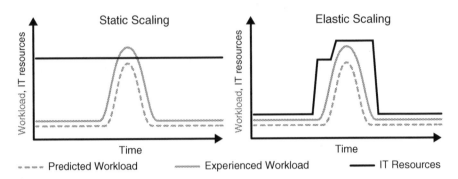

Fig. 2.5 Exemplary once-in-a-lifetime workload

decreases. The first increase is provisioned for the predicted workload. When the workload increases more than expected, the elasticity of the cloud enables the additional increase.

Result

Once-in-a-lifetime workload may be handled with the same automated mechanisms as *periodic workload* (29). In contrast to these automated mechanisms, the provisioning and decommissioning tasks necessary for *once-in-a-lifetime workload* may also be handled manually using the self-service capability of the used cloud offerings. As provisioning and decommissioning is only performed once, the benefits of an automated alignment of IT resource numbers to the experienced workload are reduced possibly making the additional effort to automate them unreasonable. Therefore, the provisioning of required IT resources, their integration into a company's IT landscape, possibly the assignment of workload to them, and their decommissioning may be handled by humans in these situations.

Related Patterns
- *Infrastructure as a Service (IaaS)* (45): this cloud service model enables the provisioning of many additional servers to be used by the *once-in-a-lifetime workload*. The integration of these servers into the customer's application, communication network etc. can often be realized as a manual task. Sometimes, the additional servers do not have to be integrated at all, but the workload assignment, it's processing, and the use of results is completely handled by users. This can be the case, if an employee needs one-time access to a powerful server provided by the *IaaS* offering.
- *Platform as a Service (PaaS)* (49): applications hosted on a provider-supplied *execution environment* (104) provided by a *PaaS* offering are often scaled automatically. However, in scope of *once-in-a-lifetime workloads*, the provider-supplied management functionality for elastic scaling may not be

reactive enough to detect and handle the extreme increase of resource demand automatically. Its behavior and configurability, therefore, has to be evaluated carefully in advance.

- *Software as a Service (SaaS)* (55): complete applications provided by *SaaS* offerings are commonly billed per month and users may sign up at any time. Therefore, a planned increase of application users to handle once-in-a-lifetime workload can usually be handled.
- *Public cloud* (62) and *community cloud* (71): all cloud deployment models are suitable for the handling of *once-in-a-lifetime workload*. The public and community cloud option is most flexible regarding the use of their resources. For workload peaks occurring only once in a lifetime, these deployment models, therefore, should be preferred.
- *Private cloud* (66): a private cloud can be less flexible as other cloud deployment models and establishing a private cloud often involves handling physical IT resources. Therefore, a *private cloud* is commonly only suitable for *once-in-a-lifetime workloads*, if the *private cloud* exceeds a critical size, thus, many applications of a company are hosted by it and experience changing workload. Problems may arise if *once-in-a-lifetime workload* peaks do occur for many of the hosted applications simultaneously.
- *Elastic infrastructure* (87) and *elastic platform* (91): these two patterns describe offerings providing virtual servers and execution environments for custom application components. Especially, they provide humans with self-service interfaces through which the resources necessary for the handling of *once-in-a-lifetime workload* may be provisioned and decommissioned.

Known Use

A good example for *once-in-a-lifetime workload* and one of the first well-known uses of cloud offerings is the digitalization of the New York Time archives. Four terabyte of digital scans of printed articles of the New York times between the years 1851 and 1980 were converted to Acrobat PDF documents using 100 virtual servers [31] dynamically obtained from Amazons Elastic Compute Cloud (EC2) [18]. The process was repeated and extended to provide full-text search by using an optical character recognition (OCR) tool [32]. The resulting article archive is available online and called the Time Machine of the New York Times [33].

2.2.4 Unpredictable Workload

IT resources with a random and unforeseeable utilization over time experience unpredictable workload.

How can random and unforeseeable utilization be characterized and how can applications experiencing this workload benefit from cloud computing?

Context

Random workloads are a generalization of *periodic workloads* (29) as they require elasticity but are not predictable. Such workloads occur quite often in the real world. For example, sudden increases of Website accesses due to weather phenomena or shopping-sprees when new products gain an unforeseen attention and public interest. The resulting occurrence of peaks or at least their height and duration often cannot be foreseen in advance under these conditions.

Solution

Unpredictable workloads require the unplanned provisioning and decommissioning of IT resources hosting applications. The necessary provisioning and decommissioning of IT resources is, therefore, automated to align the resource numbers to changing workload quickly and directly when it is being monitored. *Unpredictable workloads* are extremely hard to handle with static scaling shown at the left of Fig. 2.6. As the maximum workload peaks and the time when they occur are unknown, IT resources are often provisioned to a certain level that is economically feasible. If the workload exceeds what can be handled by these IT resources, the performance of the application degrades. Elastic scaling seen on the right of Fig. 2.6 can instead be used to monitor the experienced workload and base provisioning and decommissioning of IT resources on this information without relying on workload predictions. However, this requires a quick reaction to the workload change and very steep workload inclines can still be problematic as resources require time to be provisioned. If such strong workload inclines are anticipated, IT resources may have to be kept on standby, as described in greater detail by the *standby pooling process* (279) management pattern in Chap. 5.

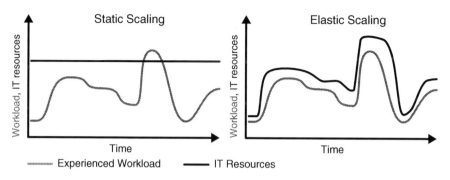

Fig. 2.6 Exemplary unpredictable workload

Result

As with *periodic workload* (29), providers have to be able to dynamically add and remove resources to customers during peak-workload times and remove them when workload intensity is lower. If one customer decommissions IT resources, the provider has to be able to assign these resources to another customer experiencing increased workload to offer a sustainable pay-per-use pricing model. Sometimes, providers move this problem partly to the customer side by offering resources for a reduced price if they are provisioned for longer time frames.

To benefit from the pay-per-use based pricing model, the customer has to be able to dynamically provision and decommission IT resources as well. As the peaks are random and unpredictable, utilization of resources is monitored and resource numbers are adjusted based on this information. The customer can either do this in custom developed management functionality or through configuration of provider-supplied management functionality. In either case, the application has to support the integration of newly provisioned IT resources as well as the removal of unused IT resources. Therefore, it has to be elastic itself as described by the cloud application property covered on Page 4 in Sect. 1.1.

Related Patterns
- *Infrastructure as a Service (IaaS)* (45): a cloud offering servers as *IaaS* commonly provides monitoring functions to detect workload increases. However, how to react to such situations often has to be configured or implemented by the customer. In this scope, it is very important to evaluate how long a server required by the application takes to be provisioned. In scope of *unpredictable workload*, the intensity of an increase may be very high creating the need to keep additional servers on standby as described by the *standby pooling process* (279) pattern.
- *Platform as a Service (PaaS)* (49): similar to the use of a provider-supplied *execution environment* (104) for custom applications experiencing *periodic workload* (29), the provider may supply management functionality handling

elastic scaling that has to be configured. Especially, the intensity of provisioning and decommissioning has to be specified directly affecting how well the application handles unpredicted peaks.

- *Software as a Service (SaaS)* (55): if complete applications are obtained as *SaaS* from a cloud offering, the workload manifests in the application being accessed by more users. As billing models are often based on monthly subscriptions, frequent workload peaks of *unpredictable workload* may hinder such offerings from being used efficiently. Nevertheless, customers still benefit from management tasks handled by the provider.
- *Public cloud* (62) and *community cloud* (71): these cloud deployment models are very flexible regarding the dynamic provisioning and decommissioning of resources and are, therefore, ideal for the handling of *unpredictable workload*.
- *Private cloud* (66): if a *private cloud* hosts few applications experiencing similar workload, simultaneous peaks of many handled applications can impose the problem of non-availability of IT resources, Therefore, the user-base must be large and diverse enough, so that workload peaks of applications can be leveled out regarding the overall utilization of the cloud.
- *Elastic infrastructure* (87) and *elastic platform* (91): to automate the provisioning and decommissioning of cloud resources, the cloud provider has to enable the customer to perform these tasks in custom applications and, thus, to monitor the utilization of an application to make good scaling decisions. The necessary provider interfaces are conceptually described by the *elastic infrastructure* (87), providing virtual servers as *Infrastructure as a Service (IaaS)* (45), and the *elastic platform* (91) hosting custom developed application components as *Platform as a Service (PaaS)* (49).
- *Elasticity manager* (250), *elastic load balancer* (254), and *elastic queue* (257): making adequate decisions when to provision and when to decommission IT resources is a challenging task. Applications and their runtime environment have to be monitored to identify overprovisioning or underprovisioning. These three patterns describe how the utilization of application components, requests assigned to them, or the number of messages exchanged with them can be used to make this decision, respectively.
- *Feature flag management process* (271) and *standby pooling process* (279): if the time it takes a cloud provider to provision new IT resources is too long for the anticipated workload increases, IT resources may have to be kept on standby. The *standby pooling process* (279) pattern describes how this can be handled. Additionally, feature flags may be used to degrade an application gracefully by keeping important functionality operational in case a sufficient amount of resources can still not be provisioned in time as described by the *standby pooling process* pattern.

Known Use

One example for *unpredictable workload* is the workload that occurs when building systems for connected vehicles. Some traffic patterns, such as rush-hour or traffic jams that concentrate workload on certain parts of the connected vehicle system can be anticipated. However, accidents and weather conditions, that require spontaneous re-routing requests or produce traffic jams that result in a higher load of requests to the central servers, cannot be predicted up front.

2.2.5 Continuously Changing Workload

> IT resources with a utilization that grows or shrinks constantly over time experience continuously changing workload.

 How can a continuous growth or decline in utilization be characterized and how can applications experiencing this workload benefit from cloud computing?

Context

Many applications experience a long term change in workload. Increasing workload often corresponds to the successful growth of a business after it was launched impacting the supporting applications. Decreasing workload is often experienced by legacy applications that still handle some of the workload that is slowly fading or by applications supporting discontinued products that are continuously used by fewer customers. In both cases – growing and shrinking workload – IT resources need to be provisioned or decommissioned with varying intensity. This growing and shrinking can be planned or unplanned, i.e., it can be previously known at which rate the growth or shrinking takes place or not.

Solution

Continuously changing workload is characterized by an ongoing continuous growth or decline of the utilization. This change can be linear, non-linear, exponential etc. but in any case, the change in utilization is consistent towards one direction. Elasticity of clouds enables applications experiencing *continuously changing workload* to provision or decommission resources with the same rate as the workload changes. Figure 2.7 shows an exemplary consistently increasing workload. The depicted static scaling and elastic scaling may be used analogous for continuously decreasing workload. In case of static scaling seen at the left of Fig. 2.7, IT resources are provisioned stepwise with the increasing workload. These large increments are present, because physical hardware, such as servers, are more efficiently provisioned in large bulks as manual tasks are involved. Elastic scaling on the other hand align the resource increments tightly to the increasing workload, because IT resources may be provisioned more flexibly and one by one as seen on the right of Fig. 2.7.

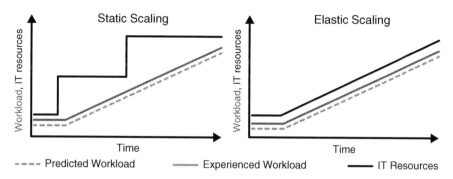

Fig. 2.7 Exemplary continuously changing workload

Result

If the rate of workload change is known and not very intense, the same effects apply as with planned *once-in-a-lifetime workload* (33). IT resource provisioning and decommissioning can be performed partially as manual activity via the self-service interface of the cloud offering. For a provider of a cloud or within a *private cloud* (66), a combination of applications experiencing increasing workload and decreasing workload can be used to level out the modification rate of IT resources. This approach is especially promising if a legacy application is replaced with a new application and both applications share a cloud, because the combined workload can be *static workload* (26).

In cases of *continuously changing workload* where the rate of workload change is varying or unknown, the same challenges arise as with the *unpredictable workload* (36), because the elastic scaling has to be adjusted automatically to the rate at which growing or shrinking takes place.

Related Patterns

- *Infrastructure as a Service (IaaS)* (45): pricing models used by *IaaS* cloud providers offering virtual servers commonly support *continuously changing workload* very well. Servers used by an application can be provisioned with increasing workload or decommissioned with declining workload. At a certain point, when an application is not used anymore at all, a *IaaS* provider often supports that virtual servers are shut down and persisted enabling the customer to restart and application on demand if it is needed again later.
- *Platform as a Service (PaaS)* (49): a provider-supplied *execution environment* (104) offered as *PaaS* behaves similar to an *IaaS* offering when facing *continuously changing workload*. As scaling may be handled by the provider, IT resources are provisioned and decommissioned automatically with increasing or declining workload, respectively. The intensity of these operations may have to be configured by the customer to match the continuously changing workload in a

concrete usage scenario. Similar to an *IaaS* offering, *PaaS* offerings often allow the suspend of an application at which point only minimal costs are generated.

- *Software as a Service (SaaS)* (55): if complete applications provided by the cloud as part of a *SaaS* offering are billed per user, use of such an offering to handle *continuously changing workload* is only beneficial if the number of users actually changes. If the same number of users access the application during a workload increase or decline – only more or less often – the costs generated by the application remain constant.
- *Public cloud* (62) and *community cloud* (71): *continuously changing workload* is especially suitable for these environments as they are less restricted regarding the number of IT resources that can be provided by them.
- *Elastic infrastructure* (87) and *elastic platforms* (91): just as for *periodic workload* (29) and *once-in-a-lifetime workload* (33), the self-service interfaces of these cloud offerings can be used to automate the provisioning and decommissioning of IT resources as the workload changes providing the required elasticity.
- *Elasticity manager* (250), *elastic load balancer* (254), and *elastic queue* (257): these three patterns describe how the change in workload may be monitored to determine the necessary adjustments in resource numbers.

Known Uses

An example for a constant decline in utilization is experienced by custom applications of manufacturers supporting specific products, i.e., provide customer manuals, service information etc. A product that is no longer in production will eventually vanish from the market, thus, continuously reducing the workload experienced by the application accessed, for example, by customers, retailers, or technicians.

2.3   Cloud Service Models

Just as the NIST cloud definition [3], the following patterns compare and categorize different cloud service models according to the layers of the application stack for which they provide IT resources. Figure 2.8 shows the application stack that we use throughout the book to illustrate on which layer certain cloud offering resides. The layers map to the NIST definition of cloud service models: *Infrastructure as a Service (IaaS)*, *Platform as a Service (PaaS)* and *Software as a Service (SaaS)*. From bottom to top the six layers comprising the stack are:

- **Physical hardware**: tangible physical infrastructure. This infrastructure contains, for example, servers, storage, networks connecting servers and racks containing the servers, as well as the building housing the data center, power lines etc.
- **Virtual hardware**: physical hardware components can be abstracted and mapped to virtual counterparts by a *hypervisor* (101) and *virtual networking* (132). The aim of this mapping is to share physical hardware between multiple

Fig. 2.8 Application stack
and associated cloud service
models

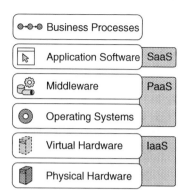

virtual counterparts, for example, virtual servers are mapped to fewer physical servers. This ensures that users of the virtual servers perceive the system as if they were the only one accessing it while physical hardware can be shared. Furthermore, virtualization reduces the need to physically adjust tangible resources, such as servers, networking switches, cables etc. in a datacenter when configurations have to be changed.

- **Operating system**: software installed directly on the physical or virtual hardware. Operating systems abstract hardware by providing functions to applications installed on the operating system, for example, to access network cards or files stored on the hard drive. Examples for operating systems on this layer are Microsoft Windows Server, Linux, or Apple OS X Server.
- **Middleware**: software on this layer is installed on an operating system and itself provides an environment for installation and execution of custom applications, processes, and data. Examples for such environments range from execution of certain programming languages, such as Python or the Java Virtual Machine to more complex middleware products hosting custom applications later described by the *execution environment* (104) pattern. Examples for more complex middleware are application servers such as JBoss or IBM Websphere, workflow engines such as Apache ODE, or IBM Websphere Process Server. Middleware can also provide communication services later characterized by the *message-oriented middleware* (136) pattern, for example, messaging by Apache ActiveMQ or IBM Websphere MQ. Data storage can also be handled by middleware, for example, MySQL, Oracle 11g, or IBM DB2. Such functionality is described by the storage offering patterns in Sect. 3.5 on Page 109.
- **Application software**: custom applications providing functionality to human users or other applications are associated with this layer. Examples for applications are software for customer relationship management systems (CRM) or enterprise resource planning (ERP).
- **Business processes**: the processes of a company that are supported by a set of applications are associated with this layer. These processes are domain specific and subsume, for example, order processing, credit approval processes, billing etc.

Cloud offerings can reside on any of these layers. *Infrastructure as a Service (IaaS)* (45) makes (virtual) hardware accessible to customers. This can be servers, network resources or storage. *Platform as a Service (PaaS)* (49) maintains an *execution environment* (104) for customers to deploy individual applications or components thereof. *Software as a Service (SaaS)* (55) offers a complete application that is accessible by humans through a graphical user interface or within the implementation of custom developed applications using an application programming interface (API).

The workload patterns that we covered in the previous section can occur on any level of the stack – be it on infrastructure, platform, software, or business process level. The level of interest for a customer is the level at which he or she outsources workload to the cloud. Thus, when outsourcing the infrastructure level, the workload patterns at the infrastructure level, i.e., server utilization and network load are of interest. Similar, the workload patterns at the software level, for example, user requests or the number of application users determine the necessity for elasticity when outsourcing on the *SaaS* level.

In the following, we cover each of the cloud service models in more detail, describe which part of the application stack is provider-supplied and which part is handled by customers, and highlight the specific features and properties with regard to the essential cloud properties: access via network, on-demand self-service, measured service (pay-per-use), resource pooling, and rapid elasticity. Also, we point to cloud offering patterns covered in Chap. 3 that describe the functionality provided on the different levels of the application stack in greater detail.

2.3.1 Infrastructure as a Service (IaaS)

Providers share physical and virtual hardware IT resources between customers to enable self-service, rapid elasticity, and pay-per-use pricing.

 How can different customers share a physical hosting environment so that it can be used on-demand with a pay-per-use pricing model?

Context

Applications often experience varying workloads that lead to different utilizations of IT resources on which these applications are hosted. Especially, in the scope of *periodic workloads* (29) with reoccurring peaks and the special case of *once-in-a-lifetime workloads* (33) with one dramatic increase in workload, IT resources have to be provisioned flexibly. One common hosting environment for applications is formed by independent servers on which applications are installed. With changing workload, the number of these servers shall be adjusted.

Solution

A provider using the *Infrastructure as a Service (IaaS)* service model offers physical and virtual hardware, such as servers, storage and networking infrastructure that can be provisioned and decommissioned quickly through a self-service interface. On these IT resources, customers install their individual operating systems, middleware, and applications software supporting their business processes as depicted in Fig. 2.9.

Result

IaaS clouds in detail offer infrastructure IT resources such as servers, storage (volatile memory and persistent disk storage) and networking. Many *IaaS* providers offer customers the choice to provision resources to multiple data center locations, allowing the distribution of applications and platforms across multiple geographic locations. How an *IaaS* cloud behaves is covered in detail by the cloud offerings patterns in Chap. 3. In this scope, the *elastic infrastructure* (87) pattern describes a common combination of cloud offering to provide *IaaS* to customers (see the

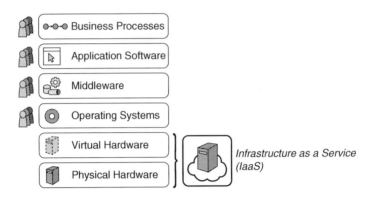

Fig. 2.9 Infrastructure as a service in the application stack

related patterns section for a detailed list). The cloud computing properties introduced in Sect. 1.1 on Page 3 are enabled in an *IaaS* cloud as follows.

Access via network: remote access to provided servers and to the storage disks is one of the key features of *IaaS*. Typically, after starting a virtual server it can be accessed remotely via a secure shell (SSH) or graphically, for example, using the remote desktop protocol (RDP) depending on the operating system running on the server and its configuration. Customers typically get full access to the servers.

On-demand self-service: customers can often access *IaaS* offerings via a Web-portal that allows customers to configure and provision servers, storage and network connectivity. One important aspect of such an on-demand self-service portal is the monitoring which allows supervising the status of the provisioned IT resources, their configuration and the corresponding charges. This information can also often be extracted from the cloud provider in an automated fashion using an application programming interface (API).

Pay-per-use: pricing models for *IaaS* are often based on an hourly charge for servers, amount of data stored per month, and amount of data exchanged via the cloud providers network per month. Prices for servers range from a few cents per hour for small servers to multiple dollars per hour for larger possibly clustered servers. To ease the calculation and comparison with traditional server processing power, volatile memory and disk storage costs are commonly determined according to a certain set of server configurations that resemble traditional servers. Often, several sizes of these server configurations are available resembling T-shirt sizes such as S, M, L, XL, XXL etc. Regarding the data exchanged with a cloud, different prices are often allocated for data uploaded to the cloud and data downloaded from the cloud. Therefore, when storing data in a cloud, the costs for transferring it and the additional monthly costs for storing it in the cloud have to be considered.

Resource pooling: resources of an *IaaS* cloud are shared between customers on the hardware infrastructure level. Thus, the IT resources pooled between different customers of an *IaaS* cloud typically are: the physical data center, physical servers, physical storage disks, and physical network components such as routers, switches, cables and firewalls as well as the personnel to maintain and operate the data centers.

Rapid elasticity: the flexibly use of servers is a key feature of *IaaS* clouds leading to their success and differentiating them significantly from other server hosting offerings. In a typical *IaaS* offering, new servers are started within minutes, firewalls and storage disks are provisioned almost instantly. Similarly all billed resources can be returned to avoid further charging, within minutes. This rapid elasticity on the infrastructure level enables adding and removing infrastructure resources on-demand.

Traditional server hosting could be compared to *IaaS*. However, these offerings often lack the dynamic pay-per-use billing model and rapid elasticity. Instead users pay monthly fees for servers whether they use them or not. Also, the ability to provision and decommission virtual servers via a self-service interface that can be accessed programmatically is often unavailable. However, the billing models of these hosting providers are sometimes also available at *IaaS* providers. Users may then decide between pay-per-use billing and a lower fixed price for resources that are provisioned for longer time periods.

Related Patterns

- *Elastic infrastructure* (87): an *IaaS* offering can subsume multiple services and functionality. A typical collection of this functionality is covered in greater detail by the *elastic infrastructure* pattern. The covered functions subsume repositories in which templates for servers including pre-installed and configured operating systems, as well as selected applications components or middleware are managed. Commonly, these images can be maintained by the cloud provider or can be created by the customer or a user community. Further-more, an *elastic infrastructure* typically offers an application programming interface (API) through which its functionality can be accessed. Thus, it becomes possible to dynamically provision and decommission (virtual) machines, storage and network elements. APIs are of particular importance when building more sophisticated *Platform as a Service (PaaS)* (49) offerings and *Software as a Service (SaaS)* (55) offerings that use these APIs to automatically scale on demand. Some of the functionality subsumed by an *elastic infrastructure* can also be offered as an independent cloud offering. Therefore, these offerings have been described as the separate patterns *hypervisor* (101), *block storage* (110), and *virtual networking* (132).
- *Hypervisor* (101): many cloud providers use hardware virtualization to host multiple servers provided to customers on an *IaaS* basis on a single physical server. The basic concepts of this virtualization are described by the *hypervisor* pattern. In almost all cases of publically available *IaaS* clouds, thus, *IaaS* offerings using the *public cloud* (62) deployment model, virtualization is used

as the basic implementation to realize the virtual server configurations. However, a few providers also offer physical servers as *IaaS* offering providing the same cloud properties described in Sect. 1.1 on Page 3.

- *Block storage* (110): as mentioned above disk storage is often provided by an *IaaS* offering in addition to servers. This storage can be kept independent from virtual servers in case a server is shut down or fails. The behavior of such offerings providing disk storage is described by the *block storage* pattern.
- *Virtual networking* (132): one of the resources typically provided and billed in an *IaaS* offering is the connection network and data exchanged through it. The network aspect of IaaS does not only include the bandwidth but often also firewalls that can be configured to allow access to and from certain ports over certain protocols to the resources started in the *IaaS* cloud. The virtual networking pattern describes how this aspect of an IaaS offering behaves.

Known Uses

Since the advent *IaaS* offerings, this type of cloud offering has gained widespread acceptance. A large number of offerings in form of *public clouds* (62) and in the form of virtual *private clouds* (66) have been established. Amazon's Elastic Compute Cloud (EC2) [18] and Rackspace [19] are *public cloud* (62) providers providing an *IaaS* offering. Other companies, such as T-Systems with their Dynamic Services for Infrastructure (DSI) [34] provide *IaaS* clouds for virtual *private cloud* (66) scenarios. In addition to these cloud offerings, a wide range of tools and data center automation products have been established, both in the open source and commercial market that enable companies and providers to build their own *private clouds* (66) offering *IaaS*. VMware's vCloud [20] is an example for a commercial implementation. OpenStack [35] is an open source implementation that is also used and supported by Rackspace [19]. Similar open source software for the management of an *IaaS* clouds is OpenNebula [36] and Eucalyptus [37]. Each of these implementations support most of the functionality common for an *elastic infrastructure* (87).

2.3.2 Platform as a Service (PaaS)

> Providers share IT resources providing an application hosting environment between customers to enable self-service, rapid elasticity, and pay-per-use pricing.

 How can custom applications of the same customer or different customers share an execution environment so that it can be used on-demand with a pay-per-use pricing model?

Context

In Sect. 2.2, various workloads have been covered and how applications experiencing them can benefit from an elastic cloud. Especially, *periodic workloads* (29), *once-in-a-lifetime workloads* (33), and *unpredictable workloads* (36) have shown suitable for this, but other type of workloads could also benefit from a cloud environment. *Infrastructure as a Service – IaaS* (45) flexibly provides servers to customers of applications for this purpose. However, this means that customers have to install and manage their own operating systems, middleware, and *execution environments* (104), such as a Java Virtual Machine, an application server, webserver, databases etc. If many customers require similar hosting environments for their applications, there are many redundant installations resulting in an inefficient use of the overall cloud. Furthermore, the management complexity to maintain an operating systems and middleware has to be handled by each customer of the *IaaS* offerings. Especially, small and medium-sized businesses may not have the manpower and skills to perform these tasks efficiently and thoroughly.

Solution

A cloud provider using the *Platform as a Service (PaaS)* service model offers managed operating systems and middleware. Customers may host individual application software supporting their business processes in this environment as depicted in Fig. 2.10. Management, such as updating operating systems or middleware is handled by the provider. Often, the provider expects custom applications to be developed in a certain style to additionally handle the elastic scaling and failure resiliency of applications for the customer.

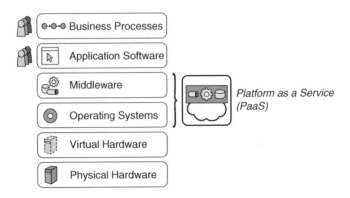

Fig. 2.10 Platform as a service in the application stack

Result

Platform as a Service (PaaS) subsumes the layers above physical and virtual hardware and below complete software applications – thus, it contains operating systems as well as middleware products, i.e., database management systems, application servers, *message-oriented middleware* (136) etc. How these individual services behave is covered in detail by the cloud offerings patterns in Chap. 3. In this scope, the *elastic platform* (91) pattern describes a common combination of these offering to provide *PaaS* to customers (see the related patterns section for a detailed list). The cloud computing properties described in Sect. 1.1 on Page 3 are enabled as follows in a *PaaS* offering.

Access via network: commonly, customers of a *PaaS* offering can access the offered *execution environments* (104) hosting an application via a network, most prevalent either an intranet or the Internet, to deploy their applications. Some *PaaS* clouds also offer development environments accessible for customers via a network to build and test their applications.

On-demand self-service: similar to an *IaaS* (45) cloud, *PaaS* clouds offer a self-service portal or an application programming interface (API) through which customers can deploy applications. In contrast to an *IaaS* cloud, the *PaaS* self-service interface often does not display virtual servers and does not allow starting and stopping individual servers. The *PaaS* self-service interface is instead focused on the offered environment that scales independently, thus, no scaling functionality is developed by the customer. The self-service portal also displays the consumed IT resources as well as their health status, i.e., their current availability and statistics for uptime and utilization.

Pay-per-use: as a *PaaS* offering provides an environment to host applications directly billing is performed based on the use of functionality provided by this environment. A *PaaS* provider can bill for different functionality, i.e., per user access to a hosted application, per message exchanged by that application etc. For example, Amazon bills per message queued in their Amazon Simple Queue

Service (SQS) [38]. Storage offerings are typically billed either per amount of items stored or per storage volume. Web application runtimes can be billed per amount of handled requests or per amount of exchanged data. *PaaS* offerings, thus, commonly bill according to the type of IT resources they offer, instead of billing for servers or network bandwidth, as *IaaS* (45) offerings do.

Resource pooling: when discussing *PaaS*, lines can be blurred between "native" *PaaS* offering and a managed *IaaS* offering with pre-installed and managed middleware components – a variation of *PaaS* covered in greater detail by the *elastic platform* (91) pattern. One important distinction is that a *PaaS* offering pools resources on the middleware layer whereas an *IaaS* offering pools resources on an infrastructure layer. Thus, in a *PaaS* storage offering, for example, multiple customers share the same middleware whereas they would have a distinguished instance of the middleware in an *IaaS* (45) cloud. However, to enable this sharing, isolation between customers has to be ensured. The consequence of sharing on the middleware layer is that the offered middleware has to be redesigned to be multi-tenant aware: for the customer it should appear that he or she is using a dedicated instance of the middleware. The provider can then balance load on the middleware layer, preventing the need to start and stop underlying virtual servers frequently. In a native *PaaS* isolation of tenants is also guaranteed through some throttling mechanisms, preventing that one customer uses up the resources assigned to the shared runtimes with faulty applications or by overloading the environment on purpose.

Rapid elasticity: flexible scaling on the platform layer requires the cloud provider to dynamically add and remove IT resources from individual customers depending on their demands. However, as *PaaS* clouds are characterized by their sharing capability on the middleware layer, this problem can be delegated to a load balancer. This load balancer distributes the requests of customers to the middleware instances that have the applications of the respective customer installed. Deployment of applications to middleware instances is handled in a transparent manner to the customer, either at deployment time or on-demand. Therefore, additional requests can be handled without modifying the applications. However, when all customers start to increase or decrease their number of requests, at some point more middleware instances need to be added to or removed from the *PaaS* cloud. This can either be done automatically via an underlying *IaaS* infrastructure or manually if the *PaaS* is not built upon an *IaaS* cloud. However, it is important that once the platform is scaled out with new middleware instances, these instances become able to serve a customer's requests. Again this is ensured by automatically deploying the customer's application on them.

Therefore, the key to be able to rapidly increase the amount of requests to be handled from one customer is the ability to dynamically and transparently distribute these requests among multiple instances of the middleware and, thus, among multiple (virtual) servers. This is similar to a traditional cluster with the addition of multi-tenancy, i.e. the ability to serve multiple customers concurrently from these middleware instances while guaranteeing isolation between those customers. In case of provider-managed scaling of the *PaaS* cloud, applications often have to be developed in a certain way to be deployed to multiple instances transparent to the user. Often, applications have to rely on external state information as described by the *stateless component* (171) pattern and by the *elastic platform* (91) pattern.

Related Patterns

- *Elastic platform* (91): a *PaaS* offering commonly consists of a certain set of functionality. As this functionality can be provided as individual cloud offerings, we described them as individual patterns. The *elastic platform* pattern describes how these other patterns are commonly combined to form a *PaaS* offering. The central functionality of a *PaaS* offering is an *execution environment* (104). Furthermore, the *elastic platform* can provide storage functionality in the form of a *blob storage* (112), *relational databases* (115), and *key-value storage* (119) as well as communication functionality to exchange information between hosted applications and external applications. This is covered in greater detail by the *message-oriented middleware* (136) pattern.
- *Execution environment* (104): this pattern describes how an environment can be provided in which customer-developed applications can be deployed and executed. Especially, it covers how functionality required by many applications can be provided by this environment so that implementation complexity is reduced for the customer.
- *Blob storage* (112), *relational database* (115), and *key-value storage* (119): an *elastic platform* (91) can provide file-system-like *blob storage*. Table-centric storage that supports more complex querying functionality that the retrieval of files is provided by *relational databases* and *key-value storage*.
- *Message-oriented middleware* (136): communication in cloud applications should be asynchronous to enable the loose coupling cloud application property described on Page 7 in Sect. 1.2. We cover how this property can be enabled in greater detail in the *loose coupling* (156) pattern as well.
- Cloud application architecture patterns (Chap. 4): applications deployed on an *elastic platform* (91) offered as *PaaS* should follow certain architectural principles to benefit efficiently from this environment. The patterns in Chap. 4 describe these principles as patterns. Most importantly, an application running on an *elastic platform* often has to be distributed, as described by the *distributed application* (160) pattern. Furthermore, it is important to consider where the application holds its state. Often, *PaaS* providers recommend or enforce that their own storage offerings mentioned above are used for this purpose, thus, the application must be implemented using *stateless components* (171). When interacting with the communication functionality, it is important to consider the delivery behavior. Messages can be delivered *at-least-once* (144) or *exactly-once* (141) using a *transaction-based delivery* (146) or *timeout-based delivery* (149) protocol. The application components interacting with this provider-supplied

functionality, therefore, may need to deal with message duplicates by implementing the *idempotent processor* (197) pattern. Furthermore, they may need to extend the delivery assurance of messages to assure their successful processing, by implementing the *transaction-based processor* (201) pattern or the *timeout-based message processor* (204) pattern. When interacting with cloud storage offerings provided as *PaaS*, data consistency assured by the provider also has to be considered as described by the *strict consistency* (123) and *eventual consistency* (126) patterns.

- Cloud application management patterns (Chap. 5): some *PaaS* providers handle the elastic scaling of hosted applications for the customer. If this task, however, has to be handled by the customer himself or herself, the cloud application may need additional management components (see Sect. 5.2 on Page 242) that monitor the workload experienced by the application and provision or decommission resources accordingly. An *elasticity manager* (250) does this based on the utilization information obtained about application components. An *elastic load balancer* (254) monitors the number of synchronous requests to the applications and an *elastic queue* (257) the number of asynchronous messages. The behavior implemented by these management components is covered in greater detail by management process patterns starting in Sect. 5.3 on Page 264.

Further Reading: there are additional patterns that cover application design. Even though most of these patterns did not have *PaaS* in mind when they were written, many of them are applicable to applications deployed on a *PaaS* offering. Hope and Woolf [1] cover patterns for message-based enterprise application integration. These patterns are also used by pattern of this book and are summarized by *the message-oriented middleware pattern* (136). Buschmann et al. [14], Gamma et al. [2], and Fowler [15] also describe patterns that can be considered when designing application components. Buschman et al. describe architectural patterns applicable to standalone and distributed applications. Gamma et al. cover best practices for object-oriented programming. Fowler's enterprise architecture patterns describes, for example, how a business usage scenario and the data and functionality it relies on may be mapped to data structures and application functions to be implemented.

Known Uses

PaaS offerings, such as Google's App Engine [21] or WSO2's Stratos Live [39] allow the deployment of (Java) Web applications. Others offer an *elastic platform* (91) to deploy and create business processes, for example, Metasonic [40], RunMyProcess [41] or Cordys [42]. In the virtual *private cloud* (66), offerings such as T-System's Dynamic Services for SAP solutions [43] also exist. Another well-known *PaaS* offering is Force platform [44] of salesforce.com which allows consumers to build extensions to the Salesforce CRM *SaaS* offering [45]. The Amazon Simple Queue Service (SQS) [38] offers *message-oriented middleware* (136) in the cloud. Other *PaaS* offerings do not only provide an *elastic platform* (91), but also additional services required in a certain business domain, for example, data about the stock market or systems to build and test customer-developed applications. An example of the latter is CloudBees [46] which offers a complete environment for software development and hosting.

2.3.3   Software as a Service (SaaS)

> Providers share IT resources providing human-usable application software between customers to enable self-service, rapid elasticity, and pay-per-use pricing.

 How can customers share a provider-supplied software application so that it can be used on-demand with a pay-per-use pricing model?

Context

The workload patterns covered in Sect. 2.2 have shown that different workloads experienced by an application make them more or less suitable for an elastic cloud environment. Especially, workload peaks experienced in scope of *periodic work-load* (29), *once-in-a-lifetime workload* (33), and *unpredictable workload* (36) can be handled efficiently by a cloud environment. However, a prerequisite for this decision is that the workload of applications has to be measured. Then, a cloud offering to host that application has to be selected. Regardless whether this offering follows the *IaaS* (45) or *PaaS* (49) service model, the application needs to be developed and deployed. Especially, small and medium enterprises may not have the manpower and know-how to develop custom software applications for this purpose. Other applications have become commodity and are used by many companies, for example, office suites, collaboration software, or communications software. However, if these applications are shipped to customers to be installed on IT resources managed by customers, the complexity to provision and maintain these resources or to select a suitable cloud provider still has to be handled by the customer.

Solution

A provider using the *Software as a Service (SaaS)* service model offers a complete software application to customers who may use it on-demand via a self-service interface. The provider, therefore, provides customers with application software to support their individual business processes as depicted in Fig. 2.11. Customers perform their individual business processes, but do not have to install and manage an application required to support these processes. Accesses to this application are billed on a pay-per-use basis.

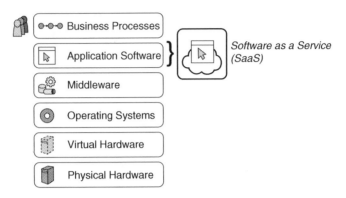

Fig. 2.11 Software as a service in the application stack

Result

SaaS is the established cloud service model in which the advantages of the cloud principles become most obvious. Instead of buying and installing hardware, paying for licenses, handling installation and configuration of the necessary middleware and software products, training and paying for system administrators on the hardware, middleware and software level, customers can simply obtain the required software from the cloud. In general, all applications could be provided by a *SaaS* cloud. Typical *SaaS* clouds provide application software for customer relationship management (CRM), collaboration, video conferencing and document management. Common to all *SaaS* offerings is the fact that a certain domain-specific functionality is offered, along with service level agreements (SLA) that guarantee the availability of that functionality. Applications offered as *SaaS* are managed, updated, and maintained by the provider. Customers can start using the provided applications in minutes instead of spending a significant amount of time to setup software applications on their own premises. Often, *SaaS* clouds allow the individual customers to configure and customize the application within defined boundaries, ranging from the specification of the user interface colors and logos to the configuration of workflows and custom data fields. The essential cloud computing properties introduced in Sect. 1.1 on Page 3 are enabled by a *SaaS* cloud as follows.

Access via network: in most cases, *SaaS* clouds provide Web-applications that offer a user interface accessed via HTTP over the Internet or an intranet of a company. Additionally, the functionality provided by the application can often also be accessed remotely via an application programming interface (API) to be integrated with other custom applications of a customer.

On-demand self-service: the Web-based user interface of a *SaaS* application provides management functionality through which customers can sign up for access to a *SaaS* offering. In this management user interface a customer can often test and evaluate the application(s) in question and can book the application. The customer will then be given access to the respective application and is also commonly provided with information about the application status, bills etc. The management interface also allows the customer to issue trouble tickets if needed. The self-service portal enables customers to add and remove additional users for the application, configure the application and provide access to the application's API in order to being able to integrate it with other applications of the customer.

Pay-per-use: the realization of pay-per-use depends on the domain of the *SaaS* application. Strictly speaking the unit of payment should be dependent on the objects this application deals with. For example, in a Web conferencing system, pay-per-use could mean that the provider charges for every minute a user accesses a Web-conference. This corresponds to the load that is put on the offering, in case customers conduct conferences, the software generates load and, thus, the provider bills the customer. Typically, for *SaaS* offerings where the load is not tied directly to an object managed by the system, or where the computation would be very complex, schemes that require a payment per user per month are established. It is assumed that each user that uses the application will put load on the system and, thus, costs occur for the provider.

Resource pooling: sharing of IT resources of a *SaaS* offering occurs on the software level. As a result different customers share not only the hardware and infrastructure resources as in the *PaaS* model but also the software resources. In this scope, customers are also called tenants, i.e., companies that have multiple employees accessing the application on their behalf. To prevent that different tenants interfere with each other, the application offered as a SaaS application must be multi-tenant aware and, thus, isolate tenants from each other, especially regarding the individual tenant's data. The advantage of multi-tenancy on the application layer is that the underlying middleware and infrastructure do not necessarily need to be multi-tenant aware as the isolation is handled on the application level. As an alternative to a multi-tenant solution, each tenant may be assigned a complete application stack for itself. This type of deployment is used by application service providers (ASP). However, the static fashion by which resources are assigned to tenants in this model hinders providers to share resources and scale elastically.

Rapid elasticity: in the context of a *SaaS* offering, rapid elasticity means that the offered software supports customers with a *periodic workload* (29), *unpredictable workload* (36), or *continuously changing workload* (40) profile, regarding the offered functionality. For example, for the teleconferencing offering this means that customers can book none or multiple teleconferences at once without necessarily having to pre-book them in advance or paying for one teleconference all the time even when they do not use it. Thus, as a consequence, the provider must balance the workload of the different tenants within the application. If this balancing is not possible an *elastic platform* (91) or *elastic infrastructure* (87) should underpin the application to be able to add and remove resources dynamically, if needed.

Related Patterns

The patterns in this book describe how cloud applications can be built on top of *IaaS* (45) or *PaaS* (49) offerings. The cloud application properties described in Sect. 1.2 on Page 5 are enabled through the use of cloud application architecture patterns of Chap. 4 and the cloud application management patterns of Chap. 5. Especially, the cloud application properties also make applications suitable to be offered as *SaaS* themselves. The following patterns are especially relevant to meet the challenges arising when offering applications to multiple tenants as a service:

- *Distributed application* (160): this pattern describes how an application's functionality may be decomposed to be distributed among several IT resources. This separation makes the application easier to scale elastically to handle the workload of all customers. It also assures that customers may configure on a finer granular which parts of the application shall be shared with other customers.
- *Stateful component* (168) and *stateless component* (171): an important aspect to consider in shared *SaaS* applications is the storage of data as customers are very sensitive to it. Therefore, application components that do not hold any state information are much easier to share between customers.
- *Data access component* (188): even though customers often require similar functionality, for example, for collaboration, schedules, project management etc. the data handled by customers may be domain specific. While every customer may, for example, manage his or her own customers using a *SaaS* application, the data associated stored for each customer is likely to be similar to other users of the *SaaS* application but may require some additional information. For example, a clothing retailer may want to store body size information for each customer in addition to common information, such as shipping addresses and billing information. In order to fulfill the requirements of all customers, a *SaaS* application, therefore, often has to be configurable regarding the data format it supports. How this can be achieved in a cloud application is covered by the *data access component* pattern.
- Multi-tenancy patterns (starting in Sect. 4.4 on Page 208): these patterns describe how application components comprising a *SaaS* application can be shared between different customers. Three different levels of sharing are covered in this section. *Shared components* (210) provide the same functionality to all tenants and do not support isolation. *Tenant-isolated components* (214) allow the tenant-specific configuration of the provided functionality and also ensure isolation between tenants. *Dedicated components* (218) are a portion of the application that is provided exclusively for a tenant. Often, *SaaS* (55) providers offer different implementations of application components and let the customer decide to which degree application functionality shall be shared with others.

Side Note: the patterns *elastic infrastructure* (87) and *elastic platform* (91) describe what kind of behavior users of *IaaS* (45) clouds and *PaaS* (49) clouds may expect, respectively. To match the cloud service model descriptions (Sect. 2.3), one could expect patterns describing the same aspects for *SaaS* (55) clouds. However, these are missing for two reasons. First, *SaaS* clouds differ significantly in behavior and functionality, depending on the business domain they support. Therefore, in these clouds, there is no common behavior by the time of this writing that could be abstracted to a pattern. The second reason, why these patterns are missing is that *SaaS* clouds do not form the basis for applications whose architecture can be based on the patterns described in this book. In scope of *SaaS* no custom code is deployed whose architecture would have to be considered. Some applications offered as *SaaS* can be extended using custom code in which case, the *SaaS* provider commonly offers a well-integrated *PaaS* cloud to host custom extensions to the *SaaS* application.

Known Uses

Saleforce.com offers a Web-based customer relationship management (CRM) software [45] as a *SaaS* offering. As customers demand extensibility and configurability of this application, salesforce.com also offers the Force platform [44] an *elastic platform* (91) as *PaaS* (49) to host such custom extensions, i.e., to integrate the SaaS CRM software with customers' other, possibly on-premise applications. Microsoft offers its complete office and collaboration suite as a Service, as part of Office 365 [47]. IBM offers collaboration software as part of its IBM SmartCloud [48]. Similar products, subsuming office and collaboration functionality, are available from Google Apps [49] as well. Telco providers, such as Deutsche Telekom started to offer *SaaS* applications, for example via their Business Marketplace [50] offering which allows independent software vendors (ISVs) to provide their applications in a *SaaS* model, where the telco provider handles automatic provisioning, billing, and support.

2.4   Cloud Deployment Models

Regardless of the service model followed by a cloud provider, a cloud can be hosted in different forms. These cloud deployment models can be mainly differentiated by the user groups accessing a cloud and the degree by which IT resources hosting the cloud itself are shared between customers. Regarding the accessibility of a cloud, the following cloud deployment types are introduced by the NIST cloud definition [3]: *public clouds* – generally accessible to everyone, *private clouds* – accessible only by a single institution, *community clouds* – accessible to a controlled group of institutions, and *hybrid clouds* – combining any set of other clouds. The NIST has further identified a number of deployment scenarios regarding the physical resources on which the different cloud deployment models may be hosted [51].

The following patterns cover these cloud deployment models and different ways to host them in detail. In this scope, we use the term "tenant" for companies or individuals that act as a customer of a cloud. Each tenant may have multiple users associated with it, i.e., a company may act as the customer of a cloud that is then used by employees of that company. We characterize each cloud deployment model regarding the number of tenants accessing the cloud and the number of tenants sharing IT resources hosting the cloud itself. For example, access to a cloud may be restricted to a certain user group, while the IT resources hosting the cloud itself may still be shared with others. Furthermore, we investigate what the different restrictions in accessibility mean for customers and providers and how the different cloud properties (see Sect. 1.1 on Page 3) access via network, on-demand self-service, measured service (pay-per-use), resource pooling and rapid elasticity influence the use of different cloud deployment models.

The restriction of the number of tenants accessing a cloud and sharing IT resources has a significant impact on the cloud properties displayed by different cloud deployment models, especially, regarding resource pooling, rapid elasticity and subsequently metered service (pay-per-use). A larger number of tenants reduces the effects of workload changes experienced by one tenant on the overall workload to be handled by the cloud provider. This is the case, because the overall workload subsumes all tenant workloads. By allowing fewer tenants to share a cloud or the underlying IT resources, the overall workload experienced by the cloud is less likely to be leveled out. The resulting workload changes make it harder for the cloud provider to ensure rapid elasticity, because resource pooling between tenants is less effective. This also affects the ability of the cloud provider to enable pay-per-use pricing models, because IT resources may become underutilized.

Figure 2.12 depicts the different cloud deployment models regarding the common level of elasticity and pay-per-use they provide. A *public cloud* (62) having the most tenants sharing it can enable the highest levels of elasticity and pay-per-use where only the operational costs are billed to customers. A *community cloud* (71) serves fewer tenants, often collaborating companies. An upfront investment may be required by these companies to establish the *community cloud* (71). Also, elasticity may be reduced as the collaborating companies may experience similar workloads. This effect is even more predominant in a *private cloud* (66) used by only one

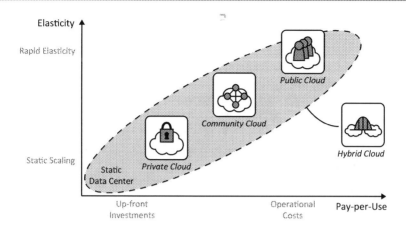

Fig. 2.12 Level of elasticity and pay-per-use of different cloud deployment types

tenant making upfront investments and reduced elasticity even more likely. A static data center is not covered by a pattern, but depicted in Fig. 2.12 as well. It does not use cloud computing technologies, requires up-front investments, and does not provide elasticity. The *hybrid cloud* (75) spans all these properties as it integrates applications hosted in the different environments. Note that the properties displayed by cloud deployment types are not generic. A *private cloud* accessed by a similar large and diverse user group as a *public cloud* is likely able to present the same properties. A *public cloud* used only by a small number of customers that experience similar workload will face similar challenges as a *private cloud*.

After reading this section you will be able to investigate which cloud deployment model is suitable for you application scenario. We cover each cloud deployment model in detail and how it deals with the essential cloud properties introduced in Sect. 1.1 on Page 3.

2.4.1   Public Cloud

> IT resources are provided as a service to a very large customer group in order to enable elastic use of a static resource pool.

 How can the cloud properties – on demand self-service, broad network access, pay-per-use, resource pooling, and rapid elasticity – be provided to a large customer group?

Context

A provider offering IT resources according to one of the cloud service models, *IaaS* (45), *PaaS* (49), or *SaaS* (55) has to maintain physical data centers that are limited in capacity. IT resources hosted in these static datacenters, nevertheless, shall be made accessible to tenants dynamically following a pay-per-use pricing model. The capacity of the data center, however, has to be planned statically and cannot be adjusted with the same elasticity, even though this behavior shall be displayed to customers. Enabling this elastic use of an otherwise static environment is especially challenging if customer experience changing workload described as *periodic workload* (29), *once-in-a-lifetime workload* (33), *unpredictable workload* (36), or *continuously changing workload* (40). Additional problems arise for the provider and the customer, as the different customers may not trust each other and, therefore, have to be isolated.

Solution

The *public cloud* is the cloud deployment model that best meets the desired cloud computing properties, because it serves a large number of customers and is, thus, large enough for customer diversity to level out peak workloads of individual applications. A *public cloud* shares a provided hosting environment between customers and this environment is accessible by many customers as depicted in Fig. 2.13 possibly reducing the costs for an individual customer. Leveraging economies of scale in this fashion, furthermore, enables a dynamic use of the static environment by customers, because workload peaks of some customers occur during times of low workload of other customers. The different workloads experienced by customers' applications are, therefore, leveled out regarding the overall customer group. This results in a more or less *static workload* (26) experienced by the provider that can be handled by a static number of physical IT resources in the

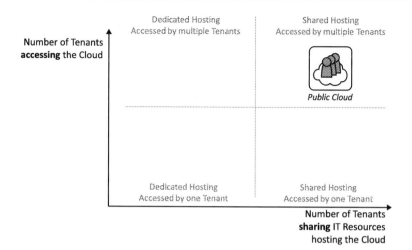

Fig. 2.13   Public cloud

data center. Security mechanisms are employed to isolate customers from each other. Often, this involves monitoring accesses and data entering and leaving the cloud in order to identify unlawful behavior. Such mechanisms are of vital importance to the success of the cloud provider, because trust is the major asset for the acceptance of *public clouds*.

Result

By sharing resources between a large number of customers and because of customer diversity, for example, due to geographic customer distribution, it is ensured that the peak workloads of customers can be handled, because other customers require fewer resources during those times. The size of a *public cloud* enables dynamic and elastic resource usage, while ensuring a leveled utilization of the static physical data center hosting the cloud. The capacity of this data center may be adjusted with much less dynamicity. The essential cloud computing properties introduced in Sect. 1.1 on Page 3 are enabled by *public clouds* as follows:

Access via network: *public clouds* are commonly made available over the Internet as they aim at being open to anyone without the need to install access software on the client. However, *public clouds* can also be available via a restricted and secured network connection.

On-demand self-service: in a *public cloud*, on-demand self-service is commonly realized as a Web-portal that allows customers to register with their credit card and then book, provision, manage, and decommission applications, platforms or infrastructure via that Web-portal. Also, an application programming interface

(API) is often provided to customers for automation of these tasks in their applications. Commonly, the allowed customer group is unrestricted enabling anybody with a credit card to sign up and use the *public cloud*. No complex setup or administration is needed on the provider side to accommodate a new customer. Customers can view their resource consumption and other monitoring information via the Web portal. The consequence of being able to rapidly sign up and then provision resources is that the Web portal and the cloud is seen as a standalone system that is not integrated in the order management and billing processes of the customer. As a consequence, even corporate users often use their private credit cards to book IT resources in *public clouds*.

Pay-per-use: *Public clouds* commonly do not require any upfront investments and bill strictly on a pay-per-use basis. Sometimes, cloud providers motivate long-term provisioning of IT resources by charging less for IT resources that are provisioned for a longer timeframe. This is beneficial for customers who may handle their *static workload* (26) with such resources and provision pay-per-use resources for workload peaks only. For the provider, the impact of workload changes on the customer side may be less and easier to predict by offering such pricing models. Some *public cloud* providers also offer cheaper resources during times when the overall utilization of the cloud is low in order to motivate time-uncritical applications to perform processing during these non-peak times and not during those times when the workload experienced by the cloud is high.

Resource pooling: *public clouds* are ideal with regard to resource pooling as they allow many customers to access and use the environment. These customers host different applications with versatile workload ensuring that workload peaks can be balanced across applications of multiple customers. As the cloud customer base and the users of applications hosted by these customers are large enough and provide enough diversity to level out peaks of individual applications, *public clouds* are often cheaper than *private clouds* (66) that sometimes have to deal with very similar usage by a few applications of a customer. One essential property that *public cloud* providers need to implement on their respective layer on the stack, i.e., the cloud service model they use, is multi-tenancy. As multiple customers (tenants) use the same IT resources, isolation is of crucial importance and must be guaranteed by the provider.

Rapid elasticity: *Public clouds* do not have any restrictions with regard to rapid elasticity as they are typically not integrated with customer-internal processes such as approval processes that sometimes hinder elasticity. Public clouds are often associated with unlimited resource availability, however, some cloud providers limit the amount of resources an individual consumer can host at the same time and implement higher quota only on request to accommodate customers with higher resource demands. The pricing models may be less dynamic than the degree of elasticity displayed by the cloud. Provisioned IT resources often become available within minutes and can be decommissioned with similar reactivity. However, the billing intervals may be longer, for example, resources may be billed for an hour even though they were provisioned only for 30 min.

Related Patterns

- *Infrastructure as a Service (IaaS)* (45): a *public cloud* offering *IaaS* provides a flexible and easy-to-use hosting environment for servers. Provider-supplied or customers-managed configurations of these servers, so called server images containing hardware configuration, operating systems, and pre-installed software, enable a quick provisioning of standardized servers. The physical hardware of *public IaaS clouds* is often virtualized through the use of *hypervisors* (101) to enable the sharing of physical hardware between customers. This resource pooling between customers eases elastic provisioning and decommissioning of servers and leads to low prices for customers all of which is relevant to provide the cloud properties covered in Sect. 1.1 on Page 3 to customers.
- *Platform as a Service (PaaS)* (49): a *public cloud* offering *PaaS* provides an open *elastic platform* (91) offering an *execution environment* (104) used by custom applications in addition to a number of offerings for communication and storage that hosted applications can use. These environments are often designed for publicly accessible Web-applications and provide functionality required in this scope.
- *Software as a Service (SaaS)* (55): *public clouds* offering *SaaS* provide standardized ready-to-use globally accessible applications over the Internet. These applications are commonly configurable in provider-defined means. The infrastructure and application components are highly shared with other customers to enable elasticity and pay-per-use. Typically, there are no upfront investments, but monthly fees per user accessing the application.

Known Uses

Public clouds providing *IaaS* are, for example, the Amazon Elastic Compute Cloud (EC2) [18], and Rackspace [19]. The Google App Engine [21], Microsoft Windows Azure [52], WSO2 Stratos Live [39], and Amazon Elastic Beanstalk [53] are examples for *public clouds* offering *PaaS* for applications developed in different programming languages. *Public clouds* using the *SaaS* service model are the Google Apps [49] or the Saleforce Customer Relationship Management (CRM) [45] offering. The Google Apps [49] provide collaboration tools, such as e-mail or scheduling. Salesforce also provides a *PaaS* (49) offering for extensions to its CRM *SaaS* offering, the Force [44] platform.

2.4.2 Private Cloud

> IT resources are provided as a service exclusively to one customer in order to meet high requirements on privacy, security, and trust while enabling elastic use of a static resource pool as good as possible.

 How can the cloud properties – on demand self-service, broad network access, pay-per-use, resource pooling, and rapid elasticity – be provided in environments with high privacy, security and trust requirements?

Context

Many factors, such as legal limitations, trust, and security regulations, motivate dedicated, company-internal hosting environments only accessible by employees and applications of a single company. These environments may follow any of the cloud service models: *IaaS* (45), *PaaS* (49), or *SaaS* (55). As they shall be used exclusively by one company, the challenge arises that physical data centers have a static capacity but shall provide a certain level of dynamicity and elasticity of IT resource use. Since the user group is, however, often smaller than in a *public cloud* (62) and often displays a similar workload behavior, economies of scale are harder to leverage.

Solution

A *private cloud* enables the cloud computing properties in a company-internal data center, thus, only one tenant accesses the cloud. Alternatively, the private cloud may be hosted exclusively in the data center of an external provider, then referred to as *outsourced private cloud* as depicted in Fig. 2.14 and according to the NIST cloud definition [3]. In case of an *outsourced private cloud*, some IT resources, such as networking infrastructure may be shared with other tenants. Sometimes, *public cloud* (62) providers offer means to create an isolated portion of their cloud made accessible to only one tenant, but still sharing hosting IT resources with all other tenants. This alternative, a *virtual private cloud*, is further described in the variation section.

Result

The main difference between a *private cloud* and other cloud deployment models is that the IT resources hosting the cloud that are shared with other customers are

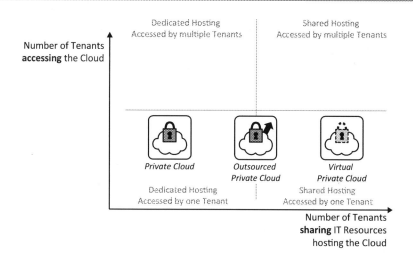

Fig. 2.14 Private cloud, outsourced private cloud, and virtual private cloud

reduced drastically, up to the point where no resources are shared. This separation may, especially, include the physical separation of networking hardware or the physical location of the data center as a whole. A *private cloud*, therefore, may provide a high level of security and privacy, which may, however, reduce its elasticity and the ability to provide a pay-per-use pricing model. This limitation is often caused by the smaller customer groups as, for example, in *public clouds* (62). The workloads of different tenants, thus, do not level each other out with respect to the workload experienced by the cloud as a whole. Static IT resources supporting the cloud then have to be provisioned for peak workloads as the peak workload of one tenant cannot be addressed with resources that another tenant does not need at that specific time. Of course, *private clouds* of a significantly large company whose employees display the same degree of diversity regarding work-load behavior as customers of a *public cloud* (62) do not experience such limitations. Such very large *private clouds* can be considered equivalent to *public clouds* regarding the level of elasticity they provide. In this book, we mostly consider *private clouds* to be smaller than *public clouds* leading to the above mentioned challenges and limitations.

To fully support the cloud computing properties as a *public cloud* (62) does, a *private cloud* has to have a certain number of globally distributed users, so that the workload experienced by different departments is leveled out. But even if a *private cloud* does not exceed the critical size to leverage economies of scale effectively, the introduction of *private clouds* to a company can still be beneficial. A *private cloud* centralizes and standardizes IT resources to leverage economies of scale as good as possible and to enable automated management. This homogenization and automation helps companies to reduce their IT management costs, which are significantly inflicted by the complexity of heterogeneous IT environments [7].

The cloud computing properties introduced in Sect. 1.1 on Page 3 are enabled as follows.

Access via network: depending on the type of *private cloud* – normal or *outsourced private cloud*, access via the connection network is different. In a normal *private cloud* hosted in a company's own datacenter, access is enabled via the company-internal network. In an *outsourced private cloud* access is often realized via secured communication channel between the customer and provider networks, a so-called a virtual private network (VPN). A *virtual private cloud* uses the same connection network as the *public cloud* (62) offered by the cloud provider.

On-demand self-service: in a *private cloud* this property is commonly assured by a Web-portal providing a self-service interface similar to a *public cloud* (62). In difference to *public clouds*, customers do not sign up with their credit card but with their company-internal billing targets, such as project names or department identifiers. Furthermore, company-internal cost-management often requires that order management, approvals, and billing are integrated with the self-service interface to reflect the company-internal procedures. Especially, approval processes are often integrated into the self-service portal of a *private cloud*. In an *outsourced private cloud* setting in which integration with a customer's on-premise IT infrastructure is required, the provider's identity management, order management and billing systems are commonly integrated with the customer's systems. This integration can make the setup of such an *outsourced private cloud* quite complex.

Pay-per-use: in a *private cloud* where a set of IT resources is used only by one individual company and then elastically assigned to projects, applications or departments of that company, pay-per-use is often not easy to ensure. This is caused by the fact that all IT resource of the *private cloud* are provided exclusively for one company and, thus, experience the workload peaks of that company. Therefore, IT resources have to be provisioned for peak workloads if the company-internal diversity of user behavior is insufficient to level-out the utilization of the overall cloud. As a consequence, IT resources may experience times of low utilization hindering pay-per-use as these resources generate costs for the provider but are not used. In an *outsourced private cloud* the initial resource provisioning is delegated to the provider. The provider may assign some resources dynamically to this *outsourced private cloud*. However, it often has to be ensured at all times that no resources are shared between customers, which may increase the complexity of the process.

Resource pooling: key for effective resource pooling and, thus, the ability to scale elastically is the right mix of applications that allow balancing the peak workload while keeping overall resource utilization high. In a *private cloud*, resources cannot be shared between customers. The number of users sharing a resource pool is commonly reduced to the employees of the company using the *private cloud*. Therefore, resource pooling in a *private cloud* cannot be established on an intra-company basis, but has to occur on an intra-department or intra-application basis by shifting IT resources between different departments, applications, or other organizational entities as the experienced workload demands. This may reduce the benefits of resource pooling to enable elasticity and pay-per-use in small *private clouds*.

Under these conditions, companies still benefit from the homogenization and centralization aspects of a *private cloud*. For example, a *private cloud* can provide standard development servers to reduce setup times for new projects.

Rapid elasticity: rapid elasticity works similarly in a *private cloud* as in a *public cloud* (62) regarding the enabling technologies. IT resources may, therefore, be provisioned and decommissioned very quickly via the self-service interface. There are two factors in a *private cloud* that may, however, hinder rapid elasticity: the limited size of data centers and a company's management processes involving human tasks. The former aspect means that elasticity in a *private cloud* may be limited if the whole company experiences a workload peak simultaneously, because rapid elasticity can only be performed within the boundaries of smaller static data centers. The second aspect considers the impact of a company's approval processes, billing processes etc. on provisioning and decommissioning times. For example, if a company requires a human manager to approve every provisioning of a new server for a project, this approval likely takes very long with respect to the actually required time to provision the server in the *private cloud*. Therefore, the integration of these processes with the self-service interface is of vital importance.

Variations

As a compromise between the flexibility of *public clouds* (62) and the security of *private clouds*, *public cloud* providers may offer so called *virtual private clouds*. These portions of a *public cloud* are often separated from other customers using the environment through networking and access configurations. This ensures that the *virtual private cloud* is isolated to some degree from other resources in the *public cloud* (62) while some IT resources may still be shared. Often, the *virtual private cloud* can additionally be integrated into the *private cloud* of a company using an encrypted communication link, such as a virtual private network (VPN) connection. The *virtual networking* (132) pattern discusses the used technologies offered by the *public cloud* provider as a communication offering in greater detail.

Related Patterns

- *Infrastructure as a Service (IaaS)* (45): a *private cloud* offering *IaaS* provides a flexible, isolated, and trusted hosting environment for servers accessible by one company. The provided virtual servers are standardized, as server images containing the server configuration, operating systems, and pre-installed software, may be shared between tenants, i.e., departments of the company. Multiple servers may be provisioned based on a server image, as described by the *elastic infrastructure* (87) pattern. As hardware is not shared with others companies, the *private cloud* provides a high degree of isolation between the hosted servers but limited elasticity. Upfront investments in hardware may be necessary when establishing this deployment model.

- *Platform as a Service (PaaS)* (49): the combination of *PaaS* and *private clouds* provides a standardized, isolated and trusted *execution environment* (104) for custom applications that provides common functionality for communication and storage used by these applications. While elasticity may still be limited, a high level of homogenization is realized by this environment as many applications of a company share it and rely on commonly accessible functions. Upfront investments may be required.
- *Software as a Service (SaaS)* (55): a *private cloud* following the *SaaS* service model offers trusted standardized applications to one company that are either standard applications or custom developed applications. This application is commonly used by many employees in a self-service manner and is integrated with other applications of the company. Similar to the other cloud service models using a *private cloud* may require upfront investments in infrastructure.
- *Batch processing component* (185): applications on a private *PaaS* or *IaaS* cloud may be designed to control the utilization of IT resources by delaying some of the workload processing. Especially, in a *private cloud*, where the overall number of IT resources that can be used elastically may be restricted, this allows processing workload when conditions are most feasible. *Batch processing components* (185) provide asynchronous application functionality that is accessible at all times, but is only processing requests when resources are available. Thus, the knowledge of the workload profiles of all applications hosted in a *private cloud* offering can lead to better resource utilization.

Known Uses

Tools to establish a private *IaaS* cloud in a company-internal datacenter are provided, for example, by the VMware product suite comprised of vCloud [20], vSphere [54], and ESX [54]. Open source software supporting similar functionality are Eucalyptus [37], OpenNebula [36], or OpenStack [35]. The mentioned variation of a *virtual private cloud* offering *IaaS* (45) is, for example, provided by Amazon Virtual Private Cloud (VPC) [55] or T-Systems' Dynamic Services for Infrastructure (DSI) [34].

2.4.3   Community Cloud

IT resources are provided as a service to a group of customers trusting each other in order to enable collaborative elastic use of a static resource pool.

 How can the cloud properties – on demand self-service, broad network access, pay-per-use, resource pooling, and rapid elasticity – be provided to exclusively to a group of customers forming a community of trust?

Context

Companies may have to collaborate for various reasons. For example, a company may be a supplier of another company. Furthermore, a group of companies or public institutions, such as university or hospitals may have to exchange information or may have to share personnel for cost reduction. Whenever companies collaborate, they commonly have to access shared applications and data to do business. While these companies trust each other due to established contracts etc., the handled data and application functionality may be very sensitive and critical to their business, thus, rendering the use of an easily accessible *public cloud* (62) impossible. Also, *private clouds* (66) may be unsuitable, because IT resources are not used exclusively by one company but need to be accessed by the collaborating community.

Solution

IT resources required by all collaborating partners are offered in a controlled environment accessible only by the community of companies that generally trust each other. This *community cloud* contains all shared data and functionality that the participating companies need to do their business. Depending on the concrete requirements on privacy, security, and trust, a *community cloud* can be provided in a private data center controlled by the collaborating companies (often, one company acts as the cloud provider). Also, the *community cloud* be hosted in a data center of a third party, then referred to as *outsourced community cloud* shown in Fig. 2.15. Another variation is the hosting of a community cloud in an isolated portion of a *public cloud* (62) called *virtual community cloud*.

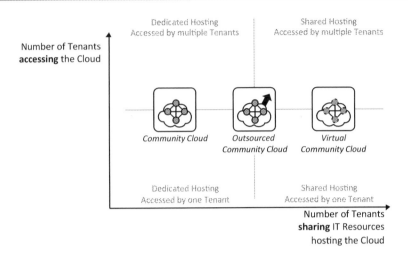

Fig. 2.15 Community cloud, outsourced community cloud, and virtual community cloud

Result

A *community cloud* hosted by one company is commonly used if this company has a central role in the collaboration, for example, a manufacturer provides a collaboration environment shared by its employees, contractors, and suppliers. *Outsourced community clouds* are, especially, suitable, if there is no company trusted enough by all the other companies to maintain the data center. *Virtual community clouds* are commonly easiest to establish as they depend on resources of a *public cloud* (62) to which access is only granted to collaborating partners. The cloud computing properties introduced in Sect. 1.1 on Page 3 are enabled by a *community cloud* as follows.

Access via network: similar to *public clouds* (62) and *private clouds* (66), the *community cloud* provides a Web-based self-service interface accessible by humans and commonly an applications programming interface (API) to be used for automation of provisioning and decommissioning of IT resources. If the *community cloud* is hosted by one company, that company may access it via its own network and grants external access to collaborating partners through a secured connection, i.e., via a virtual private network (VPN).

On-demand self-service: on-demand self-service within the *community cloud* follows the same principles as a *public cloud* (62). Any of the collaborating companies can provision and decommission IT resources, which are then billed to the ordering institution. The integration of company-internal billing and management processes is often not realized to the same degree as in a *private cloud* (66), because the individual processes of collaborating companies may differ significantly.

Pay-per-use: to establish a *community cloud*, up-front investments may be necessary for the collaborating companies. After its installment, the ability of the *community cloud* to provide pay-per-use to users mainly depends on its size and whether or not the workloads experienced by the collaborating companies lead to a leveled overall utilization of the cloud. This diversity may be less compared to customers of a *public cloud* (62), because collaborating companies may experience similar workload peaks due to tasks they perform together. The billing model supported by the *community cloud* needs to reflect that there are multiple companies that can order IT resources in the *community cloud*. This is similar to a *public cloud* (62), however, further billing models may be required. For example, one company may order IT resources to be used by its suppliers. Therefore, the tenant ordering the IT resources has no control over the users accessing them as would be the case if users were the employees of the ordering company. If IT resources are billed on a per-request basis, the ordering company may desire to define quotas on accesses performed by suppliers, which has to be supported by the *community cloud*.

Resource pooling: resources are shared between the collaborating companies. Therefore, the number tenants between which resources are shared is increased with respect to a *private cloud* (66), as sharing is possible on an inter-company basis. Because the collaborating companies trust each other more as users of a *public cloud* (62) due to established contracts etc. the desired isolation between customers of a community cloud may be reduced and, thus, easier to establish. Access control for the hosted IT resources, on the other hand, is likely to be more complex to enable the control of information exchange between companies.

Rapid elasticity: rapid elasticity in a community cloud is similar to that in a *public cloud* (62), if the customer group is large enough and displays a similar diversity. This helps to avoid the problems arising in a *private cloud* (66) due to the often smaller customer group. However, as the companies participating in a *community cloud* collaborate, they may experience similar workload behavior. The peaks of experienced *periodic workload* (29), *once-in-a-lifetime workload* (33), or *unpredictable workload* (36) may, therefore, occur at the same time hindering the ability of a *community cloud* to scale elastically.

Variations

Similar to the *virtual private cloud* variation of the *private cloud* (66) deployment model, a *community cloud* may be hosted in an isolated portion of a *public cloud* (62). This portion is commonly isolated on the networking level to avoid direct communication between the other IT resources in the *public cloud* (62) and those hosted in the *virtual community cloud*. Other hardware, for example, physical servers on which the virtual servers of multiple customers are hosted through the use of a *hypervisor* (101) may still be shared.

Related Patterns

- *Infrastructure as a Service (IaaS)* (45): *community PaaS clouds* provide a shared hosting environment where different companies may provision servers to provide data and shared functionality with each other. Preconfigured server images containing common operating systems and software combinations may be provided to provision servers in a more standardized manner, but the same level of homogenization as in *private clouds* (66) is unlikely as companies can have their own internal standardization efforts to homogenize IT resources that they also use in the *community cloud*.
- *Platform as a Service (PaaS)* (49): a *community cloud* offering *PaaS* provides a standardized, collaborative trusted *elastic platform* (91) providing an *execution environment* (104) and other offerings based on which collaborating companies may develop shared applications that rely on common functionality and data. The elasticity of this platform may be limited if the number of collaborating companies is low, but it is highly standardized to ease development and to coordinate information exchange. Often, these environments focus on the collaborative collection and evaluation of data.
- *Software as a Service (SaaS)* (55): *community SaaS clouds* often provide the same functionality as public *SaaS* offerings, but application functionality is only accessible to collaborating companies. Another difference to other *SaaS* offerings is that collaborating companies do not desire to perceive the application as if they were the only user, but want to exchange information with other companies using the *SaaS* offering, for example, to handle orders or to manage schedules.

Known Uses

The same technologies to create *private IaaS clouds* can be used to create *community IaaS clouds* in a dedicated data center. The only difference is the group of companies that are granted access to this environment. Google provides it's Google Apps [49] public *SaaS* offering also as a *SaaS community cloud* for U.S. government agencies [56].

2.4.4   Hybrid Cloud

> Different clouds and static data centers are integrated to form a homogeneous hosting environment.

 How can the cloud properties – on demand self-service, broad network access, pay-per-use, resource pooling, and rapid elasticity – be provided across clouds and other environments?

Context

The cloud deployment model used by a company in a specific use case is often determined by the required level of accessibility, privacy, security and trust, because *private clouds* (66), *public clouds* (62), and *community clouds* (71) significantly differ on these assurances. A company is, however, likely to use a large set of applications to support its business. These applications and possibly their individual application components may have versatile requirements making different cloud deployment models suitable to host them. In order to match these requirements efficiently, it is, therefore, desirable to host applications and their components in different clouds and static data centers leading to an integration challenge. Even if applications could use the same cloud, legacy and non-cloud applications may exist that also have to interact with cloud applications. A company, therefore, has to manage these different hosting environments and communication has to be enabled between them.

Solution

A *hybrid cloud* integrates multiple *private clouds* (66), *public clouds* (62), *community clouds* (71) and static date centers. Applications and their individual components are deployed to the hosting environment best suited for their requirements and interconnection of these environments is ensured. A *hybrid cloud*, therefore, integrates different hosting environments that can be accessed by different number of tenants and share underlying IT resources between different amounts of tenants as shown in Fig. 2.16.

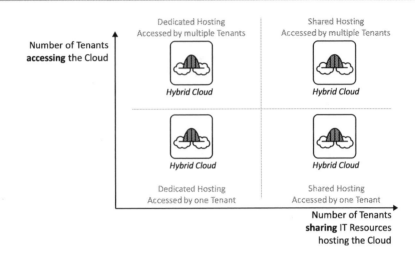

Fig. 2.16 Hybrid cloud in the cloud scope

Result

Through the establishment of a *hybrid cloud*, the applications and their components required by a company may be hosted in multiple hosting environments, for example, to use a *private cloud* (66) ho handle *static workload* (26) and deploy additional IT resources in a *public cloud* (62), if the workload increases suddenly, for example, due to a *once-in-a-lifetime workload* (33) peak. Such a workload spill-over allows *private clouds* (66) to be scaled more optimistically resulting in a higher utilization and a reduced cost of the overall environment. The cloud computing properties introduced in Sect. 1.1 on Page 3 are ensured by integrating the individual environments to form the *hybrid cloud* as follows. Especially, a *hybrid cloud* can be used to add some of these properties to a static data center by integrating it with a cloud environment.

Access via network: access via network to the separate clouds and static data centers is enabled as if they were not integrated. Additional connections are established between these environments to enable access between them as well. As the environments may assure different levels of privacy, security, and trust, this access has to be regulated in many cases. For example, *public clouds* (62) and *community clouds* (71) could be integrated with a *private cloud* (66). The *community cloud* (71) and *public cloud* (62) are accessible via a more or less public network that often can be accessed easily from the *private cloud* (66). Access from the public network to the *private cloud* is, however, often restricted. Under such conditions, a *private cloud* (66) commonly acts as the resource broker of the formed *hybrid cloud* that decides for each access request to a resource whether it is served from *private cloud* (66) resources, or *public cloud* (62) resources. This is determined by the required service level agreements, especially taking security and trust issues into account.

On-demand self-service: similar to an integrated access via network, the different self-service interfaces of integrated clouds can be subsumed to provide a unified interface to customers. Often, one cloud or data center acts as the provider of the self-service Web-portal and forwards provisioning and decommissioning requests to the other clouds if needed. The known uses section of this pattern covers some tools providing such unified interfaces to multiple clouds.

Pay-per-use: as the self-service interface of a *hybrid cloud* integrates different clouds, it has to consolidate the resource billing of the different environments as well. If possible, a *hybrid cloud* should provide a homogeneous billing model rather than just adapting the billing models of all integrated hosting environments to reduce complexity. Customers are then billed according to this billing model and the *hybrid cloud* provider pays integrated providers according their individual billing models.

Resource pooling: sharing of resources is enabled internally by the integrated *private clouds* (66), *public clouds* (62), or *community clouds* (71). However, the *hybrid cloud* may add additional management functionality on top of this resource pooling by optimizing the IT resource distribution among the integrated environments. For example, the *hybrid cloud* may consider the individual utilization of integrated environments in this decision, thus, providing a homogenous resource pool comprised of individual resource pools of different hosting environments. This integration of provisioning and decommissioning decisions has to be considered especially, when integrating a static environment that does not offer resource pooling with a cloud environment.

Rapid elasticity: elasticity regarding the overall resources in all environments should be enabled by the *hybrid cloud's* integration functionality just as resource pooling has to be enabled between the integrated hosting environments. Again, the integrated environments handle their individual elasticity and may support more or less flexibility regarding the provisioning and decommissioning of IT resources. Through this integration, a *hybrid cloud* may, for example, provision IT resources in a *public cloud* (62), if those of a static data center are insufficient during workload peaks. For this decision, the *hybrid cloud*, thus, has to monitor the integrated environments to balance resources among them.

Related Patterns
- *Infrastructure as a Service (IaaS)* (45): integration of different clouds on the *IaaS* level is commonly done by enabling networking communication between different clouds. One approach is to establish virtual private networks (VPN) between the different clouds which may make the deployment of additional servers in these environments handling the integration necessary. The involved technologies are covered in greater detail by the *virtual networking* (132) pattern.

- *Platform as a Service (PaaS)* (49): integration of different *PaaS* offerings may be enabled by special application components hosted in these environments. The *application component proxy* (228) pattern describes how application functionality may be made available in a different environment than where it is hosted. The *message mover* (225) pattern describes how messaging functionality provided in different environments may be integrated.
- *Software as a Service (SaaS)* (55): many *SaaS* applications allow customers to integrate other applications that they use in different environments. This functionality is, however, supported by the provider of the *SaaS* application. If custom developed integration functionality is required, for example, to trigger a company-internal application if a certain condition arises in a *SaaS* application custom implementations are likely to be required. Many *SaaS* providers offer *PaaS* (49) offerings for this purpose, where customers may host custom extensions to the *SaaS* application, i.e., to integrate them with other applications used by the customer.
- *Hybrid cloud applications* (starting in Sect. 6.3 on Page 303): these patterns cover different distributions of application functionality providing user interfaces, processing functionality, and data handling among different environments. The motivation to assign certain functionality to an environment is discussed as well as the integration of this functionality into one application.

Known Uses

Challenges to integrate communication between IT resources residing in different clouds have to be addressed to form a *hybrid cloud*. This can be done using an Enterprise Service Bus (ESB) that offers accesses to different resources in a seamless fashion. On-premise ESBs, such as Apache ServiceMix [57] or IBM WebSphere Enterprise Service Bus [58] can be used. Additionally, the ESB itself can be accessed as a service from a cloud providing a *PaaS* (49) offering. For example, this is offered by Microsoft AppFabric, part of Windows Azure [52]. VMWare and its partners, such as T-Systems [59], offer the VMware vCloud product that can be used to build *private clouds* (66) in a model, where the *private cloud* can be extended into a hosted cloud offering of the partner to build a *hybrid cloud*. In addition to the communication between the IT resources, the management interfaces have to be integrated by a *hybrid cloud*. Apache Deltacloud [60] offers the integration of different clouds behind one application programming interface. A similar approach is taken by Apache Libcloud [61] an Jclouds [62] offering the integration of multiple clouds in a programming library.

Cloud Offering Patterns

3

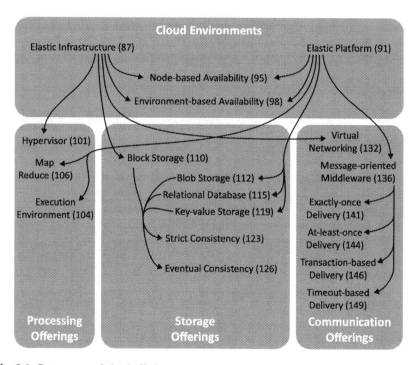

Fig. 3.1 Pattern map of cloud offerings

In this chapter, the different cloud offerings found in clouds are covered regarding the functionality they provide to customers and the behavior they display. After the overview and general discussion of the impact of cloud computing properties (see Sect. 1.1 on Page 3) on offering behavior, we describe different cloud

C. Fehling et al., *Cloud Computing Patterns*,
DOI 10.1007/978-3-7091-1568-8_3, © Springer-Verlag Wien 2014

environments (Sect. 3.3) as patterns. These patterns characterize the environments created in different cloud deployment models (see Sect. 2.4 on Page 60) in more detail. Especially, they give an overview of common combinations of the other cloud offering patterns to form an *IaaS* (45) or *PaaS* (49) cloud. In the remaining sections of this chapter, we cover cloud offerings combined to provide *IaaS* or *PaaS* individually and differentiate between three general functionality-related offering types: *processing offerings, storage offerings,* and *communication offerings.*

Processing offerings (Sect. 3.4) are used to execute workload. The required functionality to execute workload may be provided as part of the cloud offering or may be managed by the user through installation of custom software, i.e., on an *IaaS* (45) offering. Therefore, compute resources can be offered according to different cloud service models. Processing offerings host application functionality, for example, in the form of virtual servers on the *IaaS* (45) level or an application server platform on the *PaaS* level.

Storage Offerings (Sect. 3.5) can be used to store data in the cloud. Depending on the service model according to which storage is offered, it can provide physical hard drive storage resources on the *IaaS* (45) level. On the *PaaS* (49) level it may provide storage accessed as network file storage (NFS), as Windows shared folders, or table-centric storage such as a relational database management system.

Communication offerings (Sect. 3.6) are the third cloud offering type and can be used to exchange information, for example, between the different applications and their components hosted in a cloud as well as to exchange information with applications residing outside of the cloud.

3.1   Overview of Cloud Offering Patterns

The cloud service models (see Sect. 2.3 on Page 42) describe the style in which IT resources are offered by a cloud. In this chapter, we describe the properties and behavior of these offerings in a pattern format. We chose the pattern format as it allows us to describe the relevant properties of a cloud offering on an abstract architecture level. Even though these offering patterns are not implemented by developers, we argue that the pattern format makes different cloud offerings comparable and captures the impact on the application architectures making use of such offerings.

As shown in Fig. 3.1, the pattern map of this chapter starts by describing the cloud environments offered according to the different cloud service models. We cover an *elastic infrastructure* (87) offered as *IaaS* (45) and an *elastic platform* (91) offered as *PaaS*. Both of the described cloud environments, *elastic infrastructure* (87) and *elastic platform* (91) can guarantee availability of the provided service. Two approaches are covered here, *node-based availability* (95) assuring availability for individual hosted resources and *environment-based availability* (98) assuring availability only for the offered service as a whole.

Processing offerings (Sect. 3.4) are used to handle the workload of a cloud application. An *elastic infrastructure* can offer the functionality of a *hypervisor* (101) that hosts virtual servers of different customers. An *elastic platform* offers a higher level *execution environment* (104). For example, an *execution environment* for Web applications typically offers compute resources in the form of a Web-server platform. Uniform processing of large data sets can be handled by a *map reduce* (106) offering.

Storage offerings (Sect. 3.5) can be part of an *elastic infrastructure* or an *elastic platform*. An *elastic infrastructure* may provide *block storage* (110) that can be used similar to physical hard drives in virtual servers. An *elastic platform* may handle binary large objects (BLOB) in a *blob storage* (112), a directory-centric storage that can handle very large files, and a *key-value storage* (119) or *relational database* (115) for table-centric data storage. The latter two offerings mainly differ regarding data structure and data consistency. While *relational databases* are configured with a data schema by which to structure the handled data, *key-value stores* loosen the restrictions on data structures to be more flexible during runtime. Each of these storage offerings may display *eventual consistency* (126) or *strict consistency* (123). The corresponding patterns describe how data updates become visible to clients accessing the storage offering concurrently.

Communication offerings (Sect. 3.6) are provided by an *elastic infrastructure* and an *elastic platform* to enable data exchange between hosted applications and external applications. In scope of an *elastic infrastructure*, the communication offering is network hardware-centric and allows the use of *virtual networking* (132) to interconnect hosted virtual servers. In scope of an *elastic platform*, we cover asynchronous message-based communication, which is fundamental to enable the cloud properties (see Sect. 1.1 on Page 3) in cloud-native applications. A *message-oriented middleware* (136) offers message queues through which communication partners may exchange asynchronous messages. Queues may behave differently as described by the following patterns. Messages may be delivered *exactly-once* (141) or *at-least-once* (144) to communication partners. Furthermore, the delivery may be assured using transactions or timeouts as described by the patterns for *transaction-based delivery* (146) and *timeout-based delivery* (149).

3.2 Impact of Cloud Computing Properties on Offering Behavior

When revisiting the five fundamental properties of a cloud offering – *access* via *network, on-demand self-service, pay-per-use, resource pooling* and *rapid elasticity* – it becomes apparent that a cloud offering is a complex dynamic distributed system. We discussed the basic functional behavior of different *cloud service models* and *cloud deployment types* in the previous chapter. In addition to functional behavior, a cloud offering has to ensure a certain set of non-functional properties and the realization of these assurances used by a cloud provider may again affect the functionality. Given the sheer size of the distributed systems powering a cloud offering, cloud vendors are especially challenged by *availability* and *data consistency* requirements in addition to enable the cloud computing properties. Given these circumstances, cloud providers have to determine the best compromise between low costs and the guaranteed quality of non-functional properties. In the following we give an overview where cloud providers commonly accept trade-offs. The patterns covered in the remainder of this chapter then describe in detail how these trade-offs affect the functional behavior of cloud offerings.

Availability: a cloud offering is considered to be available if it is accessible via the network and the provided functionality behaves as desired. Availability, therefore, means for a storage system that it is accessible by a client and provides correct data. Driven by the need to offer on-demand self-service and pay-per-use, cloud providers have to offer elastic infrastructures, platforms, applications and processes that allow to dynamically provision and decommission resources. As a result the cloud provider has to be able to add and remove resources on the respective layer of the application stack rapidly. Resources have to be able to be started and stopped automatically to achieve this rapid elasticity. In addition, the cloud provider has to be able to deal with large amounts of IT resources while minimizing maintenance, provisioning and decommissioning costs.

These requirements can only be met by a significant amount of computing power, often realized using extremely large numbers of commodity servers as they are cheap, easy to replace and can be managed with low overhead, because their hardware is standardized. Such a setup is also referred to as warehouse-scale machines by Barroso and Hölzle [24]. Google uses a similar architecture to handle large numbers of search requests using commodity servers combined to large clusters instead of high-end servers [63], but generic large-scale data centers build on commodity hardware are also available. Vishwanath et al. [64] describe an approach to ship those data centers ready-to-use in shipping containers hosting large number of servers. These container data centers are never serviced, i.e., no individual server or hard drive is ever replaced. Rather, failures are anticipated, the failing hardware is deactivated and replaced by an already installed redundant component. If a certain number of components has failed, the data center as a whole is replaced. In such large systems, failures of individual hardware components, thus, occur constantly rather than being an exception [65]. Google Fellow Jeff Dean [66] described the failure rates in a new Google data center as follows:

> In each cluster's first year, it's typical that 1,000 individual machine failures will occur; thousands of hard drive failures will occur; one power distribution unit will fail, bringing down 500 *to* 1,000 machines for about 6 hours; 20 racks will fail, each time causing 40 *to* 80 machines to vanish from the network; 5 racks will "go wonky," with half their network packets missing in action; and the cluster will have to be rewired once, affecting 5 *percent* of the machines at any given moment over a 2-day span [...]. And there's about a 50 *percent* chance that the cluster will overheat, taking down most of the servers in less than 5 *minutes* and taking 1–2 days to recover.

To reflect this continuous presence of failures, availability assurances of many cloud offerings often state that no guarantee of the availability of individual IT resources is given, but the availability of the whole or a part of the offering is guaranteed. In essence this means that individual nodes can fail all the time but new nodes can be started to compensate for this failure. This considerably differs from the assurance that a single node is guaranteed to not fail with a certain percentage. When using cloud offerings, this behavior must be clear to customers and has to be respected in the architecture of applications relying on such cloud offerings. Other cloud offerings might guarantee a certain availability of individual nodes. Thus, when deciding to use a cloud offering it must be known to the customers if the *node-based availability* (95) pattern or *environment-based availability* (98) pattern is implemented to be able to deal with the behavior accordingly.

Consistency: as with the availability discussion above, it is important to recall that cloud storage offerings are distributed systems. Either, because of the required size of the storage capacity or because of the need to guarantee a timely accessibility of the data most, cloud storage offerings are transparently implemented as distributed, replicated data stores across multiple nodes. Consistency in this case means that independent from which replica a customer reads, the same data is returned.

Network partitioning tolerance: distributed systems are connected through a network. In this network failures may occur resulting in lost connectivity between IT resources of the distributed system. Network partition tolerance (or just partitioning tolerance) for a storage offering comprised of multiple replicas means that in case one or multiple replicas become separated from other replicas due to problems in the connection network, thus, if network partitioning occurs, the whole storage system shall still be available.

Dependencies among consistency, availability, and partitioning tolerance: the distribution of IT resources hosting a cloud offering has a significant impact on its properties and behavior. The basic theorem underlying the following discussion is the CAP theorem [67]. The CAP theorem [67] states that out of the three properties mentioned above – **c**onsistency, **a**vailability and **p**artition tolerance – any storage system can only maximize two at the same time. The efforts to ensure these properties are, thus, competing. For example, if partitioning tolerance shall be increased, the number of replicas accessed when a client retrieves data could be reduced. In case of network partitioning, fewer replicas are now required making the overall systems more robust. However, data in a different network partition may have changed while a client is provided with data. Therefore, obsolete data may be retrieved hindering high requirements on data consistency.

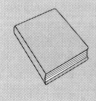

Further Reading: the CAP theorem has been researched by Gilbert and Lynch in [67]. E. Brewer gives an overview of the relationship between CAP, transactional ACID properties (Atomicity, Consistency, Isolation, and Durability), and BASE properties (Basically Available, Soft state, Eventually consistent) in [68]. Ramakrishnan covers a related Yahoo use case in [69]. Abadi discusses the tradeoffs between different CAP designs in [70].

Fig. 3.2 Eventual
consistency scenario

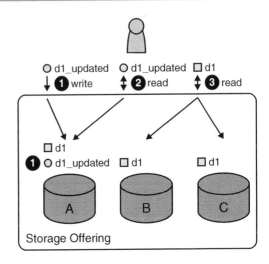

To evaluate the interdependencies between the properties consistency, availability, and partitioning tolerance in more detail consider the scenario depicted in Fig. 3.2. Storage *A, B,* and *C* are three data replicas that implement a storage offering. In the first user access, data item *d1* is written by a customer of the storage offering and changed to *d1_updated*. Transparently to the customer this update happens in replica *A*. Thus, replica *A* now holds *d1_updated* while *B* and *C* still hold the original version of *d1*. When the customer now reads from the storage offering during the depicted second and third access, either *d1_updated* or *d1* is returned depending onto which replica the access is directed. The storage offering is inconsistent. To make the storage offering consistent, only updated data must be returned to the customer. This can be done by reading and writing multiple replicas during an access while ensuring that the sets of replicas accessed during these operations overlap. For example, the storage offerings may update all three replicas during writes and reads data from only one replica. Or it may read and write two replicas. Note that these accesses can still be handled by the storage offerings transparently to the customer.

The *strict consistency* (123) pattern covers this approach to guarantee consistency in more detail. However, ensuring consistency this way always requires reading and/or writing from more than one replica depending on the setup, i.e., the ratio between replicas accessed during read and write operations. This reduces availability, because the whole system becomes unavailable if not enough replicas are available making it dependent on the availability of a large number replicas. If consistency was not required, one replica would be sufficient to write and read. This would also ensure partition tolerance as the customer could use a replica available from his or her network segment. Therefore, guaranteeing consistency and partition tolerance hinders guaranteeing availability.

Availability and partition tolerance can be increased when consistency is relaxed. As long as one replica is available even during network partitioning the whole system is still available as the customer can access the replicas available from his network segment. However, this might include only replicas that do not have current data because of the network partitioning. Therefore, consistency is affected if availability and partition tolerance shall be increased. A provider can guarantee so-called eventual consistency which means that once the network partitioning is resolved and data can be exchanged between the different replicas again, data is made consistent again. This approach is covered in greater detail in the *eventual consistency* (126) pattern.

When guaranteeing consistency and availability, customers must read from replicas that are not separated from other replicas because of network partitioning. This is the case as otherwise consistency cannot be guaranteed as replicas have to be kept in a consistent state negatively affecting partition tolerance.

Given these interdependencies between consistency, availability, and partitioning tolerance not all of these properties can be maximized at the same time. However, in large distributed systems, such as clouds, where network partitioning is likely to occur, partitioning tolerance is often vital leaving the trade-off between availability and consistency. Depending on the choice the cloud provider has made, the customer of the storage offering either has to cope with reduced availability or relaxed consistency. Instead, cloud provider may also use more reliable connection networks, however, this is also likely to result in higher costs for higher levels of consistency. Again, the two patterns *strict consistency* (123) and *eventual consistency* (126) describe which choice the provider has made and how it affects customers and their applications.

Consistency also influences communication cloud offerings. As messaging and other communication offerings often depend on an underlying data store, the properties of that data store influence the properties of the communication offerings using it. A *message-oriented middleware* (136) can guarantee so-called *exactly-once-delivery* (141), i.e., it will deliver some messages once and only once. Alternatively, messages may be delivered more than once and, thus, the *message-oriented middleware* guarantees *at-least-once delivery* (144). This delivery behavior is affected by data consistency, because when a message has been delivered to a customer it is removed from the underlying data store of the *message-oriented middleware* (136). However, in case the data store is *eventually consistent* (126) a message may be delivered more than once as it has not been removed from all replicas. Thus, whether *exactly-once delivery* (141) or *at-least-once delivery* (144) can be guaranteed for a communication offering often depends on the underlying architecture of the messaging system and its data stores. The respective patterns describe the different behaviors of a *message-oriented middleware* in more detail.

3.3   Cloud Environments

When discussing cloud computing, *hypervisors* (101) are often named as one key enabling technology. While this is certainly true, especially for *IaaS* (45) offerings, a *hypervisor* and an *elastic infrastructure* (87) or *elastic platform* (91) are considerably different. On the functional side a hypervisor typically offers hardware virtualization functionality along with some management interfaces geared towards system administrators. While a *hypervisor* often forms the basis and is offered as a part of a cloud environment, an *elastic infrastructure* and *elastic platform* are enhanced with functionality for self-service, pay-per-use pricing and rapid elasticity. The *elastic platform* then moves away from the analogy of virtual servers towards middleware runtimes that are offered to the customer. But not only the functionality of a *hypervisor* and an *elastic infrastructure* or *elastic platform* is different, but also the definition of availability in corresponding service level agreements. While a pure hypervisor is used to virtualize existing servers and, thus, the availability of an individual server often has to be guaranteed, in an *elastic platform* and also in *elastic infrastructures* the availability of the whole environment is often emphasized over the availability of individual nodes. These different availability assurances have been captured in the *node-based availability* (95) and *environment-based availability* (98) patterns, respectively. Customers must be aware of these different availability assurances and have to design their applications accordingly as many *IaaS* offerings and, even more so, *PaaS* (49) offerings often assure *environment-based availability* (98). Therefore, customers cannot rely on the *node-based availability* (95) of individual nodes, such as virtual servers or hosted applications components, as they could in a typical hypervisor-based environment. To understand the implications as an application developer, it is fundamental to be accustomed with the differences between a pure *hypervisor*-based virtual server environment and an *elastic infrastructure* or *elastic platform*.

3.3.1 Elastic Infrastructure

Hosting of virtual servers, disk storage, and configuration of network connectivity is offered via a self-service interface over a network.

How do cloud offerings providing infrastructure resources behave and how should they be used in applications?

Context

If an application experiences *periodic workload* (29), *once-in-a-lifetime workload* (33), *unpredictable workload* (36), or *continuously changing workload* (40), the number of IT resources, such as servers, it requires differs greatly over time. To adjust the size of this number of IT resources used by an application dynamically to the currently experienced workload, IT resources have to be added to and removed from an application's runtime infrastructure within very short time frames. In scope of the *IaaS* (45) service model, the applications' runtime infrastructure, thus, must support dynamic provisioning and decommissioning of virtual servers, disk storage and network connectivity. The customer of an *IaaS* offering has to be provided with functionality to handle provisioning of application components hosted on virtual servers, increase or decrease the amount of storage, adjust the networking connectivity, and monitor usage costs.

Solution

An *elastic infrastructure* provides preconfigured virtual server images and storage as well as network capability that may be provisioned by customers. Based on preconfigured images or through an upload of external server images, a customer may create individual server images containing the hosted applications and application components. This image management is fundamental to speed up the provisioning of new virtual servers. Integration into communication networks is ensured seamlessly by the provider, but may be configured by customers. Similarly, a customer is able to book necessary storage resources. Monitoring information is provided to the customer to inform about resource utilization required for traceable billing and automation of management tasks. All this functionality is offered via a self-service interface to be used by humans, automated management tools, and the applications themselves that are hosted by the environment.

Fig. 3.3 Components of an elastic infrastructure

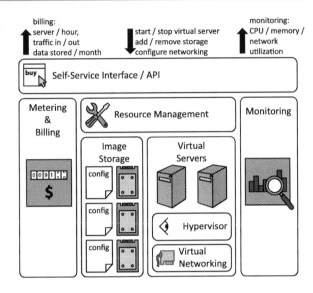

Result

Through the self-service interface or the API depicted at the top of Fig. 3.3, an *elastic infrastructure* supports the dynamic allocation of virtual servers, storage and network capability. Virtual servers are described by server images contained in an image store. These images are comprised of a description of the hardware configuration and hard drive images containing the operation system and additional software, such as middleware and custom developed applications. Based on these images, virtual servers may be provisioned and are then managed in a pool of infrastructure resources depicted next to the image management in Fig. 3.3. These virtual servers share common underlying hardware often managed by a *hypervisor* (101). Additional to this hardware virtualization, a network management component ensures that virtual servers are integrated and removed from the network infrastructure during provisioning and decommissioning, respectively. This process is completely automated to enable self-service interfaces and is one of the main differentiating factors of an *elastic infrastructure* and a pure *hypervisor*-based runtime infrastructure. A monitoring component collects information from virtual servers, such as central processing unit (CPU) and memory utilization, amount of data exchanged on the networking level etc. This information is used by the billing component and may also be extracted by the customer. Customers require this information to make manual or automated scaling decisions for the deployed applications. Monitoring ensures a common perception of virtual server utilization and, therefore, forms the basis for pay-per-use billing models as well as elasticity.

Variations

Many elastic infrastructures are built upon virtualization environments provided by one or more *hypervisors* (101). This is due to the fact, that server virtualization enables the automation of provisioning tasks and decommissioning tasks. However, these tasks may also be automated for the non-virtualized environments to allow the elastic management of physical servers without an additional virtualization layer. However, in this scope, the number of servers that may be provisioned is bound directly to the number of available physical servers and these physical servers are also not shared between different customers. Therefore, such offerings tend to target a customer group that requires higher performance or privacy, i.e., through the more direct access to hardware and the lack of hardware sharing.

Related Patterns
- *Hypervisor* (101): as mentioned above, *hypervisors* are used by an *elastic infrastructure* to abstract physical hardware and decrease provisioning and decommissioning times. It is the common processing offerings of an *elastic infrastructure*.
- *Block storage* (110): the common storage offering of an elastic infrastructure provides centralized storage to be accessed by virtual servers similar to local hard drives. The behavior of these storage offerings are described in greater detail by the *block storage* (110) pattern.
- *Virtual networking* (132): the hardware virtualization introduced by a *hypervisor* (101) can be extended further to include networking resources that enable the connectivity between virtual servers of an *elastic infrastructure*. The *virtual networking* pattern, therefore, describes the common communication offering of an elastic infrastructure.
- *Blob storage* (112): this storage offering handles large files, so called binary large objects (blob) in a directory-based fashion. It is often used internally by an elastic infrastructure to realize the image storage depicted in Fig. 3.3.
- *Watchdog* (260): if the elastic infrastructure offers *environment-based availability* (98), a *watchdog* may be used to analyze the monitoring information provided by the application hosted on the *elastic infrastructure*. Based on this analysis it detects failing resources and uses the interfaces of the elastic infrastructure to automate their replacement i.e., the decommissioning of failing resources and the provisioning of replacements.
- *Management patterns* (Chap. 5): all management patterns rely on a management interface to automate management tasks. The elastic infrastructure is a means to provide such an interface.
- *Elasticity manager* (250), *elastic load balancer* (254), and *elastic queue* (257): these require an *elastic infrastructure* or an *elastic platform* (91) as underlying infrastructure. They determine the number of required application component instances to handle experienced workload. Then, they use the interface of the elastic infrastructure to automatically provision application component instances.

Known Uses

There are many hosting providers offering virtual servers in an *elastic infrastructure*, for example, the Amazon Elastic Compute Cloud (EC2) [18]. Rackspace [19] also offers a similar service that is based on OpenStack [35], an open source implementation of the *elastic infrastructure* pattern. The mentioned variation managing physical hardware provisioning as an *elastic infrastructure* in order to avoid the limitation of the *hypervisor* (101) is offered by baremetalcloud [71]. T-Systems with their Dynamic Services for Infrastructure (DSI) [34] and other providers offer *elastic infrastructure* as virtual *private clouds* (66) with both, *environment-based availability* (98) for development and test and *node-based availability* (95) for higher-end production systems.

3.3.2 Elastic Platform

> Middleware for the execution of custom applications, their communication, and data storage is offered via a self-service interface over a network.

 How do cloud offerings providing execution environments behave and how should they be used in applications?

Context

One of the fundamental cloud properties introduced in Sect. 1.1 on Page 3 is the sharing of resources among a large number of customers to leverage economy of scale. If many of the applications hosted by customers rely on the same operating systems and middleware, customers should also share these resources to avoid redundant deployments of the same middleware products. Extending resource sharing between customers to the operating systems and middleware, thus, increases the beneficial effects of economies of scale as the utilization of these resources can be increased. Additionally, homogenization and standardization of the middleware-level is increased reducing the required skill-set and application management efforts. Customers shall, therefore, be enabled to deploy application components on a shared hosting environment that is provided according to the *PaaS* (49) service model.

Solution

Application components of different customers are hosted on shared middleware provided and maintained by the provider. Customers may deploy custom application components to this middleware using a self-service interface for component management as seen at the top of Fig. 3.4. This middleware is unified for all customers regarding the versions of used operating systems and other software as well as taken security measures, user directories, performance optimized configuration etc. This unification enables resource sharing and an automation of certain management tasks on the provider side, for example, provisioning of applications, update management etc. If the application components are developed in a certain fashion (see related patterns) the provider may also handle elastic scaling or resiliency management in case a hosted application fails. The provider ensures isolation between the deployed components to insure that the customers are not affected by the behavior of each

Fig. 3.4 Components of an elastic platform

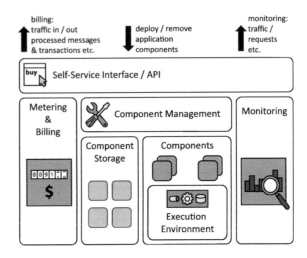

other's deployments. Furthermore, the provider offers certain platform services that can be used by customers for data storage and communication between components. Monitoring information is provided to customers to inform them about utilization caused by their deployments and to bill them based on the monitored use.

Result

By providing an *execution environment* (104) via a self-service interface or an API, the provider enables customers to deploy application components on the same shared hosting environment. This *elastic platform* hosts and executes the deployed custom applications and can provide common platform offerings. These platform offerings subsume functionality for processing, communication and storage as well as logging, security, application management and monitoring shared by all deployed applications of all customers. The behavior of the provided processing functionality is described in greater detail by the *execution environment* (104) pattern. The behavior of communication functionality and storage functionality is described by communication offerings (Sect. 3.6) and storage offerings (Sect. 3.5), respectively. Pay-per-use billing is realized regarding accesses to the deployed components, data traffic, or messages exchanged etc. Thus, the unit of payment is typically related to the type service provided by the offerings of an *elastic platform*. Scaling and other management tasks for the deployed application components can also be handled by the provider without the user noticing by dynamically provisioning or decommissioning IT resources on which the platform is hosted. This, however, often demands that component implementations follow certain architectural principles. For example, they may have to be implemented as *stateless components* (171), e.g. relying on external state stored in a provider-supplied platform service or by exchanging state in application messages (so-called REST [72] style).

The behavior of these management functionalities offered by the provider may be configured by the customer to adjust how quickly a provider shall react to different workload requirements, what maximum number of resources the application may use etc. The monitoring information about deployed applications is provided to the customer and billing is performed regarding the number of provisioned components, the number of messages exchanged by them, and the amount of data these components store using platform services. The notion of virtual servers, operating systems or middleware instances is commonly completely hidden from the user of the *elastic platform*.

Variations

As a variation, virtual servers may still be visible to the customer, but the operating system and middleware of these servers is managed by the provider of the *elastic platform*. Customers may often influence the behavior of this automated management, for example, by specifying the point in time when updates and patches are applied. This variation results in different payment models as if virtual servers are invisible to customers: pricing is more similar to that of an *elastic infrastructure* (87) where virtual servers, memory, and bandwidth use are billed. In this scope, scaling configurations undertaken by the customer may also incorporate properties of the virtual servers, such as CPU and memory utilization.

Related Patterns

- *Execution environment* (104): processing functionality of the *elastic platform* is provided by an *execution environment* that hosts application components and subsumes common functionality required by them. In addition to this processing offering, the elastic platform commonly provides a set of communication offerings (Sect. 3.6) and storage offerings (Sect. 3.5). These are described in detail by the following patterns:
- *Message-oriented middleware* (136): according to this pattern, a provider may offer message queues to enable deployed application components to exchange messages with each other and applications outside of the *elastic platform*.
- *Blob storage* (112): this storage offering may be used by deployed application components to store large data elements.
- *Key-value storage* (119) and *relational database* (115): these storage offerings can be used by deployed applications to store large amounts of table-centric data.
  Elastic platforms often require hosted applications to implement certain patterns, for example, to handle certain management tasks for the customer:
- *Distributed application* (160): cloud applications are generally componentized to be distributed among different resources. This significantly simplifies management tasks, such as scaling, failure resiliency, and load-balancing. The *distributed application* pattern covers different approaches for this decomposition and describes

how the decomposed application components may be combined to a cloud
application
- *Stateless component* (171): if deployed components do not have an internal state
  but completely rely on provider-supplied storage offerings, their handling by an
  elasticity management process (267) and *resiliency management process* (283)
  is significantly simplified.
- *Idempotent processor* (197): messaging offerings often assure *at-least-once
  delivery* (144) of messages. To cope with such message duplicates, a custom
  application component should implement the *idempotent processor* pattern.

Known Uses

Amazon Elastic Beanstalk [53] offers an *elastic platform* providing Apache Tomcat
[73] as provider-supplied and provider-managed middleware. Scalability is enabled
automatically and relies on utilization information obtained from virtual servers on
which Apache Tomcat is hosted. Windows Azure [52] is also an *elastic platform*
that maintains the notion of virtual servers, but provides pre-configured images
containing different Windows versions. These can also be updated automatically
once they are deployed by a customer. Google App Engine [21] completely hides
virtual servers from the user and allows the deployment of Python and Java
applications which is then automatically scaled for customers.

Other offerings of an elastic platform provided as *PaaS* (49) are Amazon's
Simple Queue Service (SQS) [38] which provides messaging. Billing is related to
the number of messages processed and elasticity is handled transparently to the
customer. When building *private cloud* (66) offering an *elastic platform*, products
such as OpenStack [35] often include storage offerings that can then be provided as
PaaS. Another example is WSO2's Stratos open source implementation [74], which
offers elastic multi-tenant aware runtimes for web applications, workflows and an
elastic enterprise service bus (ESB) [11].

3.3.3   Node-Based Availability

A cloud provider guarantees the availability of individual nodes, such as individual virtual servers, middleware components or hosted application components.

 How can providers express availability in a node-centric fashion, so that customers may estimate the availability of hosted applications?

Context

A provider offers an *elastic infrastructure* (87) or an *elastic platform* (91) on which customers may deploy application components. Customers of this offering need to estimate the availability of these applications to match their requirements. The provider needs a means to express the availability service level agreements for the offerings from which the customer may then compute the availability of the hosted application. Therefore, the provider has to specify two properties for offerings. First, conditions are defined that have to be fulfilled by an available offering. Second, the timeframe needs to be expressed for which the provider assures this availability.

Solution

The provider assures availability for each hosted application component or the provided virtual server, in case of an *elastic platform* (91) or *elastic infrastructure* (87), respectively. A component or virtual server is defined to be available if it is reachable and performs its function as advertised, i.e., it provides correct results. The timeframe during which this availability is assured is often expressed as a percentage. An availability of 99.95 % means that a hosted component will be available during 99.95 % of the time it is hosted at the provider. If an application is comprised out of multiple application components, customers may compute the availability of the overall application by multiplying the individual availability ensured for each component as depicted in Fig. 3.5.

Result

Through the expression of availability for individual nodes (virtual servers, middleware components, or application components – depending on the type of

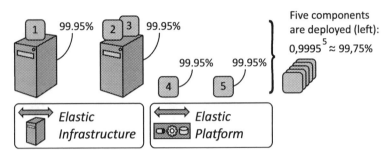

Fig. 3.5 Exemplary node-based availability

offering) the customer of an offering can determine the assured availability of a hosted application. In case this assured availability is high, the hardware employed by the cloud provider often incorporates redundant hardware components to assure its functioning. The environment, thus, monitors its own state to detect failures. In case of failure, the provider provisions a replacement for the faulty hardware. In case of a lower assured availability, the customer may have to incorporate such redundancy and failure replacement on the application level by deploying multiple instances of the same application components. In either case, monitoring information about deployed application components is provided to the customer. This information may contain utilization created by the application components, such as use of the central processing unit (CPU), memory, and disk space. While this information can be a first indicator for the runtime behavior of the applications component, proper functioning of an application component requires checks on the application level, i.e., these checks have to be incorporated in the implementation of the application component. Two common approaches used for this purpose are accessing the application functions with test data to evaluate the results and to have the application component send periodic *heartbeats*, i.e., the application component notifies the application monitoring after certain time intervals that it is still operational. Cloud providers often support such efforts through configurable checks that are performed periodically. For example, the provider may access a Web site offered by a hosted application periodically to assure the application is reachable. Furthermore, cloud providers may offer libraries to be used in an application component's implementation to send heartbeats to the provider-based monitoring infrastructure. If such functionality is not offered by a cloud provider, the monitoring of the health status of an application has to be implemented individually in each application.

Related Patterns

- *Watchdog* (260): in case the availability assured by the provider is insufficient to meet an application's requirements, a watchdog may be used to monitor and replace application components. This management component, therefore, collects the above mentioned health information and heartbeats from application components, detects faulty application components, and replaces them automatically.

- *Resiliency management* process (283): this pattern describes the process followed to replace failing components. It can be implemented by the above mentioned *watchdog* (260), in other management component, or may even by a human task.

Known Uses

Many web hosting providers assure availability in a node-centric form by stating the percentage that a hosted application is available in a given year. The same is done commonly for physical servers that are bought to be hosted in private data centers.

Hohpe and Woolf [1] cover different patterns for health monitoring in message-based applications that can also be used in scope of cloud applications using a *message-oriented middleware* (136): a *control bus* is comprised of message queues used dedicatedly for configuration messages and, especially, for heartbeat messages. This assures that heartbeat messages are not delayed by other messages processed by the application. A *test message* may be send to an application component to assure it processes it correctly. By using a *wire tap*, messages that are being processed by an application may be examined without interfering with application functionality. Finally, a *dead letter channel* and *invalid message channel* may be used to collect messages that a *message-oriented middleware* (136) cannot deliver or that are formatted incorrectly, respectively. This enables the collection of erroneous messages to detect faulty application behavior.

Further Reading: further assurances relevant for the expression of availability regards the duration of unavailability and the number of times a failure has to be expected. These factors are expressed in form of *mean time between failures (MTBF)*, the average time that a component or virtual server is available between two consecutive failures, and *mean time to recovery (MTTR)*, the time it takes to recover a failed component to become available again after a failure. Detailed information on these and other system properties as well as their computation is given by Wasson [75]. Leymann and Roller [76] discuss *hot pools* – duplicate instances of application components or processes – in greater detail. Especially, they describe how to calculate the mean time between failure and mean time to recovery of such hot pools.

3.3.4 Environment-Based Availability

A cloud provider guarantees the availability of the environment hosting individual nodes, such as virtual servers or hosted application components.

 How can providers express availability in an environmental-centric fashion, so that customers may estimate the availability of hosted applications?

Context

A cloud provider offers an *elastic infrastructure* (87) or an *elastic platform* (91) on which customers may deploy application components. The availability of this environment has to be expressed so that customers may match their requirements. Therefore, the provider defines the conditions to be fulfilled when the offering is available as well as gives the timeframe for which this availability is ensured. A customer then needs to incorporate these conditions in the deployed application to achieve the required availability.

Solution

The provider assures availability for the provided environment, thus, for the availability of the *elastic platform* or the *elastic infrastructure* as a whole as depicted in Fig. 3.6. Especially, there is no notion of availability for individual application components or virtual servers deployed in this environment as is the case for *node-based availability* (95). Instead, availability is often expressed regarding the availability of the overall set of the deployed nodes, i.e. some of them are available, as well as the availability of the management interface of the *elastic platform* (91) or *elastic infrastructure* (87). Customers of such an offering are empowered to react to failures by providing monitoring information about the environment and the deployed nodes.

Result

Environment-based availability is often used for cloud offerings comprised of commodity hardware. The cost of commodity hardware has been decreasing during the past years while its performance increased drastically. When combined in large numbers, commodity servers can, therefore, become eligible to replace high

Fig. 3.6 Exemplary environment-based availability assurances

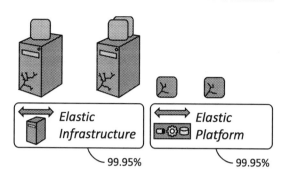

available solutions [24, 63, 64], while decreasing resource costs enabling the provider to increase the addressable customer market. Therefore, instead of aiming for high node availability, the environment is designed in a high available fashion and the customer is provided with necessary monitoring information to detect and address node failures in the deployed application. Therefore, in case a provider uses an *environment-based availability* assurance, the customer becomes responsible to assure the desired availability by incorporating failures in application architectures and their runtime management. Especially, the overall availability of the application cannot be computed from the availability of individual application components as is the case for *node-based availability* (95) but instead depends on the automated management processes coping with failures. The measures taken by cloud customers to assure availability of application under these conditions are the same taken in scope of *node-based availability* (95) assurances that are insufficient for the requirements of an application. Therefore, a cloud application hosted in an environment assuring *environment-based availability* (98) should check for correct operation of application components by accessing provided functionality and periodic heartbeats send by the application components, i.e., notifications that they are still operational. For this purpose, cloud providers often have ready-to-use functions to access an application periodically and evaluate the results. For example, a cloud provider may access a Website provided by the application to assure it is reachable. Furthermore, providers often offer libraries to be used in the application component implementation to easily send heartbeats to the provider-supplied monitoring functionality. This health information may then be evaluated by a *watchdog* (260) that detects faulty application behavior and replaces failed application components.

Related Patterns
- *Public cloud* (62): *environment-based availability* can often be found in public clouds.
- *Watchdog* (260): this pattern describes a management component that handles the evaluation of the monitoring information and corrective actions. It also describes how failing application components can be replaced more easily by implementing the *stateless component* (171) pattern and communicating via a *message-oriented middleware* (136).

- *Resiliency management process* (283): this pattern describes the steps that should be executed generally if a component fails. Especially, it describes how systems managers or automated management processes should interact with the management interfaces of used clouds.

Known Uses

Many virtual servers of public *IaaS* clouds are offered according to *environment-based availability*, thus, the implications on the cloud customer and the runtime management have to be evaluated carefully. For example, by time of this writing Amazon guarantees in its service level agreement an availability of virtual servers that are part of its Elastic Compute Cloud (EC2) of 99.95 % during a service year of 365 days [77]. As this assurance is environment based availability, this does not mean that a single virtual server instance will be available 99.95 % during this time period. Instead, unavailability is defined as the state when all running instances cannot be reached longer than 5 min and no replacement instances can be provisioned. Furthermore, the user has to make sure that redundant instances are provisioned in multiple geographically distributed "availability zones".

If a messaging application is hosted in an environment assuring environment-based availability, the same patterns introduced by Hohpe and Woolf [1] can be used as mentioned in the known uses section of the *node-based availability* (95) pattern to ensure availability on the application level. A *control bus* provides message queues exclusively used for configuration of application components and heartbeat messages to ensure that such messages are not delayed by messages processed by the application. *Test messages* may be sent to application components to assure their correct functioning. A *wiretap* can be used to evaluate messages that are being processed without interfering with the application. Finally, a *dead letter channel* and *invalid message channel* may be used to collect messages that cannot be delivered or are formatted incorrectly indicating a faulty component.

3.4   Processing Offerings

Processing offerings are used by customers to execute their workloads in the cloud. To do so, customers may deploy their own application components on the cloud provider's infrastructure. The different cloud service models covered in Sect. 2.3 on Page 42 may be used in this scope to handle the workload of an application. In this section, we cover the processing offerings provided as *IaaS* (45) and *PaaS* (49) in greater detail regarding their behavior, how to interact with them, and what has to be considered when using them in applications.

3.4.1   Hypervisor

> To enable the elasticity of clouds, the time required to provision and decommission servers is reduced through hardware virtualization.

 How can virtual hardware that has been abstracted from physical hardware be used in applications?

Context

Deploying applications directly on physical servers presents several drawbacks. It makes the application directly dependent on physical hardware failures. It may lead to unavailability if the hardware has to be re-configured, for example, for updates or replacement. And, most significantly in the area of cloud computing, it hinders the sharing or resource pooling of physical hardware between different customers, one of the cloud computing properties in the NIST definition [3], covered in Sect. 1.1 on Page 3. If multiple applications are deployed on the same physical server they may have to consider the other applications in their configuration. For example, if applications require the same network ports, access the same directories in the local file system etc. This sharing of common underlying physical hardware between different applications and their components shall, therefore, be simplified while also decoupling the application from the limitations of a physical server.

Solution

A *hypervisor* abstracts the hardware of a shared physical server into virtualized hardware. On this virtual hardware, different operating systems and middleware are installed to host applications sharing the physical server while being isolated from each other regarding the use of physical hardware, such as central processing units (CPU), memory, disk storage, and networking.

Result

Two types of hypervisors are differentiated by Goldberg [78–80] as depicted in Fig. 3.7. A *type 1 hypervisor* directly accesses physical hardware which it abstracts to provide virtual hardware to hosted virtual servers. A *type 2 hypervisor* instead

Fig. 3.7 Hypervisor types using virtualization and para-virtualization

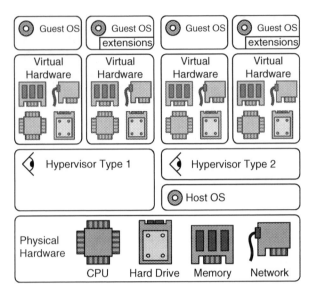

requires an operating system to be installed on the physical hardware. The hypervisor is then installed as a regular application in this operating system. In either case, the hypervisor uses the physical hardware to provide multiple virtualized hardware components. For example, the physical memory of a server may be split up into separate partitions, which are accessed by hosted virtual servers. The same is the case for virtual network cards that are mapped to fewer physical network cards shared by the virtualized servers. This setup forms two significant implications on the hosted operating systems that an application developer has to be aware of. First, the diversity of virtual hardware is significantly smaller than physical hardware, for example, the number of network card chipsets may be reduced. Therefore, even though special hardware may be installed in the host machine it may be abstracted to virtual hardware behaving very differently and offering significantly less functionality. This may, for example, be problematic if the guest operating system requires very specific hardware. Even though such hardware may be present in the host system, it may be abstracted to very different virtual hardware with which the guest cannot interact. Second, the style how guest operating systems access the virtual hardware may be very different depending on the hypervisor and its configuration: they may either access the virtualized hardware or may use functionality of the hypervisor to access the physical hardware directly, which is called *para virtualization*. In the latter case, the operating system is, therefore, tightly integrated with the hypervisor and may be rendered dysfunctional if moved to a different hypervisor. Such attempts to migrate virtual servers can additionally be hindered as *hypervisors* use different storage formats for virtual servers, different configuration formats etc.

All hypervisors have in common that the virtual servers are stored as files on the host system. Therefore, virtual servers are only loosely coupled on the physical hardware. Moving them from one physical server to another one is reduced to copying files containing the virtual server configuration and virtual hard drives. This hardware virtualization and decoupling is fundamental to in cloud computing. It enables quick provisioning and decommissioning of cloud resources (virtual servers) as the necessary tasks may be automated and no physical alterations, such as re-wiring of networking cables are required in data centers. Furthermore, it allows cloud customers to share a common hardware infrastructure enabling the exploitation of economies of scale.

Related Patterns
- *Elastic infrastructure* (87): a *hypervisor* forms the basis for the dynamicity of virtual server provisioning. This functionality is offered via self-service interfaces by an elastic infrastructure.
- *Elastic platform* (91): even though the notion of virtual servers is often hidden from customers of *elastic platforms*, *hypervisors* may still form the basis on which providers create their offering.

Known Uses

Hardware virtualization using hypervisors has been employed for a long time in mainframes, for example, IBM System Z [81]. VMware offers hypervisors for Desktop PCs [82, 83] and servers [54]. Xen [84], Hyper-V [85], KVM [86], and VirtualBox [87] are also virtualization environments that offer the functionality of a hypervisor.

Side Note: *hypervisors* pose significant implications on hosted applications. Especially, applications once deployed on a specific hypervisor may be difficult to move to a different hypervisor. As hypervisors form the basis for many clouds we included this pattern. Even though a hypervisor enables rapid provisioning and decommissioning of resources, it often lacks the following cloud properties described in Sect. 1.1 on Page 3: a *hypervisor* does not necessarily provide a self-service interface to customers. Thus, it does not necessarily ensure self-service on-demand provisioning and decommissioning of resources. Also, offerings employing this pattern often provide long-term contracts and no usage-based billing. We included this pattern to distinguish between cloud providers in terms of the NIST Cloud Definition [3] from similar products. Also, a *hypervisor* often has to be established as underlying infrastructure for a *private cloud* (66) and is used in on premise data centers that may be part of a *hybrid cloud* (75).

3.4.2   Execution Environment

> To avoid duplicate implementation of functionality, application components
> are deployed to a hosting environment providing middleware services as well
> as often used functionality.

 *How can multiple application components share a hosting
environment efficiently?*

Context

Whenever multiple applications or application components share one physical or
virtual server as runtime environment, they often use similar functions, for example, to access networking interfaces, display user interfaces, access storage of the
server etc. This effect is event increased, if the applications are developed in a
similar fashion, i.e., they use the same programming language, middleware, and
implement the same architectural patterns, such as those of this book, patterns for
enterprise integration described by Hohpe and Woolf [1], object oriented
applications described by Gamma et al. [2], or application architecture patterns of
Buschmann et al. [14]. In this case, each application implements similar
components that could be shared with other applications. Sharing such common
functionality between applications would result in a better utilization of the
environment.

Solution

Common functionality is summarized in an *execution environment* providing
functionality in platform libraries to be used in custom application implementations
and in the form of the middleware part of the application stack described on Page 43
in Sect. 2.3. The environment, thus, executes custom application components and
provides common functionality for data storages, communication etc. As depicted
in Fig. 3.8, this *execution environment* abstracts from operation system functions
and provides abstract functions for multiple applications or application
components. Platform libraries and common functionality, furthermore, are only
deployed and instantiated ones and can then be shared between all application
concurrently running in the *execution environment*.

Fig. 3.8 Execution environment in an application stack

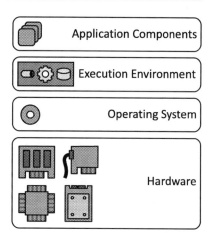

Result

By sharing common functionality provided by platform libraries, resources are used more efficiently. Custom applications may rely on platform functionality making them easier to develop and test as less custom functionality has to be implemented by developers. Through homogenization of the *execution environment* regarding the provided functionality and used middleware, supported programming languages etc., applications can be moved easier between different installations of a platform.

Related Patterns

- *Elastic platform* (91): additional to the provided execution functionality, execution environments may be offered as a service, referred to as *PaaS* (49). These environments commonly provide further properties, such as a self-service interface, described by the *elastic platform* (91) pattern.
- *Hypervisor* (101): this pattern describes another concept to share resources between multiple applications by hosting multiple virtual servers on one physical server. It, therefore, introduces a similar sharing of resources on the virtual hardware layer, while an *execution environment* shares the middleware layer among applications.

Known Uses

Many programming environments, such as the JAVA Virtual Machine [88], provide an execution environment with common functionality that is shared by applications. More complex middleware environments are provided by application servers, such as JBoss [89] or Apache Tomcat [73]. In the cloud, there is a multitude of platforms available for different programming languages, such as JAVA, Python, or custom languages, for example, Google App Engine [21], Amazon Elastic Beanstalk [53], Salesforce's Force platform [44], or VMware CloudFoundry [90] as well as WSO2s Stratos Live [39].

3.4.3   Map Reduce

Large data sets to be processed are divided into smaller data chunks and distributed among processing application components. Individual results are later consolidated.

 How can the performance of complex processing of large data sets be increased through scaling out?

Context

Cloud applications often have to handle very large amounts of data for various reasons. For example, cloud applications may have very large user groups and clouds are destined for workload that is too large to be handled in a static environment. Furthermore, the storage offerings (Sect. 3.5) found in the cloud, for example *key-value storage* (119), are designed to be scaled out to increased performance and scalability at the expense of support for complex and expressive queries. This design leads to larger data sets being returned to handling application components. These components, thus, have to cope with large data sets efficiently. As *distributed applications* (160) are designed to scale out, data processing should be distributed among multiple application component instances in a similar means. Afterwards, results of these distributed components have to be consolidated.

Solution

A large data set to be processed is split up and *mapped* to multiple application components handling data processing. During the mapping filtering functions are often used to ensure that only data is handled in the following processing that has met certain criteria. Data processing components simultaneously execute the query to be performed on the assigned data chunks. Afterwards, the individual results of all processing components are consolidated or *reduced* into one result data set. During this reduction, additional functions, such calculations of sums, average values etc. may be used.

To be efficiently handled by *map reduce*, data generally has to display three characteristics. First, it needs to be split up into subsets with no interdependencies among the resulting sets. Second, the query needs to be executable for each subset of data independently without the need of query processors to interact. Third, each individual query needs to return a result that can be consolidated afterwards.

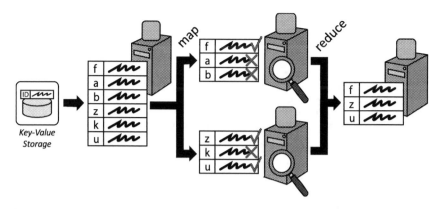

Fig. 3.9 Elastic map reduce using key-value storage

Result

Figure 3.9 exemplarily depicts the flow of data during the *map step* and the *reduce step*. In this example, an *elastic infrastructure* (87) is used as indicated by the application components hosted on servers. Alternatively, an *elastic platform* (91) could also be used to host components or the complete map reduce functionality can be provided by the platform and the user merely has to provide data and query statements. The example considered here uses a *key-value storage* (119) as source of information, but the data to be queried may also come from other sources, i.e., from large text files or large tables in *relational databases* (115). One application component divides the data to be queried into smaller data chunks that it distributes among multiple distributed querying components. This task is referred to as *mapping*. All components perform the query on the data assigned to them and return a result. This result is again *reduced* to one consolidated query result by another application component. In Fig. 3.9, the reducing component is separate, but it can also be the same as the component dividing the data. During the reduction of results a merge of the data can be performed, for example, the table entries matching the query, in Fig. 3.9, are merged. More complex operations are also possible. Consider for example, that the distributed query shall count the number of occurrences of a certain entry in a large table retrieved from the *key-value storage* (119). This table is split up and distributed among the querying components that count the occurrences in part of the table assigned to them and return the number of matching entries as their result. These individual results are summed up by the reducing application component to obtain the final result. In practice, the *map reduce* pattern can be implemented manually, but there are several ready-to-use implementations (see known uses). Often, these map reduce frameworks enforce the use of a certain programming language or programming style that enables the automated distribution of developed code among a distributed map reduce environment. In the known uses section, we cover some of these environments that can often be used according to the cloud service models covered in Sect. 2.3 on Page 42 as well.

Variations

In general, *map reduce* is used to query large amounts of weakly structured data for analysis purposes. Examples are the analysis of server logs to determine user access statistics or the analysis of order information to determine popular products. Conceptually, the underlying approach is to *divide and conquer*, also used by recursive search algorithms [91]. The data to be queried in a distributed fashion does not necessarily have to be in a table form, as depicted in Fig. 3.9. Many of the ready-to-use map reduce frameworks also expect table-centric, key-value structured or simply text based data, but the architectural concept to divide data and then process it in smaller parts can be applied to other data formats as well. Therefore, the map reduce pattern can also be used to distribute other types workload among compute nodes, such as physics simulations, video file conversion, text recognition in pictures etc. Especially, these workloads may not be data-centric, but may consider any type of processing.

Related Patterns

In messaging systems, a similar pattern exists that distributes the handling of large, complex messages among several compute nodes, called *scatter–gather* defined by Hohpe and Woolf [1]. The map reduce pattern is, furthermore, likely to be combined with the following patterns:

- *Watchdog* (260): if the used runtime environment assures *environment-based availability* (98), resources may possibly fail during query processing. A watchdog supervises such resources to replace them in case of failures. If combined with *map reduce*, the mapping component and the watchdog should work together closely, i.e., the watchdog should inform the mapping component about failures, so that the mapping component can restart the query on the corresponding data subset.
- *Message-oriented middleware* (136): query processing components should be triggered by using asynchronous message-based communication enabled by message queues provided by a *message-oriented middleware*. If multiple processing components retrieve messages from the same queue, the mapping component does not have to load balance workload among processing components itself. Hohpe and Woolf [1] describe such a setup as *competing consumer*.
- *Transaction-based processor* (201) and *timeout-based message processor* (204): if *exactly-once delivery* (141), or *at-least-once delivery* (144) is supported by the *message-oriented middleware* (136) is assures that messages are delivered successfully. However, they may still be lost, during their processing. This is, especially, critical, if the processing components using by the *map reduce* pattern need a lot of time to compute their output. A *message-oriented middleware* can support different styles of interaction to read messages transactional or acknowledge their successful read as described by *transaction-based delivery* (146) and *timeout-based delivery* (149) patterns, respectively. The assurance that messages

are processed successfully can be extended by processing components through the implementation of the *transaction-based processor* (201) pattern or the *timeout-based message processor* (204) pattern.

Known Uses

Dean and Ghemawat describe map reduce in general and cover its implementation by Google [92]. Varia [93] covers a practical example application for map reduce that crawls websites. This example application is based on Amazon's Elastic MapReduce [94] offering that provides the environment for *map reduce* according to *PaaS* (49). Thus, customers may deploy their own map reduce queries which are then executed on the Amazon runtime. The Amazon offering is based on the open source framework implementing *map reduce*, Apache Hadoop [95]. Being open source, this software may also be hosted in *private clouds* (66). *Map reduce* functionality is also part of Windows Azure [96] and Google App Engine [21]. Another open source implementation of *map reduce* that includes native support for JSON [97] documents is part of the Apache CouchDB [98] *key-value storage* (119).

3.5 Storage Offerings

This section discusses cloud storage offerings. Different types of cloud storage offerings exist that are offered in cloud environments (Sect. 3.3). They can also be characterized by the cloud service models introduced in Sect. 2.3 on Page 42. *Block storage* (110) offers (virtual) hard drives as *IaaS* (45) often used as virtual hard-drives for virtual servers offered in an *elastic infrastructure* (87). *Blob storage* (112), *relational database* (115) and *key-value storage* (119) offer different types of elastic storage according to *PaaS* (49). In these offerings the underlying hard-drives (or other physical storage mediums) are hidden from the customer. Often, these offerings are tightly integrated with an *elastic infrastructure* (87) or *elastic platform* (91) offering. The following two patterns, *strict consistency* (123) and *eventual consistency* (126), describe how cloud providers handle different requirements regarding storage availability, consistency, and partitioning tolerance (CAP). According to the CAP theorem [67] only two of these properties may be maximized for a storage offering, as described on Page 83 in Sect. 3.2. Therefore, a customer has to consider the requirements of an application carefully prior to selecting a storage offering.

3.5.1   Block Storage

Centralized storage is integrated into servers as a local hard drive managed by the operating system to enable access to this storage via the local file system.

 How can central storage be accessed as a local drive by servers and hosted applications?

Context

Virtual and non-virtualized servers can be managed significantly easier if they do not store any state information locally, i.e., on their (virtual) hard drives. This eases their provisioning, decommissioning, and failure handling. Especially, the often low availability of individual servers offered as *IaaS* (45) by cloud providers requires a central data storage offering that assures a higher availability for stored data. This way, if a server fails the data is not lost, but a new server can be started to use the centralized data. However, in many cases, the software running on the managed servers uses locally stored data and possibly cannot be altered to access a centralized storage offering. Therefore, the impact of this centralization on the hosted applications shall be minimized by hiding the complexities of accessing centralized storage from applications.

Solution

Centralized storage is accessed by servers as if it was a local hard drive, also referred to as block device. This *block storage* is integrated into an operating systems running on a physical or virtual server as a local hard drive as shown in Fig. 3.10. This integration is enabled through operating systems functionality or third-party software. Once integrated into the server, the operating system provides access to this storage via the local file system. Applications can, therefore, access the centralized block storage as if it was a local hard drive of the server they are hosted by.

Result

The operating systems running on the (virtualized) servers integrate remote storage into the operating system as if they were local hard drives or as a folder in the file

Fig. 3.10 Images of a block storage being mapped to virtual drives

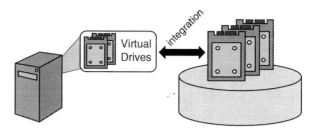

system. On the storage offering side, these files may be formatted similar to a hard drive. Common access protocols used by operating systems to integrate remote storage as local drives are, for example, the network file system (NFS), WebDav [99] or Microsoft's Common Internet File System (CIFS) [100]. Virtualization of the servers accessing such virtual hard drives significantly eases the integration task. Many *hypervisors* (101) come with functionality to integrate remotely stored hard drive images in the virtual servers managed by them.

Related Patterns
- *Environment-based availability* (98): if an *elastic infrastructure* (87) offers a virtual server according to *IaaS* (45), a *block storage offering* may be used to avoid data loss in case this server fails and, thus, helps to cope with the possibly low-availability assured by these resources.
- *Blob storage* (112): a *block storage* offering may use a *blob storage* offering to create snapshots of the hard drive image files that are integrated into remote servers, for example, for backup purposes.

Known Uses

Block storage is offered as a component of Windows Azure [101] from where it may be integrated into virtual servers running in Azure or into other remote servers. Amazon Elastic Block Storage (EBS) [102] also offers functionality of *block storage*. For virtual servers running in Amazon EC2 [18] this integration may be done by the hypervisor used by Amazon so that the use of a centralized block storage offering becomes completely invisible to hosted virtual servers.

3.5.2   Blob Storage

Data is provided in form of large files that are made available in a file
system-like fashion by storage offerings that provide elasticity.

 *How can large files be stored, organized, and made available over a
network?*

Context

Distributed cloud applications often need to handle large data elements, also
referred to as binary large objects (blob). Examples are virtual server images
managed in an *elastic infrastructure* (87), pictures, or videos. These files may be
too large for efficient handling in table-based storage. Due to the distribution of
applications components in *distributed applications* (160), the large data elements
shall be made available in a central storage offering. Access has to be enabled in an
agreed upon, standardized, elastic fashion that enables addressing, access and
retrieval of large data elements.

Solution

A *blob storage* organizes data elements in a folder hierarchy similar to a local file
system. Each data element is given a unique identifier comprised of its location in the
folder hierarchy and a file name. This unique identifier is passed to the storage offerings
to retrieve a file over a network. Access control mechanisms may be established to
ensure that users only access certain data elements. A *blob storage*, therefore, abstracts
from individual hard drives installed in servers. In particular the customer typically
does not know where his or her data is physically located. Some providers do allow
customers to specify data centers or geographical regions in which the physical storage
mediums powering the *blob storage* offering should be located.

Result

The data elements are stored centrally and in hierarchical folders. Within each folder
every data element is given a unique name. Folders also have unique names within
the scope of other folders in which they are contained. The address of a data element
is then determined by the protocol used to access it, the address of the storage

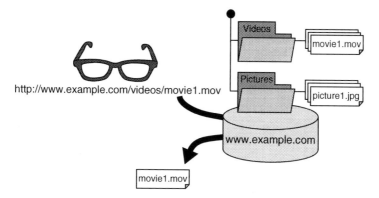

Fig. 3.11 Blob storage accessed via HTTP

offering, its location within the folder hierarchy, and its file name. In Fig. 3.11, the hypertext transfer protocol (HTTP) is used to access a video file maintained by a storage offering addressed by the domain name "www.example.com". The file is called "movie1.mov" and is located in the folder "videos".

Variations

The number of hierarchy levels in the directory structure is sometimes limited by the storage offerings. Further limitations can include naming conventions, such as length of identifiers or the use of special characters. Also, automatic distribution of data among multiple geographically distributed blob storages can be offered to guarantee locality of data.

Related Patterns

The data storage used for virtual images or software artifacts used by *IaaS* (45) and *PaaS* (49) is often realized as *blob storage*. A *blob storage* offering itself is realized according to *PaaS* (49). It may display *strict consistency* (123) or *eventual consistency* (126) regarding the handling of data manipulations. Blob storage offerings are often combined with the following patterns:

- *Block storage* (110): a *block storage* offering offers (virtual) hard-drives as *IaaS* (45). To scale, customers have to manually (or automatically) add new (virtual) hard-drives and must manually ensure that data is replicated to other (virtual) hard-drives in other data centers if replicas are needed. Billing is then done per size of the provisioned (virtual) hard-drives. In a *blob storage* offering replication is done by the storage platform which also adds and removes resources to create just the amount of storage for a customer that he needs and only bills for storage that is actually used.

- *Processing component* (180): these components handle the workload of applications and may work on very large files. These files may then be stored in a *blob storage* offering to reduce the state information contained in processing components. This makes them easier to scale within the scope of *elasticity managers* (250), *elastic load balancer* (254), or *elastic queues* (257). It also eases failure handling by the *resiliency management process* (283).

Known Uses

Traditional Web servers and FTP servers function according to the *blob storage* pattern. Amazon's Simple Storage Service (S3) [132] services offers similar functionality. Amazon CloudFront [104] provides similar access to streaming content that is automatically replicated geographically to increase performance. In Windows Azure *blob storage* functionality is provided by Windows Azure Blob storage [105].

3.5.3   Relational Database

Data is structured according to a schema that is enforced during data manipulation and enables expressive queries of handled data.

 How can data elements be stored so that relations between them can be expressed and expressive queries are enabled to retrieve required information effectively?

Context

The data handled by a storage offering is often comprised of large numbers of similar data elements, for example, the same information is stored for every customer of a company. Furthermore, these data elements have certain dependencies among each other, for example, each customer may have an associated sales agent who handles the customer's orders. If such structured data is stored in a storage offering, clients querying the data elements, therefore, make certain assumptions about the data structure. Furthermore, the client expects consistent relations between the retrieved data elements. In scope of stored information about customers, a querying client could, for example, expect that a data element describing a sales agent exists, if a customer data element has a reference to it. Inconsistencies in this data structure may lead to failure of the querying clients, because they assume the presence of certain data elements. If these data elements cannot be retrieved, errors may occur. This consistency should be enforced for the overall storage offering during the manipulations of individual data elements. For example, if a sales agent leaves the company, the data element representing this agent is deleted and it should be assured that there is not customer data element that is still associated with this agent, as this would leave the overall stored data in an inconsistent state.

Solution

In a *relational database*, data elements are stored in tables where each column represents an attribute of a data element with a well-defined semantic. These attributes may be used in data queries to make them more expressive. Furthermore, table columns may have dependencies in the way that entries in one table column must also be present in a corresponding column of a different table. These dependencies are enforced during all data manipulations.

Fig. 3.12 Exemplary
relational storage

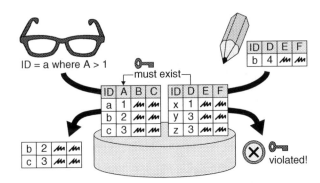

Result

Data elements are represented by rows of tables and table columns are attributes of
these individual data elements. Therefore, the table structure enforces a certain
number of attributes with well-defined semantics for each data element. In
Fig. 3.12, these semantics are depicted as column headers. This homogenous
structure of data elements ensures that the client querying the storage offering
may assume that certain attributes are present in retrieved data elements. Data
elements are identified uniquely by so-called *key attributes* that differentiate them
from all other data elements in the same table, as seen in the ID column of Fig. 3.12.
Furthermore, it is ensured that dependencies between data elements are always
consistent: relationships between elements are specified as special attributes, so-
called *foreign keys*, depicted in Fig. 3.12 as a dependency between column A of the
left table and column D of the right table. For entries in column D to be assigned a
certain value, that value must, therefore, also exist in a key attribute column of
column A. This description of data tables and their dependencies is referred to as a
database schema.

   This data consistency regarding individual data element attributes as well as the
dependencies between attributes of different data elements makes the structure of
retrieved data predictable. Whenever a data element is created, altered, or deleted it
is verified that the relations described in this schema are still fulfilled. The
consistencies of these relationships are, therefore, evaluated and enforced during
all data manipulating operation. In Fig. 3.12, a write operation is depicted on the
right that violates the foreign key dependency between the two tables and, therefore, does not succeed. Again, an example for data structured in this fashion would
be customers represented by data elements that have dependency on a sales agent
data element. This dependency is represented by a foreign key of a customer data
element that is a key attribute of a sales agent, maybe an employee ID. The database
schema then ensures that a sales agent data element is not removed from the storage
offering as long as there are customer data elements referencing it and that a
customer data element is not altered to point to a non-existing sales agent.

   The database schema enforced by the *relational database* has to be defined
during design time. It is deducted from the *domain model* of an application

describing the data elements used by an application as well as the functionality to access them in order to support the applications usage scenario. Fowler [15] covers best practices to create a domain model in his *domain model* pattern. Changes of the domain model and subsequently in the database schema during the runtime of the *relational database* when it is already filled with data may be complex and time consuming. Therefore, if the domain model supported by an application is well-known during design time and contains a lot of dependencies between data elements a relational database can support this structure efficiently and enforce the dependencies during runtime. This move the task to keep data dependencies consistent from the application to the storage offering. If the domain model is instead very simple with few dependencies and can possibly change during runtime, a *relational database* may introduce too many restrictions making it difficult to extend and adjust the application. Under these conditions, a *key-value storage* (119) may be a better choice as it enforces less structure on handled data and is, therefore, more adaptable.

During queries to the *relational database*, the attributes names defined in the database schema may be used to make queries more expressive and, thus, to reduce the amount of data that is returned to the querying client. Queries can be sent to the database and express ranges of and conditions on data element attributes as depicted in the left side of Fig. 3.12. Only the attributes that match the specified conditions are returned to the querying application. The structured query language (SQL) is a common and standardized query language for this purpose [106, 107]. The more precise these queries can describe the required elements, the less stress is put on the network transporting data elements and on the application processing them. Relational databases may use different techniques, such as indexing to increase query performance. Much like the index of this book, a *relation database* can generate specific tables to answer often used queries more quickly. If you were to search for a specific term in this book, an alphabetical index generated based on the book content is easier to search. *Relational databases* similarly generate indexes. As these may be generated in advance, query processing times may be reduced.

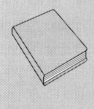

Further Reading: the *relational database* pattern describes how such a storage offering behaves to customers. The relational model to store data is covered in more detail by Codd [106]. For more information on how to structure data in a relational form and for a detailed introduction to query languages refer to Silberschatz et al. [108] or Elmasri et al. [109]. These sources, especially, discuss how indexes mentioned above may be created and updated to speed up database queries.

Related Patterns

If expressive queries are not needed, scalability and performance of the data base can often be increased, as described by the *key-value storage* (119) pattern. *Relational database* often display *strict consistency* (123). *Relational database* offerings are likely to be used in conjunction with the following patterns:

- *Stateless component (171):* components implemented according to this pattern do not hold any internal state information, thus, completely rely on storage offerings. They may use the *relational database* for this purpose.
- *Data access component (188):* in order to isolate other application components from the idiosyncrasies of data querying, data access components may be used to execute queries on relational databases. This separation of querying functionality from the rest of the application also help to ensured *loose coupling* (156) between the other application components to the database schema used by relational databases.

Known Uses

A *relational database* is offered by data base management systems, such as IBM DB2 [110], Oracle 11g [111], MySQL [112], or Microsoft SQL Server [113]. These can be also realized on top of an *IaaS* (45) cloud. Virtual servers offering such functionality are already available in Amazon EC2 [18, 114, 115]. Alternatively, *PaaS* (49) offerings, such as Amazon Relational Database Service [116] or Microsoft SQL Azure [117], can be used.

 Side Note: a complex and well-known domain model with lots of dependencies among data elements is an indicator for the use of *relational databases* (115) as the complexity to enforce consistent data dependencies is moved to the storage offering. A simple domain model that may change during runtime and contains few dependencies may make the *key-value storage* (119) a better choice.

3.5.4 Key-Value Storage

Semi-structured or unstructured data is stored with limited querying support but high-performance, availability, and flexibility.

 How can key-value elements be stored to support scale out and an adjustable data structure?

Context

To ensure availability and performance, a data storage offering shall be distributed among different IT resources and locations. Furthermore, changes of requirements or the fact that customers share a storage offering and have different requirements, raises the demand for a flexible data structure. *Relational database* (115) storage offerings systems depend on user-defined database schemas that they enforce on handled data. They are also harder to scale horizontally, as data structure validation during queries requires high-performance connectivity between distributed resources storing the data elements. An example for such dependencies would be foreign keys used in a table. Refer to the *relational database* (115) pattern for more information on this data structure. The complexity of query operations, if data from remote systems has to be combined, forms an additional challenge in scope of a *relational database* (115), as these database systems aim to utilize the resources of a holistic server or cluster of servers that are connected via high-performance networks optimally: in this setup, a query should be as expressive as possible to avoid too large data sets being returned to querying clients. However, cloud offerings may not have access to centralized, high performance servers but instead employ a large number of distributed commodity servers [24, 63, 64]. The networks connecting these servers may also be less powerful and unreliable reducing the performance of a clustered relational database systems deployment in the cloud [118]. The focus for many cloud storage offerings is instead the need to handle very large amounts of data that are globally distributed and whose structure has to be adjustable to new requirements quickly and flexibly. This flexibility enables providers to adjust storage offerings to the requirements of different customers and, especially, share the same offering between customers storing very different data. Therefore, a storage solution is required that focuses on scaling-out rather than on optimizing the use of a single server or cluster and that can adjust flexibly to changes of the data structure.

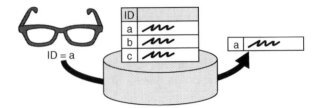

Fig. 3.13 Exemplary read operation on a key-value storage

Solution

A *key-value storage* offering stores pairs of identifiers (key) and associated data (value) in a table. It supports no database schema or only a very limited schema to enforce a data structure. Therefore, the expressiveness of queries is reduced significantly in favor of scalability and configurability. Semi-structured on unstructured data can be scaled out among many IT resources without the need to access many of them for the evaluation of expressive queries, as supported by *relational databases* (115). Configurability is enabled as only few fields of data elements have a predefined semantic, for example, there may be only the unique identifier (key) associated with arbitrary data fields. The number and semantic of these fields may then be interpreted by the client accessing the *key-value storage* offering and cannot be used in expressive queries that have to be interpreted by the key-value storage.

Result

Key-value storage offerings either do not enforce any data schema at all or a very limited one. Often, they only allow querying the key attribute as depicted in Fig. 3.13. The remainder of the data element structure is outside the control of the *key-value storage* offering. An application's ability to use such a storage offering efficiently largely depends on its *domain model*. The domain model describes the data handled by an application as well as the required functionality to access it. Fowler [15] describes best practices to obtain this model. If the domain model is rather simple with few dependencies between data elements the functionality provided by a *key-value storage* is an ideal match. On the other hand, if the domain model contains many complex dependencies among handled data elements an application using a *key-value storage* would have to ensure the consistency of data dependencies, which possibly increases implementation complexity. Under these conditions a *relational database* (115) enforcing a data structure and data dependencies internally may be a better option as the application's implementation is simplified.

The reduced data structure supported by a *key-value storage* enables data to be distributed among very many resources without affecting query performance significantly. Furthermore, the supported data structure remains extremely flexible and may be adjusted to changing requirements of different customers. This design of course adds additional complexity to the applications that use such a data store as changes to the implicit structure of the data need to be respected and enforced by the application. Since the expressiveness of queries is reduced, this storage offering may return more data to the application initiating the query. *Relational databases* (115) aim to reduce this amount of data through sophisticated queries, such as *join* operations [108]. Therefore, *key-value storage* offerings possibly put a lot more of the querying workload on the application than *relational databases*, where more expressive queries are supported. This has to be addressed in the architecture of the cloud application using *key-value storage* offerings, for example, by implementing the *map reduce* (106) pattern.

Further Reading: data storage that reduces the degree of data structuring are summarized by the term "NoSQL". Tiwari [119] gives a quick overview on NoSQL concepts and current NoSQL implementations. A more thorough and complete coverage of common underlying concepts, the fundamental differences, and use cases of NoSQL databases can be obtained from Sadalage and Fowler [120].

Variations

There is not one standard implementation of the *key-value storage* pattern and, therefore, *key-value storage* offerings may differ in supported functionality. These versatile implementations may also blur the boundaries between *key-value storage* and *relational database* offerings. Some implementations allow only one unique identified as described above, others allow more data fields to be queried similar to *relational database* and also support additional structuring. Therefore, for each application the ability to scale out, the structuring of data and the expressiveness of querying capability has to be weighted when selecting a *key-value storage* variations or a *relational database* (115).

Related Patterns

To further increase the ability to scale out among multiple resources and to cope with network failures as well as the resulting network partitions, *key-value storage* offerings often display *eventual consistency* (126). But *strict consistency* (123) solutions are also possible. The *key-value storage* offering is, furthermore, likely combined with the following patterns:

• *Map reduce* (106): as the expressiveness of queries is reduced, *key-value storage* offerings generally return more data than what a client actually requires. To handle the filtering in an application, additional data queries may again be scaled out among distributed resources as described by the *map reduce* pattern.

- *Data access component* (188): the functionality to handle access to a *key-value storage* offering and possibly the required coordination of *map reduce* (106) should be encapsulated into a *data access component*. This hides the idiosyncrasies of the data access from the rest of the application and aims at making it *loosely coupled* (156) to the used *key-value storage* offering.

Known Uses

There are stand-alone implementations of *key-value storage* systems that can be installed as regular middleware, such as Apache Cassandra [121], Apache CouchDB [98] or MongoDB [122]. Cloud-based *key-value storage* offerings include Amazon's SimpleDB [123] and Amazon Dynamo [124], or Windows Azure Tables [125]. In case of Amazon Dynamo, the consistency behavior of the offerings (eventual or strict) may be specified on a per-query basis. Google's Big Table is another *key-value storage* implementation and is described in [126].

 Side Note: a *key-value storage* (119) can be scaled out efficiently due to few enforced dependencies among data elements and a simple data structure. If the domain model of an application is simple and contains few dependencies, it can use such a storage offering efficiently. However, if the domain model is complex containing a lot of dependencies, a *relational database* (115) can enforce this data structure instead of handling this task in the application functionality.

3.5.5 Strict Consistency

> Data is stored at different locations (replicas) to improve response time and to avoid data loss in case of failures while consistency of replicas is ensured at all times.

How can data be distributed among replicas to increase availability, while ensuring data consistency at all times?

Context

To ensure failure tolerance, a storage offering duplicates data among multiple replicas. These replicas store the same set of data, so in case any of these replicas is lost, data may still be obtained and recovered from the other replicas. In this scope, the consistency of the data contained in these replicas shall be pertained at all times. The highest level of consistency is granted if all replicas are updated when the data contained by them is altered. However, this can lead to a decreasing availability of the overall storage solution regarding such write operations, because all replicas have to be available for data alterations to take place. This may, for example, happen if network connectivity between the replicas is reduced, thus, if the number of replicas experiences so called *network partitioning*. Instead, it shall be ensured that the storage offering is available even if not all replicas are available and that the correct version of the data is accessed.

Solution

Data is duplicated among several replicas to increase availability. A subset of data replicas is accessed by read and write operations to increase network partitioning tolerance. The ratio of the number of replicas accessed during read and write operations guarantees consistency: it is ensured that at least one replica with the most frequent data version is accessed during each operation.

Result

A storage offering usually incorporates multiple replicas transparently to the user. A read or write operation performed by a customer is internally executed as a

Fig. 3.14 Exemplary strict
consistent replicas

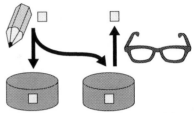

number of replicas (n) = 2
replicas accessed to write (w) = 2
replicas accessed to read (r) = 1

number of read or write operation on the replicas. Subsets of the available replicas
are accessed during these internal read and write operations. Thus, the system is
available even if not all replicas are accessible. *Strict consistency* is guaranteed
through the size of the subsets of replicas that are read or written. Considering the
overall number of replicas (n), the number of replicas accessed during read (r), and
those accessed during write (w), it is ensured that $n < w + r$ holds true for every
read and write operation. In Fig. 3.14, these ratios and operations are depicted
exemplarily for two replicas. In this example, both replicas are accessed during
write operations and one is accessed during read operations. Therefore, every
operations accesses at least one replica with the most current version. The values
for w and r are usually fixed at design time and reflect the different requirements on
read and write performance. In case of the above example, two replicas are used and
both are accessed by write operations. Read operation only have to access one
replica, thus, their performance is increased. Common examples for such a setup
would be a corporate address book, where write operations are performed rarely
while read operations take place often. If instead write performance shall be
increased, the number of replicas accessed during a write is decreased and those
during read increased. This would be the case in a logging system to which data is
written often, but evaluated less-frequently, thus, the ration between replicas
accessed during reads and replicas accessed during writes may be adjusted to
require less replica accesses for write operation.

For consistency, these read and write operations accessing multiple replicas are
additionally subsumed in one transaction that guarantees ACID properties. These
properties are ensured for the managed data replicas and are what the customer of
the storage offering experiences when performing read and write operations:

- *Atomicity*: all operations of the transaction have to be successful for the external
  read or write operation to be successful. This ensures that the required set of
  replicas is really accessed successfully to ensure consistency.
- *Consistency*: after the transaction, the overall system is in a consistent and valid
  state. This property is ensured by the ratio of replicas accessed during read and
  write operations.

- *Isolation*: no other transaction may interfere with a transactional read or write access to the set of replicas.
- *Durability*: all alterations performed by the transaction are stable and will not be revoked.

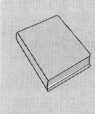 ***Further Reading:*** transactions are a common concept to coordinate the alteration of data stored in distributed databases. An excellent coverage of fundamental concepts is given by Tanenbaum et al. [127]. More practical information on how to build applications that have to handle transactions is given by Bernstein et al. [128] and Gray et al. [129].

Variations

Some storage offerings allow the specification of consistency behavior on a per request basis. Therefore, critical information can be retrieved following *strict consistency*; less critical information is retrieved granting *eventual consistency* (126). While the *strict consistency* pattern is mostly being implemented by providers, application developers may also have to consider the consistency of data when they integrate different cloud providers or replicate data between a cloud environment and a non-cloud environment, such as a static data center or a legacy application.

Related Patterns

All storage offering patterns described in Sect. 3.5 of this Chapter can guarantee *strict consistency* or *eventual consistency* (126). The latter is often used if consistency requirements can be relaxed in favor of increased performance and availability to serve very large user groups. Some of the storage offerings, like *relational database* (115) are more likely to display strict consistency, while other such as *key-value storage* (119) and are more likely to use *eventual consistency* (126).

Known Uses

Database management systems, such as MySQL [112] or IBM DB2 [110] ensure *strict consistency*. The replicas may be realized by multiple instances of the database installations that comprise a cluster. Since these clusters rely heavily on connectivity, their performance may degrade in a cloud environment [118]. This is due to the fact, that connectivity between cloud resources of the cluster may be not as powerful as in a local data center, where the network topology may be specifically optimized for a database cluster setup.

3.5.6 Eventual Consistency

> If data is stored at different locations (replicas) to improve response time and avoid data loss in case of failures. Performance and the availability of data in case of network partitioning are enabled by ensuring data consistency eventually and not at all times.

 How can data be distributed among replicas with focus on increased availability and performance, while being resilient towards connectivity problems?

Context

Using multiple replicas of data is vital to ensure resiliency of a storage offering towards resource failures. Keeping all these replicas in a consistent state, however, requires a significant overhead as multiple or all data replicas have to be accessed during read and write operations. The availability of the storage offering, therefore, becomes dependent on a certain number of replicas during read operations and write operations. To cope with unavailable replicas, *strict consistency* (123) ensures that these read and write operations only access a subset of replicas, so it is guaranteed at all times that the retrieved data is current and consistent. Depending on the priority of read accesses and write accesses the ratio of replicas that have to be read or written can be adjusted. While making the offering dependent on fewer replicas during accesses, still more than half of the replicas need to be accessed by one or both of these operations to ensure consistency as described by the *strict consistency* (123) pattern in greater detail. If a large number of replicas is distributed among a large connection network, this may result in an inacceptable performance of the offering. Also, the connection networks may be less reliable in this large distributed setup making connection problems more likely. When this occurs and the replicas are divided into so called network partitions, the read and write operations may not be able to access the necessary number of replicas to ensure *strict consistency*. And even during times of connectivity, the transmission time of the data updates over such large distributed networks may be too high for the desired performance of read and write operations. Assuring consistency among many geographically distributed replicas can, therefore, reduce the availability and performance of the storage offering to a degree that becomes inacceptable.

Fig. 3.15 Exemplary
eventual consistent replicas

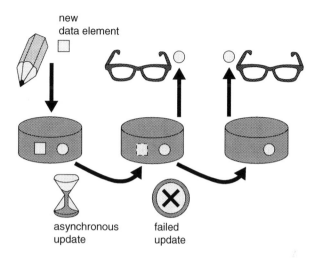

Solution

The consistency of data is relaxed. This reduces the number of replicas that have to be accessed during read and write operations. Through this relaxation, the storage offering, therefore, becomes more tolerant towards network partitioning and node failure, because fewer replicas have to be accessed, thus, increasing its availability. The performance of read and write operations is also increased, as replicas may be accessed that are close to the accessing entity reducing delays in the distribution network. Instead of enforcing *strict consistency* (123) among the data replicas during read and write operations, data alterations are eventually transferred to all replicas by propagating them asynchronously over the connection network. Figure 3.15 depicts three *eventually consistent* replicas. Read and write operations are only executed on one replica. Data alterations are propagated eventually. However, if this propagation has not yet been executed as indicated by the dashed data element, or if it fails, read operations do not return a data element that was previously written. Data returned under such conditions is, therefore, inconsistent.

Result

While *strictly consistent* (123) storage offerings ensure that always at least one replica containing the current version is read, eventually consistent databases allow that obsolete versions may also be read. The CAP theorem [67] gives an overview of the relation between consistency, availability, and partitioning tolerance. It states that in a distributed storage environment, only two of those properties can be optimized. By reducing data consistency, the properties availability and performance of the storage offering are increased. The impact of network partitioning and network delays is reduced as fewer replicas have to be accessed during read and write operation. After an update to this small number of replicas, other replicas are updated asynchronously, for example, via message queues provided by a *message-oriented middleware* (136). The term *consistency window* is often used to refer to the time it takes for these asynchronous updates to reach all replicas in absence of network partitioning. In case of a network partitioning, updates are eventually propagated to all replicas once the partitioning is resolved. Additional challenges arise when replicas in different network partitions have been changed independently. This condition may also occur due to the *consistency window* when there are no network partitions, but data is accessed concurrently by many clients while updates traverse trough the set of replicas eventually. For some offerings, the latest data update simply wins such conditions. Others do not make any assurances for concurrent access to the offering. Therefore, provider service level agreements and offering behavior descriptions should be carefully evaluated to ensure that they fit the expected and required behavior of the application using the storage offering.

Similar to the ACID properties guaranteed by *strict consistency* (123), an eventual consistent offering also displays a certain set of generic properties. We will now cover these BASE properties [130] prior to covering in detail what this means for the accesses executed by one **single client** and a set of **concurrently accessing clients**:

- *Basically Available:* the system providing data is available event if parts of it fail. BASE systems try to maintain the operability in case of failures as long as possible for as many users as possible and accept data inconsistencies in this attempt leading to the next two properties.
- *Soft State:* BASE systems do not have a discrete state such as ACID systems. Therefore, they may display a different state to different users or the same user at a certain point in time.
- *Eventually Consistent:* the soft state of data propagates through a BASE system and eventually reaches a state that is consistent regarding the complete system.

Respecting the BASE properties, it is important to consider the behavior of a storage offering regarding the accesses of a **single client**. In detail, eventually consistent storage offerings may display one or multiple of the following *client-centric consistency behaviors* [127, 131] to a client. If multiple behaviors are supported, they may have to be selected on a per-access-basis.

- *Monotonic Reads – One client will never read data that is older than what it has read before.* Therefore, if a client has read a certain version of a data element any later read operations performed by that client will return the same or a more recent version.
- *Monotonic Writes – Write operations of one client are executed in the order they were issued.* Therefore, a client will never update data that does not reflect changes of previous writes. On the data replica side, a more recent write operation will, thus, only be executed by a data replica, if it has executed all previous write operations of one client.
- *Writes Follow Reads – A client will never write to replicas that are older than what it has read before.* Therefore, a client always writes to the same or a more

recent version that it has previously read. This consistency behavior is closely related to monotonic writes, but a little less powerful: if a client desires monotonic-writes behavior, it has to execute a read operation prior to every one of its write operations.

- *Read Your Writes – One client will immediately see data alterations performed by it.* Therefore, if a client writes a data element, any read operations it performs after that will retrieve this data version or a more recent one.

Cloud offerings may tighten the consistency that is guaranteed for **concurrent accesses of multiple clients** [132, 133], by guaranteeing one or more of the following assurances:

- *Read-After-Write – a newly created data element will be visible to all clients immediately.* Therefore, if a client creates a new file or data base table entry, the data element will be immediately visible to all consecutive read operations executed by all clients.

- *Read-After-Update – the effect of an update to a data object will be visible to all clients immediately.* Therefore, if a client changes a data object all consecutive read operations on that object will return the updated value. In contrast to read-after-write consistency, this behavior regards changed data not only newly created data.

- *Read-After-Delete – if a data element is removed clients will be unable to retrieve it.* Therefore, after a data element is deleted all consecutive read operations will be unsuccessful by all clients.

Finally, *eventual consistent* storage offerings can use a concept called *conditional writes* to coordinate the update of data elements. If an update operation is executed conditionally, the client updating a data element passes a condition to the storage offering under which the update shall be executed. This approach is used to pass the expected current value of the data element or the expected version to the storage offering. Therefore, it can be avoided that a client changes a data element that has been changed since that client has been last accessed the data element. If the condition is not fulfilled, the update operation fails.

Side Note: *eventual consistency* can have many characteristics regarding the behavior displayed to a single client and concurrently accessing clients. We captured commonly found behavior here. However, this behavior may be changed by providers and the terms covered here may be used for different behavior. Therefore, eventual consistent behavior of cloud offerings has to be evaluated carefully in every usage scenario.

Related Patterns

All *storage offering patterns* can guarantee *strict consistency* (123) or *eventual consistency*. Many storage offerings found in *public clouds* (62) display *eventual consistency*, as they target very large user groups and are globally distributed. This distributed often hinders a timely distribution of data updates.

Known Uses

Amazon SimpleDB [123] uses two consistency models, *strict consistency* (123) and *eventual consistency*. For every request to the storage offering, a user can specify the required consistency model. In case of *eventual consistency* fewer replicas are read to increase the availability and performance. In case *strict consistency* is required, the number of replicas that are read is increased to guarantee accessing the current version. Also, this storage offering supports the above mentioned conditional writes. Apache CouchDB [98] and Apache MongoDB [122] also support *eventual consistency*.

Eventual consistent behavior is, however, not dedicated to cloud computing. Probably the largest as best-known eventual consistent systems is the domain name system (DNS) [134]. It handles the resolution of domain names to addresses and is, therefore, fundamental to the proper functioning of the Internet. As it is comprised out of a huge number of globally distributed DNS servers, changes to a domain name or the address that name maps to are propagated eventually.

 *Further Reading:* the *eventual consistency* pattern only describes how an eventual consistent data store behaves and what motivates providers and customers to use such data stores. It does not describe how to actually build such a data store that is comprised out of multiple replicas. For a detailed description how *eventual consistency* can be ensured by a replica management system, please refer to Tanenbaum et al. [127].

3.6 Communication Offerings

Applications running in the cloud rely on different communication offerings. These communication offerings are used cloud internally and externally, for example, to exchange messages between application components or to communicate with applications in on-premise datacenters. This section first describes a fundamental communication offering to configure networking connectivity via a self-service interface, which is *virtual networking* (132). Then, it covers communication offerings providing functionality for message exchange. This functionality is provided by a *message-oriented middleware* (136) that manages different queues, routes messages between them and also handles message format transformation. A *message-oriented middleware* can assure different delivery behavior for handled messages. The assurance that messages are not lost is described by the *exactly-once delivery* (141) pattern and *at-least-once delivery* (144) pattern. This assurance may also be extended to ensure the successful receive of messages by clients interacting with the message-oriented middleware as described by the *transaction-based delivery* (146) and *timeout-based delivery* (149) pattern.

3.6.1   Virtual Networking

Networking resources are virtualized to empower customers to configure
networks, firewalls, and remote access using a self-service interface.

 *How can network connectivity between IT resources hosted in a
cloud be configured dynamically and on-demand?*

Context

Application components deployed on *elastic infrastructures* (87) and *elastic
platforms* (91) rely on physical network hardware to communicate with each
other and the outside world. On this networking layer, different customers of a
cloud shall be isolated from each other to increase security and avoid performance
influences between them. Furthermore, networking connectivity between the cloud
and other environments, i.e., an on-premise data center shall be enabled.

Solution

Just as *hypervisors* (101) introduce a virtualization level to physical hardware
enabling the isolated hosting of multiple virtualized servers, *virtual networking*
abstracts physical networking resources, such as networking interface cards,
switches, routers etc. to virtualized ones. These virtual networking resources may
share the same physical networking resources enabling sharing between multiple
customers. The physical hardware of the connection networks often has to support
this virtualization. The necessary technologies have been supported by networking
hardware for quite some time but are made available to customers through self-
service interfaces as depicted in Fig. 3.16.

Result

Customers may configure the connectivity between the provisioned IT resources
and hosted applications, as well as integrate other network environments, such as
their own data centers. In many cases, the configurable network entities are virtual
local area networks (VLAN), virtual routers, firewalls, and virtual private networks
(VPN), all covered in the following.

Fig. 3.16 Self-service
interface for configuration of
virtual networking

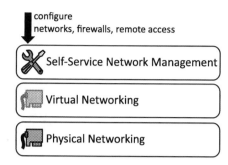

Further Reading: just as a *hypervisor* (101) enabling hardware virtualization, virtual networking is an enabling technology for cloud computing as it allows customers to configure networks, routing, firewall rules, and remote access via a self-service interface without any physical alterations in the providers' data centers. For an in-depth description of the networking technologies covered briefly by this pattern please refer to Harpence [135], Odom [136], or Deal [137].

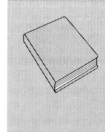

Virtual local area networks (VLAN): networking switches – physical hardware interconnecting servers can support VLANs to define the network segments on which servers may communicate directly with each other regardless of their actual physical connectivity. Figure 3.17 depicts and exemplary VLAN setup comprised of two physical switches connecting six servers. Through the configuration of two different VLANs ("v1" and "v2") on the ports of these two switches, the servers one, two and six can communicate directly with each other just as the servers three through five, because they reside on the same virtual network segment. This virtualization of network segments is used in clouds to enable self-service configuration of network connectivity by customers and to ensure isolation of network traffic between customers.

Virtual routers: similar to virtual configuration of switches to specify different VLANs, providers offer network routers connecting multiple network segments that can be configured through ha self-service interface. These connected network segments can be multiple VLANs, for example. While communication between servers in a VLAN is enabled directly between the servers, a router acts as one communication partner on such a segment and forwards communication to other networks it is connected to based on customer-specified routing rules.

Firewalls: this networking resource is used to restrict the networking traffic exchanged over communication networks to ensure security. Many cloud providers allow the separation of their environments into separate networks through the definition of VLANS. Connectivity between these network segments may then be controlled by virtual routers and virtual firewalls through the definition of routing

Fig. 3.17 Exemplary VLAN setup

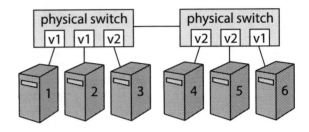

Fig. 3.18 Firewall setup for an example application

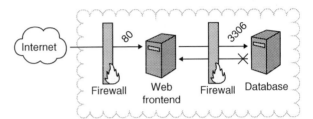

rules and access rules specified by the customer. Consider, for example, an application deployed in an *IaaS* (45) offering depicted in Fig. 3.18. It is comprised of a Web frontend that is accessed through the standard HTTP port 80. Therefore, a virtual firewall between the virtual server hosting this component and the Internet only allows this port for inbound communication. The Web frontend also accesses a data base hosted on a different virtual server through the port 3,306. Both servers are again separated by a virtual firewall that only allows this form of communication. Again, the virtualization of firewalls is used in clouds to enable the self-service definition of access rules by customers.

Virtual private network (VPN): many cloud providers offer functionality to create virtual private networks as a service, thus, an encrypted communication channel may be established between the cloud and a different network, commonly an on-premise datacenter or *private cloud* (66). Figure 3.19 depicts such an encrypted channel from a server in a corporate network to an *IaaS* (45) provider. Through this encrypted channel, servers hosted by the cloud provider may, for example, be accessed as if they resided in the same local network as the server connecting to the cloud.

Related Patterns

- *Elastic infrastructure* (87): virtual networking is often provided in conjunction with an *elastic infrastructure* where it used to configure the network connectivity between virtual servers. In scope of an *elastic platform* (91), the networking is instead often hidden from customers as communication is enabled through higher-level communication services, such as messaging provided by a *message-oriented middleware* (136).

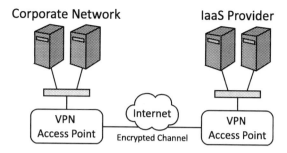

Fig. 3.19 VPN from a corporate network to an IaaS provider

- *Hypervisor* (101): some *hypervisors* allow the definition of virtual networks between virtual servers hosted on them as well as the virtual configuration of connectivity to the outside world.

Known Uses

Amazon AWS [138] allows the definition of so called security groups [139], network segments on which virtual servers of its Elastic Compute Cloud (EC2) [18] reside. The communication between these security groups and the outside world is restricted by user-defined firewall and routing rules. Other products and offerings offer similar functionality to group virtual servers into groups that restrict access from and to outside servers.

3.6.2 Message-Oriented Middleware

> Asynchronous message-based communication is provided while hiding complexity resulting from addressing, routing, or data formats from communication partners to make interaction robust and flexible.

How can communication partners exchange information asynchronously with a communication partner?

Context

The application components of a *distributed application* (160) are hosted on multiple cloud resources and have to exchange information with each other. Often, the integration with other cloud applications and non-cloud applications is also required. These different applications possibly use different programming languages, data formats, and *execution environments* (104). When one application directly exchanges information with another application, the address and data format of the target application has to be respected. Even within one homogeneous *distributed application* (160), the communicating application components must be available at the time when the information shall be exchanged. These dependencies can significantly reduce the availability of the overall application as the failure of one application component would directly affect all components communications with it. The resulting dependency between communication partners regarding their location, availability, and data format is called *tight coupling*. It also increases the complexity of the management of the overall application or the landscape of applications, because changes to one communication partner, for example, regarding the format of exchanged data or the address used, also affect the other communication partner directly. This should be avoided to increase the availability of the overall application and ease continuous alterations by making communication flexible.

Solution

Communication partners exchange information asynchronously using messages handled by a *message-oriented middleware*. For this purpose, a *message-oriented middleware* provides different communication functionality:

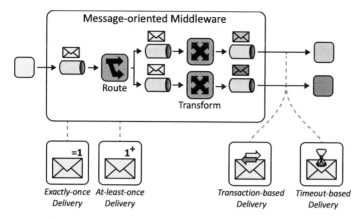

Fig. 3.20 Message-oriented middleware and related patterns

A *message queue* also called message channel by Hohpe and Woolf [1] stores messages until they are retrieved from a receiver. Multiple receivers can send messages to a queue and retrieve them from it. This behavior enables the scalability of cloud applications using messaging. In this book, we will mostly use message queues in the covered patterns.

A *pub-sub* channel [1] may be used to broadcast a message to multiple receivers. While a message queue conceptually delivers messages to only one receiver, a pub-sub channel delivers messages to multiple receivers.

> ***Further Reading:*** the *message-oriented middleware* pattern summarizes selected messaging patterns of Hohpe and Woolf [1]. These messaging patterns are applicable in scope of cloud applications in their original form and should, especially, be considered when building a message-oriented middleware offering. Here, we give an overview of messaging functionality. We focus on the cloud-specific behavior of such an offering and the properties relevant in cloud applications.

Result

When interacting with a *message-oriented middleware*, a sender puts a message on one message queue or pub-sub channel and receivers can retrieve it from possibly different queues. In between these two access points the *message-oriented middleware* handles the complexity of addressing, availability of communication partners and message format transformation as shown in Fig. 3.20. Therefore, in addition to message queues, the *message-oriented middleware* provides components that route messages to intended receivers as well as handle message format transformation. Communication partners may communicate via messages without the need to know the message format expected by the communication partner or the address at which it can be reached. Furthermore, communication partners can send and receive messages at their own pace and without relying on the availability of communication partners.

The *message-oriented middleware*, therefore, suggests a *pipes-and-filters* application architecture as covered by Hohpe and Woolf [1], Bushmann et al. [14] and in the *distributed application* (160) pattern in Chap. 4. In this scope, application components act as independently operating *filters* that are interconnected through *pipes*, i.e., the message queues provided by the *message-oriented middleware*. Hohpe and Woolf [1] describe the behavior of these pipes and how they may be connected. Regarding the *filters*, i.e., the application components, Hohpe and Woolf also described how to interface with the messaging systems in the *adapter* pattern.

The more intermediaries a message passes through while traversing a *message-oriented middleware*, the more likely it becomes that an intermediary fails. To address this issue, messages are often stored in persistent storage by *the message-oriented middleware* from where they can be recovered in case of failures. This approach is described by the *guaranteed delivery* pattern introduced by Hohpe and Woolf [1].

Variations

A *message-oriented middleware* is used if small amounts of data need to be exchanged frequently, as messages are often restricted in size so they can be handled more easily. If larger amounts of data have to be exchanged, messages may either contain a pointer to this data that is actually stored at a different location, for example, a storage offering (see Sect. 3.5) or the data may be split up among multiple messages. Hohpe and Wolf [1] cover patterns for this exchange of large data elements: the *file transfer* pattern describes how data may be exported from one application and imported by a different one. A *message sequence* may be used to split large data elements among a set of messages.

Related Patterns

Figure 3.20 shows how the other messaging patterns of this section are related to the message oriented middleware:

- *At-least-once delivery* (144): it is ensured that messages traversing the *message-oriented middleware* are delivered once or multiple times. This is achieved through acknowledgements for message receives. If an acknowledgement is not received, a message is retransmitted.

- *Exactly-once delivery* (141): messages traversing the message-oriented middleware are delivered once and only once to the receiver. This involves reliably storage of messages in the *message-oriented middleware* and, often, transactional message exchange during its traversal of *the message-oriented middleware*.
- *Transaction-based delivery* (146): the transactional behavior used to assure *at-least-once delivery* of messages can be extended to the client receiving the message. This assures not only that messages are delivered exactly once, but also that they are received exactly once.
- *Timeout-based delivery* (149): the acknowledged receive of messages can be extended to the client receiving the message, to assure not only that messages are delivered at-least-once, but also successfully received by message receivers.

 Side Note: the patterns *at-least-once delivery* (144) and *exactly-once delivery* (141) describe assurances of the *message-oriented middleware* regarding the **end-to-end message delivery** from sender to receiver.
The patterns *transaction-based delivery* (146) and *timeout-based delivery* (149) describe the behavior of the *message-oriented middleware* when **interacting directly with the receiver** of messages.

In addition to these communication patterns, there are several related patterns that should be considered to be implemented in applications and their components interacting with a *message-oriented middleware*:

- *Transaction-based processor* (201): if the *message-oriented middleware* uses transactions to assure that messages are delivered *exactly-once* (141), the transaction can be extended to include the message processing performed by the receiver as well. Therefore, the *transaction-based processor* enables the application to assure that messages are processed *exactly-once*. A similar behavior is also described by Hohpe and Woolf's [1] *transactional client* pattern. The transaction-based processor pattern summarizes this behavior and extends it to the transactional interaction with a storage offering.
- *Timeout-based message processor* (204): if the *message-oriented middleware* assures *at-least-once delivery* (144) by acknowledging message receives, the client can extend the acknowledgment to the successful message processing. Therefore, the *timeout-based message processor* enables an application to assure that messages are processed *at least once*.
- *Distributed application* (160): applications that are comprised of multiple *loosely coupled* (156) application component usually employ a message-oriented middleware to exchange information between components. In this scope, an *idempotent processor* (197) may be used to cope with duplicate messages created by a *message-oriented middleware* assuring *at-least-once delivery*.

- *Message mover* (225): this component may be used to integrate different *message-oriented middleware* instances offered by different cloud providers or that are installed in on-premise datacenters.
- *Watchdog* (260): a watchdog may be used to cope with failing resources, especially, in scope of *environment-based availability* (98). It uses message queues to store information securely even in case of failures.
- *Batch processing component* (185): message queues may be used to actively delay messages. A *batch processing component* does so to process messages only when conditions are feasible, for example, if cloud resource prices are low or the overall application experiences a low utilization.

Known Uses

Using messaging to integrate distributed applications is a common architectural approach. Many additional messaging patterns have been identified by Hohpe and Woolf [1]. Amazon offers a *message-oriented middleware* as a service, called Amazon Simple Queue Service (SQS) [38]. A similar service is provided by Windows Azure Messaging [140]. Apache Camel [141], IBM WebSphere MQ [142], and Apache ActiveMQ [143] are open source and commercial *message-oriented middleware* products designed for on-premise use. Many of the cloud-based offerings offer *at-least-once delivery* (144) unlike many on-premise solutions, which typically also provide *exactly-once delivery* (141). When switching between different *message-oriented middleware* products, a change in delivery behavior has to be carefully evaluated.

3.6.3 Exactly-Once Delivery

> For many critical systems duplicate messages are inacceptable. The messaging system ensures that each message is delivered exactly once by filtering possible message duplicates automatically.

 How can it be assured that a message is delivered only exactly once to a receiver?

Context

Message duplicity is a very critical design issue for *distributed applications* (160) and or application components that exchange messages via a *message-oriented middleware* (136). A *message-oriented middleware* may try to avoid message duplicates by storing messages in persistent storage and acknowledge the successful transmission of every message from one persistent storage to the next, as described by Hohpe and Woolf [1] as *guaranteed delivery*. In case of failures, the recovery time may, however, be inacceptable to an application if it exceeds a certain threshold. In this scope, messaging systems may retransmit a message, which is a concept that is commonly used by *message-oriented middleware* to guarantee *at-least-once delivery* (144). A critical design decision affecting message duplications is how long to wait for a system to recover eventually from its persistent storage after a failure occurred. Waiting for message recovery may only be acceptable in a given timeframe as a timely delivery may demand that messages are resend instead.

Solution

Upon creation, each message is associated with a unique message identifier. This identifier is used to filter message duplicates during their traversal of a *message-oriented middleware* (136).

Result

The identification and removal of message duplicates may be offered by the *message-oriented middleware* (136) itself or may be implemented by the cloud

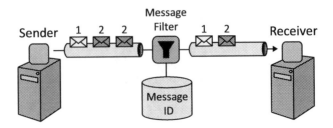

Fig. 3.21   Message filter used to guarantee exactly-once delivery

application using messaging. In the latter case, the component accessing the *message-oriented middleware* that identifies message duplicates is implements the *idempotent processor* (197) pattern. If the filtering is handled by the *message-oriented middleware*, it associates each new message with a unique identifier. This is used by a *message filter* as described by Hohpe and Woolf [1] on the message path to delete duplicates. To identify message duplicates, the message-oriented middleware stores the identifiers of messages it has already seen passing through it and deletes those it has already seen as depicted in Fig. 3.21. A central design decision is the size of the list that stores message identifiers, because it dramatically affects how well the *message-oriented middleware* (136) may detect message duplicates as well as the performance of duplicate identification. These two factors have to be weighted carefully. To balance these factors, messages are often also associated with a time frame in which they are valid to limit the size of message identifier lists. This means that a message identifier may be dropped when it is too old.

Variations

As pointed out, the filtering of messages can be implemented in the *message-oriented middleware*, or as a specific application component residing outside of the *message-oriented middleware*. This implementation would then form an *idempotent processor* (197).

Related Patterns
- *Message-oriented middleware* (136): *exactly-once delivery* is a property that can be assured of a *message-oriented middleware*.
- *Transaction-based delivery* (146): exactly-once delivery can be combined with transaction-based delivery to incorporate the receive operations of a communication within a transaction. This assures that a message is successfully received prior to being removed from a message-queue. If this transactional-receive of messages shall also be extended to assure not only a successful receive of messages, but also their successful processing, the receiver of messages may implement the *transaction-based processor* (201) pattern.

Known Uses

Exactly-once delivery is described in greater detail by the WS-Reliable Messaging standard [144]. It is implemented, among other message-oriented systems, by IBM WebSphere MQ [142]. Tanenbaum et al. [127] describe methods for failure tolerance during a message exchange if a failure occurs during message receive or message processing.

3.6.4   At-Least-Once Delivery

In case of failures that lead to message loss or take too long to recover from, messages are retransmitted to assure they are delivered at least once.

 How can communication partners or a message-oriented middleware ensure that messages are received successfully?

Context

Whether or not messages exchanged through a *message-oriented middleware* (136) by two communication partners actually reach their destination may be uncritical. For example, messages may be interchanged for informational purposes only. For other messages, guaranteed delivery and the number of times a message is delivered may be very critical, for example, in stock trading and financial systems. For such messages, the additional overhead and complexity to assure *exactly-once delivery* (141) is adequate. However, there are other use cases, where message duplicity can be coped with by the application or a cloud provider may simply decide to relax the *exactly-once delivery* (141) behavior as it is easier to implement and scale possibly reducing the price of an offering. Therefore, for scenarios where message duplicates are uncritical, it shall still be ensured that messages are received.

Solution

For each message retrieved by a receiver an acknowledgement is sent back to the message sender. This interaction protocol may be used each time a message is transmitted inside a *message-oriented middleware* (136). In case this acknowledgement is not received after a certain time frame, the message is resend.

Result

Since the sending communication partner resends unacknowledged messages, a message that is lost on the way to the receiving communication partners is eventually received. However, duplicate messages may be generated, if an error occurs during the transmission of the acknowledgement message itself as depicted in Fig. 3.22. In this case, the sending communication partner will mistakenly assume that the message has not been received and will retransmit it.

Fig. 3.22 Communication
between a sender and a
receiver to ensure at-least-
once delivery

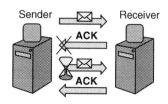

This acknowledged transmission of messages may be implemented between communicating applications or may be used internal of a *message-oriented middleware* (136). The former case may be used in custom applications to even use very unreliable message queues. Especially, this interaction protocol may be used when a receiver interacts with a *message-oriented middleware* as described by the *timeout-based delivery* (149) pattern.

Variations

Acknowledgement messages can be sent either after each individual message or after an agreed upon number of messages. This variation reduces the necessary communication overhead, if messages are not lost often. However, if a message is lost, it may lead to a retransmission of multiple messages, even though these have already been received successfully.

Related Patterns

- *Idempotent processor* (197): if a message queue provided by a *message-oriented middleware* (136) guarantees *at-least-once delivery*, the receiver of messages needs to be able to detect and handle message duplicates. Alternatively, the receiver functionality can be designed to be immune to duplicate messages. Both approaches are described by the *idempotent processor* pattern.
- *Timeout-based delivery* (149): this delivery method is used to assure that a message is received by a communication partner. It does so by extending the *at-least-once delivery* pattern to incorporate the receive operation performed on a message queue provided by a *message-oriented middleware* (136).

Known Uses

Most cloud messaging services guarantee the described *at-least-once delivery* behavior [38, 140]. Just as *exactly-once delivery* (141), the *at-least-once delivery* behavior is also included in the WS-Reliable Messaging standard [144]. Tanenbaum et al. [127] covers methods to generally implement *at-least-once delivery* between a sender and receiver as part of creating fault-tolerant distributed systems.

3.6.5   Transaction-Based Delivery

Clients retrieve messages under a transactional context to ensure that messages are received by a handling component.

 How can it be ensured that messages are only deleted from a message queue if they have been received successfully?

Context

While traversing a *message-oriented middleware* (136), thus, while being passed from message queue to message queue provided by this offering, the *message-oriented middleware* itself can assure that messages are not lost by assuring *at-least-once delivery* (144) or *exactly-once delivery* (141). Eventually, handled messages are received by clients, such as application components comprising a *distributed application* (160). While the *message-oriented middleware* can control how messages are passed between the components it provides, additionally it may be necessary to assure that messages are actually received successfully prior to removing messages from the message queue accessed by the client interacting with the *message-oriented middleware* to retrieve messages.

Solution

The *message-oriented middleware* (136) and the client reading a message from a queue participate in a transaction to ensure *transaction-based delivery*. All operations involved in the reception of a message are, therefore, performed under one transactional context guaranteeing ACID behavior, which is also described by the *strict consistency* (123) pattern. As depicted in Fig. 3.23, the message transmission starts by the sender writing a message to the queue. Then the ACID transaction is initialized when a receiver reads the message from the queue. As a third step the message is deleted from the queue, still under transactional context. If one of these operations performed under this transactional context fails, no alterations performed by the other operation are persisted. Therefore, it is ensured that a message is only removed from the message queue if it has been read successfully by the receiver.

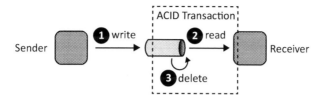

Fig. 3.23 Operations of the transactional reception of a message

Result

By delivering messages in a transactional fashion to receivers, the messaging systems may, therefore, ensure that messages are always delivered successfully prior to their deletion. The transaction ensures the ACID properties for the message exchange operations:

- *Atomicity*: either both, the read operation and the delete operation are executed or none of them.
- *Consistency*: after the transaction, the messaging system is in a valid state, thus, the message is at a specific location, the client, and not somewhere in transit or lost during transit.
- *Isolation*: a message is always only handled by one transaction, thus, there may be multiple clients concurrently reading transactional from the same queue without interfering with each other.
- *Durability*: after the transactional message delivery, the message has been successfully received and this state cannot change in case further network or system failures occur.

Variations

A similar approach to the *transaction-based delivery* of messages may be used to send messages transactional as well. In this scope, the sender of a message participates in a transaction with the message queue to send a message to it. Extending the transactional interaction with the *message-oriented middleware* (136) to sending of messages can, thus, be used to ensure that message senders do not create messages twice if unsure if the message was sent successfully. Hohpe and Woolf [1] summarize this variation and the transaction-based delivery in the *transactional client* pattern.

Related Patterns

- *Transaction-based processor* (201): the transactional message receive pattern only assures that a message is delivered successfully to a client. If this client fails, the message can still be lost and is not processed. The transaction may be extended further on the client side to include the message processing operation as well. This approach is described by the *transaction-based processor* (201) pattern.

- *Timeout-based delivery* (149): instead of using a transaction to ensure that a message is delivered, the *message-oriented middleware* (136) may resend messages that may not be received properly as described by this pattern.
- *At-least-once delivery* (144) and *exactly-once delivery* (141): these two patterns describe different assurances that a *message-oriented middleware* may make regarding the number of times a message is delivered to a handling application component. *Transaction-based delivery* is closely related to *exactly-once delivery* (141) as it is assured that a message is deleted from a message queue after it has been received by a client. However, note that the *transaction-based delivery* pattern only considers the message exchange between a queue and the handling application component. Other message processing performed as the message traverses the *message-oriented middleware* may still result in message duplicates. Therefore, if a *message-oriented middleware* supports *transaction-based delivery* of messages, these messages cannot be considered to be delivered exactly-once as well.

Known Uses

Message-oriented middleware, such as IBM Websphere MQ [142] and Apache ActiveMQ [143] support the described transactional delivery of messages. Several standards, such as the Java Message Service (JMS) [145, 146], describe the protocols used between the message-oriented middleware and the message receiver [38, 140, 147].

3.6.6 Timeout-Based Delivery

Clients acknowledge message receptions to ensure that messages are received properly.

How can it be ensured that messages are only deleted from a message queue if they have been received successfully at least once?

Context

Internally, *message-oriented middleware* (136) often assures that messages are not lost while traversing it. At some point, these messages, however, leave the *message-oriented middleware* when being read from a provided message queue by a client, for example, an application component part of a *distributed application* (160). In addition to ensuring that messages are not lost while they are traversing the *message-oriented middleware* it may, thus, also be required to assure that they are actually received by a client before they are deleted from a message queue.

Solution

To assure that a message is properly received, it is not deleted immediately after it has been read by a client, but is only marked as being invisible. In this state, a message is still stored by a message queue but may not be read by another client. After a client has successfully read a message, it sends an acknowledgement to the message queue upon which reception the message is deleted. The different steps of this interaction are depicted in Fig. 3.24. First, a message is written to a queue by a sender. Second, it is set visible by the queue to be retrieved by receivers. Third, the message is read and, fourth, set as invisible by the message queue. After the following acknowledgement given by the receiver as the fifth step, the message is deleted as step six. However, if a *visibility timeout*, also referred to as *visibility window*, is reached while a message is invisible, thus, if the receiver does not acknowledge the successful read, the message is made visible again. It may then be retrieved by other receivers.

Result

A message is only deleted from the message queue if its reception is correctly acknowledged. In case a message could not be read successfully or the success is

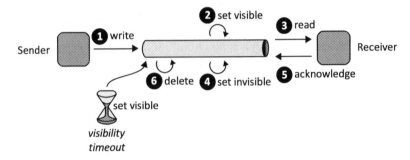

Fig. 3.24 Operations of timeout-based reception of a message

unclear, it is retransmitted. Therefore, the delivery behavior between the message queue and the client is *at-least-once* (144), thus, a message may be received multiple times by the same or different clients reading messages from the queue. Commonly, visibility timeouts of *message-oriented middleware* (136) range from a few seconds to minutes and may be configured by customers. Especially, if an applications wants to extend the receive assurance of messages to assure their processing as well, as described by the related pattern *timeout-based message processor* (204), the visibility timeout should be increased

Related Patterns
- *Timeout-based message processor* (204): to additionally ensure the proper processing of a received message, a receiver can acknowledge not only success- ful reading of a message, but the acknowledgement is sent after a message has been processed completely. Therefore, a *distributed application* (160) can then assure that all messages handled by it are processed *at least once* (144). In this scope, a problem may occur if the visibility timeout is shorter than the time it takes to process the message. The message would then become visible while it is being processed. The used *message-oriented middleware* should be configured carefully to avoid such a condition.
- *Transaction-based delivery (146):* alternatively to the retransmission of messages that may not have been received, the message reception and its deletion from the queue may be summarized in a transaction guaranteeing ACID behavior, as described by this pattern.

Known Uses

Distributed transactions required for *transaction-based delivery* can reduce the performance in large distributed environments and are very complex to implement. Many cloud-based *message-oriented middleware* offerings, therefore, provide timeout-based delivery of messages. Examples are Amazon's Simple Queue Ser- vice (SQS) [38] and the messaging service part of Windows Azure Messaging [140].

Cloud Application Architecture Patterns

4

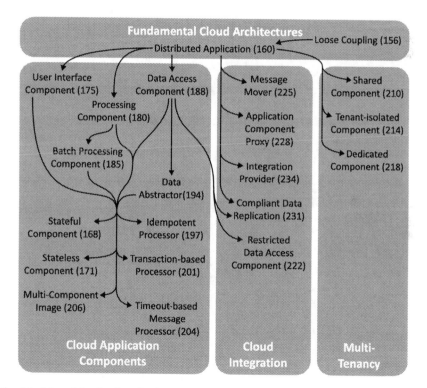

Fig. 4.1 Map of the cloud application architecture patterns

This chapter covers architectural patterns that describe how applications have to be designed to benefit from a cloud environment. Additionally, it is described how applications themselves can be offered as configurable cloud services. Having

---

All figures published with kind permission of © The Authors 2014. See list of figures.

C. Fehling et al., *Cloud Computing Patterns*,
DOI 10.1007/978-3-7091-1568-8_4, © Springer-Verlag Wien 2014

introduced cloud service models (see Sect. 2.3 on Page 42) and cloud deployment types (see Sect. 2.4 on Page 60), this chapter describes patterns that architects and developers can use to build *cloud-native applications*, i.e., applications that display the cloud application properties introduced in Sect. 1.2 on Page 5. Following the overview, *fundamental application architectural patterns* cover the architectural principles found in most cloud-native applications to enable the cloud application properties. *Application component patterns* then specify patterns on how to design and build individual components of a cloud-native application, so that the overall application can be built on top of an *elastic infrastructure* (87) or *elastic platform* (91). *Multi-tenancy patterns* describe how cloud applications and individual components can be shared by multiple customers, so called tenants, on different levels of the application stack. *Cloud integration patterns* finally describe mechanisms on how to integrate multiple cloud environments or cloud environments and on-premise datacenters as well as applications both in and outside the cloud.

4.1   Overview of Cloud Application Architecture Patterns

A cloud-native application is an application that embraces the essential cloud properties: *access via network, on-demand self-service, pay-per-use, resource pooling* and *rapid elasticity*. To be able to incorporate pay-per-use and rapid elasticity, cloud native applications must be able to elastically scale to be able to deal with varying workload (see Sect. 2.2 on Page 23). Often, the workload imposed on different components of the same application is different.

The two fundamental cloud architecture patterns, shown at the top of the pattern map depicted in Fig. 4.1, form the entry point to this section by describing what cloud-native applications have to support to enable independent elastic scaling of different parts of the application. *Distributed applications* (160) should be comprised of several *loosely-coupled* components. *Loose coupling* (156) means that application components make few assumptions about each other regarding the format of exchanged data or the communication channels used, for example. Components should also not be influenced by the failure of other components. In essence, the fundamental concepts covered by these patterns are, therefore, the decomposition of application functionality into separate components and the reduction of dependencies among these components. The following patterns describe how different application components of such cloud-native application can be implemented.

Cloud application components (Sect. 4.3) are characterized by three central patterns. *User interface components* (175) provide application functionality to users. *Processing components* (180) handle computational tasks. How this processing can be delayed to be handled when it is most feasible is described by the *batch processing component* (185) pattern. *Data access components* (188) handle data stored in storage offerings (see Sect. 3.5 on Page 109). They can deal with storage offerings at different cloud providers with different consistency levels.

Data access components can further be adjusted to inherently support *eventual consistency* (126) by abstracting data to hide that there may be data inconsistencies. This approach is described in the *data abstractor* (194) pattern. The remaining application component patterns describe general application component behavior that can be combined with all other application component patterns. The *stateful component* (168) pattern and its alternative, the *stateless component* (171) pattern describes how application components can maintain their own internal state or rely on external state information maintained in storage offerings (see Sect. 3.5 on Page 109), respectively. In this scope, we consider state to subsume session state – the state of interactions with components and application state – the data handled by the application, as introduced on Page 6 in Sect. 1.2. When dealing with state different consistency patterns such as *eventual consistency* (126) or *strict consistency* (123) have to be considered by developers.

With respect to the cloud properties, *stateless components* (171) should be preferred in applications by storing all state of an application in provider-supplied elastic storage offerings, because application components can be made *elastic* easier. Processing power can be adjusted by merely adding and removing instances of individual application components without having to respect the state handled by them. This also enables cloud applications to benefit from the elasticity and pay-per-use pricing models, because cloud resources can flexibly be added to and removed from the application. How elasticity is handled during cloud application management (Chap. 5) and the complexity involved, therefore, largely depends on the fact whether a component is a *stateful component* or a *stateless component*. Thus, splitting applications into stateless *user interface components* and stateless *processing components* coupled *via* asynchronous messaging over a *message-oriented middleware* (136) is good architectural approach to elastically scale user interfaces independently from processing components. We describe this architecture in greater detail in the *two-tier cloud application* (290) and *three-tier cloud application* (294) patterns in Chap. 6. The *batch processing component* (185) pattern processing workload only when it is most feasible, i.e., because of resource price or utilization can also be used to decouple user interfaces from backend processing.

As distributed components are often *loosely coupled* (156) *via* messaging, the behavior displayed by the *message-oriented middleware* (136) becomes important for the overall application. In case the messaging system assures *at-least-once delivery* (144), receiving components must deal with duplicate messages and, thus, implementing the *idempotent processor* (197) pattern. Furthermore, a *message-oriented middleware* can ensure that messages are received successfully, either using transactions described by the *transaction-based delivery* (146) pattern or by re-transmitting messages if the receive is not acknowledged after a timeout as covered by the *timeout-based delivery* (149) pattern. The assurance that a message is received by an application can be extended by application components to ensure that messages are successfully processed by them as well. The patterns *transaction-based processor* (201) and *timeout-based message processor* (204) describe the assured processing of messages delivered according to the respective delivery patterns. The *transaction-based processor* (201) can also be used to interact with storage offerings in the same fashion.

Having described the different application components, the following section describes multi-tenancy patterns (Sect. 4.4) on how to deal with resource sharing among different applications and customers. The *shared component* (210) provides functionality to different tenants without maintaining a notion of tenants itself. The *tenant-isolated component* (214) does the same but ensures that tenants do not influence each other while they access shared functionality. The *dedicated component* (218) pattern enables some functionality to be provided exclusively to tenants without sharing it with others.

Cloud integration patterns (Sect. 4.5) describe special application components to enable the communication across cloud boundaries, as applications are often not standalone and must be integrated with other cloud applications and non-cloud applications. A *restricted data access component* (222) extends the functionality of the *data access component* (188) to incorporate data obfuscation if sensitive data may not be retrieved completely from a less secure environment. Alternatively, data may be replicated between environments. During this replication data may be altered transparently to adhere security regulations, laws, etc., as described by the *compliant data replication* (231) pattern. These different environments may be integrated using an *integration provider* (234). When using asynchronous messaging, *message movers* (225) ensure that queues at different providers can be integrated into logical queues and, thus, applications can be split across different *hybrid clouds* (75). An *application component proxy* (228) makes complete application components accessible in different environments even if the communication between these environments is restricted.

Side Note: we covered best practices how to design application functionality to provide user interfaces, processing, or data access in separate patterns, however, the implementation of these patterns does not have to result in multiple application components in a built application. Depending on the deployment type, it may be more efficient to have a single developed application component implement multiple application component patterns described in this section. Thus, the architecture of a cloud application should consider logical components that are subsumed to tiers hosted on cloud resources. The *distributed application* (160) pattern describes this decomposition of application functionality into components and their assignment to tiers. We, furthermore, cover common tiers in cloud application in the *two-tier cloud application* (290) and *three-tier cloud application* (294) patterns in Chap. 6.

4.2   Fundamental Cloud Architectures

The patterns in this section cover the fundamental architectural styles that architects and developers have to be aware of when building a cloud-native application. From the areas of grid computing, service-oriented architectures, and messaging systems, certain architectural best practices have emerged. These are generally applicable to distributed systems and, therefore, can also be used in cloud computing. For application developers and architects it is of great importance to understand that a cloud-native application almost always is a distributed application. This is the fact as a cloud-native application is almost never deployed on one single (virtual) server but is scaled-out, thus, it spans at least two or more distributed nodes because of the need for horizontal scalability (see Page 6 in Sect. 1.2) and availability. With the adoption of the different cloud service models (see Sect. 2.3 on Page 42) – *IaaS*, *PaaS*, and *SaaS* – and the corresponding cloud offerings (see Chap. 3) cloud-native applications become even more distributed as different layers and functionality of the application can be handled by different cloud offerings. In the *distributed application* (160) pattern we describe various architectural approaches for decomposing application into distributed components.

When building cloud-native distributed applications, regardless of the concrete approach chosen, *loose coupling* (156) among the distributed components is a key success factor. Symptoms of tightly coupled components such as fixed addressing or the assumption of synchronous instantaneous communication hinders elastic scaling one of others, because they depend on each other's location and availability.

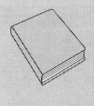

Further Reading: the architectural styles fundamental to cloud computing are similar to those of distributed systems, service-oriented architectures, and messaging systems. Tanenbaum [127] covers the fundamentals of distributed systems that are also relevant in many patterns of this book. An introduction to services-oriented architectures is given by Krafzig et al. [10] and Weerawarana et al. [9]. Messaging concepts have been captured by Hohpe and Woolf [1]. Most of these messaging patterns can be applied in cloud computing without change and are also used in this book.

4.2.1   Loose Coupling

A communication intermediary separates application functionality from concerns of communication partners regarding their location, implementation platform, the time of communication, and the used data format.

 How can dependencies between distributed applications and between individual components of these applications be reduced?

Context

Resources provided by clouds are distributed by design and often enforce a similar distribution of application functionality among these resources. How applications can be decomposed into distributed components is described in the *distributed application* (160) pattern. In this scope, the individual application components have to be integrated to form a uniform application. For such applications information exchange and management tasks, such as scaling, failure handling, or update management can be simplified significantly if application components can be treated individually and the dependencies among them are kept to a minimum. For example, the effects that a failing component has on other components should be minimal to reduce the amount of components to be replaced or reconfigured if one of them fails. Similar challenges are also faced when multiple applications, such as cloud applications and legacy applications have to be integrated, thus, they have to communicate and exchange data. Therefore, the dependencies among components shall be reduced, so that the addition, removal, replacement, or update of one component has minimal to no impact on other components communicating with it.

Solution

Communicating components and multiple integrated applications are decoupled from each other by interacting through a *broker*. This broker encapsulates the assumptions that communication partners would otherwise have to make about one other and, thus, ensures *separation of concerns*. The broker concept has also been introduced as a pattern by Buschmann et al. [14]. To ensure *loose coupling*, a broker enables four degrees of autonomy between communication partners:

- *Platform autonomy:* communication partners may be implemented in different programming languages and are executed by different *execution environments* (104). Differences in these platforms regarding data representation, processor architecture etc. are unimportant for the communication.
- *Reference autonomy:* communication partners have to be addressed on the network. They shall be unaware of the concrete address of each other and also of the number of communication partners with which they interact.
- *Time autonomy:* communication partners can exchange information even if one of them is temporarily unavailable. Also, they may send and receive information at their own speed, thus, if one communication partner transmits information faster than another one, both remain operational.
- *Format:* when data is sent over a remote connection, it has to be serialized into an exchange format by the sender and de-serialized by the receiver. Communication partners shall be unaware of the other party's format and shall receive data in the format they support.

The broker can, therefore, be accessed from different implementation languages, handles addressing of communication partners, request routing and the transformation of exchanged data if the serialization formats used by communication partners differ. These concerns may be handled more efficiently in a specifically designed broker than in each communication partners' implementation. Therefore, the implementation complexity is reduced as communication partners may rely on a highly specialized, highly available intermediary. The fewer assumptions two components make about each other, i.e., the more degrees of autonomy are ensured, the looser they are coupled and the more robust and flexible is their integration.

Result

Many cloud offerings already support such a *loose coupling*. Here, we cover the use of a *message-oriented middleware* (136) and an enterprise service bus (ESB) realizing the intermediary depicted in Fig. 4.2.

A message queue offered by a *message-oriented middleware* (136) enables asynchronous communication for application components, takes care of message addressing and routing as well as message format transformation. But it is important to note that *loose coupling* is not ensured alone by the intermediary. The communication partners integrated by an intermediary have to ensure that the format of the exchanged information can be processed by the intermediary to fulfill its purpose. If the exchanged information is serialized to a format that cannot be read by the intermediary, it likely needs to be extended with custom functionality. Assuming that the used intermediary supports such an extension, the format transformation complexity still has to be completely handled by the developer. To ensure *loose coupling* a standardized serialization format should, therefore, be used to transfer data to rely on intermediary functionality that still has to be configured but not implemented individually. Examples of such data

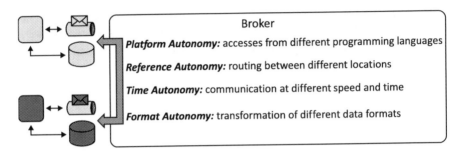

Fig. 4.2 Realization of loose coupling through an intermediary

format standards are the Extensible Markup Language (XML) [148], the Java Script Object Notation (JSON) [97], or SOAP [149], which is also normally serialized as XML.

An enterprise service bus (ESB) [10, 11] can also serve as an intermediary to ensure *loose coupling* in a service-oriented architecture (SOA) [10]. This architecture style considers functionality to be provided by services accessible over a network *via* a well-defined interface. Services are, therefore, one way to realize the application components of a *distributed application* (160). An ESB acts as a broker between service consumers and service providers enabling the above mentioned separation of concerns. Especially, it may subsume the functionality of a *message-oriented middleware* (136) and bridge between asynchronous message exchange and synchronous service invocations, for example, by supporting synchronous and asynchronous protocols for SOAP [149] messages.

By following the *loose coupling* pattern regardless of the used middleware, applications and their components, thus, do not know the concrete address of a communication partner, or the data formats supported by it, and do not rely on the partner to be available at the time when they communication is initiated or to support the necessary communication speed. *Loose coupling* can, however, can have some drawbacks. Application performance can be impacted as communication through a broker may add overhead to the information exchanged. Data needs to be serialized and de-serialized by communication partners and for the processing performed by the broker. Additionally, the communication path is longer and includes address resolution and format transformation functionality.

Therefore, when designing an application it commonly has to be weighed between loose coupling, application performance, and the complexity of implementation and debugging. In clouds where applications shall scale out elastically, *loose coupling* is, however, often more desirable than the efficient use of individual cloud resources.

Related Patterns

- *Distributed application* (160): this pattern describes fundamentals for the logical decomposition of application functionality into components. These components may be summarized to multiple tighter-coupled tiers to ensure performance. The individual tiers are then integrated according to the loose coupling pattern.

- *Two-tier cloud application* (290) and *three-tier cloud application* (294): two common summarizations of application components to *loosely coupled* tiers of a cloud application are covered by the *two-tier cloud application* (290) pattern and the *three-tier cloud application* (294) pattern. These patterns describe how the discrepancy between performance and flexibility should be weighted for smaller and larger cloud applications, respectively.
- *Hypervisor* (101): this pattern ensures loose coupling of a virtual server and the physical hardware on which it is deployed. The application that may be installed in such a virtual server, however, loses access to any physical hardware that it may require.
- *Eventual consistency* (126): storage offerings providing eventual consistency aim at making replicas of data required for availability coupled looser. By doing so, the storage offering becomes more resilient towards network partitioning and can be distributed among a large number of resources more efficiently.
- *Message-oriented middleware* (136): as pointed out in the result section, a *message-oriented middleware* and provided message queues allow avoiding connectivity dependencies between communication partners and may also handle message format transformations.
- *Watchdog* (260): loose coupling simplifies the implementation of this pattern significantly. A *watchdog* monitors resources and application components for failures, especially, needed if the cloud provider assures *environment-based availability* (98). If a failure is detected, the watchdog decommissions the failed component and replaces it with a newly provisioned one automatically. If the components supervised by a watchdog are loosely coupled, this resiliency management becomes significantly easier. Loosely coupled components have a lesser impact on each other if one of them fails and the integration of a replacement component into the application requires fewer to none reconfiguration of existing component.

Known Uses

Loose coupling is one of the fundamental concepts of service oriented computing (SOC). Its realization in a service-oriented architecture (SOA) is described in great detail by [9], [11] and [10]. Loose coupling between applications and their components through messaging is described by Hohpe and Woolf [1]. They also motivate the use of a *canonical data model* to simplify format translation between different message formats.

4.2.2 Distributed Application

A cloud application divides provided functionality among multiple application components that can be scaled out independently.

 How can application functionality be decomposed to be handled by separate application components?

Context

Cloud applications have to rely on multiple, possibly redundant IT resources to ensure that the unavailability of one IT resource does not affect the application as a whole. Furthermore, clouds are designed to scale out and not scale up, as described by the essential cloud properties in Sect. 1.1 on Page 3, thus, applications have to add more IT resources rather than increasing the capabilities of a single resource to increase their performance. However, applications have to respect the distribution and the scaling-out support of this environment in their architecture to efficiently benefit from it.

Monolithic applications that are not distributed, but subsume all functionality of an application for user interaction, processing, and data handling into a single component and are deployed on a single IT resources, i.e., one server. Such applications are often less suitable for a cloud environment due to two characteristics. First, the individual availability and performance of a single IT resources offered by a cloud can be insufficient for the requirements of the applications. This can especially be the case if the cloud provider assures *environment-based availability* (98) – the availability of the complete environment and not of single IT resources hosted in it. For example, the provider could only assure that customers can provision servers and does not assure availability of running servers at all. Even if the provider assures *node-based availability* (95) – the availability of individual IT resources, such as servers, the assurance may be insufficient for the application calling for a redundant deployment. The second characteristic making monolithic applications less suitable for a cloud environment is their inability to be scaled out efficiently as multiple instances of the whole application have to be provisioned instead of scaling the different functionality offered by the application independently.

Solution

The functionality of the application is divided into multiple independent components that provide a certain function. Later, these components are integrated to form a *distributed application*. This componentization of application functionality introduces a logical decomposition of the application. These logical components are subsumed to multiple *tiers* to denote that they shall be deployed together physically, i.e., on one server (cluster). Tiers are, thus, deployed separately on distributed IT resources provided by the cloud environment. When integrating the tiers to a complete *distributed application, loose coupling* (156) is ensured to reduce the impact of component failures on other components.

> *Side Note:* the terms "layer" and "tier" are often used interchangeably. In this book, we wanted to differentiate between a decomposition that can be based on logical layers of an application into components and the summarization of these components to physical tiers hosted in a cloud environment. Sometimes, especially, in scope of *PaaS* (49), each component can be a tier, but the summarization of logical application components into physical tiers should always be considered carefully, because communication between components in a tier is usually more efficient while *loose coupling* (156) between tiers makes the application more robust and scalable. In Chap. 6, we cover a *two-tier cloud application* (290) and a *three-tier cloud application* (294) in greater detail.

Result

The mapping of application components to tiers is mainly influenced by the cloud service model used by the provider. If a provider offers and *elastic platform* (91) as *PaaS* (49), each application component is often deployed individually and integrated with other application components using provider-supplied communication offerings, for example, a *message-oriented middleware* (136). However, logical application components may also be summarized to be deployed together. If the provider offers an *elastic infrastructure* (87) as *IaaS* (45), the application architect can influence the summarization of application components to a higher degree as the customer has to specify the distribution of application components among the provided virtual servers. In the following, we cover three different logical decomposition approaches of applications into separate components and the corresponding physical tiers for *IaaS* (45) and *PaaS* (49) environments. The covered decompositions are based on layers of the application stack on which a component resides (*layer-based decomposition*), centered on the processes that an

Fig. 4.3 Exemplary
decomposition into three tiers

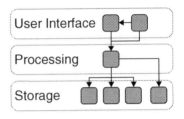

Fig. 4.4 Process-based
decomposition

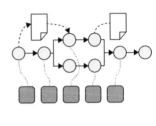

Fig. 4.5 Pipes-and-filters-
based decomposition

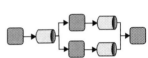

application supports (*process-based decomposition*), and focus on data elements
handled by the application that traverse a set of components for processing (*pipes-
and-filters-based decomposition*).

Layer-based decomposition: this decomposition approach divides the application into separate logical layers. Often, the three layers, user interface, processing,
and storage are used as depicted in Fig. 4.3, but more layers may also be introduced.
Each layer is comprised of application components providing a certain function.
Components are restricted to access components of the same layer or one layer
below. This restriction avoids complicated interdependencies among components
and enforces a well-defined interface description for communication between
layers.

Often, layers used during the decomposition are mapped to tiers to be deployed
to an *elastic infrastructure* (87) or *elastic platform* (91). For the above example, this
results in a three-tier architecture also described by Tanenbaum [127]. In scope of
an *elastic platform* (91) components may also be deployed directly without group-
ing them. In this case, the communication offerings used to *loosely couple* (156) the
different layers is also used within a layer to exchange information between
components.

Process-based decomposition: this decomposition style focuses on the business
processes supported by the application. These processes are comprised out of
activities that are executed in a specific order. Activities, their execution order,
and data elements handled by the process are described by executable business
process models, as depicted at the top of Fig. 4.4. The functionality accessed by the

activities of the processes is decomposed into separate components. Activities interact with these components comprising the *distributed application*. During this enactment required information is passed to the invoked application component and results are stored in the business process. Business process models are executed by a specific runtime, called a process engine. A process engine can handle multiple process models and instantiates a model every time a process is started. The running process instance then contains the values of data elements handled by the process and maintains the state of execution, i.e., it controls which activities of the process are active.

One tier of an application decomposed in this fashion is often the process engine handling the execution of the business process. It can be hosted on a virtual server provided by an *elastic infrastructure* (87), but may also be provided by an *elastic platform* (91) to which process models can be deployed directly. Other application components should be summarized to tiers regarding similar functionality they provide to the process.

Pipes-and-filters-based decomposition: the pipes-and-filters pattern for application architecture for data-centric processing of an application has been described by Gamma et al. [2], Buschman et al. [14], and Hohpe and Woolf [1]. Each filter provides a certain function that is performed on input data and produces output data after processing. Multiple filters are interconnected with pipes ensuring that the output of one filter is fed to the next filter in a processing chain. In a *distributed application*, filters map to application components that provide a certain function and are interconnected using communication offerings provided by a cloud. Pipes-and-filters-based decomposition, therefore, identifies components performing a certain function on input data that traverses different processing steps. Data may be provided as fixed data elements or as a stream of data that is continuously processed by the application.

Pipes and filters are, for example, used in Unix operating systems to connect multiple commands [14] or in digital picture processing to manipulate images in a certain order. In scope of *distributed applications* and the realization of multiple tiers, components should be deployed independently. To ensure *loose coupling* (156) the communication through pipes should be asynchronous, for example, using message queues provided by a *message-oriented middleware* (136) as depicted in Fig. 4.5. This implementation is also suggested by Hohpe's and Woolf's [1] use of the pipes-and-filters pattern. Each component receives input from a queue, processes the messages, and writes it to an output queue. Larger data elements may be exchanged using other communication channels, for example, folders provided by a *blob storage* (112). Due to this asynchronous communications, applications components never interact directly with other components making them significantly easier to scale or replace in case of failures.

Regardless of the decomposition style followed, the application is divided into multiple components, each providing a certain set of the required application functions. These components are then composed to form the integrated functionality that the *distributed application* shall offer. Due to this architecture, the application remains extensible as boundaries between components are clear and interface and communication styles are well-defined. Therefore, new components can be added and integrated with the application easier. Furthermore, the integration of other applications, for example, legacy applications, is simplified as whole applications can be integrated similarly to individual components.

A critical design decision for *distributed applications* is the number of physical tiers to which logical application components are summarized. The distribution of functionality among separated components and tiers, thus, the optimal granularity of components has to be found. If too few components are created, integration of new functionality and changing the application flexibly, i.e., for scaling, can still be a complex task. If the functionality is distributed among too many components assigned to too many *loosely coupled* (156) tiers, the necessary communication overhead can become too high for the application to be executed efficiently. The *two-tier cloud application* (290) and *three-tier cloud application* (294) patterns discuss the efficient assignment of application components of a *distributed application* under different conditions.

 ***Further Reading:*** Cheesman and Daniels [150] describe how to use components in object-oriented programming. Eels and Cripps [151] cover the process to design a software architecture. Especially, they cover different viewpoints on the architecture to design functional and structural aspects. Daigneau [152] covers patterns for service design that can be used to create the orchestrated application components in scope of the above mentioned process-centric decomposition. Weerawarana et al. [9] describe technologies used for the implementation of these services. Leymann and Roller [76] cover the modeling and execution of business processes in depth.

Related Patterns

- *Loose coupling* (156): it is very important, that a *distributed application* avoids dependencies between application components to scale components independently and to avoid that failing components impact each other.
- *Message-oriented middleware* (136): asynchronous communication between application components of a *distributed application* is very important to enable *loose coupling* (156). A message queue provided by a *message-oriented middleware* offers functionality for such asynchronous message exchange.
- *Blob storage* (112): as pointed out above, this storage offering may be used in *distributed applications* to exchange larger data elements than those that can be transmitted using messages.

- *Two-tier cloud application* (290): this pattern describes a common layer-based decomposition used for cloud applications. It describes the different tiers and the patterns implemented by them.
- *Three-tier cloud application* (294): this pattern describes a more complex layer-based decomposition than the *two-tier cloud application* (290) resulting in three *loosely coupled* (156) tiers that may be scaled independently. The IT resources used by this application can, therefore, be aligned even more flexibly to the current demand experienced by each tier.
- Cloud application components (Sect. 4.3): the patterns covered in the following section describe how different functionality decomposed into application components may be implemented to support the cloud computing properties described in Sect. 1.1 on Page 3.
- *Processing component* (180): the processing component pattern covers an exemplary decomposition of processing functionality for a video conversion application.

Known Uses

The decomposition of application functionality into application components and the later summarization of these components to tiers is also described by Youngs et al. [153]. Varia [93, 154] generally motivates why applications should be split into separate components when using the Amazon AWS [138] cloud. Zimmerman et al. describe the decomposition of an application in the finance industry [155] as well as a process-centric decomposition of an order management scenario [156]. The T-Systems Process and Service Platform (PSP) uses service-oriented principles to offer services and processes of the public sector [157] in a *community cloud* (71). Languages for such process model specification are, furthermore, the Business Process Execution Language (BPEL) [158] or the Business Process Model and Notation (BPMN) [159]. Leymann and Roller [76] give detailed background information about composition languages. Application components invoked by a process instances in such a fashion are often implemented as Web services [9] and provide interfaces in the Web Service Description Language (WSDL) [160] format.

Buschmann et al. [14] cover the *layers* pattern describing how application functionality may be decomposed into separate layers to structure an application. A similar decomposition is used by a Service Oriented Architecture (SOA) [9, 10] introducing the separation of application functionality into multiple independent services. Both approaches are, therefore, applicable in the domain of cloud computing even though they have been established long before the concept of cloud computing arose. Actually, the approach to layer application can be traced back even further to distributed systems in general as covered by Tanenbaum [127] where it is predominant to ensure their manageability and reduce complexity. Also, operating system architectures use this approach to manage complexity. The Open Systems Interconnection Reference Model (OSI-Model), for example, separates networking functionality into different layers.

4.3   Cloud Application Components

When building a cloud-native application following the two fundamental principles of *distributed applications* (160) and *loose coupling* (156) covered in the previous section, an important follow-up design activity of an architect is to define how the application handles state. With elasticity in mind, one of the cloud application properties described in Sect. 1.2 on Page 5, it is important to specify which components of the application are *stateful* and which are *stateless*. As defined in the introduction on Page 6 in Sect. 1.2, we use these the term "state" to refer both *session state* – the state of client interaction with an application component and *application state* – the data handled by the application. *Stateful components* (168) carry state that is lost if the component or the underlying platform or infrastructure fails. *Stateless components* (171) are components that can be added and removed more easily as they delegate all their non-transient state to *stateful components* (168) or storage offerings (see Sect. 3.5 on Page 109). This distinction between *stateful components* (168) and *stateless components* (171) is important when dealing with cloud-native applications as it gives a good first hint which components can be elastically scaled more easily and where state needs to be kept and, thus, elastic scaling is harder to implement or should be delegated to a provider-supplied offering. Additionally, it is important to identify whether a consistent state is required or not by the business usage scenarios. If not, *user interface components* (175) or other application components may become *data abstractors* (194) that hide data inconsistencies from other application components.

When dealing with elasticity requirements it may also be helpful to implement processing-intensive business logic as separate *processing components* (180), that handles requests as they receive them (asynchronously or synchronously), or as *batch processing components* (185) that collect requests and work on them in batch.

Regarding the access to *storage offerings*, for example, in a processing component, the *data access component* (188) pattern describes how to encapsulate the data access. The *idempotent processor* (197) pattern, then, deals with the situation, that requests may arrive multiple times but should only affect the state of an application once. Requests may arrive multiple times, for example, when they are routed by a *message-oriented middleware* (136) that supports *at-least-once delivery* (144). Similar challenges may arise if the data processing component accesses an *eventually consistent* (126) data store. Thus, it is important to deal with such situations in cloud-native applications.

Two other patterns deal with the processing of messages that are received *via* a *message-oriented middleware* (136) to assure that messages are processed successfully. The first approach is to implement the *transaction-based processor* (201) pattern that interacts in a transaction with the *message-oriented middleware*. The transaction begins by reading of the message from the queue. The message is then locked until the transaction is committed or aborted by the *transaction-based processor*. In case of a successful processing, the message is deleted from the message queue and the transaction is committed. If the processing fails, the transaction is aborted and the message remains in the message queue.

The transaction-based processor also describes this style of interaction with storage offerings. The second approach to assure message processing is to implement a *timeout-based message processor* (204) accessing a corresponding *message-oriented middleware*. In this case, a message is made invisible once a receiver has taken it from the message queue and the *messaging middleware* waits for the receiver to acknowledge message processing. If processing has not been explicitly acknowledged after a certain timeout period by the receiver the message is made visible again to all receivers. The last pattern we cover in this section is the *multi-component image* (206) pattern which describes how multiple components of one or several applications can be deployed on one the same virtual server of an *elastic infrastructure* (87).

4.3.1 Stateful Component

Multiple instances of a scaled-out application component synchronize their internal state to provide a unified behavior.

 How can applications components that are scaled-out maintain a synchronized internal state?

Context

To benefit from a distributed cloud runtime environment, components of a *distributed application* (160) are deployed to multiple cloud resources. *Loose coupling* (156) between these components ensures that they may be instantiated multiple times for scaling them out. Some of these application components may need to maintain an internal state. This state may, for example, reflect a list of items that a user of a Web shop has added to his or her shopping basket. As an application component is scaled-out, the challenge arises that individual instances should contain the same internal state, so that they present a unified behavior.

Solution

The internal state maintained by application component instances is replicated among all component instances as depicted in the right side of Fig. 4.6. Only small portions of shared information are used, for example, all instances of a *stateful component* may still share a configuration file stored centrally or have the configuration send to them by clients with every request. The application developer, therefore, faces similar challenges as the provider of a cloud storage offering and has to decide whether this replication should be performed ensuring *strict consistency* (123) or *eventual consistency* (126). Each client request is associated with a unique identifier as shown in the left side of Fig. 4.6. This identifier is used by the *stateful component* to retrieve the correct data associated with a client request from its internal storage.

Result

Upon each data manipulation accessing the *stateful component*, the new state is updated among the deployed instances. This update may be performed in a *strict*

Fig. 4.6 Stateful application components

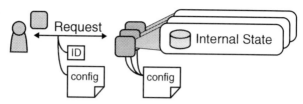

consistent (123) or *eventual consistent* (126) manner, which significantly affects the behavior that the application component displays to users. In the following both approaches are described in greater detail.

In case of *strict consistency* (123), read and write operations access a subset of the instances. These subsets are configured to overlap regarding the overall number of deployed instances, so it is ensured that each read operation accesses at least one instance with the most current data version. For more information about this replication and how the ratio should be between instances accessed during read operations and write operations, refer to the *strict consistency* (123) pattern. The application component keeps an internal state that may be altered externally. Such *stateful components* assuring *strict consistency* (123) are, for example, obtained when installing database software on virtual servers provided by an *elastic infrastructure* (87). Clustering abilities of this software may then be used to distribute the state among multiple virtual servers increasing the availability of the *stateful component*.

In case of *eventual consistency* (126), read and write operations access a reduced number of instances, possibly only one instance. After data has been manipulated, the new data version is replicated asynchronously to all instances. For this purpose, message queues offered by a *message-oriented middleware* (136) may be used. Therefore, the availability of the *stateful component* is increased as fewer instances have to be available to execute a read or write operation. Performance may also be increased if the component instances are distributed among a large, possibly global, connection network. In such a setup, accessing large sets of instances required for *strict consistency* may be ineffective due to network communication delays and is, therefore, avoided. The downside of this *eventual consistent* update propagation is that users may be served with obsolete data if they access an application component instance that has not been updated. Similar to the *strict consistent stateful component*, database software exists that handles data updates between replicas in an asynchronous eventually consistent fashion.

Variations

Based on the identifier associated with requests of customers or their components, requests may be routed only to a specific number of component instances. In very large setups handling many customers, this may simplify the data replication as the number of instances handling specific customers is reduced. This approach may, thus, be used to create smaller clusters of component instances handling a specific customer among which replication may be performed more efficiently.

Related Patterns
- *Stateless component* (171): to implement stateful application components, developers have to handle the complex replication of state information among component instances. If possible, this should be avoided by storing all state information in storage offerings (see Sect. 3.5 on Page 109) accessed by *stateless components* (171). In this scope, the developer is only concerned about the custom application functionality that is implemented in *stateless components*. All instances of these components share an external state held by the storage offerings. Furthermore, *stateful components* are significantly harder to manage than *stateless components* (171), because the management patterns (see Chap. 5) implemented in the cloud application have to respect the internal state of the *stateful component* instances.
- *Managed configuration* (247): the above mentioned concept to manage common configuration files centrally is described in further detail by this separate pattern.

Known Uses

Tanenbaum [127] covers different approaches to store an update state in distributed applications as well as the related interaction protocols. Fowler [15] also discusses different approaches to handle state on the client side and the server side. In general, a *stateful component* is any implementation of the storage offerings *relational database* (115), *key-value storage* (119), *blob storage* (112), or *block storage* (110) that is not provider-supplied or managed by the application itself. Therefore, if a customer obtains a virtual server from an *IaaS* (45) cloud providing an *elastic infrastructure* (87), an installed *relational database* (115), for example, MySQL [112] or *key-value storage* (119), for example, Apache MongoDB [122] can be considered a *stateful component*. As these installations of storage offerings are managed by the customer, the challenges described in the *stateful component* pattern have to be handled by the customer himself or herself.

4.3.2   Stateless Component

> State is handled external of application components to ease their scaling-out and to make the application more tolerant to component failures.

 How can elasticity and robustness of an application component be increased?

Context

The components of a *distributed application* (160) are deployed among multiple cloud resources to benefit from this distributed runtime environment through scaling out. As resources may fail, this distribution of components among multiple resources makes the application dependent on the availability of all these resources. The chance that a resource failure occurs that affects the application is increased with a higher degree of distribution. Especially, resources of *public clouds* (62) may display a low *node-based availability* (95) or *environment-based availability* (98) that makes no assurances regarding individual resources. Therefore, *distributed applications* often have to be enabled to cope with failing application components and need to handle their replacement. But not only failures demand that application components are removed from or added to a *distributed application*. If the application is scaled out elastically, component instances are also added and removed regularly according to the currently experienced workload. This is especially the case if the application has to handle *periodic workload* (29), *unpredictable workload* (36) or *continuously changing workload* (40).

The most significant factor complicating addition and removal of component instances is the internal state maintained by them. In case of failure, this information may be lost. If an instance shall be removed from the application, the internal state has to be extracted and stored elsewhere. If a new instance shall be added to the application, its internal state has to be initialized before it may function properly.

Solution

Application components are implemented in a fashion that they do not have an internal state. Instead, their state and configuration is stored externally in storage offerings (see Sect. 3.5 on Page 109) or provided to the component with each

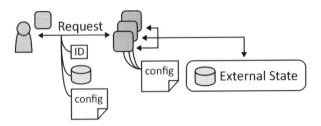

Fig. 4.7 Stateless application components

request, as shown in Fig. 4.7. An identifier (ID) may be associated with requests to retrieve the required information from the external storage.

Result

In scope of Web applications, the term "stateless" is commonly used to refer to the state of a session between a client and a Web server. This *session state* can hinder spreading client requests among multiple servers to scale an application horizontally. As every request could possibly be handled by a different server, this server may be unaware of previous interaction with a client hindering it to produce correct results. For example, if the content of a shopping cart of an online shop application was to be stored on the server-side, multiple servers would have to keep the content of the shopping cart, i.e., the session state in sync. Therefore, it is a best practice in Web applications to keep the session state on the client-side and send it with every request of a client to the Web applications, so called REST [72] style interaction (see known uses). This interaction style allows every request to be handled by an arbitrary server. The *stateless component* pattern extends this best practice by not only considering *session state*, but also *application state* – the data handled by application components. Applications state is a result of client accesses to functions provided by the cloud application by which they manipulate the data handled by the application. Keeping this state in sync between multiple instances of an application component hinders the cloud application to be scaled elastically. Therefore, the *stateless component* pattern motivates to provide the *session state* with every request just as the best practices for Web applications. Furthermore, it extends this notion of statelessness by keeping the *application state* external of its implementation making instances of the *stateless component* easier to provision and decommission.

Since the *stateless component* instances do not have an internal state, no data is lost if an individual instance fails. This statelessness significantly increases the capability of the *distributed application* (160) to scale out, because multiple components can share a common external state and, thus, act as if they all had the same internal state. Furthermore, no data is lost if one component instance fails. Provisioning and decommissioning of components, part of elastic scaling operations, is simplified by this. However, the ability to scale out now depends significantly on the scalability of a provider-supplied storage offering or application component handling the external state – a *stateful component* (168). In both cases, the performance of the communication between *stateless components* and *stateful components* (168) or storage offerings is also of vital importance.

Variations

To reduce the amount of requests to the central data store and to avoid the delay that may occur from remotely accessing this storage, component instances may keep local replicas of the centrally stored state information. For this purpose, they usually store results of queries to the central data store temporarily, a concept known as caching [127]. Data stored in these caches may, however, be of an older version than the data stored centrally. Therefore, the use of caching can lead to an *eventually consistent* (126) behavior of the application.

Related Patterns

Stateless components may use cloud offerings to manage a central state:
- *Relational database* (115), *key-value storage* (119): these storage offerings may be used for table-based centrally stored data. *Relational databases* may, however, be less scalable due to the complexity and interdependencies caused by the enforced data structure. Due to this complexity relational database offerings can also be more expensive as they are more complex, but they often guarantee *strict consistency* (123). *Key-value storage* enforces much less structure on the data handled by them and do often not perform data integrity checks. Therefore, this complexity will then have to be handled in the *distributed applications* (160). The required functionality may be encapsulated in *data access components* (188).
- *Blob storage* (112): this type of central storage offering is commonly used for large data elements. It is good practice that components of a *distributed application* do not communicate *via* these data elements but reference them in *relational databases*, *key-value storage*, or pass references *via* messages. Messages can be exchanged through message queues provided by a *message-oriented middleware* (136).
- *Message-oriented middleware* (136): if application components process messages, the state may be contained completely in the messages. In this scope, components often have to assure that messages are only deleted from a message queue if they have been successfully processed. Possible implementations are described by the *transaction-based processor* (201) pattern and the *timeout-based message processor* (204) pattern.

Known Uses

It is a central principle of the REST [72, 161] architectural style to transmit the state each time a component is accessed. As mentioned above, shopping baskets in Web stores are often realized this way. Web services [9] can be developed with a similar approach [162] where state is provided with each request. If a *message-oriented middleware* (136) is used to keep the external state, it has to assure that messages are not lost, as summarized by the *message-oriented middleware* (136) pattern and described by Hohpe's and Woolf's [1] *reliable messaging* pattern in greater detail. This externalization of state through the use of messaging is also covered by Varia [154] as a best practice for applications using Amazon Web Services (AWS) [138]. Fowler [15] also discusses different approaches to handle state in applications. *Client Session State* refers to the above mentioned state attached to each request, thus, the state is managed by the client accessing the application. *Database Session State* refers to storing state information in a database. In this scope, the *stateless component* pattern would introduce the additional restriction that this database should be provided by a storage offering, such as *relational database* (115), *key-value storage* (119), or *blob storage* (112).

4.3.3 User Interface Component

Interactive synchronous access to applications is provided to humans, while application-internal interaction is realized asynchronously when possible to ensure loose coupling. Furthermore, the user interface should be customizable to be used by different customers.

 How can user interface components be accessed interactively by humans while being configurable and decoupled from the remaining application?

Context

Distributed applications (160) componentize their functionality and deploy the resulting application components to *elastic infrastructures* (87) or *elastic platforms* (91). The individual application components are scaled out and instantiated multiple times. Therefore, user interface component instances have to be added and removed easily from the application without affecting the user experience. The dependencies on other application components should be reduced as much as possible. Furthermore, user interface components may be used by many different customers if the cloud application itself is offered as a service. Therefore, the user interface should be configurable to the individual requirements of these customers.

Solution

The *user interface component* serves as a bridge between the synchronous access of the human user and the asynchronous communication used with other application components. *User interface components* are implemented as *stateless components* (171). All data handling and processing functionality is, therefore, externalized to simplify adding and removing component instances for scalability or due to instance failure. State information is attached to requests, may be held in a part of the user interface that is deployed on the user's access device, or may be obtained from external storage. In a similar fashion, a configuration may be managed for the *user interface component* to adjust display languages, color schemes etc.

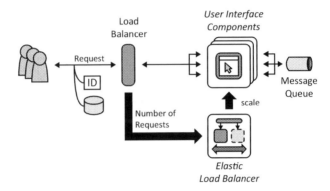

Fig. 4.8 User interface components in a common setup

Result

The functionality provided by the *user interface component* should be as minimal as possible and should only subsume user input validation and enrichment of the provided data from other sources necessary to initialize processing in other components of the application. Such separation of duty also simplifies addition or removal of the user interface component instances. Requests to *user interface components* that are instantiated multiple times are distributed on a per-request-basis, thus, each user request to the application is load-balanced individually. As depicted in Fig. 4.8, *user interface components* should be accessed through an *elastic load balancer* (254). This component distributes requests among the individual *user interface component* instances based on the observed requests. Alternatively, the load balancer may only handle the assignment or requests while the user interface component itself handles elasticity by implementing the *elasticity manager* (250) pattern. For either approach used for load balancing, users are not associated with a specific component instances. This allows component instances to be added and removed more easily and user experience is not affected by the failure of an individual instance of a user interface component. Handling of elasticity may be further simplified by asynchronous interaction of the user interface with other application components to increase *loose coupling* (156) between them. In Fig. 4.8, this asynchronous access is enabled by a message queue offered by a *message-oriented middleware* (136) that the *user interface component* uses to communicate with other application components.

State information required by user interfaces is provided by the user accessing the application with each request as depicted in Fig. 4.8. User interface components may rely on an external state as described by the *stateless component* (171) pattern. But in this case, a possible *eventual consistency* (126) of the used storage offering has to be considered carefully. Depending on the consistency guaranteed by the storage offering, a user may, for example, not directly see the data manipulations he or she has performed. If more state information is needed in the user interface than what can be transported with each request or obtained from storage offerings, part

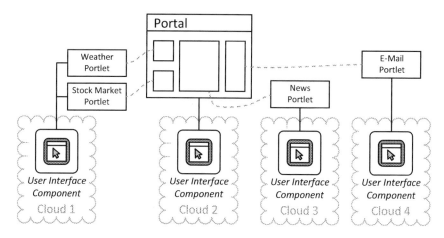

Fig. 4.9 Integration of different portlets into a portal

of the user interface may be deployed on the device through which a user accesses the application. Such deployments also increase the level of interactivity as the local parts of the user interface may be accessed similar to native applications, for example, using the Google Web Toolkit (see known uses).

Configurability of the user interface is supported by a configuration file managed in a similar fashion as state information. In this file, user requirements, such as UI colors or interface languages, and device type are specified. A *user interface component* may also be adjusted transparently to the user, for example, to reflect the security privileges and access rights granted to the user. Information about the device used to access a user interface should be associated with every request, so that the interface can be adjusted for screen size etc. respectively. Other configuration information, for example, the user-specific layout of user interface elements should be stored on the server side, as a user may use different devices to access the user interface component.

In scope of user interface configurability, *portal* technologies [9, 163] may be used to enable users to compose their individual interfaces from content provided by separate user interface components. The concept of portals is not cloud-specific or has been introduced by cloud computing. Instead, it is a long established technology to enable user of Web applications to compose user interface functionality into custom Web sites. Figure 4.9 depicts an exemplary use of portal technology in user interface components hosted by different clouds. The portal itself is provided by one user interface component that retrieves content from other user interface components and combines it in a unified user interface. The retrieved content, referred to as *portlets*, is commonly not fully configured, i.e., colors, text formats etc., are not specified. This configuration is kept in the portal configuration specific to every user. Each user of the portal may, therefore, define individual compositions of portlets provided by other user interface components hosted in different clouds.

Variations

Under some conditions, users have to be associated with specific user interface instances, for example, if a secure communication session has been established. In this case, user requests may be routed to this specific user interface component instance for the duration of the communication session.

Related Patterns

- *Managed configuration* (247): if the user interface component is scaled out, the configuration should be stored in a central storage offering as described by the *managed configuration* pattern.
- *Relational database* (115), *key-value storage* (119): these storage offerings may be used to keep state information that cannot be transmitted with each request. If used, the consistency guaranteed by these offerings has to be evaluated carefully, as it is likely to be directly reflected in the user interface experience provided to human users. A *data abstractor* (194) can be used to hide data inconsistencies from users in case of *eventual consistency* (126).
- *Processing component* (180): longer running tasks that are initiated by the human user are handled in separate processing components. As interaction with these components should be asynchronous, a user interface component may have to provide information to the human user about the processing state prior to its completion. This separation of user interfaces from the rest of the application is also a successful best practice in stand-alone applications, where it is called three-tier architecture [127]. We describe this in more detail as well in the *two-tier cloud application* (290) and *three-tier cloud application* (294) patterns.

Known Uses

Some cloud provider offer special libraries to create user interface components suitable for their own and other runtime environments. Google, for example, provides the Google Web Toolkit [164] for this purpose. The above mentioned deployment of part of the user interface on the client side to enable a more interactive user-experience can be realized using Asynchronous Java Script and XML (AJAX) [165], a technology on which the Google Web Toolkit also relies. In essence, AJAX decouples human interaction from requests to a server, thus, a user may be given feedback directly from the application he or she is using while longer running requests to a server are executed transparently and asynchronously in the background. Yahoo and other portal providers provide users with means to integrate versatile information into a customized portal [166, 167] effectively enabling the above mentioned portal configuration.

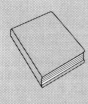 ***Further Reading:*** Tatnall et al. [163] give an overview of portal technologies. Architectural styles to build AJAX applications have also been captured in a pattern format by Mahemoff [168] and Gross [169]. General patterns on user interface design are available in the Yahoo Design Pattern Library [16]. Fowler [15] covers *Web Presentation* patterns for Web-based user interfaces and *Session State* patterns describing how these may store managed state information.

4.3.4   Processing Component

Possibly long running processing functionality is handled by separate components to enable elastic scaling. Processing functionality is further made configurable to support different customer requirements.

 How can processing be scaled out elastically among distributed resources while being configurable regarding the supported functions to meet different customers' requirements?

Context

A *distributed application* (160) divides application functionality among different cloud resources. These application components shall be instantiated multiple times to scale out elastically among multiple cloud resources. The processing functionality offered by an application, therefore, has to be handled by different application component instances that operate independently. Furthermore, instances of these components have to be added and removed easily to the application. To ease this provisioning and decommissioning of component instances, the dependencies of the processing components on each other as well as other application components should be minimized. This *loose coupling* (156) of components would also limit impacts of component instance failures on other running instances.

Solution

Processing functionality is split into separate function blocks and assigned to independent *processing components*. Each processing component is scaled out independently. To ease these tasks, processing components should be implemented in a stateless fashion as described in the *stateless component* (171) pattern. Therefore, they should obtain data required for processing with requests to them or from storage offerings, for example, *relational databases* (115), *key-value storage* (119), or *blob storage* (112). Such offerings may also be used to persist the results after the completion of processing.

Result

The interaction of multiple *processing components* with each other and with other components of the application is realized in an asynchronous fashion. Through this asynchronous communication, they can be *loosely coupled* (156) from the

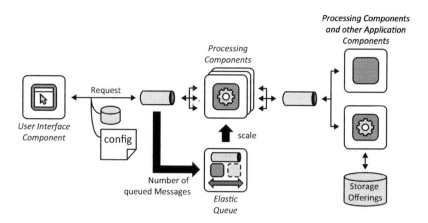

Fig. 4.10 Processing component in a standard setup

interacting application components. As depicted in Fig. 4.10, processing component instances should share a common message queue offered by a *message-
oriented middleware* (136) for requests to enable load balancing. This concept
has been introduced by Hohpe and Woolf [1] as a *competing consumer*. In scope
of a cloud application, the processing components should be scaled-out by an
elasticity manager (250) or an *elastic queue* (257) as shown in Fig. 4.10. These
management components handle the provisioning and decommissioning of
processing components based on the number of requests. Regardless of the used
load balancing technique, the separated *processing components* may, thus, be
scaled individually enabling a more efficient use of cloud resources. A critical
design decision is, however, the level of granularity at which processing functionality is divided into individual components. Too small components may not utilize
underlying resources, for example virtual servers offered by an *elastic infrastructure* (87), efficiently and lead to a significant amount of communication overhead.
Too large components may run inefficiently on single cloud resources that are
limited in capabilities. If an *elastic platform* (91) is used for deployment of the
distributed application (160), the distribution of application components among
cloud resources, such as virtual servers is handled internally by the cloud provider.
Therefore, the developer is alleviated from this design decision, but a too fine
granular of processing components may still result in a performance drawback due
to a high level of communication overhead. The *distributed application* (160)
pattern describes this decomposition of application functionality in greater detail
and covers how application components may be distributed among cloud resources.
In scope of processing components, thus, the level of parallelization has to be
weighted regarding an efficient use of cloud resources and the required communication overhead.

Once separated, the processing components should be implemented as *stateless
components* (171) to avoid data loss in case of failures. Therefore, processing

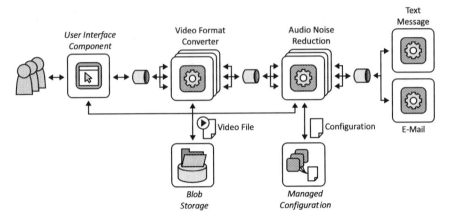

Fig. 4.11 Exemplary pipes-and-filters video processing application

components should be provided with data in requests or should obtain the data required for processing from storage offerings. In this scope, data should only be persisted after a component has finished processing a request. Storing intermediate processing results could leave the application in an inconsistent state in case a processing component fails.

Configurability of processing components is enabled by passing configurations information with every request or storing a customer-specific configuration that shall influence all requests. To ensure a flexible configurability, processing components should be decomposed into smaller components providing a specific processing function. These components can then be composed in a loosely-coupled fashion. As dependencies among components are, therefore, avoided, customer-specific configurations can be used to adjust the processing performed by such composed processing components easily, for example, by re-routing requests. The *distributed application* (160) pattern describes several approaches that may be used to decompose applications functionality into separate components. Processing components are especially suited for the decomposition based on *pipes-and-filters* [1] or *processes* [76].

For example, consider a video processing application, depicted in Fig. 4.11. Separate processing components are created for video format conversion, reduction of audio signal noise, and informing a customer when a video has been converted. These components or "filters" are then connected using "pipes", i.e., message queues provided by a *message-oriented middleware* (136), to provide a processing path traversed by each request, i.e., a video. As messages are too small to contain video files, these are stored in a central *blob storage* (112). Configuration about the processing of a specific video file is now passed to the application in the input message to adjust the setting for the format converter components and noise reduction components. After the video has been processed as specified, the user can decide how to be informed about the outcome. This configuration is specified

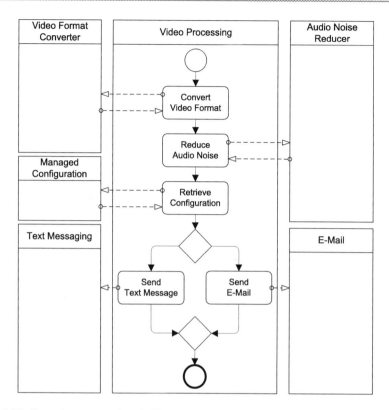

Fig. 4.12 Exemplary process-based video processing application

once and then stored centrally as a *managed configuration* (247). Based on this configuration, the last video processing component specifies the desired communication channel in the notification message it sends out. This message is put into a message queue that is accessed by the e-mail *processing component* and text message *processing component*. Each of these components only retrieves the messages to be processed by them and notifies the user accordingly.

A process-based decomposition of the same example application is depicted in Fig. 4.12. We used the Business Process Model and Notation (BPMN) language [159] for the graphical modeling of this process and its interaction with the individual processing components. The order of video format conversion, signal noise reduction, and customer notification is described by a process model. For every video to be converted, this processes model is instantiated and executed on a process engine [76]. The state of the process instance is, therefore, kept by the process model instance and does not traverse the separate processing components, which differentiates the approach from a pipes-and-filters architecture. Upon instantiation, the process is provided with configuration parameters that are passed as input parameters to processing components to specify which video should be converted and what setting should be chosen for conversion and noise reduction. *Processing component* interfaces and enactment protocols are often specified in the form of WSDL files [9, 160] in this scope. As the process instance cannot directly access remote files, a separate activity is used to retrieve the customer configuration about the desired notification style form the *blob storage* (112). After this retrieval, the content of the file is mapped to process instance variables that can be used in the conditional branch containing the notification activities.

Related Patterns

- *User interface component* (175): this component receives requests from human application users and forwards them asynchronously to the processing components.
- *Blob storage* (112): the size of data that can be transmitted *via* message queues through which processing components are accessed is often limited. In case a processing component has to work on larger data, a pointer to a data element stored in a *blob storage* may be included in the request message.
- *Data access component* (188): if a processing component has to access storage offerings, the complexity of this access, such as the concrete interface, access protocols etc. should be encapsulated into a *data access component*.
- *Message-oriented middleware* (136): the message queue may be provided by a message-oriented middleware that can further increase the *loose coupling* (156) between the processing components and other application components by handling message format transformations.
- *Managed configuration* (247): as described above, configuration parameters of processing components may be managed centrally.

Known Uses

Varia covers the decomposition of processing functionality into separate processing components as one a fundamental architectural style for cloud applications [93, 154] built on Amazon Web Services [138]. Processing components should, especially, be loosely coupled through the use of Amazon's *message-oriented middleware* (136), called Simple Queue Service (SQS) [38]. Furthermore, each component should handle its own elasticity and should keep any state information externally. Chapell suggests a similar approach as a good Windows Azure Programming Model [170]. Processing components in Windows Azure are called worker roles as opposed to web roles providing user interfaces. It is suggested to communicate between multiple instances of these worker roles using messaging, as described by the processing component pattern.

4.3.5 Batch Processing Component

> Requests are delayed until environmental conditions make their processing feasible.

 How can asynchronous processing requests be delayed to be handled when conditions for their processing are optimal?

Context

Distributed applications (160) divide processing functionality among different *processing components* (180) to scale out processing among multiple cloud resources. If such processing components are accessed asynchronously, some or all of the three following conditions may make it unfeasible to process the requests sent to such components immediately: *seldom accesses* to processing functionality, *powerful processing component instances* accessed continuously, *environmental conditions*, such as resource costs. In case of seldom accesses, it may be more efficient to provision the handling processing component on-demand and only when a certain number of requests are present to utilize it. Similar, if the capabilities of a processing component instance are significantly higher than what can be utilized by requests continuously sent to it, a processing component instance should only be provisioned, when there are enough requests to make processing feasible. These first two conditions are more likely to arise in an *elastic infrastructure* (87) where the application controls when virtual servers are provisioned and decommissioned. However, the approach may be applicable to an application deployed on an *elastic platform* (91) as well. The third condition considers the environment as cloud resources used by the processing component may be provided under varying conditions (availability only during certain time frames, varying price etc.). In this case, requests should be processed when environmental conditions are matching, for example, the desired price or availability of required IT resources.

Solution

The *batch processing component* accepts asynchronous processing requests at all times, but stores them until conditions are optimal for their processing (Fig. 4.13). Usually, a message queue provided by a *message-oriented middleware* (136) is

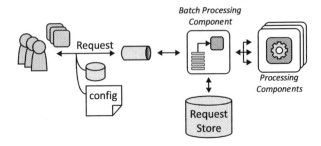

Fig. 4.13 Batch processing component in a standard setup

used to store requests, but storage may also be handled a separate *stateful compo-nent* (168) or storage offerings (see Sect. 3.5 on Page 109). Based on the number of stored requests, environmental conditions, and custom rules, processing compo-nents are instantiated to handle the requests. Furthermore, request handling has to respect the service level required from the batch processing component, thus, provisioning processing components under non-optimal conditions if requests cannot be delayed any longer.

Result

Processing requests are accepted and their execution is coordinated by the *batch processing component*. It stores these requests using a storage offering, a message queue, or *stateful component*. Requests sent to the *batch processing component* either contain information regarding the desired service level or the service level is a fixed configuration. The *batch processing component* continuously monitors the delayed and stored requests and environmental conditions, such as cloud resource availability and pricing. If these conditions make processing feasible or the assured service level requires it, processing components are instantiated. This approach may also be used to better utilize cloud resources accessed on a pay-per-use basis. Such resources are often billed by a certain time-slot (hourly, daily etc.). A batch processing component may be used to collect processing requests until a complete time-slot may be utilized. Configurability of the *batch processing component* is handled in a similar fashion as for *processing components* (180).

Variations

The component monitoring the delayed requests and the environment may also contain the processing functionality to handle requests immediately. In this scope, it would only initiate the provisioning of additional processing components if its own capabilities are insufficient.

Related Patterns

The batch processing component functions similar to an *elastic queue* (257) and such a queue can be used to implement the functionality of a batch processing component. However, if load balancing functionality is offered by the provider, the application may have to provide an additional batch processing component. Based on the functionality that may already be implemented by other application components, a batch processing component, therefore, uses the following other patterns:

- *Message-oriented middleware* (136): this communication offering provides message queues for storage of messages until they are retrieved for further processing. It is, therefore, ideal to delay request messages in scope of the *batch processing component*.
- *Elastic queue* (257): an *elastic queue* provisions and decommissions the components handling requests depending on the number of messages stored in a queue. An *elastic queue* may, therefore, be configured to provide the behavior desired from the *batch processing component*.
- *Elastic infrastructure* (87): the *batch processing component* has to provision and decommission *processing components* (180) that may be hosted on virtual servers provided by an *elastic infrastructure*. Through the management interface of the *elastic infrastructure*, a *batch processing component* may handle the required scaling tasks automatically.
- *Elastic platform* (91): in contrast to an *elastic infrastructure*, application components deployed to an *elastic platform* are often not associated with a virtual server. In this environment, the *batch processing component*, therefore, decides when to provision and decommission the *processing components* (180) directly. Especially, the load balancing of the *processing components* once instantiated, may be handled completely by the *elastic platform*. The only decision that has to be made by the batch processing component is then, when processing should be started and stopped.

Known Uses

Amazon provides virtual servers, Spot Instances [171], part of its Elastic Compute Cloud (EC2) [18] that have a variable pricing based on the current workload experienced by Amazon. Amazon already allows users of such instances to specify rules for which price range virtual servers may be started or stopped. A *batch processing component* may delay requests until processing is cheaper, but can also supervise other influencing factors, such as the desired response time.

4.3.6   Data Access Component

Functionality to store and access data elements is provided by special components that isolate complexity of data access, enable additional data consistency, and ensure adjustability of handled data elements to meet different customer requirements.

 How can the complexity of data storage due to access protocols and data consistency be hidden and isolated while ensuring data structure configurability?

Context

A *distributed application* (160) may use different storage offerings (see Sect. 3.5 on Page 109), for example, *relational databases* (115) and *key-value storages* (119) to store data. Alternatively, these applications may also use *stateful components* (168) developed individually. Handling the complexity of accessing this data, i.e., handling of authorization, querying for data, failure handling etc. in *user interface components* (175) or *processing components* (180) tightly couples those components to the used storage offering and complicate the implementation of these components as a lot of the idiosyncrasies of data handling have to be respected by them. Therefore, a later change to the application, for example, the replacement of a storage offering with another one causes significant changes to other application components. Instead, different data sources should be integrated to provide a unified data access to other application components. Also, data may be stored at different cloud providers that have to be integrated as well.

Solution

Access to different data sources is integrated by a *data access component* (Fig. 4.14). This component coordinates data manipulation if different storage offerings are used. In case a storage offering shall be replaced or the interface of a storage offering of a cloud provider changes its interface, the *data access component* is the only component that has to be adjusted, thus, ensuring a *loose coupling* (156) between the rest of the application and used cloud offerings.

Fig. 4.14 Data access components integrating stateful components and storage offerings residing in two clouds

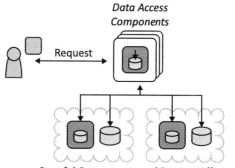

Data Access Components

Request

Stateful Components and Storage Offerings

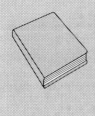

Further Reading: Fowler [15] motivates a similar separation of data handling and application logic as is ensured by the use of data access components. He also covers different styles to structure data, i.e., in tables or rows and discusses how data access can be integrated with other application components.

Gamma et al. [2] apply a similar approach to object oriented applications called *adapter*. Buschmann et al. [14] cover a *proxy* pattern to enable remote access to functions an data that may be used to control and restrict these accesses.

Result

The complexity of accessing different storage offerings due to different interfaces, interaction protocols, authentication methods etc. is subsumed by a data accesses component that is used by other application components. This ensures that the cloud providers among which data storage is distributed may be hidden from other application components to ensure a unified data access behavior to them. If a cloud provider that stores data shall be exchanged with a different one, the application components to be adjusted may be easily identified. Furthermore, these data access components can enable client-centric consistencies in addition to the consistency assured by the provider and can be designed to assure configurability of the handled data elements. Both concepts are described in the following:

Client-centric consistencies: the data access component may be used to provide a different consistency behavior to other components than what is provided by the integrated cloud storage offerings. If the *data access component* can access stored data in a transactional context, it can ensure strict consistency of integrated data as described in the *strict consistency* (123) pattern. In case of *eventually consistent* (126) storage offerings, the *data access component* can use the following approaches to enable client-side consistencies regardless of the eventually consistent behavior initially supported by a storage offering, as adapted from Tanenbaum et al. [127] and Vogels [131]. For these naïve implementations to assure client-side consistency models, the data handling uses *versions on data elements*, and *histories of operations* executed by clients. We first cover briefly how different client-side consistency assurances can be realized by a *data access component*. These consistency assurances are also covered in detail by the *eventual consistency* (126) pattern. Afterwards, we cover how the consistent knowledge in both approaches regarding versions numbers and operations identifiers can be ensured if the *data access component* itself is scaled out.

- *Monotonic Reads – One client will never read data that is older than what it has read before.*
- *Read Your Writes – One client will immediately see data alterations performed by it.*

These two consistency levels can be realized by *data access components* using version identifiers associated with each data element. Upon every write of a data element, this version identifier is increased. The *data access component* may then know the last version accessed by a client and can drop any results of read and write operations that are too old. If the *data access component* is scaled out, all instances of it need to have consistent information about the version last seen by a client (*consistency for that client*) or all clients (*consistency for all clients*).

- *Monotonic Writes – Write operations of one client are executed in the order they were issued.*

This client-side consistency can be ensured by storing the unique identifiers of client's operations in an operation history. If a *data access component* retrieves an operation that it shall execute but the data to update does not reflect all previously executed operations in the history, it can wait. Again, this requires that all instances of a scaled-out *data access component* have a consistent knowledge about the operation history of a client (*consistency for that client*) or all clients (*consistency for all clients*).

Scaling of the *data access component* is significantly hindered if it enables a client-side consistency assurance that is not assured by the storage offerings, because the version identifiers and operation identifiers have be consistent among data access component instances. This can be realized in two ways. First, the *data access components* are *stateful components* (168), thus, they maintain the identifiers internally. If an identifier shall be increased, the data access component instances do so in an ACID transaction, as described in the *strict consistency* (123) pattern. The second approach is to implement the data access component as a *stateless component* (171) and store the version identifiers and operation identifiers in a *strict consistent* (123) storage offering that is accessed by all data access component instances. In either case a hybrid access to data elements can now be realized: clients can decide on every read if they would like to retrieve consistent data (the version identifier and operation identifier is accessed) or if eventual-consistent data is sufficient (only the eventual consistent storage offering is accessed).

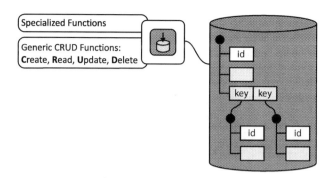

Fig. 4.15 Data access component interface and data structure

This hybrid approach is also used by to some storage offerings and also reflected in pay-per-use pricing models: customers pay less if they decide for eventual consistent reads as consistent reads are harder to realize. Therefore, introducing any consistency to an eventually consistent storage or a set of storage offerings that are integrated always has to be weighted with performance and partitioning tolerance, because according to the CAP theorem [67] not all of these can be optimized at the same time. Especially, the initial consistency behavior of a storage offering can significantly impact performance if changed. Consider, for example, a storage offering, that assures no client-side consistency, for which read-your-write consistency shall be enabled. Therefore, a versioning identifier is associated with every data element and all operations retrieving an obsolete data version are dropped and re-executed by the *data access component*. However, that means that a write operation executed after a read operation may take very long to return, as the *data access component* waits until it retrieves the last or a newer version, thus, significantly affecting the performance experienced by the client. Also, when the *data access component* computes the new version identifier it has to coordinate with all other instances in case it is scaled-out. Reintroducing the problems of *strict consistency* (123) to the eventually consistent storage offering it accesses.

Configurability: to adjust the data structure supported by *data access components* two characteristics have to be ensured. First, the data elements and their structure have to be extensible to support additional data elements and to extend existing data elements with additional data fields. Second, configured or new data elements have to be queried using generic functionality. Therefore, the interface of the *data access component* and the structure of handled data elements have to support configurability as depicted in Fig. 4.15.

The extensibility of data elements is realized by a certain data structure, where each data element is associated with a list of arbitrary data elements. This list may either be filled directly with data values or may be used as a pointer to other data elements that shall be associated with the extended data element. For example, if an application handles children of a school and the result of a test not commonly made by schools shall be stored with data elements representing children, one of the data fields may be used for it. If the test shall instead be modeled as a different data element containing more information, for example, when a child took it, the test result can also be modeled as a separate data element referenced in a field.

The second characteristic of configurable *data access components* is generic portion of their interfaces. To increase comprehensibility, interfaces usually provide specialized application specific functions as depicted in the left part of Fig. 4.15. These functions, for example, can be used to specifically query children data elements in the above example. The semantic of these functions is well-defined in scope of the application they are used in an, thus, significantly ease interaction with the interface. However, if the data elements provided by the *data access component* are extended, new data fields and new data elements cannot be respected in specialized functions defined for an application. Therefore, a *data access component* should also provide generic functions to access arbitrary data elements handled by it. These generic functions should at least be usable to create, read, update, and delete data elements, thus, they are called CRUD functions [172]. Using these functions, data elements may be accessed using a unique identifier, which is passed to the operations as parameter. Arbitrary data elements provided by the *data access component* can, therefore, be queried and manipulated using the generic functions, if no specialized functions exist for this purpose. A drawback of such extensible data elements and generic access functions is that readability of the *data access component* interface is drastically reduced, as a lot of the provided functionality is hidden behind the same interface. Furthermore, if multiple components access the same *data access component*, each of these components needs to implement specialized functionality, i.e., to query children using the generic functionality, rather than using an interface function specifically created for it. This may lead to a lot of redundancy in the application implementation. Therefore, interface readability always needs to be weighed against the flexibility of generic data manipulation interfaces.

Related Patterns
- *Restricted data access component* (222): if the components accessing data do not have the same level of privacy, security, and trust as the rest of the application, the data access component can be extended to restrict access to data, obfuscate data, or delete confidential data elements transparently to the other components accessing it.
- *User interface component* (175), *processing component* (180), and *batch processing component* (185): if the data access component is implemented as a separate component, the required serialization and deserialization of data to communicate with these other application components can degrade performance of the application. The functionality described by the data access component pattern is, therefore, often implemented together with another application component patterns to form one larger application component of the *distributed application* (160).
- *Data abstractor* (194): if the data access component provides data that is *eventually consistent* (126) it can additionally implement the data abstractor

pattern to hide the fact that data is eventually consistent from other application components and application users if the application's use case allows it.

- Storage offerings (see Sect. 3.5 on Page 109): the *data access component* may be used to integrate different storage offerings and then provides a unified access to them. All storage offerings covered in Chap. 3 are suitable for this integration. The *data access component* may even provide application specific functionality to access data, so rather than just providing operations to execute general queries, it may offer operations to query users, customers, stock items etc. adding more semantics to its interface than what generic interfaces of storage offerings provide.

- *Provider adapter* (243): the unification and abstraction that a data handling pattern provides for integrated storage offering should be used internally by every application component accessing a provider interface. This best practice is described generally in the *provider adapter* (243) pattern ensuring that application component implementations are loosely coupled to cloud provider interface specific.

Known Uses

The above mentioned CRUD functions are also used in the REST architectural style [72]. It limits the functions of interfaces to these fundamental operations. Often, this style of interaction is found in storage offerings, such as Amazon's Simple Storage Service (S3) [132]. How access methods exceeding these basic data manipulation functions can be designed is discussed by Fowler in [173]. The covered configurability of data elements has also been described by Chong et al. [174] to adjust database tables to the need of different customers. They saw this as a major enabling factor to share database instances between multiple customers in order to reduce costs and, thus, address a larger customer market.

4.3.7   Data Abstractor

> The data provided to users or other application components is abstracted to inherently support eventually consistent data storage through the use of abstractions and approximations.

 How can eventually consistent data be presented, so that possible inconsistencies are hidden from other application components and application users?

Context

Storage offerings (see Sect. 3.5 on Page 109), especially, *key-value storage* (119) and *blob storage* (112) may display *eventually consistent* (126) behavior to increase availability and partitioning tolerance. According to the CAP (consistency, availability, and partitioning tolerance) theorem [67], these desirable properties of a storage offering compete with each other (see Page 83 in Sect. 3.2 for a detailed discussion). As *strict consistency* (123) demands that more data replicas among which data is distributed for availability are accessed during read and write operations, the tolerance of the storage offerings towards network partitions is decreased, also decreasing its availability. Instead, *eventually consistent* (126) storage offerings allow that data manipulation operations access fewer data replicas to increase the performance of these operations and to make the offering more robust. Changes to stored data are then propagated between replicas asynchronously after the data alternating operations have already completed. However, if the *distributed application* (160) using these eventually consistent storage offerings is designed for consistent data, data consistency has to be reassured by higher-level components in the application stack. The *data access component* (188) pattern covers some approaches for this purpose. Reassuring data consistency on the application level can, however, void the benefits introduced by eventually consistent storage offerings regarding performance and availability.

Solution

The style of data representation is adjusted to allow data retrieved from storage offerings to be *eventually consistent* (126). Therefore, the data representation always reflects that the consistent state is unknown by approximating values or

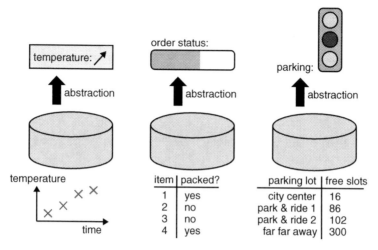

Fig. 4.16 Exemplary data abstractions

abstracting them into more general ones, such as *progress bars*, *traffic lights*, or *change tendencies (increase/decrease)* as depicted in Fig. 4.16. If the application scenario for such abstractions and approximations, thus, if the user of the applications does not require consistent data values, a *data abstractor* should be implemented to increase the beneficial effects of *eventually consistent* storage offerings.

Result

A *data abstractor* reads eventually consistent data and provides it in an abstracted, approximated, or summarized form to users and other application components. Additional consistency checks during read and write operations are not required as the abstraction reduces the impact of inconsistent data. This incorporation of *eventual consistency* (126), especially, simplifies scaling out of the *user interface component* (175) as the component instances do not have to coordinate consistency verification information, such as a versioning number kept with data elements. However, the adjustment of the user interface affects the look-and-feel of the application and, therefore, has to be acceptable in the concrete application scenario. Figure 4.16 depicts three examples for application scenarios that may be suitable for *data abstractors*. On the left, a large number of sensors store temperature readings in an *eventually consistent* storage offering. The application approximates theses values to determine the average and uses prior values to display a tendency (temperature increase or temperature decrease).

In the middle of Fig. 4.16, a progress bar approximation is depicted. Consider, for example, a logistics center where workers pick items from a large storage and prepare them for packaging. If a worker has picked up an item, this status is stored in the eventually consistent storage. The application approximates the number of prepared items, the active workers, and the overall number of concurrent packing processes into an approximated progress bar for each order.

On the right of Fig. 4.16 a traffic light abstraction is used. A Web application shall display the available free space of multiple parking lots. For this purpose, the entry gates report cars entering or leaving the properties. Due to the *eventual consistency* of the storage offering, the exact number of parked cars cannot be determined. Using the overall amount of parking lots, the *eventually consistent* number of parked cars, and the current tendency (drivers are generally leaving or drivers are generally entering the parking lot), the data is approximated to a traffic light to indicate how soon the parking lot is likely to be filled completely.

All of these application scenarios not only ensure the use of *eventually consistent storage* offerings in the applications user interface, but also provide information to users in a more useful fashion. Instead of providing consistent numbers, leaving their interpretation up to the user, approximations and tendencies are provided that can be interpreted by humans much more easily. For example, if a user was only provided with the absolute number of free parking slots in the last example, he or she would have to guess about the maximum available parking slots and the current behavior of other drivers to determine how soon the parking lot will be utilized fully.

Related Patterns

- *Stateless component* (171): the *data abstractor* pattern avoids consistency validation in application components, therefore, limiting the state that has to be stored by these components. Ideally, they should not keep any internal state as described by the *stateless component* pattern.
- *Loose coupling* (156): the interactions of the data abstractor with other application components should be realized in a loosely-coupled fashion, as described by the *loose coupling* (156) pattern.

Known Uses

This pattern has originally been described by us in [27]. SFPark [175] is an application provided by the city of San Francisco. It provides the above mentioned abstraction of available parking space in parking lots distributed among the city. As consistent state information is hard to retrieve from the large number of parking lots, availability is indicated only as *high*, *medium*, or *low*. Similarly, many online stores indicate the availability of products as "in stock", "limited quantity", and "out of stock", for example. In both cases, the representation of the data to users is better suited semantically than providing the consistent numbers.

4.3.8 Idempotent Processor

Application functions detect duplicate messages and inconsistent data or are designed to be immune to these conditions.

 How can an application component cope with message duplicates or data inconsistencies that could lead to duplicate function execution?

Context

The information on which a *distributed application* (160) operates can be inconsistent due to properties of used storage offerings (see Sect. 3.5 on Page 109), for example, *key-value storage* (119) and *blob storage* (112) assuring *eventual consistency* (126). Similar inconsistencies may occur due to *message-oriented middleware* (136) assuring *at-least-once delivery* (144) of messages. This behavior of storage offerings and communication offerings can result in duplicate execution of application functions as follows.

In case of *storage offerings* displaying *eventual consistency*, application components can possibly read obsolete information that has already been processed and, thus, may have already been changed. However, this change is currently propagated internally of the storage offering. Therefore, some application components, even those that performed the data change, may read obsolete data and would, thus, decide to execute the same function again.

The same problem arises, if application components of the distributed application exchange information asynchronously *via* a *message-oriented middleware* assuring *at-least-once delivery*. Cloud applications may also use messaging to communicate with separate application, non-cloud applications, and legacy applications. If the *message-oriented middleware* does not guarantee *exactly-once delivery* (141) behavior, the receiver of a message must be able to cope with duplicate messages. Even if *exactly-once delivery* (141) is guaranteed, it may still be beneficial to implement receivers that can handle duplicate messages. This is especially the case if non-cloud applications or legacy applications have to be integrated, which do not support the transactional message exchange that is often necessary for *exactly-once delivery*. Furthermore, even in *exactly-once delivery* (141) messaging implementation failure recovery may still lead to very rare message duplicates.

Solution

The *idempotent processor* ensures that duplicate messages and inconsistent data do not affect application functionality either through *inconsistency detection* identifying message duplicates and data inconsistencies or through *idempotent semantics* of application functions enabling them to be erroneously executed multiple times with the same outcome.

Inconsistency detection is ensured by a message filter as introduced by Hohpe and Woolf [1] removing received messages prior to processing them or by a data version identifier used to identify inconsistent data retrieved from a storage offering that has already been processed.

Idempotent semantic of application functions is ensured if a duplicate execution of a function due to duplicate messages or obsolete data results in the same outcome. Therefore, the state of the overall application is not affected if some functions are accidentally executed multiple times.

 ***Further Reading:*** the idempotent processing of messages has originally been covered as a messaging pattern, called *idempotent receiver* by Hohpe and Woolf [1]. Respectively, the *idempotent processor* pattern extends this concept to the interaction with *eventually consistent* (126) storage offerings to avoid the duplicate execution of application functionality.

Result

Figure 4.17 depicts the two approaches how an idempotent processor may be implemented for messaging (left) and eventual-consistent data stores (right).

Idempotent message processing: the first approach as described by Hohpe and Woolf [1] is to associate each message with a unique identifier. The message filter analyses a unique identifier associated with each message. For each message passing through it, the identifier is stored by the filter in a message ID store. Upon receiving new message, its message identifier is compared to message identifiers already in this store. If a match is found, the message is dropped and not forwarded. A critical design issue is how long message identifiers shall be stored by the message filter, since a large list of message identifier may decrease the filter's performance. Therefore, messages are often also associated with a timestamp specifying how long they are valid to enable the removal of message identifiers from filter lists.

The second approach considers the semantics of functions offered by the receiver. It is ensured that these functions have the same effect even when they are executed multiple times. An example of such a message is depicted at the top

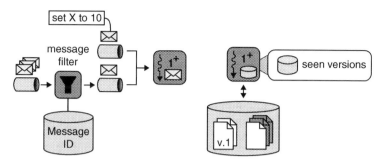

Fig. 4.17 Idempotent component for messaging (*left*) and storage offerings (*right*)

left of Fig. 4.17, instead of sending a message saying that the value of a variable "X" shall be increased by a certain amount, the message specifies the concrete amount to which the variable has to be set, in this case "10". Therefore, a duplicate handling of this message will still result in the same variable value. This can of course result in concurrency problems if messages are received out of order. In such cases message identifiers may also contain sequence numbers. For further information on message sequencing and their reordering also refer to the patterns *message sequence* and *re-sequencer* described by Hohpe and Woolf [1].

Idempotent data processing: the first approach is to associate each data element with a version identifier to enable the idempotent processor to identify data that was already read. To do so, the idempotent processor internally stores the version identifiers it has already processed. Alternatively, this version identifier may also be stored in a storage offering, however, only *strict-consistent* (123) storage offerings may be used. Detailed information on how to use such version identifiers and, especially, how to keep them consistent among multiple application component instances, is given by the *data access component* (188) pattern.

The second approach is to implement idempotent application functionality. Functionality is often idempotent, if data is transformed from one format to a different format. Consider, for example, an application that accesses pictures in a storage offering, performs a color adjustment on them, and stores them again. If an obsolete picture is read that has already been processed, processing it again and storing the results again will lead to the same overall outcome. If multiple idempotent processors access storage in this fashion, some optimization can be ensured by reading data elements randomly instead of ordered to avoid duplicate processing of the same element, and to check prior to processing if the data element has already been changed.

Related Patterns

- *Exactly-once delivery* (141): a *message-oriented middleware* (136) may use a similar functionality as the message filter employed by the *idempotent processor* to filter messages internally prior to delivering them to receivers. Therefore, if the *message-oriented middleware* assures this property, *idempotent processors* are likely to become unnecessary.

- *Timeout-based delivery* (149): this pattern describes how a *message-oriented middleware* (136) may assure that a communication partner successfully receives a message. Due to the used interaction protocol, messages are often delivery *at-least-once* (144), thus, the need for an *idempotent processor* may be created.
- *Eventual consistency* (126): storage offerings (see Sect. 3.5 on Page 109) assuring this kind of consistency should be considered for access by an *idempotent processor*.
- *Data access component* (188): if the *idempotent processor* uses version identifiers, it ensures a higher level of consistency than the storage offering provides. It, therefore, implements so-called *client-side consistency*. The different kinds of client-side consistencies and how to assure them is covered in detail by the *data access component* (188) pattern.

Known Uses

The *idempotent processor* for messaging has originally been introduced by Hohpe and Woolf [1]. Amazon's messaging system, the Amazon Simple Queue Service (SQS) [38], guarantees *at-least-once delivery* (144), and, therefore, Amazon also suggests the implementation of idempotent receivers [147]. The same is suggested by Mizonov and Manheim for messages that are exchanged using the Windows Azure Queues [176].

4.3.9 Transaction-Based Processor

> Components receive messages or read data and process the obtained information under a transactional context to ensure that all received messages are processes and all altered data is consistent after processing, respectively.

 How can an application component ensure that all messages it receives are processed successfully and altered data is persisted successfully after processing?

Context

A *message-oriented middleware* (136) can use *transaction-based delivery* (146) of messages to ensure that messages are only deleted from provided message queues if they have been received successfully by a client. However, using this approach no assurances can be made regarding the processing of that received message. Especially if application components of a *distributed application* (160) can fail during the processing of messages, additional means shall be established to ensure that messages are not only received properly, but that they are also ensured to be processed by the application. The same challenge arises, if an application component accesses data from a storage offering (see Sect. 3.5 on Page 109) and it shall be ensured that retrieved data is processed and successfully persisted again after processing.

Solution

Transaction-based delivery (146) subsumes reading the message from a queue and deleting it from a queue in one transaction. Therefore, these operations either both complete or both fail leaving the message on the queue to be received by a different client. The *transaction-based processor* extends the transactional context to the processing of the message in the receiver as depicted in the left of Fig. 4.18. Therefore, it is additionally ensured that every message received and deleted from the queue is also processed by the receiving component.

Analogous, a *transaction-based processor* interacting with a *storage offering*, reads, processes and writes data in one transactional context. This ensures that data is only altered if it was processed successfully and that data is not changed by other clients interacting with the storage offering while it is being processed. Avoiding changes from other clients may also motivate pure transactional read operations

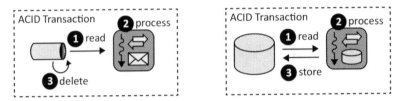

Fig. 4.18 Operations of the transactional processing of a message (*left*) and data (*right*)

that do not alter data in the storage offering to ensure that data remains unchanged while the application component processes it.

Further Reading: the transactional interaction with a *message-oriented middleware* (136) supporting *transaction-based delivery* (146) has been covered by Hohpe and Woolf [1] as the *transactional client* pattern. Transactional processing and transactional processing using message queues is also discussed in detail by Bernstein and Newcomer [128]. Respectively, the *transaction-based processor* pattern summarizes these concepts and the transactional interaction with storage offerings. The use of transactions to interact with storage offerings, such as *relational databases* (115) is also long established and described in detail by Silberschatz et al. [108] or Elmasri et al. [109].

Result

Through the use of (distributed) transactions, the *transaction-based processor* ensures atomicity, consistency, isolation and durability for the processing of a received message or accessed data. These are the following ACID properties in scope of these interactions:

- *Atomicity*: all operations to receive, process, and delete a message or to manipulate data are either completed as a whole or fail completely, thus, making no changes to the message queue or the storage offering.
- *Consistency*: after the transaction, the messaging system or the storage offering is in a valid state, thus, the message or accessed data has been successfully processed.
- *Isolation*: a retrieved message or accessed data is always handled by only one transaction within a transaction-based processor.
- *Durability*: after the transactional operations have been completed, changes are permanent, thus, the message is processed, has been deleted, and will not reappear on the messaging queue and altered data will remain in that state.

Related Patterns

- *Transaction-based delivery* (146): this pattern describes the transactional delivery behavior that must be supported by the used *message-oriented middleware* (136) to enable the extension of the transactional context to the processing of received messages by receiving application components.
- *Relational database* (115): this storage offering often supports the transactional interaction required by the *transaction-based processor*.
- *Watchdog* (260): if transactional processing of messages is used to avoid message loss in case of application component failure, a *watchdog* may be used additionally to detect and replace failing application components.
- *Timeout-based message processor* (204): transactional interaction with a *message-oriented middleware* (136) often makes the middleware harder to scale out. This is due to the fact that the state of message queues, i.e., the messages currently stored as well as the operations performed on these messages have to be coordinated between the IT resources among which the *message-oriented middleware* itself is scaled out. The challenges are similar to keeping a consistent state among instances of a *stateful component* (168). Therefore, many cloud providers, instead, use *timeout-based delivery* (149) to ensure successful delivery of messages by retransmitting messages. In this case, the component processing messages can implement the *timeout-based message processor* (204) to ensure that messages are processed successfully.

Known Uses

The *transaction-based processor* pattern describes how *transaction-based delivery* (146) assured by a *message-oriented middleware* (136) can be extended to include message processing performed by application components. Protocols of this interaction are, for example, specified by the Java Message Service (JMS) [145, 146]. Especially, if the message-processors are subject to fail transaction-based processor can help to ensure that messages are not lost. Perry et al. [177] cover transaction-based message processing for IBM Websphere MQ [142] in a pattern format and especially focus on this transactional message processing. Many *relational database* (115) products, such as IBM DB2 [110], Oracle 11 g [111], or MySQL [112] support the transaction-based interaction with these storage offerings.

4.3.10 Timeout-Based Message Processor

Clients acknowledge message receptions and processing to ensure that all messages are handled by an application. If a message is not acknowledged after a certain timeout, it is processed by a different client.

How can an application process messages while guaranteeing that all messages handled by the application are processed at-least-once?

Context

A *message-oriented middleware* (136) uses *timeout-based delivery* (149) to ensure that messages are received successfully by at least one client. It requires these clients to acknowledge a successful message reception. Until this acknowledgement, messages are still stored in the queue but are invisible to other clients retrieving messages from the queue. If an acknowledgement is not received in a specific time frame, often called the *visibility window or visibility timeout*, a message is again made visible to be received by other clients. Certain conditions, for example, unreliable application components processing messages, may demand to extend the assurance that a message has been received. Therefore, it shall be assured by the application that a message has also been properly processed after its reception.

Solution

Instead of sending an acknowledgement right after receiving a message, a *timeout-based message processor* sends this acknowledgement after it has successfully processed the message. Therefore, if the processing fails after a successful message reception, the message is made visible to other clients as if it had never been received successfully at all. The operations necessary for this extended assurance are depicted in Fig. 4.19. First, the message is written to a message queue supporting *timeout-based delivery* (149). Second, the message is read by the client, i.e., an application component of a *distributed application* (160) and, third, marked as invisible by the message queue. Forth, the message is being processed. Fifth, the application component implementing the *timeout-based message processor* pattern acknowledges the processing of the message to the message queue followed by the final deletion of the message from the queue in step six. At any time after setting a message invisible, a visibility timeout may be reached at which point the message is set visible again.

Fig. 4.19 Operations of the timeout-based processing of a message

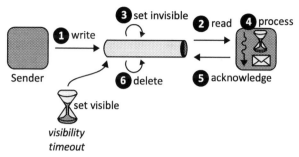

Result

Every message is only deleted from a queue when it was received and processed successfully. In case one of these operations fails, the message is made visible again to be received again. A critical design parameter in this scope is the length of the visibility timeout after which messages become visible again. If this timeout is shorter than the amount of time required for processing of messages, messages are never deleted but processed over and over again. Therefore, the *message-oriented middleware* (136) used in an application containing *timeout-based message processors* has to be configured carefully.

Related Patterns

- *Timeout-based delivery* (149): this pattern describes the behavior of the *message-oriented middleware* (136) to assure messages receptions. The behavior described there is extended by the *timeout-based message processor* to ensure successful message processing.
- *Watchdog* (260): if the application components processing messages are unreliable, a watchdog may be used to identify and replace failing ones.
- *Transaction-based processor* (201): if the *message-oriented middleware* (136) supports *transaction-based delivery* (146), the application component processing messages can implement the *transaction-based processor* (201) pattern instead of the *timeout-based message processor* pattern to ensure message processing.

Known Uses

Timeout-based message processing in the cloud is common, as cloud providers often assure *environment-based availability* (98) and *at-least-once delivery* (144) of messages. Therefore, the application component instances processing messages are subject to fail. The communication offerings of these providers, additionally often only assure *at-least-once delivery* of handled messages. Therefore, messages traversing a cloud application from component to component should be processed according to the *timeout-based message processing* pattern. This best practice is described for Amazon AWS [138] by Varia [93, 154] and for Windows Azure [52] by Chapell [170].

4.3.11 Multi-Component Image

Virtual servers host multiple application components that may not be active at all times to reduce provisioning and decommissioning operations.

 How can a virtual server provide the functionality of multiple application components to be used flexibly in applications?

Context

A *distributed application* (160) may deploy its application components among virtual servers provided by an *elastic infrastructure* (87). The individual application components may, however, not fully utilize the servers if only one component is hosted per server. Therefore, mapping each application component to a single server may lead to underutilization. Furthermore, the workload experienced by different application components may differ during the runtime of the cloud application. This is especially the case for *periodic workload* (29), *unpredictable workload* (36), and *continuously changing workload* (40). If each component is scaled individually and hosted on separate servers, changes in the workload ratios between components may require provisioning activities even though workload experienced by the overall application could be handled by the same number of virtual servers.

Solution

Multiple application components (possibly including middleware) are hosted on a single virtual server to ensure that running virtual servers may be used for different purposes without making provisioning or decommissioning operations necessary. Figure 4.20 exemplarily shows two application components managed as one *multi-component image*. Both application components may be provisioned based on this image, but not all of the application component instances are actively processing workload at all times.

Result

Since different types of application components share a virtual server, the running virtual servers can be used more flexibly. Furthermore, less server images have to

Fig. 4.20 Two application components managed as one multi-component image

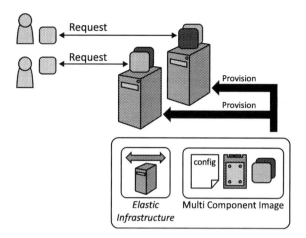

be maintained for the application in the image database of the *elastic infrastructure* (87). Regarding the management of the cloud application, it can also be beneficial to provision inactive application components on virtual servers, thus, a virtual server hosts a multitude of application components, but only a subset of these components is active. Through this design, provisioned servers become much more flexible regarding the application functionality they are used for. A challenging design decision in this scope is how to distribute application components among images in an optimized fashion. A problem that may arise in this scope, are licensing issues if application components require licensed software on the virtual server. In this case, having a multitude of inactive application components provisioned on servers can result in licensing costs without providing a benefit to the application.

Related Patterns
- *Elasticity manager* (250), *elastic load balancer* (254), and *elastic queue* (257): these management patterns describe the process how application component instances are added and removed from a running application. If an *elastic infrastructure* (87) is used, they are, therefore, concerned about starting and stopping virtual servers. If these servers provide different functionality they can be reassigned instead of being decommissioned, which simplifies and optimizes elasticity management.
- *Feature flag management process* (271): if an application has to be scaled up, but necessary resources cannot be provisioned quickly enough, the *feature flag management process* (271) enables a fallback on less resource-demanding application functionality. If combined with a *multi-component image*, servers used by application components of lesser importance to the application's overall functionality may be repurposed quickly to support critical functionality instead.
- *Resiliency management process* (283): as cloud resources may fail, failures have to be detected and addressed. If *multi-component images* are used by an

application, replacements of failing component may be executed more quickly, as other running components may be used as substitutes while new application component instances are provisioned.

- *Standby pooling process* (279): pay-per-use cloud resources are often billed for specific time-slots, for example, on an hourly basis. This pattern describes how they can be kept on standby to be used again as long as they have been paid for instead of decommissioning them right away. In case of a combination with a *multi-component image*, cloud resources that are kept on standby can be reassigned a lot more flexibly.

Known Uses

Abbot and Fisher [178] describe how to determine the optimal configuration of a (virtual) server, for example, regarding the amount of memory to host an application through a set of tests. In [179], we evaluate optimal distribution of application components among virtual servers in greater detail.

4.4   Multi-Tenancy

Resource sharing is one of the five *essential cloud properties* established on Page 3 in Sect. 1.1. When dealing with the architecture of cloud-native applications, the discussion is important which components of that application are shared with other applications or, more specifically, which resources of underlying cloud environments can be shared with other instances of the same or other applications. Additionally, it is important to consider for applications, cloud infrastructures, cloud platforms as well as execution environments that are offered to multiple customers, which components are shared among the different customers, also referred to as "tenants", and which are not. The patterns in this section are, therefore, targeted at applications build on top of cloud offerings that shall themselves be offered as a service to multiple tenants, thus, these applications have to support multi-tenancy.

During the design of *aaS applications, three degrees of multi-tenancy have to be considered that we captured in patterns: *shared component* (210), *tenant-isolated component* (214), and *dedicated component* (218). These patterns apply to infrastructure resources, platform components, application components and business processes alike. For the sake of simplicity we call all these artifacts "components" when discussing the multi-tenancy patterns. The degree of isolation between tenants enabled by the multi-tenancy patterns is the main differentiating factor. Isolation, in this scope, has three aspects. First, *performance* experienced by one tenant shall not be affected by the performance required by other tenants. Second, the stored *data volume* needed by one tenant shall not affect the storage available to other tenants. Third, tenants shall not be able to *access* application components and data that belong to other tenants.

In case of a *shared component* (210), all tenants access the same component instance that is unaware of the fact that is used by different tenants. Tenants may provide individual configurations to adjust the component behavior, but isolation among individual tenants is not guaranteed.

Instances of a *tenant-isolated component* (214) are also shared by all tenants, but it is guaranteed that tenants are isolated against other tenants regarding the above mentioned isolation aspects.

If a *dedicated component* (218) is used, tenants do not share this component. Each tenant is associated with one instance or a certain number of instances of the component.

When analyzing the different cloud offerings on the infrastructure and platform level, it becomes clear that with an *elastic infrastructure* (87) offered as *IaaS* (45) the hardware is run in a *shared component* (210) fashion where the *hypervisor* (101) ensures multi-tenancy and isolation among the virtual servers, virtual data stores and virtual networks, thus, implementing the *tenant-isolated component* (214) pattern. In an *elastic platform* (91) offered as *PaaS* (49), even the middleware is deployed following the *tenant-isolated component* (214) pattern. When a *SaaS* (55) application is built on top of a *PaaS* (49) offering that is built on top of an IaaS offering, the notion of a multi-tenancy differs in the *SaaS* level – different customers with different users using the application, the *PaaS* level – different applications using the platform, and the *IaaS* (45) level – different platforms and applications using the infrastructure.

In custom cloud applications that shall themselves be offered as *SaaS* (55), application architects can then decide how they implement individual components of their applications regarding multi-tenancy. For example, they can implement the data layer as a *tenant-isolated component* (214) based on a *PaaS* cloud storage offering and implement the user interface as *dedicated component* (218) for each tenant, because the user interface is very specific for individual tenants. In this design, the architect always has to consider the tradeoff between IT resource homogenization, which is necessary to share resources between tenants, and customizability that has to be taken into account when opting for one of the multi-tenancy patterns.

4.4.1   Shared Component

> A component is accessed by multiple tenants to leverage economies of scale.

 How can an application component be shared between multiple tenants enabling some individual configuration?

Context

A *distributed application* (160) is offered to multiple tenants. Motivation for this may be to address a large number of customers to leverage economies of scale, but tenants may also be different departments of one company that access an application. These tenants share IT resources required by applications provided to them. This sharing may be introduced by an *elastic infrastructure* (87) or *elastic platform* (91) to which the instances of the application components are deployed. But the deployment of application component instances can be optimized by sharing them between tenants and not only the IT resources that are hosted on. Sharing of components is especially feasible for application components that provide the same functionality to all tenants. If tenants can share the same instance of such application components, underlying resources can be utilized more efficiently as deployment redundancy is avoided. The provisioning of application component instances shall be optimized by limiting the portion of the application stack and the number of application components deployed exclusively for one tenant.

Solution

The most important property of a *shared component* is that the provided functionality is equal for all tenants accessing the component. In particular, if the component merely provides data and does not store data of tenants, all tenants can be treated as a uniform user group to which a common user experience and service level is guaranteed. The *shared component* can be used by all tenants, thus, each *shared component* instance handles requests of all tenants as depicted in Fig. 4.21. These components behave equally for every tenant, but display, process, and store tenant-specific data. Therefore, the corresponding *user interface components* (175), *processing components* (180), or *data access components* (188) are configured equally for all tenants and may not even be aware of the fact that they handle workload of different tenants. Only minor configurations of component behavior

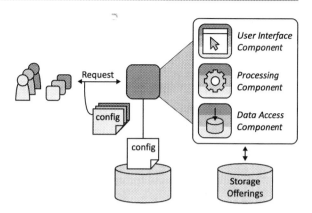

Fig. 4.21 Clients accessing a shared component

may be passed to the application component instance with each request, for example, to specify different display resolutions supported by user interface components.

Result

Instances of *shared components* can be scaled out regarding the overall workload of all tenants using the application. As individual tenants may not fully utilize an application component instance, subsuming the individual workloads of tenants leads to a reduced number of necessary application component instances, because tenants share the same component instances. Also, as *shared component* instances can be scaled for all tenants, the number of provisioning and decommissioning operations is reduced when the workload of different tenants changes. Due to these two effects, the runtime cost per tenant is reduced, allowing the cloud provider to address a larger customer market. As depicted in Fig. 4.21, the shared component is configured equally for every tenant. The functionality provided by this shared component, regardless whether it is located on the user interface, processing, or data layer of the application handles workload of every tenant, as shown on the right side of Fig. 4.21. It is important to note that this functionality provided by the *shared component* is unaware of the actual tenant for which a request is being executed. Therefore, the behavior of one tenant may possibly influence other tenants, for example, if a tenant generates a very high workload and the application does not scale up accordingly, the performance experienced by other tenants may be impacted as well.

Related Patterns

Two factors can render sharing application components as described by this pattern unsuitable for tenants. First, the influences between tenants that may occur when sharing components have to be avoided. Second, other requirements of tenants, for example, legal obligations disallow the sharing of resources with other tenants. In these situations, the following patterns should be used instead of a shared component:

- *Tenant-isolated component* (214): this pattern describes how application components can be implemented to be made tenant-aware. Therefore, the application components implement additional functionality to separate tenants, thus, assuring isolation of access, performance, and data storage.
- *Dedicated component* (218): this pattern describes how some application components may be deployed exclusively for a tenant, while other application components of the *distributed application* (160) may remain shared.

Furthermore, the following patterns may be relevant if the *shared component* pattern is used:

- *Managed configuration* (247): the configuration of the shared component may be managed centrally as described by the *managed configuration* pattern.
- *Periodic workload* (29), *once-in-a-lifetime workload* (33), *unpredictable workload* (36), and *continuously changing workload* (40): if the different tenants using an application component experience these workloads, the application may benefit from a *shared component* if the workload peaks experienced by different tenants happen during different timeframes. Sharing of component instances reduces the amount of necessary provisioning and decommissioning operations in this case.
- *Private clouds* (66): the elasticity of this cloud deployment type may be limited if the *private cloud* is used by a small number of tenants. *Shared components* may help to level out the utilization of resources by sharing application component instances between tenants.
- *Hypervisor* (101): if a *hypervisor* is used as a shared component to which different tenants may deploy their individual machines, it should be considered if it supports the *shared component* pattern or the *tenant-isolated component* (214) pattern. In case it supports the *shared component* pattern it is unaware of the fact that it is being used by different tenants and may not ensure tenant-isolation. Therefore, if one tenant utilizes the physical hardware, networking bandwidth, storage space etc. too much, the performance experienced by other tenants may be affected.

Known Uses

Within the scope of one company, thus, a *private cloud* (66), many common services, for example those used for authentication or user rights management, may implement the *shared component* pattern. Chong and Carraro [174] discuss the dedicated hosting for software applications for tenants on two levels: "Level 1: Ad Hoc/Custom" and "Level 2: Configurable". Level 1 deploys an instance of a standard application for a tenant. Level 2 allows tenants to configure their instance to their needs. The shared component pattern breaks this down to the level of application component and motivates that many application components can be provided as one instance on these levels – configurable or not – and can then be used in different applications of tenants. An example for such a shared component is the National Weather Service provided by the National Oceanic and Atmospheric Administration (NOAA) [180]. It offers a Web service interface to be integrated in applications, but it is unaware of the different tenants and their applications accessing the provided functionality.

4.4.2   Tenant-Isolated Component

A component shared between tenants avoids influences between tenants regarding assured performance, available storage capacity, and accessibility of functionality and data.

 How can an application component be shared between multiple tenants enabling individual configuration and tenant-isolation regarding performance, data volume, and access privileges?

Context

A *distributed application* (160) is offered to multiple tenants sharing IT resources to leverage economies of scale. In this scope, tenants may be separate customers or departments of one company, each accessing a *distributed application* (160). The offered application is, therefore, offered to multiple tenants, however, application components should be shared between tenants to utilize resources better by avoiding redundant deployments of components. While resource sharing can be enabled to a certain degree by hardware virtualization, i.e., functionality provided by a *hypervisor* (101), sharing higher level application components further minimizes the portion of the application stack provided exclusively for a single tenant. The resulting setup can then be scaled better, because tenants' applications can be scaled up or down regarding the workload of all tenants. Such a consolidation of workload would also reduce the number of necessary provisioning and decommissioning operations as application component instances can serve arbitrary tenants. However, the sharing of application components is hindered by three factors. First, tenants may have unique requirements and, thus, expect application components to be configurable to their individual needs, for example, specifying the language, color schema, date format etc. used by the user interface. Second, tenants may not trust each other, thus, they demand strong access controls to their application. Third, tenants expect an application to behave as if a single tenant was the only one accessing it, therefore, the workload behavior of one tenant must not impact the performance that can be assured to another tenant.

Solution

Components on all layers of the application stack are specifically developed to be used by different tenants. Especially, they ensure isolation between tenants by controlling tenant access, processing performance used, and separation of stored data. Also, the *tenant-isolated component* can store an individual configuration for each tenant.

Result

As shown in Fig. 4.22, the *tenant-isolated component* is accessed under tenant context: every tenant has to be authenticated. Authenticated accesses to the application component are associated with a *tenant identifier* (tenant ID) attached to the requests. Based on this identifier, a tenant-specific configuration is identified according to which the *tenant-isolated component* adjusts its behavior. Regardless whether the *tenant-isolated component* provides user interfaces, processing, or data handling, the tenant identifier is further used to separate requests of tenants and ensure a proper isolation.

The *tenant-isolated component* enables the highest degree of sharing application functionality between tenants, while keeping them isolated simultaneously. In contrast to the *shared component* (210), the *tenant-isolated component* ensures that tenants do not influence each other. Depending on the level of the application stack, tenant-isolation may be realized differently. *User interface components* (175) may handle access control to ensure that human users of a tenant may gain access to the user interface configured by for that tenant and cannot log into the user interface of a different tenant. In a multi-tenant *processing component* (180), the performance consumed by every tenant may be monitored to enable isolation, thus, avoiding that one tenant consumes so much processing capacity that the performance assured to other tenants is impacted. In *data access components* (188) data of different tenants is stored in an isolated fashion. In case of table-based storage offerings, such as *relational database* (115) and *key-value storage* (119), it can be differentiated between *table-based tenant isolation* and *row-based tenant isolation* [174, 181] as depicted in Fig. 4.23. Table-based tenant isolation creates a different set of tables for every tenant with the respective access rights. These tables are used exclusively by a tenant. Row-based tenant isolation adds a tenant identifier to each data element of that tenant. Therefore, the same table may contain data elements of different tenants. In either case, the queries performed by the data handling component are adjusted respectively to isolate access to the stored data elements.

In scope of table-based and row-based tenant isolation, tenants share the same database. Of course multi-tenancy can also be introduced by installing the database software multiple times on a shared server or by using a *hypervisor* (101) and, thus, hardware virtualization to share resources. Resource sharing is, however, more efficient the larger the shared the portion of the application stack is.

Through the use of tenant-isolation application components, the runtime cost per tenant is reduced and utilization of underlying IT infrastructure is increased. If the *tenant-isolated component* is scaled out, the number of instances may respect the workload of all tenants sharing the component. The cost savings achieved with this

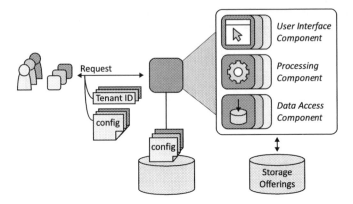

Fig. 4.22 Clients accessing a tenant-isolated component

Tenant1_TableName			
ID	A	B	C
∿∿	∿∿	∿∿	∿∿
∿∿	∿∿	∿∿	∿∿
∿∿	∿∿	∿∿	∿∿

TableName				
TenantID	ID	A	B	C
1	∿∿	∿∿	∿∿	∿∿
2	∿∿	∿∿	∿∿	∿∿
3	∿∿	∿∿	∿∿	∿∿

Fig. 4.23 Table-based tenant isolation (*left*) and row-based tenant isolation (*right*)

sharing of resources often enables the cloud application provider to target a larger target market.

Variations

If the configurations file that is specific to every tenant size is small enough, the configuration may be provided to the *tenant-isolated component* with every access request. This REST style [72, 161] is, for example, used by Web browsers that can inform an accessed Web server about the preferred language.

Related Patterns

Components may be provided to tenants in two other fashions, each more suited to specific requirements:

- *Shared component* (210): if tenants do not require tenant-isolation as enabled by the *tenant-isolated component*, a *shared component* (210) may be used instead. Components implemented according to this pattern are unaware of the fact that they are used by different tenants. Therefore, they often only support one configuration and do not isolate tenant access, assured processing performance, or access to stored data.

- *Dedicated component* (218): the customer-required level of tenant-isolation between tenants may be even higher than what a *tenant-isolated component* can offer. Especially, certain laws and regulations may not permit critical application functionality to be shared with any other tenants. If a tenant has such requirements, the corresponding application component should be provided exclusively to the tenant according to the *dedicated component* (218) pattern. A *dedicated component* may also be more suitable if the component configuration desired by tenants differs to a high degree making the implementation of a *tenant-isolated component* handling different configurations too complex.

Known Uses

Chong et al. [174] cover different levels of multi-tenancy in *SaaS* (55) applications. *Shared components* (210) and *dedicated components* (218) can be associated with the first two levels defined by the authors: "Level 1: Ad Hoc/Custom" – application instances are hosted exclusively for a tenant – and "Level 2: Configurable" – configurable application instances are hosted exclusively. The tenant-isolated component pattern describes the means of the next two levels: "Level 3: Configurable, Multi-Tenant Efficient" and "Level 4: Scalable, Configurable, Multi-tenant Efficient". Level 3 introduces the need for tenant isolations within one instance of a component. Level 4 adds the scaling of this application for the combined workload of all tenants. Both levels are broken down from complete applications to the application component level by the *tenant-isolated component* pattern. Especially, this allows the combination of *tenant-isolated components* with *shared components* – functionality that does not have to be tenant-aware – and *dedicated components* – custom functionality of tenants – into a *distributed application* (160) that can be scaled elastically.

Guo et al. [182] evaluate the different isolation capabilities that should be considered in this scope: *Authentication isolation* refers to the ability of tenants to incorporate the *tenant-isolated component* with on-premise applications. When they do so, access to their on-premise environment must not be enabled for other tenants sharing the *tenant-isolated component*. Access control isolation enforces access rights within the tenant-isolated component. *Information protection isolation* refers to the related access controls for tenant data handled by the tenant-isolated component. *Performance isolation* ensures that the workload created by a tenant does not affect the performance experienced by a different tenant. If one tenant overloads the application, a different tenant may not experience performance degradation. *Fault isolation* ensures that failures in tenant-isolated components only affect one tenant and do not propagate to others. Finally, the authors cover *administration isolation*, thus, administrators of tenants may only change access rights etc. for the user of the associated tenants. Therefore, multi-tenant applications often employ a two-level administration: administrators for every tenant and one administrator managing tenant administrators.

4.4.3   Dedicated Component

Components providing critical functionality shall be provided exclusively to tenants while still allowing other components to be shared between tenants.

 How can application components that cannot be shared be integrated into a multi-tenant application?

Context

A *distributed application* (160) is provided to multiple tenants, who shall share the application components of the application as much as possible. This sharing increases the utilization of underlying resources by reducing duplicate deployment of application components. However, while some application components may be shared easily between tenants, others may offer functionality that is too critical for this purpose or needs to be configured very specifically for individual tenants. Tenant-specific requirements, such as laws and corporate regulations, may hinder the degree to which tenants may share resources even further. Also, tenants may require the integration of custom developed and legacy application components into the distributed application, but these components were often not designed to be shared by tenants.

Solution

Dedicated components are provided exclusively for each tenant using the application (Fig. 4.24). If a component is available as *shared component* (210) or *tenant-isolated component* (214) as well, the decision whether or not to deploy these components exclusively can be made by every tenant based on individual requirements. Using a tenant identifier associated with requests, requests are routed to different application component instances to integrate dedicated components seamlessly with other *shared components* or *tenant-isolated components*.

Result

The deployment of *dedicated application component* instances enables tenants to adjust components very flexibly to their requirements. If laws and corporate regulations restricting resource sharing are the sole motivation for using dedicated

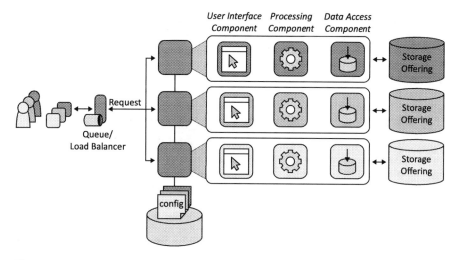

Fig. 4.24 Clients accessing dedicated components

components, often the same implementations used for *shared components* (210) or *tenant-isolated components* (214) can be used and are merely instantiated exclusively for one tenant. *Dedicated components* can also be developed exclusively for a tenant. In this case, the provider may offer an *elastic infrastructure* (87) or *elastic platform* (91) where customers may deploy self-developed components to be included in the application. Often, such *dedicated components* are used to extend the applications functionality to make it suitable for a customers' application scenario. However, implementing application components as *dedicated components* reduces the degree of sharing between tenants. Therefore, the ability of the provider to benefit from economies of scale is reduced.

Related Patterns

The dedicated component hinders sharing of application functionality between tenants, thus, limiting resource sharing to lower layers such as the platform or virtualization layer of the application stack. Therefore, the following two multi-tenancy patterns should be preferred whenever possible to maximize the degree of resource sharing between tenants leading to better resource utilization and reducing the running cost of the application.

- *Shared component* (210): components implementing this pattern are unaware that multiple tenants use them. Therefore, they provide the same functionality to every tenant and only support one configuration.
- *Tenant-isolated component* (214): components implementing this pattern are used by multiple tenants and ensure tenant isolation. Therefore, tenants are unaware of other tenants using the components. This is realized by making sure that tenants may not access other tenants' information and an equal level

of performance is guaranteed for every tenant regardless of the workload caused by other tenants.

Known Uses

Salesforce.com [45] started out as a *SaaS* (55) provider for customer relationship management (CRM) software. Quickly the need of customers arose to extend the functionality of this software with custom functionality, for example, to integrate existing applications with it. Therefore, salesforce.com started its *PaaS* (49) offering, Force [44], providing an *elastic platform* (91) on which custom-developed *dedicated components* may be deployed. Therefore, the customer may choose to use a tenant-isolated *SaaS* application to handle most of the required application functionality. The functionality not provided by this application can be custom developed and hosted as dedicated application components on an *elastic platform* (91) offered as *PaaS*.

Chong et al. [174] cover this deployment model for complete applications offered as *SaaS*. They differentiate between dedicated hosted applications on "Level 1: Ad Hoc/Custom" and "Level 2: Configurable". On the first level, dedicated standard applications are hosted exclusively for every tenant. On the second level, these applications still offer standardized functionality, but can be customized for every tenant. The *dedicated component* pattern motivates to break down this behavior to the application component level, so that customers may use standard application components offered as *shared components* (210) or *tenant-isolated components* (214) when they are sufficient and can integrate dedicated custom application functionality when required.

4.5   Cloud Integration

Having introduced the different patterns on how to build cloud-native applications and their components in the previous section, we cover another dimension in the following set of patterns. The integration dimension is very important when building cloud-native applications that are distributed among different cloud environments of a *hybrid cloud* (75) or have to be integrated with other applications of one or several customers hosted in different environments on-premise and in the cloud.

Similar to the *data access component* (188) described previously, the *restricted data access component* (222) makes data of an application or storage offering (see Sect. 3.5 on Page 109) available to other application components. However, it ensures that only certain parts of the data are made available that are characterized as non-critical. Other parts of the data can be obfuscated or removed transparently.

The *integration provider* (234) pattern describes how to offer a service to customers that enables them to flexibly integrate on-premise and cloud applications.

The *message mover* (225) pattern describes how to transparently integrate on-premise and cloud-based *message-oriented middleware* (136) so that it becomes transparent for the sending and receiving applications whether their messages end up in a cloud-based application or in an on-premise application.

When integrating cloud-applications with on-premise applications it is often difficult to make the functionality of an on-premise application available in the cloud, because of firewalls restricting inbound communication to the corporate network. However, it is often acceptable to poll for external messages or initiate outbound synchronous communication from on-premise applications. The *application component proxy* (228) pattern describes how to handle the requirement to send messages to on-premise applications or access them synchronously from the outside if communication in this direction is restricted.

4.5.1   Restricted Data Access Component

> Data provided to clients from different environments is adjusted based on access restrictions.

 How can an application component alter provided data based on access restrictions imposed on different environments?

Context

A *distributed application* (160) may host application components at different providers to match the individual requirements of components with best fitting providers. One factor may be that application components experience different workload, as described by the workload patterns in Sect. 2.2 on Page 23. For example, a *processing component* (180) may only be active during certain times of the month, when financial reports are generated resulting in *periodic workload* (29). Other differentiating factors of the used environments may be assured privacy, security, and trust. For example, an application may be hosted primarily in a secure cloud, often a *private cloud* (66) and performs annual report generations using resources from a more elastic, but insecure cloud, often a *public cloud* (62). However, due to the reduced level of privacy, security, and trust of the public environment, only anonymized data may be used to generate reports. While the anonymized data is sufficient for report generation, it has to be provided to the environment in this form. One approach could be to replicate the data to the insecure cloud and importing it to the secure environment after processing has completed. However, problems may arise for various reasons. Data may change in the secure environment while being processed externally hindering its later import. Furthermore, the export and import functionality of the application would have to be adjusted every time the restrictions on data elements changes.

Solution

Data storage restrictions and access privileges are defined for each data element and the attributes comprising them as shown in Fig. 4.25. Access to these data elements is provided by separate *restricted data access components* that interpret the information associated with data elements. It adjusts data accordingly through deletion or obfuscation during every access from an insecure environment.

Fig. 4.25 A data access
component and a restricted
data access component
providing data to a secure and
an insecure environment

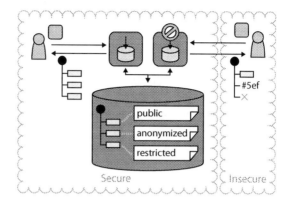

Result

The *data access component* (188) interacting with components in the secure environment as depicted in the left of Fig. 4.25, may provide the data in an unaltered form to clients in the secure environment as the assured level of privacy, security, and trust is sufficient. The *restricted data access component* providing data to the insecure environment with a lower level of privacy, security, and trust alters data elements transparently during accesses. Data element attributes that are, for example, unrequired for the workload handled in the insecure environment may be deleted (if they are not required to uniquely identify a data element). Data element attributes required for the data element identification may instead be obfuscated. In this case, their values are replaced by random identifiers. The mapping of the original value and its obfuscation is stored by the restricted data access component, so data manipulations possibly performed from the insecure cloud can be de-obfuscated prior to persisting them in the secure environment.

Variations

If a *restricted data access component* provides read-only access to data elements, the information used to map obfuscated and original data may be omitted.

Related Patterns
* *Managed configuration* (247): ideally, both data access components depicted in Fig. 4.25 are based on the same implementation and are then configured regarding the treatment of different restriction attributes of data elements. The *managed configuration* pattern describes how to provide such a configuration centrally for multiple components and their instances.

- *Data access component* (188): this more general pattern describes how the idiosyncrasies of accessing storage offerings (see Sect. 3.5 on Page 109) can be encapsulated. These concepts are also applicable in scope of the *restricted data access component* pattern. However, while the *data access component* (188) is often implemented together with another component pattern to avoid unnecessary data serialization and deserialization, the *restricted data access component* pattern is implemented as a separate component more regularly as other components communicating with it are hosted in a different environment. In the *data access component* pattern, it is further described how the structure of data elements can be made configurable to be adjusted later on.
- *Application component proxy* (228): the restricted data access component communicating with the insecure environment often has to be hosted in the secure environment as the component itself still handles the unaltered data elements. Therefore, it is often hosted in a *private cloud* (66) and shall be accessible from a *public cloud* (62). However, this direction of access is often restricted by corporate firewalls. The *application component proxy* (228) pattern describes how communication may still be enabled under these conditions.

Known Uses

As the restricted data access component extends the functionality of the *data access component* (188) pattern, its known uses are also closely related. For design of the functions exposed by a *restricted data access component*, the REST architectural style [72] and Fowler's data access routines [173] may be considered similarly. In addition to this overlap, there are cloud providers focusing on the exposure of access controlled data. WSO2 offers an integration component, the so called Cloud Services Gateway [183] exposing application functionality and data hosted in one environment to a different environment. For Windows Azure [52], there is the related *OData Service* [184] that enables the integration of different data sources to provide data to a large user group with different access privileges.

 Further Reading: the *restricted data access component* uses concepts similar to the *adapter* pattern described by Gamma et al. [2] and the *proxy* pattern described by Bushmann et al. [14]. Fowler [15] describes in the *remote façade* pattern how the access functions used to retrieve remote data can be adjusted to improve efficiency.

4.5.2 Message Mover

> Messages are moved automatically between different cloud providers to provide unified access to application components using messaging.

 How can message queues of different providers be integrated without an impact on the application components using them?

Context

The application components comprising a *distributed application* (160) often exchange data using messages. These messages are stored in message queues provided by a *message-oriented middleware* (136) to which communication partners may send messages and from which messages are received. If these queues reside in different cloud environments that form a *hybrid cloud* (75) accessibility to queues of one environment may be restricted for application components that are deployed in another environment. In such a setup, the idiosyncrasies of bridging these environments shall be hidden from the communicating application components. Especially, application components should still be able to send messages regardless of connectivity between the two environments. Therefore, each of the application components shall access a message queue hosted in the cloud environment where the application component itself is hosted in order to ease the access to this queue. The integration of the environments shall be enabled in a specialized application component transparently to the rest of the application.

Solution

A *message mover* is used to integrate message queues hosted in different environments by receiving messages from one queue and transferring it to a queue in other environments as depicted in Fig. 4.26. This process is completely hidden from other application components.

Result

The *message mover* integrates queues in different environment to provide one logical queue to all components hosted in the same environment. Communicating application components may always access a local queue, even though the communication partner may reside in a different environment and accesses a message

Fig. 4.26 Message mover
integrating queues of two
environments

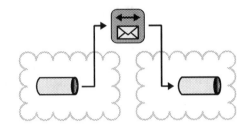

queue provided by a different *message-oriented middleware* (136). The *message mover*, thus, may also have to handle message format transformation if the different environments expect different message formats to be used. If multiple environments are integrated this way, a common message interchange format may be agreed upon for an application to ease the creation of *message movers*. Hohpe and Woolf [1] cover best practices for creation of a message format – the *canonical data model* pattern, transformation of message formats – the *message translator* pattern, and message format normalization – the *normalizer* pattern.

The integration of the environments regarding the creation of communication links is also simplified by the message mover, as only the message mover has to be enabled to access both integrated environments. The deployment location of the message mover is commonly based on the communication restrictions of the environments. For example, if the message mover integrates queues in a *private cloud* (66) and a *public cloud* (62), it is most likely to be hosted in the *private cloud*, as communication leaving the *private cloud* is more likely to be allowed than inbound communication initiated from the outside.

Variations

The *message mover* may be implemented internally by other application components. In this variation, the component itself maintains a local queue that is directly accessible by the implemented application functions. A local message mover takes messages from this internal queue and sends it to a message queue provided by a *message-oriented middleware* (136). This makes the component more resilient to connectivity problems and it may operate for some time even if the component itself does not have connectivity to any other application components.

Related Patterns
- *At-least-once delivery* (144) and *exactly-once delivery* (141): a *message-oriented middleware* (136) may assure that messages are delivered successfully at least once or exactly once as described by the corresponding patterns. In this scope, the *message mover* should assure the same delivery behavior as the integrated queues, if possible.

- *Idempotent processor* (197): if one of the integrated queues assures *at-least-once delivery* (144) and the other queue assures *exactly-once delivery* (141), the message mover should implement the idempotent processor pattern. When it receives messages from the queue assuring *at-least-once delivery*, the message mover, therefore, should filter the messages it has already forwarded to assure *exactly-once delivery* to components expecting this kind of behavior.

- *Transaction-based processor* (201) and *timeout-based message processor* (204): clients may interact with a *message-oriented middleware* (136) according to these patterns, to assure that messages are processed successfully exactly once (*transaction-based processor*) or at least once (*timeout-based message processor*). The *message mover* should implement one of these patterns. The successful processing, in this scope, would mean that the *message mover* has successfully moved a message from one of the integrated message queues to the other message queue.

Known Uses

Functionality to create *message movers* is often provided by a *message-oriented middleware* (136). The only task left for application developers is to define routing rules in a specific format understood by the *message-oriented middleware*. These routing rules are then deployed to the *message-oriented middleware* where messages are then moved between message queues managed internally and message queues provided externally based on defined rules. A common example for an open source implementation that supports the definition of message routing rules is Apache Camel [141], which is also part of the Apache Service Mix [57] enterprise service bus (ESB) [11].

4.5.3 Application Component Proxy

An application component is made available in an environment from where it cannot be accessed directly by deploying an application component proxy. The communication between this proxy and the application component is initiated and maintained from the environment where communication is unrestricted.

How can an application component be accessed if direct access to its hosting environment is restricted?

Context

Application components of a *distributed application* (160) are deployed in different cloud environments that form a *hybrid cloud* (75). These environments often have different privacy, security, and trust properties. The communication from environments with lower privacy, security, and trust to environments with higher privacy, security, and trust is often restricted through the use of firewalls. However, application components hosted in unrestricted environments, for example, a *public cloud* (62), may have to access application components hosted in a restricted environment, for example a *private cloud* (66) or corporate data center, but direct access may be unavailable. Only the components hosted in the restricted environment may access others in unrestricted environments.

Solution

The interface of a restricted application component is duplicated to form a proxy component as depicted in Fig. 4.27. Synchronous and asynchronous communication with this proxy component is initiated and maintained from the restricted environment that may access the unrestricted environment directly. Application components hosted in the unrestricted environment may then communicate with the proxy component that forwards any communication to the restricted application component.

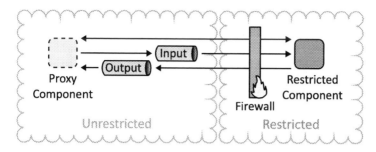

Fig. 4.27 Application component proxy bridging two environments

Result

Direct access to the restricted component is avoided as its functionality is accessed through its proxy component. The establishment of the communication channel between the restricted component and its proxy component depends on the style of communication.

If the restricted component shall be accessed synchronously, its functionality must return results immediately. A synchronous communication channel is initialized similarly to accessing a webserver on the Internet from the restricted environment, where the firewall has to allow the requested website to be transferred back into the restricted environment. A synchronous communication is established with the proxy component by initiating such a synchronous request that the firewall allows. The reply to this synchronous request then contains the requests send to the proxy component from other application component. As these requests, therefore, appear to be an answer to a request sent out from the restricted environment, they may pass through the firewall. In case the request initialized from the restricted component times out, it reinitializes the synchronous communication channel by re-requesting communication with the proxy component, thus, always maintaining a connection.

If the restricted component is accessed asynchronously, communication is realized through the use of message queues provided in the unrestricted environment by a *message-oriented middleware* (136). Asynchronous messages to the proxy component are put into an input queue from which the restricted component retrieves them. Result messages are put into an output queue from where the proxy component retrieves them.

Variations

In case of asynchronous communication with the proxy component, other application components may access the message queues in the unrestricted environment directly. In this variation, it may, therefore, be unnecessary to deploy a separate proxy component in the unrestricted environment.

Related Patterns

- *Message mover* (225): to hide the fact from the restricted component that it accesses a queue in a different environment than where it is hosted, a *message mover* (225) may be used to let the restricted component transparently access a different queue hosted in the secure environment.
- External patterns: the *application component proxy* pattern is based on concepts of the *proxy* pattern [2] and the *façade* pattern described by Gamma et al. [2] that cover a similar proxy for interfaces of objects in the scope of object-oriented programming. Buschmann et al. [14] also define a *proxy* pattern used in distributed applications.

Known Uses

The *application component proxy* has originally been described by us in [26], where it was called "application component gateway". Microsoft guides the implementation of this pattern for synchronous communication between the Windows Azure cloud and another environment. The Azure Service Bus Relay [185] integrates application components developed for Windows Azure through the automatic generation of proxy components. WSO2 provides an enterprise service bus [183] that can be installed in different environments and may then be used to create so called Cloud Services Gateway to access services in these different environments regardless of where they are hosted.

4.5.4 Compliant Data Replication

Data is replicated among multiple environments that may handle different data subsets. During replication data is obfuscated and deleted depending on laws and security regulations. Data updates are adjusted automatically to reflect the different data structures handled by environments.

 How can data be replicated between environments if some environments may only handle subsets of the data due to laws and corporate regulations?

Context

Distributed applications (160) that are hosted in a *hybrid cloud* (75) often require access to the same data from different application components of the application. For this purpose, data could be hosted exclusively in one cloud environment and accessed from all others. Such a setup is described by the *data access component* (188) pattern and the *restricted data access component* (222) pattern. However, if application components accessing the data are globally distributed, data access performance may be reduced drastically if data is only stored in one geographic location. Therefore, data may have to be replicated among different cloud environments.

Due to laws and corporate regulations, some of these environments may only handle a subset of the available data or data has to be obfuscated. Furthermore, the level of trust in the provider and especially in other users of the environment may be too low to store the complete data set. The data replication, therefore, needs to be compliant to these laws and regulations and has to reflect different levels of privacy, security, and trust. Often, the complete data set may only be stored in the most secure environment and shall be replicated to other, less secure environments in an automated fashion. Therefore, during the automatic updates of replicas in different environments data has to be altered automatically.

Solution

Data replicas in different environments are updated asynchronously using messaging, thus ensuring *eventual consistency* (126) of the replicas. As seen in Fig. 4.28, *message filters* introduced by Hohpe and Woolf [1] are used to delete and obfuscate

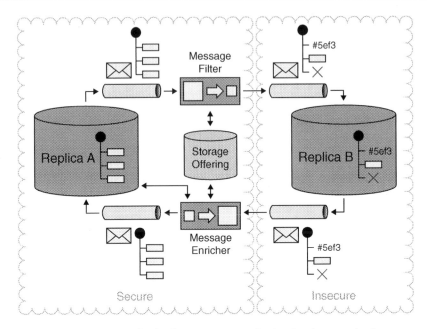

Fig. 4.28 Compliant data replication between a secure cloud and an insecure cloud

certain data elements in these messages as they leave the trusted environment.
Information about the data manipulations, for example, the original data that has
been obfuscated or values that have been deleted are stored in a storage offering, for
example, a *key-value storage* (119) or a *relational database* (115). If data is then
altered in the less secure environment, the corresponding update message is enriched
by a *message enricher,* also introduced by Hohpe and Woolf [1], as it enters the
secure environment. This enrichment is performed using information previously
stored by the message filter and may also query the original data replica.

Result

Since the replicas are updated following an *eventually consistent* (126) approach, a
message is generated when replica A is updated. When this message leaves the
trusted environment, its content is filtered. During this filtering process, data
elements may be deleted completely from the messages or are obfuscated, for
example, by replacing them with random data. The latter is required, if the filtered
data element resembles a data identifier or "key" required to correlate messages to
data elements. Replica B is updated according to the adjusted message it receives. If
replica B is then changed, the message is enriched when it enters the secure
environment. During this enrichment, obfuscated elements are de-obfuscated
using information stored during the filtering process. Deleted information can be

enriched if necessary by querying replica A. Note that access privileges on replica B may differ from the original replica. For example, clients should not be allowed to alter obfuscated data as this would hinder the correlation with the original data element. A challenge that arises from this setup is that the application components provisioned in the less secure environment have to be able to cope with the reduced and obfuscated data. These requirements have to be maintained during the application development and must be considered also during its deployment.

Related Patterns

- *Data access component* (188) and *restricted data access component* (222): if data does not have to be replicated but can be accessed from the less secure environment, these two patterns may be used. In this scope, an *application component proxy* (228) may also be necessary, if the access to the secure environment is further restricted using firewalls, for example.
- *Hybrid backend* (317): this pattern describes how data-intensive processing may use a cloud environment while the remainder of the application resides in a different environment. The *compliant data replication* pattern is often applicable here to replicate the data between these two environments.
- *Eventual consistency* (126): the consistency behavior of the data replicas is eventually consistent as messages are used by the compliant data replication pattern.
- *At-least-once delivery* (144) and *exactly-once delivery* (141): if the data update messages are exchanged using a message queue provided by a *message-oriented middleware* (136), the delivery behavior of this queue must be considered by the implementation of the message filter and the message enricher. Especially, if *at-least-once delivery* is assured, thus, messages may be received multiple times, the message filter and message enricher should implement the *idempotent processor* (197) pattern to cope with message duplicates.

Known Uses

Many *key-value storage* (119) offerings use messaging internally to propagate changes. If these can be configured to use a *message-oriented middleware* (136) for this message exchange, the routing functionality and message-transformation functionality provided by the *message-oriented middleware* may be used to perform the transformation required by the *compliant data replication* pattern. For example, the *key-value storage* Apache CouchDB [98] can be configured to use Apache Camel [141] for message exchange. In this scope the transformation functionality of Apache Camel may be used to adjust the messages as desired.

4.5.5   Integration Provider

> Integration functionality such as messaging and shared data is hosted by a separate provider to enable integrate of otherwise separated hosting environments.

 How can application components that reside in different environments, possibly belonging to different companies, be integrated through a third-party provider?

Context

When companies collaborate or one company has to integrate application of different regional offices, different applications or the components of a *distributed application* (160) are distributed among different hosting environments. Communication between these environments may be restricted. Especially, hosting environments may restrict any incoming communication initiated from the outside. Communication leaving the restricted environments is, however, often allowed. Therefore, additional integration components are required that have to be accessible from restricted environments. The establishment of demilitarized zones (DMZ) [137] at the restricted environments to contain shared integration components may be complicated and time-consuming. Especially, if the integration is only needed during a small time frame the use of DMZs may not be feasible. Company regulations may even prohibit it completely.

Solution

The distributed applications or their components communicate using integration components offered by a third party provider. This provider hosts, for example, a *message-oriented middleware* (136) or an enterprise service bus (ESB) [11] to enable *loose coupling* (156) between environments. The cloud of this provider is made accessible from all other environments. Communication with this environment is always initialed and maintained from the restricted ones through the use of *application component proxies* (228) or *message movers* (225). Shared data is either stored in storage offerings provided by the *integration provider* or through the use of *restricted data access components* (222) exposing data stored in the restricted environments to the integration environment.

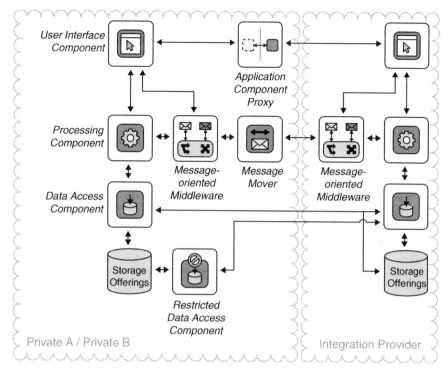

Fig. 4.29 Integration provider integrating two private environments

Result

The restricted environments communicate through the third-party provider. Figure 4.29 depicts such a scenario for two *private clouds* (66) (A and B) on the left integrated through an *integration provider* depicted on the right. Communication may be asynchronous or synchronous. In addition to the communication between the environments, data handling may be integrated through provider- supplied storage offerings accessed by private *data access components* (188) and *restricted data access components* (222) that enable the access to private data from the integration environment. The individual challenges to enable asynchronous communication, synchronous communication, and data access can be addressed as follows.

Asynchronous communication: information is provided in the integration environment *via* message queues or pub-sub topics provided by a *message-oriented middleware* (136). This communication offering is often provided in both environments and integrated using a *message mover* (225) depicted in the middle of Fig. 4.29. As inbound communication to the private environments is commonly restricted, the message mover in the restricted environments polls for new messages at the integration provider and moves them to the restricted environment.

Synchronous communication: an *application component proxy* (228) deployed in the private environments enables synchronous communication if a privately hosted application component shall be accessible in the integration environment and inbound communication to the private environment is restricted. This is depicted exemplarily for *user interface components* (175) in Fig. 4.29. The *application component proxy* (228) accesses a proxy component in the integration environment to which it maintains a communication channel at all times. Inbound communication to the private environment is then enabled through this channel. The *application component proxy* (228) may also be used to integrate message queues for asynchronous communication in a similar manner to the *message mover* (225).

Data access: shared data is either handled by storage offerings provided by the integration provider or by *restricted data access components* (222). Storage offerings of the integration provider are either accessed from inside the integration environment or from the *data access components* (188) deployed in the private environments. If data shall be stored in the private environments but shall be made accessible from the integration environments, *restricted data access components* (222) may be used to alter exposed data according to access privileges. *Compliant data replication* (231) can be used alternatively, if data in the private environment and the integration environment shall be kept in sync.

Related Patterns
- *Hybrid processing* (308) and *hybrid backend* (317): these two patterns describe in more detail how processing functionality and data-intensive processing functionality can be distributed among the different environments of a hybrid cloud. These concepts can be used in scope of the *integration provider* pattern as well.
- *Hybrid data* (311): if only data shall be shared between the integrated environments, the *hybrid data* pattern may be considered.
- *Restricted data access component* (222): if data shall not be moved to the integration provider, but shall still be made accessible to other parties, this pattern can be used. It describes how access to some data elements may be restricted and how data can be obfuscated.
- *Application component proxy* (228): this pattern describes how a component that is hosted in a restricted, possibly private environment can be made accessible in a different environment. It may, therefore, be used to make internal application components accessible in the integration provider environment. It covers both synchronous and asynchronous communication approaches mentioned above to interact with application components.
- *Message mover* (225): if application components access message queues provided by a *message-oriented middleware* (136) in both the internal environment and the environment of the integration provider, the application implementation can be complicated and could become tightly coupled to the used integration provider. The message mover pattern describes how the physical location of a message queue can be hidden from a message sender and receiver, thus, making the application more *loosely coupled* (156).

- *Compliant data replication* (231): this pattern describes how data may be replicated between different environments while alternating data transparently to adhere laws, corporate regulations, as well as different levels of security, privacy, and trust.

Known Uses

In many cases, cloud providers offer functionality to connect a private environment with their cloud in a secure manner. There is Amazon's Virtual Private Cloud (VPC) [55] a separated virtual part of the Amazon cloud that is not publicly accessible. It can be integrated with a private environment using a virtual private network (VPN) as described in the *virtual networking* (132) pattern. A similar feature is available in Microsoft Windows Azure's virtual networking offering. When connected to different *private clouds* (66) and hosting environments, for example, from different branch offices, these services may be used to serve as an integration provider.

Cloud Application Management Patterns

5

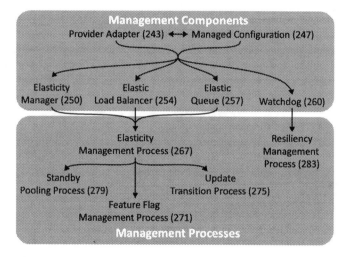

Fig. 5.1 Map of the cloud application management patterns

This chapter covers architectural patterns that describe how cloud applications as described in Chap. 4, can be managed automatically by separate components (Fig. 5.1). These management components (Sect. 5.2) handle the automated management of cloud-native applications regarding dynamic elasticity, resiliency, updates etc. Due to the *pay-per-use* property of cloud applications covered in Sect. 1.1, scaling tasks should be automated, because the number of provisioned IT resources, i.e., the number of provisioned virtual servers, the size of booked storage or the number of application component instances directly affects the runtime costs of an application. Furthermore, *environment-based availability* (98) assurances, where individual cloud resources can fail at any time, or a *node-based availability* (95) that

All figures published with kind permission of © The Authors 2014. See list of figures.

C. Fehling et al., *Cloud Computing Patterns*,
DOI 10.1007/978-3-7091-1568-8_5, © Springer-Verlag Wien 2014

does not meet requirements of an application, as well as network partitions, may create the need to monitor applications and automatically react to resource failures.

The management processes (Sect. 5.3) executed by management components are described as separate patterns. They address tasks such as elasticity management, version updates, or failure resiliency. In the overview, we introduce the covered patterns and show how the management components are integrated into a cloud native application.

5.1   Overview of Application Management Patterns

Management components (Sect. 5.2) form the execution environment for management processes (Sect. 5.3). Therefore, they describe the architectural components that enable the automated execution of management processes handling application components and system resources. *Provider adapters* (243) are used to encapsulate provider interfaces. The encapsulated functionality may then be accessed from other non-provider-specific management components. Especially, encapsulation can be used to trigger other management processes when a certain provider function is called, for example, if a failure in a provider-supplied function has to be addressed. Most management patterns handle a large set of application components and, often, a coordinated behavior of these components is required. *Managed configurations* (247) centrally control the behavior of application component instances and distributed management components in a unified fashion. An *elasticity manager* (250) enables automated horizontal scalability based on resource utilization. To manage elasticity and distribute workload across horizontally scaled instances based on the number of handled requests the *elastic load balancer* (254) is needed. When communicating asynchronously via queues, similar behavior can be realized via an *elastic queue* (257) that dynamically adjusts the number of message processing components depending on the number of pending requests. If one of these elasticity management components is used, it can implement the *elasticity management process* (267) describing the basic process to be followed when scaling and application up or down. This process can then be extended further. A *standby pooling process* (279) optimizes the provisioning and decommissioning of resources by considering the timeframe for which resources have been paid for prior to decommissioning them. Additionally, it can be used to keep component instances on standby to speed up provisioning for critical application components. If new resources still cannot be obtained fast enough from the cloud provider during a workload increase, the *feature flag management process* (271) enables an application to degrade gracefully by replacing or disabling less important functionality. Finally, when new application component versions have been developed, an *update transition process* (275) can be used to seamlessly switch between different versions with minimal or no downtime of the application component.

Similar to the elasticity considerations, availability of applications is typically a very important topic. Depending on the requirements of an application or platform, the *node-based availability* (95) assured by *elastic infrastructures* (87) or *elastic*

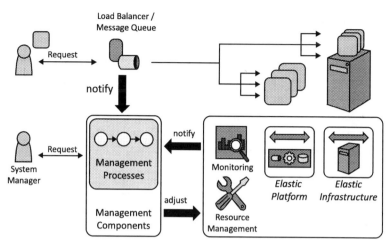

Fig. 5.2 Abstract management architecture

platforms (91) may be insufficient. In case of *environment-based availability* (98) no assurance is made regarding the availability of individual hosted IT resources. Under these conditions, a *watchdog* (260) monitors applications and platforms and starts new IT resources or application components in case of failures. It does so by following a *resiliency management process* (283) to cope with failures.

The management components and management processes presented in this chapter are commonly integrated into the cloud application and cloud environment as depicted in Fig. 5.2. An *elastic platform* (91) or an *elastic infrastructure* (87) as seen on the lower right side of the figure provides a runtime environment to application components. Both of these patterns provide monitoring and resource management functionality with which the management components and management processes interact. Application components are either hosted directly in the environment provided by the *elastic platform* or on virtual servers deployed on the *elastic infrastructure*. Requests sent to these components from application users or other application components usually traverse a load balancer or a message queue to distribute the workload among multiple component instances. The management components described in Sect. 5.2 interact with these load balancing components and react to certain conditions, for example, an increased number of queued messages. Similar notifications and runtime information about the application are also provided to management components by the monitoring interface of the *elastic infrastructure* or the *elastic platform*. Section 5.3 describes the behavior of management components in the covered management process patterns.

5.2   Management Components

In order to manage cloud applications automatically, management functionality has to be integrated with components providing application functionality. Due to their nature, this management functionality is often tightly coupled with the interfaces offered by cloud providers, i.e., they depend on the provider-specific operations and protocols used. To avoid a tight-coupling of the overall application with the provider, management functionality should be encapsulated into separate components. This can be used to control dependencies of applications on interfaces of a specific vendor and also simplifies the reuse of management functionality in multiple applications hosted at the same cloud provider. Some of the management components may be provider-supplied and then have to be integrated with custom applications.

5.2.1 Provider Adapter

> Provider interfaces are encapsulated and mapped to unified interfaces used in applications to separate concerns of interactions with the provider from application functionality.

 How can the dependencies of an application component on a provider-specific interface be managed?

Context

Cloud providers offer many interfaces that can be used in application components of a *distributed application* (160). *Elastic infrastructures* (87) and *elastic platforms* (91) offer interfaces through which resources may be provisioned, decommissioned, and monitored. Cloud offerings (see Chap. 3) providing computation, storage, and communication functionality each offer individual interfaces with specific operations, authentication mechanisms, communication protocols etc. If a component directly interacts with these interfaces, its implementation becomes strongly interleaved with the specific functions offered and the protocols used. This may complicate future adjustments to an application components implementation if a different provider shall be used or a provider interface changes. Therefore, the concerns to interact with a provider shall be separated from application functionality to identify necessary adjustments easier if a provider interface changes.

Solution

A *provider adapter* wraps the provider interfaces into an abstract interface to be used within the scope of the *distributed application* (160). In doing so, the *provider adapter* encapsulates all provider-specific implementations required for authentication, data formatting etc. *Provider adapters* may consolidate multiple different provider interfaces. The provider adapter pattern, thus, ensures *separation of concerns* between application components accessing provider functionality and application components providing application functionality. Therefore, if a provider interface changes or a provider shall be exchanged, the part of the distributed application to be adjusted may be identified easier. Of course, this separation of concerns does not reduce the complexity of this adjustment for provider exchange or leads to a general exchangeability of cloud providers. For

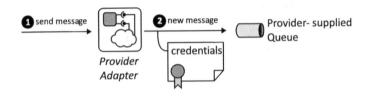

Fig. 5.3 Exemplary provider adapter component accessed synchronously

this purpose, the interfaces of providers would have to be standardized. Only if a customer decides to use a small number of cloud providers and develops *provider adapters* that are standardized internally to his or her company, provider interchangeability may be realized to a certain degree, i.e., within one company. Similarly, a *provider adapter* may be used by a company to control the subset of the provider-supplied functionality that may be used by developers to create custom applications. Such restrictions may also reduce necessary changes to application code if a provider is changed. A *provider adapter* may, therefore, also be used to enforce that developers may only use certain provider functionality to reduce or control the chance of vendor lock-ins.

Result

The *provider adapter* accesses interfaces of processing offerings, communication offerings, and storage offerings and maps provided functions to its own interface. The interface of the *provider adapter* can then be accessed by other application components. Especially, protocols, authentication, and communication styles (synchronous or asynchronous) may differ between the provider interfaces and the interfaces offered by the *provider adapter*. The provider adapter, therefore, enables *loose coupling* (156) between the provider interface and the application's implementation. In Fig. 5.3, an exemplary *provider adapter* is depicted encapsulating the access to a provider-supplied message queue offered by a *message-oriented middleware* (136). Other application components may interact with the provider adapter component synchronously even though the messaging offered by the cloud provider is asynchronous. When supporting different communication styles in this way, the provider adapter faces challenges regarding timeouts of synchronous interactions that may be significantly smaller than the asynchronous communication via messaging actually requires.

The exemplary *provider adapter* depicted in Fig. 5.4 encapsulates the provisioning functionality of an *elastic infrastructure* (87) and an *elastic platform* (91). Even though these accesses are synchronous, other application components may send messages to the *provider adapter* in order to provision new application components. Depending on the environment where the requested application component is hosted, the provider adapter automatically forwards the provisioning request to the *elastic infrastructure* (87) or the *elastic platform* (91).

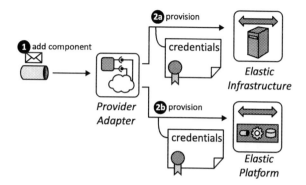

Fig. 5.4 Exemplary provider adapter component accessed asynchronously

The encapsulation of provider interface specifics makes the effort for the replacement of cloud offerings easier to determine, because the amount of implementation code to be adjusted can be easier identified. In case a cloud offering shall be replaced, the adapter implementation needs to be adjusted to the different interface provided by the new cloud offering. This adjustment may still be difficult and complex, but through the encapsulation of provider-specific interfaces, the amount of application code that has to be revised can be controlled more efficiently. The use of *provider adapters*, therefore, makes the effort to switch cloud providers more predictable and manageable. However, the actual adjustments may still be hard to realize, especially, if providers use different communication styles.

Variations

A *provider adapter* can be realized in form of a programming library to be used in the implementation of another application component. This reduces the need for serialization and deserialization of requests as the *provider adapter* functionality is directly available in the other application components code.

Related Patterns
- *Data access component* (188): if provider interfaces of storage offerings are accessed, this pattern describes how to implement a *provider adapter* and, furthermore, how to change data consistency behavior in the adapter implementation.
- *Multi-component image* (206): similar to the above mentioned variation the provider adapter may be deployed close to the application components accessing it, for example, on the same virtual server. This summarization of application component implementations is described by the multi-component image.

Known Uses

In object-oriented applications, there is a similar concept to encapsulate interface interaction functionality in special components. Gamma et al. described this in the *adapter pattern* and *façade pattern* [2]. Buschmann et al. [14] describe a *proxy* pattern used in distributed applications that is also used to encapsulate interfaces. Apache Libcloud [61] is a programming library to abstract from the differences and idiosyncrasies of multiple cloud providers. If application developers use this interface in their applications, the used cloud provider remains interchangeable to a certain degree as the concrete behavior of accessed functions may still differ. Deltacloud [60] or Jclouds [62] adapts to different cloud providers in a similar fashion and provides a common REST [72, 161] interface.

Further Reading: *provider adapters* only make the involvement of a cloud application with provider interfaces manageable. For a desirable exchangeability of cloud providers, their interfaces would have to be standardized. The *provider adapter* pattern can only be used for this purpose company-internally, if the company decides to use a small number of cloud providers and standardizes the interface of *provider adapters* used to access these providers. To solve the issue of interchangeability in general, industry standardization efforts have been initialized, for example:

OASIS: Topology and Orchestration Specification for Cloud Applications (TOSCA) [186]

DMTF: Cloud Infrastructure Management Interface (CIMI) [187]

IEEE: Cloud Profiles Working Group (CPWG) [188]

IEEE: Intercloud Working Group (ICWG) [189]

5.2.2 Managed Configuration

Scaled-out application components should use a centrally stored configuration to provide a unified behavior that can be adjusted simultaneously.

 How can the configuration of scaled out application component instances be controlled in a coordinated fashion?

Context

Application components of a *distributed application* (160) are likely to have particular configuration parameters. Exemplary configuration parameters are colors, logos and language of *user interface components* (175), data storage locations used by *processing components* (180), or the location of credentials used by *data access components* (188) to interact with storage offerings. Storing this configuration information together with the application component implementation can be unpractical as it results in more overhead in case of configuration changes as each instance of the application component must be updated separately. Whenever a change occurs, the corresponding machine image stored in an *elastic infrastructure* (87) or the component image stored in an *elastic platform* (91) would have to be adjusted, so that newly provisioned application component instances use the new configuration. Alternatively, the configuration could be adjusted after a component has been provisioned and then has to be maintained during the runtime as well. Instead of configuring each running instance and adjusting provisioning images in case of configuration changes, the configuration of application component instances should be managed in a more coordinated fashion. This is especially needed if a large number of application component instances have to be configured or if the configuration changes very frequently.

Solution

As all application component instances of the same type expect the same configuration specification, this configuration is stored in a central storage offering, commonly, a *relational database* (115), *key-value storage* (119), or *blob storage* (112) from where it is accessed by all running component instances. Application

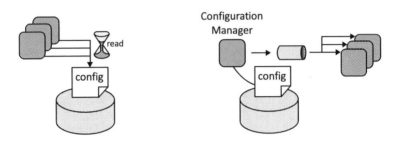

Fig. 5.5 Polling (*left*) and pushing (*right*) of managed configurations

component instances can obtain the configuration following two approaches –
polling and *pushing*. Component instances poll the storage offering by accessing
it periodically to check for configurations and configuration changes as depicted
in the left side of Fig. 5.5. Pushing means that the configuration is send to the
application component instances when they are provisioned or the configuration
changes. This is commonly done asynchronously through the use of pub-sub
channels provided *by a message-oriented middleware* (136). Pub-sub channels
are also described as a pattern by Hohpe and Woolf [1].

Result

As the component instances access externally stored configuration, component
images handled by *elastic infrastructures* and *elastic platforms* do not have to be
adjusted if the configuration changes and the configuration of running application
components is easier to adjust. The design decision whether to push or to pull the
configuration from the central storage offerings is mainly influenced by the reactiveness required during configuration changes. If changes have to be reflected
quickly, application components would have to pull configuration often. This could
result in a larger load on the storage offering. Especially, if the configuration
changes seldom, this approach may be inefficient. In this case, pushing configuration changes to the application component instances may be a better solution.

Related Patterns
- *Blob storage* (112), *relational database* (115), and *key-value storage* (119):
  these storage offerings can be used to handle pulled configurations centrally. If
  a reactive and coordinated adjustment of component behavior is required, the
  storage offering should ensure *strict consistency* (123) to ensure that all application components can retrieve the new configuration at a distinct point in time. If
  the storage offering is *eventually consistent* (126), application component
  instances might be provided with different configuration versions even if they
  query the storage simultaneously.

- *Message-oriented middleware* (136): configurations may be pushed to application components using a message queue provided by a *message-oriented middleware* (136). Message queues are used to deliver messages to one receiver. In scope of configuration updates, messages, however, have to be received by a multitude of application components in many use cases. In scope of this delivery behavior a pub-sub channel also provided by a *message-oriented middleware* should be used instead.

Known Uses

Chef [190] provides centralized configuration management that pushes information to managed systems or allows a client to pull it. Puppet [191] follows a similar approach to manage configuration files centrally. Amazon's best practices [93, 154] motivate the use of a centralized configuration that is pulled from virtual servers during startup.

5.2.3 Elasticity Manager

The utilization of IT resources on which an elastically scaled-out application is hosted, for example, virtual servers is used to determine the number of required application component instances.

 How can the number of required application component instances be determined based on the utilization of hosting IT resources?

Context

Application components of a *distributed application* (160) shall be scaled-out automatically. They are, therefore, instantiated multiple times to exploit the distributed nature of a cloud environment better by leveraging the capabilities of multiple cloud resources. The instances of applications components shall be provisioned and decommissioned automatically based on the current workload experienced by the application. This is, especially, effective if the application experiences *periodic workload* (29), *unpredictable workload* (36), or *continuously changing workload* (40). It enables the application to benefit from the pay-per-use pricing models of the *IaaS* (45) and *PaaS* (49) cloud service models, because the number of deployed component instances directly affects the running cost of the application. The applications considered here, therefore, use an *elastic infrastructure* (87) or an *elastic platform* (91) as runtime environment, respectively. Through such automation scaling, the number of used resources can be aligned to changing workload dynamically and quickly.

Solution

The utilization of cloud resources on which application component instances are deployed is monitored by an *elasticity manager*. In many cases, this information is the utilization of a virtual server on which an application component is hosted. This information is used to determine the number of required instances.

Result

As depicted in Fig. 5.6, users, other components or applications send requests to application components managed by the *elasticity manager*. The workload

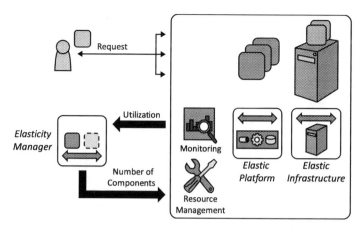

Fig. 5.6 Elasticity manager interacting with an elastic platform or elastic infrastructure

resulting from these accesses is determined by monitoring the utilization of the hosting environment provided by the *elastic infrastructure* or *elastic platform*. Utilization is, often, measured on the hardware level, for example, in form of load on central processing units (CPU), memory usage, network I/O etc. The monitored utilization information is then extracted from the *elastic infrastructure*, *elastic platform*, or from the component itself and passed to the *elasticity manager*. This manager uses the utilization information to determine the number of required component instances and adjusts it using provisioning and decommissioning functionality of the *elastic infrastructure* (87) or *elastic platform* (91) to ensure resource utilization within defined thresholds.

If an *elastic infrastructure* is used server images containing the application components, are maintained in the image storage of the *elastic infrastructure* to speed up provisioning. The distribution of application components among server images is a critical design decision in this scope since it affects the granularity by which the application can be scaled out. More information about this issue is given by the *multi-component image* (206) pattern.

In case of an *elastic platform*, the notion about virtual servers and their utilization is commonly hidden from the customer. The *elasticity manager*, therefore, requires the variation of the *elastic platform*, where virtual servers are still visible to customers, but the operating systems and middleware is completely maintained by the provider.

Related Patterns

- *Elastic load balancer* (254) and *elastic queue* (257): the *elasticity manager* may be substituted by the *elastic load balancer* (254) or *elastic queue* (257) pattern if the utilization of hosting IT resources cannot be used to make scaling decisions. This is especially the case, in an *elastic platform* where this information may not provided to customers. Even if the utilization of hosting IT resources is made available, the use of *elastic load balancers* and *elastic queues* may still enable a more sophisticated scaling behavior for two reasons. First, they can monitor the utilization of individual application components independent on their actual distribution among IT resources. This is especially helpful if multiple application components share the same virtual server. Second, *elastic queues* can be used to actively influence the point in time when workload is processed. Therefore, they can respect environmental factors, such as fluctuating resource prices in scaling decisions.

- *Provider adapter* (243): as an *elasticity manager* interacts with a cloud provider interface, it may become dependent on that interface. To control this and to enable an *elasticity manager* to be easier reusable, the functionality accessing the provider interface may be encapsulated in a *provider adapter* (243) to assure separation of concerns between the functionality of the *elasticity manager* handling elastic scaling and functionality accessing the provider interface.
- *Stateless component* (171): the scaled-out application component should ideally rely on external state information, either passed to it with every request or retrieved from a storage offering (see Sect. 3.5 on Page 109). Implementation of the *stateless component* pattern, therefore, simplifies the provisioning and decommissioning of component instances, as no data handled by the component has to be extracted prior to decommissioning or inserted during the provisioning.
- *Transaction-based processor* (201) and *timeout-based message processor* (204): when a component instance is removed from the application while it is processing a message or accesses data in a storage offering, the *elasticity manager* has to coordinate decommissioning to ensure that no data is lost. This can be simplified if application components process messages or data in transactions or acknowledge the successful processing to a *message-oriented middleware* (136), as described by the *transaction-based processor* pattern and *timeout-based processor* pattern, respectively. A *message-oriented middleware* needs to support this kind of interaction with message processing components, as described by the *transaction-based delivery* (146) pattern and *timeout-based delivery* (149) pattern.

Known Uses

Many providers, such as RightScale [192] and Scalr [193], offer external monitoring of virtual servers deployed in Amazon EC2 [18] to enable elastic scaling. Amazon also has its own service for this purpose, called Amazon Auto Scaling [194]. In Windows Azure, there is the Application Autoscaling Block [195] that enables developers to scale applications based on workload.

The scaling functionality of many cloud providers has in common that it may be configured by rules. Therefore, developers can, for example, specify that two more application component instances shall be started once an average utilization of instances exceeds a defined threshold. In this rule-based scaling environments, the implementation of an *elasticity manager* as a custom management component may, however, still be feasible to supervise the rule-based scaling and change the rules according to additional heuristics from past experiences or based on user input etc.

5.2.4 Elastic Load Balancer

> The number of synchronous accesses to an elastically scaled-out application is used to determine the number of required application component instances.

 How can the number of required application component instances be determined based on monitored synchronous accesses?

Context

Application components of a *distributed application* (160) shall be scaled out automatically. They are, therefore, instantiated multiple times to handle the currently experienced workload. A tight alignment of the provisioned component instances to this workload is especially effective if the application experiences *periodic workload* (29), *unpredictable workload* (36), or *continuously changing workload* (40). The required flexibly provisioning of application components is enabled by an *elastic infrastructure* (87) or *elastic platform* (91). Moreover, the pay-per-use pricing models of these environments are exploited best if cloud resources are provisioned and decommissioned timely while manual scaling approaches are less suitable. Therefore, requests sent to an application shall be used as an indicator for the currently experienced workload from which the required number of components instances shall be deducted.

Solution

An *elastic load balancer* is a management component that is provided with information from a load balancer that spreads out synchronous requests from human users or other application components among multiple component instances. Based on the number of distributed requests and possibly other utilization information, the required number of required component instances is determined. When determined, the necessary provisioning or decommissioning operations to reflect this number in the application are executed. The *elastic load balancer* invokes these operations provided by the interface of the *elastic infrastructure* or the *elastic platform*.

Result

As seen in Fig. 5.7, a load balancer distributes requests of human users and other application components among a set of application component instances hosted on

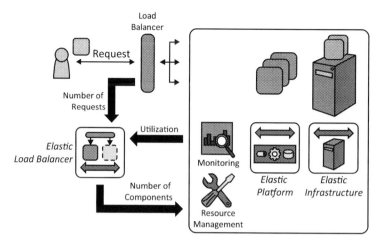

Fig. 5.7 Elastic load balancer interacting with an elastic platform or elastic infrastructure

an *elastic platform* (91) or an *elastic infrastructure* (87). Information about the number of these requests and utilization information of the individual component instances are provided to the *elastic load balancer* management component. This component uses the monitored information and employs heuristics about the capabilities of application component instances, for example, how many concurrent requests one component instance can handle to determine the number of required instances. These heuristics are a crucial design parameter, since they significantly affect how efficient the application is scaled. Heuristics should, therefore, also be monitored, evaluated, and possibly adjusted during runtime. The *elastic load balancer* can, for example, observe execution times required by the application components to handle requests. Information about the time it takes to provision new applications instances is also necessary to make efficient scaling decisions. Once the required component instance numbers have been determined, they are reflected by initiating the corresponding provision operations and decommission operations.

Further Reading: capacity planning techniques to estimate the number of requests that an application component can handle are described in more detail by Menasce and Almeida [196]. Allspaw [23] also incorporates how heuristics about user behavior, i.e., a higher demand during Christmas, may be incorporated in scaling decisions.

Related Patterns

The *elastic load balancer* is used for requests that are synchronous and, thus, are handled immediately. If the application, or some of the application components, handle asynchronous requests, delaying requests to actively influence the workload may be more effective than processing them immediately. This is especially the case in less elastic environments, i.e., environments supporting a smaller maximum number of application component instances or if the resource costs of the *elastic infrastructure* differ over time. Such asynchronous scenarios in which workload can be delayed are handled more effectively using an *elastic queue* (257). The *batch processing component* (185) also describes this delay of workload. The *elastic load balancer* is, furthermore, likely to be combined with the following patterns:

- *Stateless component* (171): the *elastic load balancer* is most efficient if the scaled out application components are implemented as *stateless components*. This significantly eases their addition and removal from the application during the provisioning and decommissioning operations.
- *Watchdog* (260): if application component instances do not guarantee the required availability, they can be monitored by a *watchdog* to be replaced in case of failures. During this replacement, the *watchdog* has to interact with the *elastic load balancer* to inform this component about the newly provisioned application component instances that shall be assigned requests to. Similarly, components that have failed should not be assigned any workload.
- *Provider adapter* (243): the functionality provided by the *elastic load balancer* to handle elastic scaling may be similarly applicable to multiple cloud providers. In this case, a *provider adapter* (243) may be used to encapsulate the functionality accessing a provider interface from the rest of the *elastic load balancer* implementation making it easier to reuse.

Known Uses

Amazon offers an *elastic load balancer* for application components running on its *elastic infrastructure* (87), called Elastic Compute Cloud (EC2) [18], and its elastic platform, called Elastic Beanstalk [53]. In both cases, resources are scaled based on the number of accesses as well as the load of virtual servers on which application components are hosted. Customers may specify rules for Amazon's Auto Scaling [194], i.e., to describe how many component instances shall be deployed for a certain number of requests. Even though this means that a significant amount of functionality described by the *elastic load balancer* pattern is provided by Amazon, the customer should still monitor the application to adjust the heuristics that were considered during the creation of these scaling rules. Especially, to reflect heuristics about user behavior, rules should be adjusted periodically. In case of Windows Azure, a so called traffic manager distributes requests among application components [197]. This Traffic Manager and the application components called Web Roles provide interfaces through which and *elastic load balancer* implementation may obtain the information necessary to make scaling decisions.

5.2.5   Elastic Queue

The number of asynchronous accesses via messaging to an elastically scaled-out application is used to adjust the number of required application component instances.

 How can the number of required application component instances be adjusted based on monitored asynchronous accesses?

Context

A *distributed application* (160) is comprised of multiple application components that are deployed to an *elastic infrastructure* (87) or an *elastic platform* (91). To benefit from the dynamicity of these runtime environments, the number of application component instances shall be scaled-out and adjusted to the currently experienced workload. Especially, if a pay-per-use pricing model is used by the *elastic platform* or *elastic infrastructure*, the reactiveness of the scaling operations directly affects running costs of the application. In scope of workloads that require different number of resources frequently, manual scaling approaches are less optimal. This is the case for *periodic workload* (29), *unpredictable workload* (36), and *continuously changing workload* (40). Therefore, the required provisioning and decommissioning operations should be performed in an automated fashion. Another property of an application that poses an opportunity for scaling optimization is the handling of asynchronous requests. In this scope, additional optimization of the workload execution can be performed by delaying some of the requests to process them when it is most feasible as described by the *batch processing component* (185) pattern in greater detail. For example, such delayed processing can be advantageous, if resource costs fluctuate or the elasticity of the environment is limited, for example, in a small *private cloud* (66). In the former case, workload should be delayed until processing is beneficial due to cheap resource costs. In the latter case, non-business-critical or non-time-critical workload can be moved to times when resources of the small *private cloud* (66) are less utilized.

Solution

An *elastic queue* monitors queues provided by a *message-oriented middleware* (136) used to distribute asynchronous requests among multiple application components instances. It adjusts the number of application component instances handling these requests via provisioning and decommissioning operations. These operations are provided by the management interfaces of the *elastic infrastructure* (87) or *elastic platform* (91). The number of required component instances is determined from the number and type of messages contained in the monitored queue, utilization information of the scaled application component, and environmental information about the *elastic infrastructure* or *elastic platform*. If the application components are implemented as a *batch processing component*, the handling of messages may additionally be delayed to wait for optimal processing conditions.

Result

As depicted in Fig. 5.8, all requests to the scaled-out applications components are stored in a message queue. The application components retrieve messages from this queue for processing. Information is collected about the number of messages contained in this queue at a given time and passed to an *elastic queue* management component. The *elastic queue* may use defined thresholds regarding the number of queued messages to determine if more or fewer component instances are required. The *elastic queue* can, furthermore, respect environmental information, such as the overall utilization of the cloud or resource prices. For example, when the overall utilization is high, the *elastic queue* may be used to delay less important messages and to prioritize business-critical ones by reducing the number of handling application component instances respectively. Also, the less important messages can be delayed, if resources prices are too high to process them at acceptable costs. The importance of messages can be modeled as an attached state that is set by the application component initializing the request. For example, message could be characterized as "informational", "critical", "status event" etc. Numbers may also be used to indicate the importance of a message. For example, the Java Message Service (JMS) [145, 146] standardizes a *JMSPriority* field that may be used in every message to define priority values ranging from "0" – lowest priority – to "9" – highest priority. The *elastic queue* may be configured with thresholds for each message type to deduct provisioning and decommissioning of application component instances.

If an *elastic infrastructure* (87) is used, application components are hosted by virtual servers deployed on the *elastic infrastructure*. If an *elastic platform* (91) is used, scaling a deployed application component is possibly handled completely by the platform. In this case, the elastic queue only determines the times when processing components are active and inactive and not how many to provision. However, the automatic scaling functionality of platforms is commonly configured by customers. Therefore, even when relying on such provider-supplied scaling automation, a customer should monitor the application behavior and could use an elastic queue to adjust the configuration of the provider functionality.

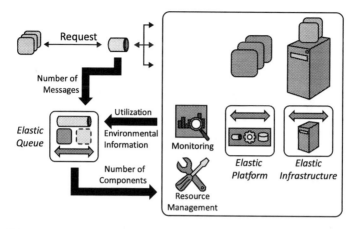

Fig. 5.8 Elastic queue interacting with an elastic platform or an elastic infrastructure

Related Patterns

- *Stateless component* (171): implementing the components handled by the *elastic queue* in a stateless fashion significantly eases the scaling tasks as components may be provisioned and decommissioned without considering data handled by them.
- *Watchdog* (260): if the used *elastic infrastructure* (87) or *elastic platform* (91) assures *environment-based availability* (98) or a low *node-based availability* (95), a *watchdog* can supervise to application components scaled by the *elastic queue* for failures to replace failing ones automatically. The *elastic queue* and the *watchdog* may even be summarized in one component.
- *Provider adapter* (243): as message queues are offered by different cloud providers, an implementation of the *elastic queue* pattern may be applicable for different providers. In this case, a *provider adapter* (243) may be used to separate the functionality of elastic scaling from functions accessing provider interfaces.

Known Uses

Amazon provides a messaging service, the Simple Queue Service (SQS) [38]. It may be monitored by Amazon's monitoring service, CloudWatch [198]. Especially, with respect to the size of the *elastic queue*, rules may be defined to provision or decommission application components hosted on virtual servers based on the number of messages present in the queue.

5.2.6   Watchdog

Applications cope with failures automatically by monitoring and replacing application component instances if the provider-assured availability is insufficient.

How can applications automatically detect failing application components and handle their replacement?

Context

Many *distributed applications* (160) deploy their application components on *elastic infrastructures* (87) and *elastic platforms* (91), which assure *environment-based availability* (98), thus, availability is assured for the environment itself, i.e., regarding the ability of the customer to provision new application components. If a provider assures *node-based availability* (95), i.e., the availability for each hosted application component instance the whole application may have to display a higher availability than the provider assures. Furthermore, if a *distributed application* is comprised of many application components it is dependent on the availability of all component instances. To enable high availability under such conditions, applications have to rely on redundant application component instances and the failure of these instances has to be detected and coped with automatically.

Solution

Individual application components rely on external state information by implementing the *stateless component* (171) pattern. Components are scaled out and multiple instances of them are deployed to redundant resources. In scope of an *elastic infrastructure* (87), these resources are usually virtual servers hosting application components. In case of *elastic platforms* (91), the application component itself is deployed multiple times to the same or different *elastic platforms* (91). Highly available communication between these components is assured, for example using a *message-oriented middleware* (136). Components are monitored by a *watchdog* component and replaced in case of failures.

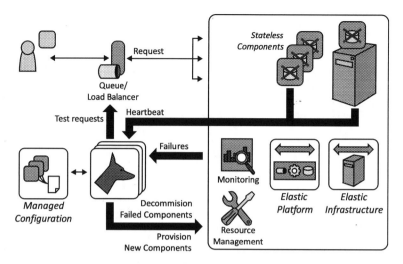

Fig. 5.9 Watchdog supervising application components hosted on IaaS and PaaS

Result

Multiple instances of application components are deployed. Either these application components are hosted on an *elastic infrastructure* (87) or an *elastic platform* (91). Application component instances are accessed synchronously through a load balancer or asynchronously using message queues provided by a *message-oriented middleware* (136) as shown in Fig. 5.9. This communication offering guarantees that messages are delivered successfully as described by the *at-least-once delivery* (144) pattern *and exactly-once delivery* (141) pattern. The application components are implemented as *stateless components* (171) and, therefore, rely on state information contained by the messages, the synchronous requests, or in storage offerings provided by the *elastic infrastructure* or *elastic platform*. Refer to Page 6 in Sect. 1.2 and the *stateless component* (171) pattern for a detailed discussion of our notion of state: *session state* – the state of interactions with a component and *application state* – the data handled by a component. Keeping state externally ensures that no data is lost in case of application component failures and that replacements may be provisioned more easily. The *watchdog* can monitor these components for failures using three information sources. First, application components can send periodic heartbeats to notify proper functioning. Second, the watchdog may rely on monitoring information provided by the *elastic platform* or *elastic infrastructure*, for example, regarding the network connectivity of components, their memory use etc. Third, the watchdog can send test requests and test messages to the application components and can compare the results of these requests to expected results. Hohpe and Woolf [1] describe patterns to supervise message processing: a *control bus* can provide dedicated message queues for heartbeat messages; *test messages* are used to ensure correct processing; a *wire tap* may be used to analyze messages processed by the application.

As the *watchdog* shall ensure high availability, it must be implemented highly available itself. One approach depicted in Fig. 5.9, is to use multiple instances of the watchdog supervising each other that are hosted on the *elastic platform* (91) or *elastic infrastructure* (87) just like other application components. To coordinate the operation of these *watchdogs* a *managed configuration* (247) to provide information to all *watchdog* instances about the number of the components to be monitored, the status of these components, performed provisioning and decommissioning operations etc.

Variations

The *watchdog* can randomly treat long running application component instances as failed and replace them. This approach can be chosen if application component implementations were never tested for long term execution. Since the transition between failed and replaced application component instances takes place seamlessly, there is no need to keep long running instances anymore.

Related Patterns

- *Elasticity manager* (250), *elastic load balancer* (254), and *elastic queue* (257): the *watchdog* supervises application component instances and replaces failing ones. If these components are also scaled out, thus, if multiple component instances are provisioned to handle workload, the *watchdog* has to be coordinated with elasticity patterns. If new instances are provisioned or decommissioned as workload changes, the watchdog needs to be notified to supervise more or less application component instances, respectively. Due to these interdependencies, elasticity management and watchdog functionality are often subsumed into one component.
- *Transaction-based processor* (201): if the *message-oriented middleware* (136) provides *transaction-based delivery* (146), messages can be read from a queue under transactional context. In this case, the processing component has to implement the *transaction-based processor* (201) pattern to assure that messages are not lost in case the component fails during message retrieval or message processing. The component, therefore, performs operations to read from the input queue, process the message within the scope of one transaction. This transaction assures that if a component instance fails during one of these operations, none of the operations are successful. Especially, the processed message is not deleted from the input queue, but can be retrieved again from an operation application component. The *transaction-based processor* (201) pattern also describes this style of interaction with storage offerings to assure that data is retrieved and processed successfully. The *transaction-based processor* pattern also describes this style of interaction with storage offerings. It may, therefore, be implemented by the application components if state information is

kept in storage offerings. This assures that data processed by the application is not lost if components fail.

- *Timeout-based message processor* (204): as an alternative to the *transaction-based processor* (201) pattern, application components can implement the *timeout-based message processor* (204) pattern. Thus, they send an acknowledgement to the input queue that they have successfully retrieved and processed a message. This requires that the *message-oriented middleware* (136) provides *timeout-based delivery* (149). If the acknowledgement is not received by the message queue in a specified time frame, the message is put back on the queue to be processed by a different application component instance. Following this approach, late receives of acknowledgement messages can result in duplicate messages, which can be detected by an *idempotent processor* (197).

- *Idempotent processor* (197): if the messaging system used by a *watchdog* displays *at-least-once delivery* (144) behavior, the application components supervised by the watchdog can be implemented as *idempotent processors* (197) to cope with message duplicates. If application components exchange data using a storage offering, the *idempotent processor* may also be useful to deal with data inconsistencies, if the storage offering displays *eventual consistency* (126).

Known Uses

Companies such as RightScale [192] and Scalr [193] implemented *watchdog* functionality on top of Amazon EC2 [18], but similar functionality is also made available by Amazon itself, called Amazon CloudWatch [198]. Application developers may have to implement some application-level failure detection in addition to these provider-supplied services. The *watchdog* pattern is also described by Douglass [199] and Hanmer [4]. How the redundancy used by this pattern affects the overall availability of a so-called *hot pool* of monitored processes is described by Leymann and Roller [76].

5.3   Management Processes

The following management process patterns describe how distributed and componentized cloud applications may address runtime challenges, such as elasticity and failure handling in an automated fashion. The automation of management tasks is required to increase the beneficial effects of some cloud properties discussed in Sect. 1.1 on Page 3: *elasticity* – resources may be provisioned and decommissioned quickly and on-demand; *pay-per-use* – only the actually used resources result in costs for the cloud customer; and *homogenization* – the (re)use of available cloud offerings and infrastructure platforms homogenizes the environment in which cloud applications are hosted. This homogenization reduces costs because of reduced complexity of the overall environment [7, 8] resulting from a reduced number of middleware, storage options etc. In this scope, the automation of cloud application management leads to a better exploitation of pay-per-use billing, because unused resources are freed without any human interaction. Thus, the number of resources is efficiently aligned with the experienced workload. Furthermore, homogenization of the environment should also be extended to the management of cloud resources to allow the reuse of management processes in different application contexts. If the cloud application shall itself be offered as a service, automation of management processes is fundamental to enable self-service interfaces. Only if the management processes of an application are executed automatically, customers may sign-up independently. If human tasks are required for this purpose, the application may be hindered to handle new users or changing demand of users efficiently.

These management process patterns describe the management tasks and challenges addressed by them. They specify an abstract management process expressed in the Business Process Model and Notation (BPMN) [159] language. These management processes provide a template for the implementation of an automated management process in a concrete application runtime environment. The following BPMN modeling elements are used in this section:

Start Events None Message Timer	The *none start event* indicates the start of a process without giving any specific condition or event. A *message start event* indicates that a message is received to start the process. A *timer* triggers a process periodically or at a given time.
Intermediate Events Message Timer	During the process execution, intermediate events are used to wait for a certain *message* to be received or to delay a process until a *timer* runs out.
Exclusive Event-based Gateway	This instantiating *exclusive event-based gateway* is used to connect multiple intermediate events. We use it to start a process as soon as one of these events is observed.

(continued)

End Event

The *empty end event* indicates when the process ends. When all active sequence flows reach this state, the process is completed and, thus, no longer active.

Activity

A process contains multiple *activities* that handle the management tasks. *Multiple instances* of activities may be executed to handle the same tasks multiple times in parallel.

Sequence Flow

Activities are interconnected using *sequence flow* arrows. When an activity is completed the sequence flow points to activities to be executed or the gateways to be evaluated next.

Sub-process

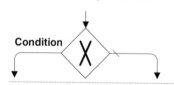

A *sub-process* is an activity whose internals are modeled using other activities, events etc. Especially, sub-processes may have events attached to its boundary that stop the sub-processes if observed.

Collapsed Sub-process

A *collapsed sub-process* hides the internals of a more complex activity implementation. We use it in diagrams to indicate that an activity has to be refined additionally to a usage scenario.

Exclusive Gateway: Decision

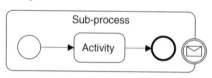

Only one of the sequence flows leaving an *exclusive gateway* becomes active based on associated *conditions*. A slash marker indicates the *default* sequence flow to follow, if none of the other conditions is true.

Exclusive Gateway: Merge

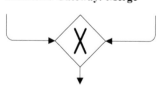

One of the sequence flows entering the *exclusive merge* must be active for the leaving sequence flow to be triggered. We always use this element in combination with an *exclusive decision*.

(continued)

Parallel Gateway: Fork 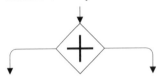	When the sequence flow entering a *parallel fork* becomes active, all outgoing sequence flows are triggered. Unlike the *exclusive gateway*, there are no conditions.
Parallel Gateway: Join 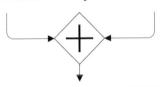	All of the sequence flows entering a *parallel join* must be active for the outgoing sequence flow to be triggered. We always use this element in combination with a *parallel fork*.
Data Store 	Activities may write to *data stores* or read from them as indicated by the dotted arrows. We use this element for data generated by activities to be used by other activities (possibly across process boundaries).
Message Flow 	Activities may send and receive messages. In this case, they are connected with a message flow. An attached *message graphic* and *content* description is optional.
Pools and Lanes 	Participant	 	Lane	Lane		*Pools* are used to describe participants in a process. We used this element to model the components of the abstract management architecture introduced in Sect. 5.1. Activities executed by a participant are contained in *lanes*. Commonly, we only used one lane per participant in a process.
Description description]······	Descriptions can be annotated to arbitrary elements for further information.

5.3.1 Elasticity Management Process

Application component instances are added automatically to an application to cope with increasing workload. If the workload decreases application component instances are removed respectively.

How can the number of resources to which application components are scaled-out be adjusted efficiently to the currently experienced workload and anticipated future workload?

Context

A *distributed application* (160) is hosted on an *elastic infrastructure* (87) or *elastic platform* (91). This application uses *elasticity managers* (250), *elastic queues* (257), or *elastic load balancers* (254) to ensure an elastic scaling of application components for an efficient utilization of cloud resources. This is especially important if the cloud employs pay-per-use billing and the application experiences *periodic workload* (29), *unpredictable workload* (36), or *continuously changing workload* (40). To handle this task adequately, the current resource demand has to be obtained automatically from the application and has to be reflected in provisioning and decommissioning of cloud resources.

Solution

An *elasticity management process* analyzes the utilization of application component instances in intervals, when a system manager requests it, or if certain conditions are observed by the monitoring component. Based on this information, the current workload of the application is computed and reflected by adjusting the assigned resource numbers accordingly.

Result

The *elasticity management process* can be triggered by a condition observed by the monitoring component or periodically as depicted by the message event and timer event in Fig. 5.10, respectively. Alternatively, the message can also be issued by a human system administrator, for example, because he or she knows that a number of new employees will start using the application at a certain date. This alternative

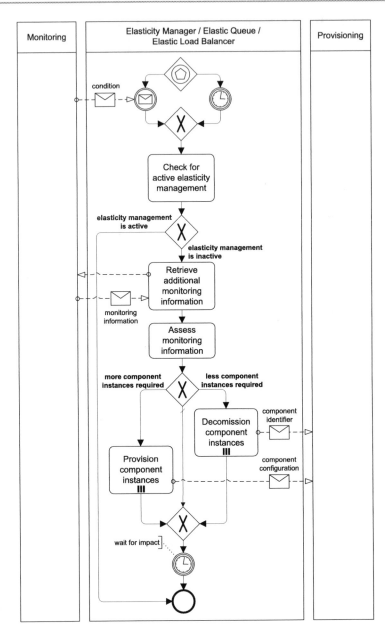

Fig. 5.10 Elasticity management flow

is omitted from the *elasticity management process* depicted in Fig. 5.10 for space reasons. As further alternatives, the process can be triggered by a message originating from the monitoring functionality implemented by the *elasticity manager*, *elastic load balancer*, or *elastic queue*. For example, the size of a queue may exceed a certain threshold triggering the *elasticity management process* from an *elastic queue* (257). After it has been triggered, the *elasticity management process* checks if elasticity management is already currently handled. If so, it terminates. This check assures that multiple events generated by the monitoring component are given enough time to be handled by the active *elasticity management processes*. After this check, additional information may be retrieved and the number of required component instances is computed. Afterwards, the provisioning or decommissioning of instances is initiated followed by a pause to give these instances time to start up or shut down, respectively.

The *elasticity management process* optimizes application component utilization and adjusts component instance numbers to correctly reflect the experienced workload. The first critical design decision in this scope is the time interval at which system utilization is evaluated in case of time-based triggers. If this interval is too large, the system may be underutilized or overloaded without notice. If the interval is too short, the system may not be given enough time to react to the resource number adjustments. The second critical design decision for this pattern is to ensure adequate reactions to the performed workload analysis. If too few application component instances are added when a workload increase is observed the performance of the application may still be insufficient. If too many resources are added at once, the application will not be utilized optimally. Both design decisions mainly depend on heuristics and prior experiences. When determining the time interval at which utilization is measured, it has to be considered how quickly utilization has changed in the past or the workload behavior may be compared to previously experienced workloads. Also, the time required to provision new resources has to be respected here. Historic information, such as user behavior during holidays may be used to adjust these variables as described by Allspaw [23].

Variations

Manual triggering of the *elasticity management process* may not only originate from cloud customer and their system administrators. Who is responsible for this task mainly depends on the employed *cloud service model*. In case of *IaaS* (45), the customer of the cloud likely performs this task. However, in case of *PaaS* (49) and *SaaS* (55), the *elasticity management process* may be hidden from the customer. In this case, the task instead may be performed by the cloud provider. The *elasticity management process* may also be offered by a provider different than the used cloud provider.

Autonomic computing described, for example, by Murch [200] also realizes functionality of an *elasticity management process*. It assumes the existence of an autonomic manager that takes care about an application's self-management, i.e., self-configuration to optimize behavior properties or in case certain failures occur. This autonomic manager may also handle elasticity. This can be completely outside of the application and may be invisible to the application itself.

Related Patterns

- *Elasticity manager* (250), *elastic queue* (257), and *elastic load balancer* (254): these three patterns form the basis for the *elasticity management process* that can be implemented by them.
- *Elastic infrastructure* (87) and *elastic platform* (91): these two cloud environments provide the required monitoring information used by the *elasticity management process* to determine scaling decisions.
- *Stateless component* (171): components managed by the *elasticity management process* should keep their state externally, for example, in storage offerings (see Sect. 3.5 on Page 109) as described by this pattern.

Known Uses

The *elasticity management process* has originally been introduced by us in [25]. Varia [93, 154] describes how to scale Amazon AWS Resources. Especially, the different events and conditions are covered when elasticity management should be executed. Hill et al. [201] evaluate the scaling capabilities of Windows Azure, for which ParaleapTechnologies [202] offers a scaling software as a Service. RightScale [192] and Scalr [193] offer a similar service for Amazon EC2 [18]. The concept to scale out applications automatically is, however, not only seen in cloud computing and has been used by the IT industry for quite some time. Self-adaptive autonomous systems perform a similar management task to adjust their size, structure, communication channels etc. to react to environmental conditions. They undergo a so-called MAPE loop [127] comprised of similar steps as the *elasticity management process* contains.

5.3.2   Feature Flag Management Process

> If the cloud cannot provide required resources in time, the features provided by application components are degraded gracefully to replace or disable unimportant ones in order to keep vital features operational.

 How can the performance of an application degrade gracefully, if the experienced workload increases but additional cloud resources are unavailable or take too long to provision?

Context

A *distributed application* (160) resides in an elastic cloud and experiences varying workload, i.e., *periodic workload* (29), *unpredictable workload* (36), or *continuously changing workload* (40). While the elasticity of clouds generally allows a tight alignment of resource numbers to the current workload experienced by the application, the time it takes to provision new resources remains as a limiting factor. If the workload increases too drastically, it may take too long to provision new cloud resources to handle it. Especially, since many cloud providers do not guarantee a specific provisioning time of new cloud resources or even for the availability of this function, cloud applications have to be able to cope with increasing demand if new resources do not become available.

Solution

Less important application functionality provided by application component instances is disabled or replaced with a less demanding implementation, if the cloud provider cannot fulfill current workload demands. When resources can eventually be provisioned again, the application components return to normal operation. While the *feature flag management process* degrades application functionality, the regular *elasticity management process* (267) is disabled to avoid unnecessary provisioning requests. Also, the utilization information on which *elasticity managers* (250), *elastic load balancers* (254), or *elastic queues* (257) base their decision to provision or decommission application component instances may be obfuscated. A degraded application component instance may seem less utilized as it executes less demanding replacement functionality.

Result

Less important functions (features) of the application degrade first if a shortage of resources is experienced. This shortage is detected in a *provider adapter* (243) encapsulating the provider's resource management interface, for example, when it receives an error from encapsulated provisioning interfaces. If this condition occurs, it triggers the *feature flag management process*, commonly executed by an *elasticity manager* (250), *elastic load balancer* (254), or *elastic queue* (257), as depicted in Fig. 5.11. After notification from the *provider adapter*, the *feature flag management process* degrades application functionality in a separate sub-process. This sub-process is immediately stopped if the provider adapter notifies that resources may be provisioned again. This is indicated by the boundary message event on the sub-process in Fig. 5.11. As mentioned above, during the degradation, the *feature flag management process* deactivates elasticity management. To degrade application component functionality, features are identified and their state, for example, "active", "limited", "inactive" may be specified via flags in the configuration of application components. This enables the *feature flag management process* to reduce or completely avoid load from these functions in case new resources cannot be provisioned at desired speed. After each degradation, the management process waits for an impact in and then checks the application performance. The performance check involves multiple requests to application components and the monitoring component, thus, it is depicted as a collapsed sub-process in Fig. 5.11.

The degradation is continued, i.e., going from "active" to "limited" to "inactive", until the performance is acceptable. Note that this does not always have to be the case, but the feature flag degradation of functionality can by design not be performed indefinitely.After the ability to provision new resources is re-obtained and notified by the *provider adapter*, application component instances are upgraded to their regular functionality and the regular *elasticity management process* (267) is reactivated.

As an example for a *feature flag management process*, consider the forum of a web site that may experience a significant workload increase. Therefore, the elasticity management requests the provisioning of new resources. Since these resources do not become available within an acceptable time-frame, the load resulting from the forum's search function shall be reduced. Therefore, instead of considering all entries in the forum during a search, only cached entries from earlier search queries are considered, thus, reducing the computing power required by the application component providing the search function. Other functionality, such as news tickers, tagging functions etc. may be turned off completely to reduce the overall load. A challenge arising in this scope is that the approach is only successful, if degraded application components share a common underlying infrastructure with vital application components. The distribution of application components among cloud resources, described in detail by the *distributed application* (160) pattern, is, therefore, a fundamental design issue.

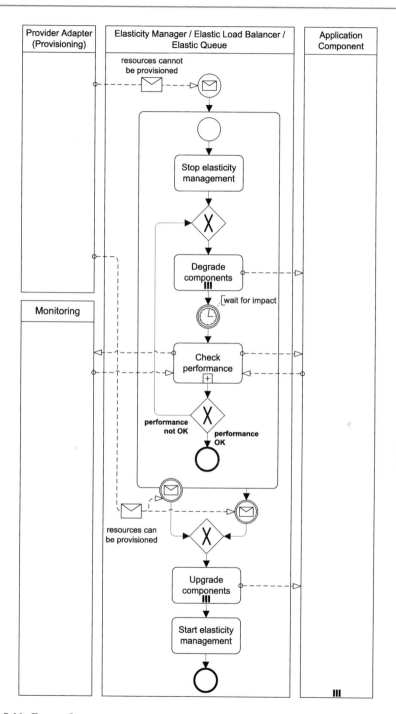

Fig. 5.11   Feature flags management process

Variations

In a similar fashion as functions are degraded, when resources are unavailable, certain functions may also only be enabled, when there are superfluous resources. These may, for example, be indexing tasks of *relational databases* (115) or other maintenance issues improving the application's performance during times of higher workloads. This approach is especially powerful in *private clouds* (66), where maximal resources numbers may be limited. In *public clouds* (62), varying prices may motivate this kind of application management.

Another variation of the *feature flag management process* may be used during the provisioning of application component instances to reduce provisioning times. If application components provide complex functionality they may need a long time to start up. Therefore, the functionality that is available and its capabilities may be reduced right after startup of an application component. During runtime more complex functions are then enabled. This approach to startup additional functionality after core functions are active is also referred to as *lazy loading*.

Related Patterns
- *Managed configuration* (247): to set application components' feature flags, their configuration may be stored centrally as described by the *managed configuration* pattern. From a central storage offering it may then be pulled from application components periodically or pushed to them using messages in case of configuration changes. In scope of feature flag management, pushing configuration changes may be more effective as resources provisioning shortages happen seldom and pushing ensures a timely reaction of application components if feature flags change.
- *Multi-component image* (206): the challenge to find an adequate distribution of vital and non-vital application components among cloud resources may be simplified if not all components sharing a cloud resource are active at all times. This concept is described by the *multi-component image* pattern.
- *Standby pooling process* (279): application component instances may be kept on standby to increase the speed of provisioning tasks and to optimize the utilization of pay-per-use billing slots.

Known Uses

Hull [203] describes how feature flags should be used in internet applications handling large amounts of users. The use of an *elastic infrastructure* (87) or *elastic platform* (91) is not considered explicitly by Hull, but Hoff [204] shows that even in such an elastic environment provisioning functionality may be unavailable or less responsive during times of high demand.

5.3.3   Update Transition Process

When a new application component version, middleware versions etc. become available, running application components are updated seamlessly.

 How can application components of a distributed application be updated seamlessly?

Context

During the runtime of a *distributed application* (160), new versions of used middleware, operating systems, or application components may become available. If the application has to ensure high availability, the elasticity of an underlying *elastic infrastructure* (87) or *elastic platform* (91) should be employed to enable a seamless switch from the old to the new version of application components. During this update process to a new version of a component, the transition time shall, therefore, be minimized to avoid a downtime of individual application components and of the overall application. Updating a running component may be too error-prone in this scope. Additionally, aside from updating running application components, it also has to be ensured that after a distinct point in time new component versions are provisioned in scope of automated elasticity and resiliency handling tasks.

Solution

The new component version is created and stored as a new virtual server image or component image in the *elastic infrastructure* (87) or *elastic platform* (91). Based on this image, a system administrator triggers the *update transition process* commonly implemented as part of an *elasticity manager* (250), *elastic load balancer* (254), or *elastic queue* (257). Additional application component instances of the new version are provisioned. These components are executed simultaneously with the application components of the old version. If necessary, load balancing is then switched to the component instances of the new version. If the application components access a queue, this step is unnecessary. Finally, the old application component instances are decommissioned. During this transition, problems may arise if components of different versions are incompatible, for example, because their interfaces and the used data structure or if their functionality differs too much.

These conditions may prevent both versions to be active simultaneously. Having provisioned two versions at the same time may still be beneficial as it leaves more flexibility. For example, if an error occurs during the switch having the old component version still running may provide a fallback option.

Result

Due to the ability of the *elastic infrastructure* (87) or *elastic platform* (91) to dynamically start additional application component instances, no running application component instances are updated by the *update transition process* depicted in Fig. 5.12. Instead, new versions are created and tested independently by system administrators and developers, or automatically via an automated testing procedure as part of a DevOps [205] scenario. Thus, new virtual server images are created for an *elastic infrastructure* and new component images are created for an *elastic platform*. Then, the *update transition process* is triggered. It starts by provisioning the new application components additionally to the old ones. Load balancing functionality may have to be adjusted after this as an *elastic load balancers* (254) actively assign requests to provisioned component instances and, thus, have to be reconfigured for the switch. *Elastic queues* (257) do not assign requests to components, as components retrieve messages from queues independently. After load balancers have been reconfigured, application components of the old version are decommissioned. This switchover guarantees a graceful transition between the new version and the old version of application components.

This graceful transition, however, requires the versions of application components to be compatible, i.e., regarding their data structure, data serialization format, interfaces, or interaction protocol. Additional challenges may arise due to incompatibilities of the application component versions. If different versions must not handle requests simultaneously, the transition must be executed instantly. Load balancers have to switch between components at a distinct point in time respectively. In case of an *elastic queue* (257), there are two approaches. First, application components can be decommissioned and then the new ones are provisioned. During the timeframe when no components are active, the message queue serves as a buffer for requests. Second, an immediate switch is realized by sharing a *managed configuration* (247) between all application component instances that is kept in a storage offering, commonly, a *relational database* (115), *key-value storage* (119), or *blob storage* (112). In this *managed configuration* (247), it is stated whether application components should start or stop processing requests. A *managed configuration* can, therefore, help to activate and deactivate large numbers of application components simultaneously without a significant impact of the time it takes the *elastic infrastructure* (87) or *elastic platform* (91) to provision or decommission them.

In either case, limitations of the runtime environment used may still result in a small downtime of the application during the immediate switchover between

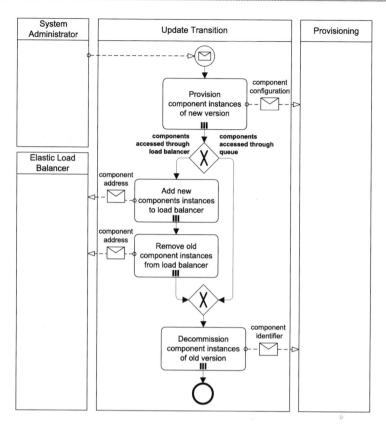

Fig. 5.12 Update transition process for application components accessed through load balancers and queues

application versions. Assurances made by providers should be considered when selecting one for hosting an application.

Variations

If the components are monitored by a *watchdog* (260) handling the *resiliency management process* (283), the watchdog hay have to be notified after the provisioning task and prior to the decommissioning tasks depicted in Fig. 5.12. This ensures that the *watchdog* starts monitoring provisioned component instances and stops monitoring if component instances are decommissioned. Otherwise, the *watchdog* could mistake these operations for failures.

Related Patterns

- *Stateless component* (171): the complexity of the transition process is reduced drastically, if no state information has to be extracted from old component versions and inserted into new component versions. Also, a possible data synchronization during the time when both versions are active is rendered unnecessary.
- *Loose coupling* (156): the dependencies between update components and other application components communicating with them should be kept to a minimum, as described by the *loose coupling* pattern. Especially, if the new component version uses a different data structure or serialization format, the necessary format transformations should be hidden from other communication partners.
- *Managed configuration* (247): as mentioned above, this pattern describes how a large number of application components may be configured from a central location.

Known Uses

An *update transition process* has to be implemented separately for every application to respect the individual order in which application components have to be updated. Windows Azure [52] supports transition functionality between a staging and a productive version of compute nodes.

5.3.4 Standby Pooling Process

> Application component instances should be kept on standby to increase provisioning speed and utilize billing time-slots efficiently.

 How can defined provisioning times for application component instances be ensured while utilizing pay-per-use resources in an optimal fashion?

Context

Even though application component instances may be provisioned and decommissioned dynamically, it usually requires some time to actually provision and decommission them. If a cloud application, however, experiences drastic and quick workload changes, these provisioning times may limit its capability to obtain the required resources quickly enough. Decommissioning of component instances immediately when no longer needed may also be ineffective, if cloud resources are charged for fixed time-slots. To reduce costs in this scope, provisioned component instances should be decommissioned when they are no longer needed with respect to the amount of time they have been paid for. For example, if a cloud provider charges for every hour that a resource is provisioned, decommissioning it after 30 min results in the same cost as if it was active for a full hour. Decommissioning the resource after 30 min may be inefficient, if it turns out to be required again after 45 min.

Solution

Instead of decommissioning application component instances instantly when they are unused, they are assigned to a standby list by the *standby pooling process*. They are decommissioned only when the time-slot they have been paid for has been utilized and they are still not needed. Additionally, the standby list may always contain a certain number of component instances to ensure timely provisioning.

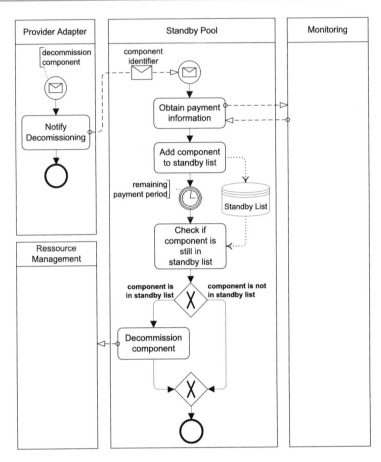

Fig. 5.13 Decommissioning executed by the standby pooling process and interacting components

Result

As depicted in Fig. 5.13, the *standby pooling process* uses the *provider adapter* (243) pattern. This pattern describes that provider interfaces should be wrapped by a separate component that can provide more abstract functionality to other application components. It also encapsulates functionality to deal with authentication and provider-specific access protocols. In scope of the *standby pooling process*, the *provider adapter* is accessed to initiate the provisioning and decommissioning of application component instances. If an *elastic infrastructure* (87) is used, this would be functionality to start and stop virtual servers. If an *elastic platform* (91) is used, application component instances are likely to be deployed directly. When accessed, the *provider adapter* triggers two standby pooling processes handing provisioning and decommissioning of application components depicted in Figs. 5.13 and 5.14. Whenever a component instance is decommissioned as shown in Fig. 5.13, the

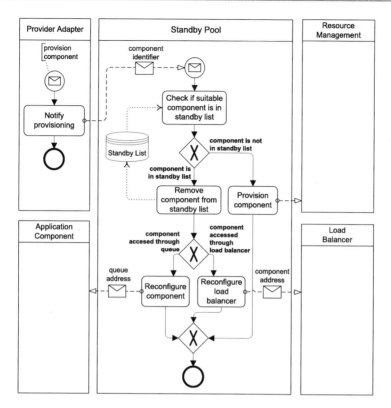

Fig. 5.14 Provisioning executed by the standby pooling process and interacting components

standby pooling process obtains payment information about this component and assigns it to a standby list. This standby list is a central data store and shared between the decommissioning process and provisioning process. The decommissioning process waits for the payment period to be over and then checks if the component instance has been reactivated in the meantime. If not, the instance is decommissioned. The reactivation of application component instances in the standby list is handled by the provisioning process seen in Fig. 5.14. When it is notified by the provider adapter that a new component instance is required, it first checks for a suitable component in the standby list. If no suitable component instance is on standby, a new instance is provisioned. If a suitable instance is in the standby list, the *standby pooling process* removes it from the list. In either case, the *standby pooling process* reconfigures a load balancer assigning requests to the component or configures the component to accesses a queue.

Component instances in the standby list are decommissioned at the last possible moment. Until then, they may be put to work again quickly. This reduces the number of provisioning and decommissioning operations and, therefore, results in a more efficient and economic use of cloud resources. Also, the application is less vulnerable, if the cloud is unable to provide new component instances in time if a certain number of component instances is kept on standby at all times.

Variations

In a *private cloud* (66), the *standby pooling process* may be beneficial, because provisioning times may still be too long for certain workload changes. However, in this environment the *standby pooling process* may have to use a different decommissioning strategy, because a time-slot-based pay-per-use billing model may not be in place.

Related Patterns

- *Multi-component image* (206): if an elastic infrastructure is used, the *standby pooling process* should be combined with multi component resources. Such virtual servers contain more than one application component implementation and can, thus, serve multiple purposes. This significantly increases the flexibility how virtual servers kept in the standby pool may be reused in the application.
- *Resiliency management process* (283): this pattern describes the process how component failures can be detected and how failing component instances can be replaced. The speed at which this replacement may be performed can be increased by the *standby pooling process* as the provisioning times of replacement component instances are avoided.
- *Feature flag management process* (271): if critical provisioning times cannot be met even though instances are kept on standby, the feature flag management process can help to degrade application functionality gracefully. This pattern also describes how lazy loading can be used to startup application component instances more quickly.

Known Uses

Almost all *public cloud* (62) providers are billing compute resources by the hour and are candidates for the efficient implementation of *standby pooling processes*. This can also be used for the mentioned reduction of provisioning times. If provisioning times are critical, Hoff [204] states that Amazon EC2 [18] instances should be kept on standby to assign them to applications more quickly.

5.3.5 Resiliency Management Process

Application components are checked for failures and replaced automatically without human intervention.

How can the overall availability of an application be ensured automatically even if individual application component instances fail?

Context

If an application depends on the availability of many individual cloud resources, the overall availability of the application is reduced drastically. This is due to the fact that the chance of resources failures is higher the more resources are used by an application. Therefore, it has to be ensured that individual resources may fail without affecting the availability of the overall application. To address failing application components, a *distributed application* (160) provisions application components to redundant cloud resources offered by an *elastic infrastructure* (87). In scope of an *elastic platform* (91), this redundant provisioning is often handled transparently to the customer. Nevertheless, the custom developed application component may malfunction in a way that the provider cannot detect. A *watchdog* (260) provides the infrastructure to monitor application components and react to failures. To handle this task, the component functionality must be verified and failing components must be replaced with newly provisioned components in a coordinated fashion.

Solution

Application components are scaled out among multiple cloud resources and are supervised by a *watchdog* (260) that executes a *resiliency management process*. This process is triggered by the monitoring functionality provided by an *elastic infrastructure* or an *elastic platform* or by the *watchdog* if it detects a component failure, for example, if an application component did not send heartbeat messages. Additionally, the *resiliency management process* periodically verifies application component health. If a failure is detected, the faulty application component instance is decommissioned and replaced by a newly provisioned instance.

Result

The monitoring functionality of providers can often be configured to generate notifications in case a certain condition is observed. For example, the monitoring functionality may check that a Web site offered by an application component is reachable. If such a preconfigured condition is observed, the monitoring generates a message that triggers the *resiliency management process* depicted in Fig. 5.15. Alternatively, this message may be generated by the *watchdog* (260) if heartbeats of application components are not received. Also, the *resiliency management process* executed by the *watchdog* periodically checks for malfunctioning application component functionality. Checks performed for this purpose may especially include test requests sent to application components' functionality. Such tests may be necessary as application level failures may otherwise remain undetected.

If a failure is observed, the *resiliency management process* simultaneously issues the provisioning of a replacement component using the provisioning functionality of a provider and stops the access to the failed component. In case a queue is used to access the component, the latter step is omitted as the component proactively retrieves requests from the queue. After access to the component is stopped, the component is decommissioned. This step is executed after the access has been stopped, as the faulty component may still function in a limited fashion. If it is decommissioned simultaneously to reconfiguring the load balancer, accesses assigned to are certainly not handled.

The first critical design decision in this scope is the time interval at which the correct functioning of component instances is verified periodically. Adequate intervals mainly depend on the required recovery time and, therefore, have to respect the provisioning time of cloud resources. Often, providers do not make assurances for these times and heuristics have to be employed to predict them.

The second critical design decision is how failures shall be detected in the monitored information. To detect a component failure, providers may offer monitoring of network availability, for example. The *resiliency management process* executed by the *watchdog* (260), however, is obligated to interpret these values and deduct information about application component availability from them. Furthermore, none of this information can assure that the component functions correctly on the application level. Such tests have to be implemented individually for each cloud application.

Variations

Failures may be hard to detect on the application level. Especially, the long-term behavior of application components may be hard to test. To address these challenges, application components may be randomly treated as failed after certain time intervals and are then replaced with newly provisioned instances.

Hohpe and Woolf [1] describe detailed patterns to detect and manage failures in an application using messaging provided by a *message-oriented middleware*

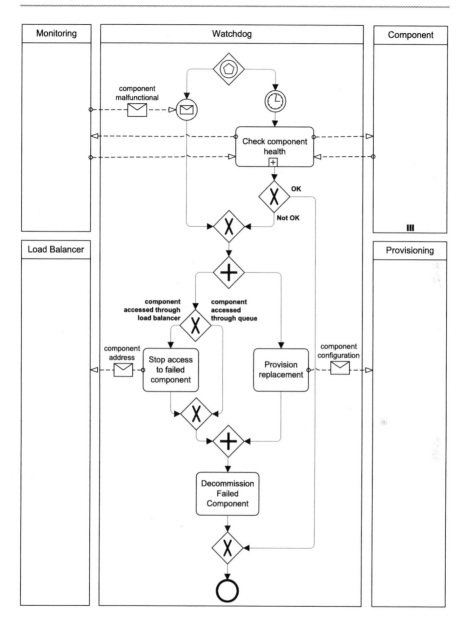

Fig. 5.15   Resiliency process handled by the watchdog

(136). The fundamental approach is to use a *control bus* comprised out of message queues dedicated for health information messages. Monitored messaging components publish heartbeat messages to the control bus to state that they are still available. To verify the proper functioning of a messaging application Hohpe and Woolf introduce the concept of *test messages* these messages are injected to the messaging application. After the processing of these messages, results are compared to expected results to detect faulty components. Furthermore, a *wire tap* may be used to inspect messages while they traverse a *message-oriented middleware* (136) without affecting processing application components.

Related Patterns
- *Stateless component* (171): application components managed using the *resiliency management process* should implement this pattern. It describes how application components may completely rely on external state information rather than maintaining their own internal state. This makes them significantly easier to replace as the information that is lost in case of failures is reduced.
- *Elasticity management process* (267): the *resiliency management process* is often integrated with an *elasticity management process* (267) that scales the number of application components up and down according to the experienced workload. Especially, the variation to treat application components as failed after a long runtime can be incorporated here by replacing them during necessary scaling operations.
- *Standby pooling process* (279): this pattern describes how application component instances can be kept on standby to integrate them into an application more quickly than the provider-supplied provisioning functionality allows. In scope of resiliency management, this could be used to speed up the replacement of failing application components significantly.

Known Uses

The concept of the *resiliency management process* pattern has also been described as a *hot pool* by Leymann and Roller [76]. Amazon suggests a similar approach to assure fault tolerance in applications using their Elastic Beanstalk offering [53] by using its monitoring service Amazon CloudWatch [198]. Users of Elastic Beanstalk can configure a website address provided by the hosted application, which is then periodically retrieved to monitor application health.

Composite Cloud Application Patterns

6

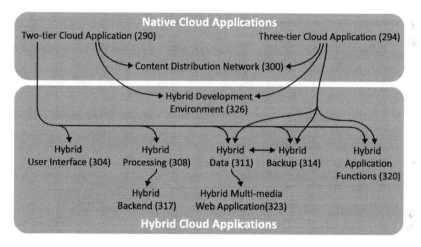

Fig. 6.1 Map of composite patterns for cloud computing

This chapter contains patterns that compose patterns covered in previous sections to describe cloud applications (Fig. 6.1). Furthermore, it describes possible distribution scenarios of the composed patterns among different cloud environments forming a *hybrid cloud* (75).

Native cloud application patterns (Sect. 6.2) cover fundamental structures of *distributed applications* (160), how to scale them elastically, and how to integrate cloud offerings (see Chap. 3) with their custom application components.

Hybrid cloud application patterns (Sect. 6.3) refine these fundamental composite patterns further. They describe how the requirements of application components may differ regarding elasticity, availability, accessibility, privacy, security, and trust, which makes them suitable for different environments comprising a *hybrid*

C. Fehling et al., *Cloud Computing Patterns*,
DOI 10.1007/978-3-7091-1568-8_6, © Springer-Verlag Wien 2014

cloud (75). These patterns, therefore, describe different distributions of *user interface components* (175), *processing components* (180), *data access components* (188), and data stored in storage offerings among cloud environments.

6.1   Overview of Cloud Application Patterns

The native cloud applications start with two fundamental composite patterns. A *two-tier cloud application* (290) subsumes *user interface component* (175), *processing component* (180), and *data access component* (188) functionality in one application component that is scaled-out among cloud resources. Data is handled in storage offerings (see Sect. 3.5 on Page 109). In this scope, *relation databases* (115), *key-value storage* (119), and *blob storage* (112) are commonly used. A *three-tier cloud application* (294) decomposes application functionality further in order to be more flexible. It separates *user interface components* (175) from *processing components* (180), and *data access components* (188). Data is again kept in the third tier in storage offerings. Each of these tiers' components may then be scaled out independently. Both native cloud applications may use a *content distribution network* (300) to distribute application component instances and data replicas globally in order to assure the necessary performance for a globally distributed user group.

Following this description of native cloud applications, the distribution of their components among different environments in a *hybrid cloud* (75) is described. A *two-tier cloud application* (290) is more restricted in this scope, as a larger portion of the application functionality is subsumed into one application component. The corresponding distributions of the application components lead to the patterns for *hybrid user interface* (304), *hybrid processing* (308), *hybrid data* (311), *hybrid backup* (314), and *hybrid application functionality* (320) – arbitrary application functions are distributed among a *hybrid cloud* (75). As a specialization for data-intensive processing the *hybrid backend* (317) pattern is given. A *hybrid multimedia web application* (323) distributes static web content and streaming multimedia content among different environments. Finally, all of the described applications may be developed and tested using a *hybrid development environment* (326) that uses different runtime environments for application development, test, and production use.

6.2   Native Cloud Applications

The *distributed application* (160) pattern describes how the functionality of cloud applications can be decomposed into separate application components. It covers three styles of decomposition. The first decomposition style separates the layers of an application, for example, user interface, processing, and data handling. Second, an application can be decomposed using a process-centric approach, where functionality is assigned to multiple components that are then orchestrated by a process model. Third, a pipes-and-filters based decomposition covered dividing application functionality in components that are interconnected by data channels through which data is passed and processed continuously.

In the following, we cover two concrete approaches to decompose a cloud application. The *two-tier cloud application* (290) and *three-tier cloud application* (294) patterns describe the result of a layered decomposition. The other decomposition approaches can be used in a similar fashion.

We cover in detail which application components (see Sect. 4.3 on Page 166) and cloud offerings (see Chap. 3) are used to form a cloud-native application. Furthermore, this section describes the *content distribution network* (300) pattern that can be used in conjunction with applications to make large amounts of data available efficiently.

6.2.1   Two-Tier Cloud Application

> Presentation and business logic is bundled to one stateless tier that is easy to scale. This tier is separated from the data tier that is harder to scale and often handled by a provider-supplied storage offering.

 How can application functionality be separated from data handling to scale them independently?

Context

A *distributed application* (160) is decomposed into *loosely-coupled* (156) application components to scale individual application functions independently by automatically provisioning and decommissioning application component instances. The main influencing factor regarding this elastic scaling is the data handled by the application. Data handling functionality is significantly harder to scale than *stateless components* (171), because scaled out *stateful components* (168) have to coordinate state information between instances. Therefore, the application shall be decomposed in a fashion that separates the easy-to-scale functionality from the hard-to-scale functionality. The application shall, furthermore, exploit the elasticity of an underlying cloud environment to benefit from the cloud properties described in Sect. 1.1 on Page 3, especially, pay-per-use and rapid elasticity. This enables the application to offer elasticity and possibly pay-per-use pricing models itself.

Solution

The *two-tier cloud application* decomposed application functionality into data handling functionality, provided by one or several storage offerings (see Chap. 3), and application components handling presentation and business logic. The two tiers are depicted in Fig. 6.2. The first tier is comprised of a load balancer and one application component subsuming the necessary presentation and business logic functionality that is scaled out elastically by an *elastic load balancer* (254). The second tier provides data handling functionality and is commonly realized by one or more provider-supplied storage offerings. It handles the data accessed by the application component providing presentation and business logic functionality. This separation enables the two tiers to elastically scale independently with their workloads.

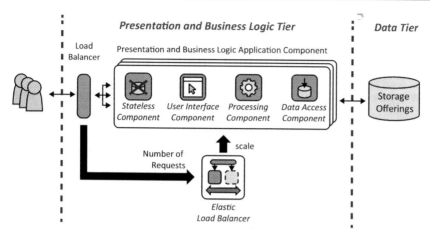

Fig. 6.2 Exemplary architecture of a two-tier cloud application

Result

A *two-tier cloud application* implements the *distributed application* (160) pattern separating the data tier from the presentation and business logic tier. As seen in Fig. 6.2, the presentation and business logic is provided by one scaled-out application component that implements the patterns *stateless component* (171), *user interface component* (175), *processing component* (180) and *data access component* (188). This application component, therefore, handles accesses by users, workload processing, and data access in a holistic fashion. It is implemented as a *stateless component* (171) so that additional instances can be provisioned and decommissioned efficiently to support rapid elasticity. Application state – data handled by the application is kept in the separate data tier commonly delegated to provider-supplied storage offerings, for example, a *relational database* (115) offering or *key-value storage* (119). Session state – the state of user-interaction with the application is provided with every request or also managed by a storage offering as described by the *stateless component* (171) pattern. These offerings assure the necessary elasticity and also offer a pay-per-use pricing scheme. Depending on the requirements in a concrete usage scenario, the application logic tier may be extended with other application component patterns (see Sect. 4.3 on Page 166), such as the *batch processing component* (185) pattern to actively delay workload, or *data abstractor* (194) to cope with *eventual consistent* (126) storage offerings comprising the data tier.

An *elastic load balancer* (254) determines the number of required instances of application components and provisions and decommissions them as needed, commonly, via an *elastic infrastructure* (87) or *elastic platform* (91). The *elastic load balancer* (254) ensures that the right number of component instances is provisioned based on the number of user accesses notified by the load balancer, and possibly also monitors the utilization of the application components. A pay-per-use pricing scheme can be offered by the *two-tier cloud application* itself due to this elastic scaling, because the number of application component instances and, thus, the cost of running the application correlates with the experienced requests.

Variations

Instead of using provider-supplied storage offerings, the data tier may be implemented by the application developer using *stateful components* (168). In this variation, the elastic scaling of the data tier has to be ensured by the application developer as described by the *stateful component* (168) pattern. The other variants of the *two-tier cloud application* pattern use provider-supplied storage offerings and have to cope with different consistency behavior displayed by these offerings – *strict consistency* (123) and *eventual consistency* (126).

In case the chosen storage offering implements the *strict consistency* (123) pattern no additional measures regarding consistency need to be taken in the presentation and business logic tier. It must, however, be ensured that the implementation of the data tier can scale enough to accommodate the potentially high number of presentation and business logic components accessing it concurrently.

In case the storage offering implements the *eventual consistency* (126) pattern the presentation and business logic tier must deal with data inconsistencies that may lead to the following challenges:

- *Duplicate reads*: if data is retrieved from the data tier, processed, and stored again, the effect of data manipulations may not be visible immediately. There is a chance that an unprocessed version of a data element may be read again even though it has already been processed and stored successfully before. To deal with this issue, the application components should be implemented as *idempotent processors* (197) that can deal with duplicate reads of the same data element by implementing idempotent operations or by detecting duplicate reads.
- *Inconsistent view*: if large amounts of data are processed and accumulated by the *two-tier cloud application*, data may change during processing and while it is being retrieved from the storage offering. To deal with this issue, the application component may implement the *data abstractor* (194) pattern. Data is then approximated and abstracted to hide inconsistencies. For example, instead of providing a concrete number of items that a Web shop has in store, item availability could only specified as "available", "low", or "unavailable". However, such data abstractions have to be acceptable in the usage scenario supported by the application.

Related Patterns

In addition to the patterns mentioned above that are used by the *two-tier cloud application*, it is related to the following patterns:

- *Three-tier cloud application* (294): if the processing handled by the cloud application is computation intensive, it may be feasible to separate it from the user interface functionality as it allows to elastically scale these tiers individually, instead of scaling the presentation and business logic as a combined tier.

- *Content distribution network* (300): if the *two-tier cloud application* needs to handle a globally distributed user group, a *content distribution network* can be used to provide local application component instances and data replicas to users in order to increase access performance.
- *Hybrid data* (311), *hybrid backup* (314), and *hybrid application functions* (320): these patterns describe how the two tiers of a *two-tier cloud application* can be distributed among different runtime environments forming a hybrid cloud application. Especially, it is motivated in which business usage scenario a certain distribution should be used.
- *Hybrid development environment* (326): this pattern describes how different runtime environments may be used during the development, test, and production use of a *two-tier cloud application*.

Known Uses

PaaS (49) offerings for web applications such as the Google App Engine [21] and Amazon ElasticBeanstalk [53] tend to imply applications to be build using the *elastic two-tier cloud application* pattern, separating the application in a presentation/business logic tier hosted on an *elastic platform* (91) and a data tier hosted on a cloud storage offering. Varia [93, 154] discusses this decomposition for Amazon Web Services (AWS) [138]. Guest [206] discusses a similar decomposition approach to create elastic cloud applications on Windows Azure [52].

One common technology stack to build *two-tier cloud applications* is to use a light-weight frontend technology such as PHP [207] or Active Server Pages (ASP) [208] and elastically scale the underlying Apache Web Server [209], Microsoft Internet Information Services (IIS) [210] or Servlet Container, such as Apache Tomcat [73] along with the applications implemented as *stateless components* (171). The data tier is often implemented as MySQL [112] database cluster in traditional setups or one of the cloud storage offerings in more cloud-native settings. Often, with high-volume PHP/MySQL Web-applications, you will find this pattern implicitly implemented: a stateless PHP frontend backed by a MySQL cluster.

The main problem in these settings is session handling. Often, mechanisms such as sticky-sessions are employed to redirect individual users to the same of the horizontally scaled frontend servers that served the previous requests. This allows keeping sessions in memory to improve performance sometimes with asynchronous session-replication to a central data tier. This prevents having to synchronously write session information to a central data store with all persistent session data accessible to all frontend servers. In case of *environment-based availability* (98) of the frontend servers, sessions are either lost on crash of a server or the replica in the central data store can be retrieved.

6.2.2   Three-Tier Cloud Application

> Presentation logic, business logic, and data handling are realized as separate tiers to scale stateless presentation and compute-intensive processing independently of the data tier, which is harder to scale and often handled by the cloud provider.

 How can presentation logic, business logic, and data handling be decomposed into separate tiers that are scaled independently?

Context

A *distributed application* (160) is decomposed into separate application components that are *loosely-coupled* (156) and scaled independent of each other. In scope of a *two-tier cloud application* (290), the main issue that motivated decomposition is that *stateful components* (168) are harder to scale than *stateless components* (171) and, thus, are separated from the remainder of the application. However, there can be more differentiating factors of application tiers. For example, if *processing components* (180) are more computation intensive or are used less frequently than *user interface components* (175), aligning the elastic scaling of these two components by summarizing their implementation in one tier can be inefficient. This issue arises every time components comprising a *distributed application* (160) experiences different workloads introduced in Sect. 2.2 on Page 23: *static workload* (26), *periodic workload* (29), *unpredictable workload* (36), or *continuously changing workload* (40). The number of provisioned component instances cannot be aligned well to the different workloads if they are summarized to coarse grained tiers. A further decomposition may allow a tighter alignment of application component instances to experienced workload under such conditions, especially important, if the application shall offer elasticity and pay-per-use pricing models itself. While tiers are elastically scaled independently regarding their workloads they have to be integrated to ensure the end-to-end functionality of the application.

Solution

The *distributed application* (160) is decomposed into three tiers shown exemplarily in Fig. 6.3, where each tier is elastically scaled independently. The presentation tier is comprised of a load balancer and an application component that implements the

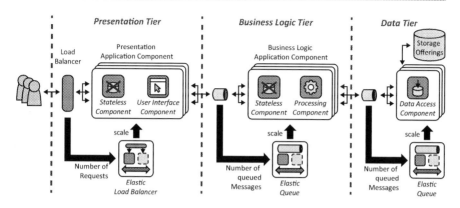

Fig. 6.3 Exemplary architecture of a three-tier cloud application

stateless component (171) pattern and *user interface component* (175) pattern. New instances of this application component are provisioned on demand by an *elastic load balancer* (254) based on the number of requests issued by application users. Communication between the presentation tier and the business logic tier is realized via asynchronous messaging provided by a *message-oriented middleware* (136). This communication through an intermediary ensures *loose coupling* (156) between those tiers, which is essential to allow the business logic tier to be scaled independently of the presentation tier.

The business logic tier is comprised of an application component implementing the *stateless component* pattern in addition to the *processing component* (180) pattern. This business logic component interacts with the *message queue* provided by the *message-oriented middleware* (136) retrieving the requests from the presentation tier. It is scaled elastically by an *elastic queue* (257), which provisions and decommissions instances of the business logic application components based on the number of messages buffered by the message queue.

The data tier is again accessed by the business logic tier through a message queue to ensure *loose coupling* (156) between these two tiers. The data tier is comprised of storage offerings accessed by an application component implementing the *data access component* (188) pattern. The data access component interacts with the used storage offerings, for example, *relational databases* (115), *key-value storage* (119), or *blob storage* (112) that are obtained from the cloud provider and provides data using message queues provided by the *message-oriented middleware* (136). Multiple message queues may be used between each tier, omitted in Fig. 6.3 for space limitations. If large amounts of data have to be exchanged between tiers that cannot be handled in single messages, application components may also access the storage offerings directly. In this case, the messages only contain the addresses of to be accessed data elements.

Result

In contrast to a *two-tier cloud application* (290), a *three-tier cloud application* needs to be able to scale presentation, business logic, and data handling independently, because the requirements of these functions regarding the necessary number of application component instances to handle workload differ greatly. To exploit the cloud computing properties introduced in Sect. 1.1 on Page 3, especially, rapid elasticity and pay-per-use this functionality is, therefore, assigned to different tiers. To be able to scale each tier independently these tiers are decoupled from each other. As in a *two-tier cloud application* (290) the business logic and the data tier are decoupled. Therefore, the communication mechanism between business logic and data tier is asynchronous. The access between data handling components and storage offerings is commonly synchronous via interfaces provided by the storage offering. The presentation tier is also decoupled from the business logic tier via asynchronous messaging enabled by a *message-oriented middleware* (136). The message queues assure *at-least-once delivery* (144) or *exactly-once delivery* (141) of messages leading to two variations of a *three-tier cloud application* (see variations). Asynchronous messaging enables independent scaling of both tiers and reliably stores messages exchanged between both tiers. Thus, the business logic application component can be scaled according to the number of messages in the queue. To enable this, the number of queued message are monitored by an *elastic queue* (257) that accesses the resource management interface of the *elastic platform* (91) or *elastic infrastructure* (87) underpinning the business logic components.

An exemplary communication path in the *three-tier cloud application* works as follows: a request is sent to the presentation tier via the load balancer seen on the left of Fig. 6.3. Depending on the number of requests assigned this way, the elastic load balancer provisions or decommissions presentation application components. After handling the request and validating the necessary user inputs the presentation application component sends the request to the message queue for the business logic tier and informs the user respectively. If the workload experienced by the business tier has reached a certain threshold the *elastic queue* (257) provisions a new instance of the business logic components. When one of the business logic components is idle, it consumes the message from the queue. The message is now invisible to all other business logic component instances either through a transactional messaging mechanism, described by *transaction-based delivery* (146) or for a certain timeout-window, as described by *timeout-based delivery* (149). This sharing of one queue between multiple component instances is also described by the *processing component* (180) pattern and by Hohpe and Woolf [1] as the *competing consumer* pattern. The business logic component processes the message and stores necessary data in the data tier. Having finished processing, the business logic component commits the message from *a transaction-based delivery* queue or acknowledges the message to the queue in a *timeout-based delivery* queue. This behavior is described in the *transaction-based processor* (201) and *timeout-based message processor* (204) patterns, respectively. In case the business logic component fails to process a message from the queue due to a failure of the node on which it runs or through any other cause, the transaction is aborted or the message is not acknowledged and the message appears in the queue again where it can be processed by another processing component instance. Using these mechanisms it is possible to only have *environment-based availability* (98) for the presentation tier components and business logic tier components, as the state of the application is always securely and persistently stored in the queues and the data tier.

Variations

Regarding the interaction of the *data access components* (188) with the storage offerings, two additional variants exist for the use of storage offerings displaying *strict consistency* (123) and *eventual consistency* (126). These variants are equivalent to the two variants of the *two-tier cloud application* (290) described on Page 292. Additional variants of the *three-tier cloud application* exist depending on the delivery behavior displayed by the used message queue between the presentation application component and business logic application component – *exactly-once delivery* (141) and *at-least-once delivery* (144).

In case the used queues have *exactly-once delivery* (141) behavior, there are no additional measures required to deal with duplicate messages as messages exchanged between the tiers will always be delivered exactly once.

In case the queues used only guarantee *at-least-once delivery* (144), duplicate messages may arrive in the business logic tier, or the presentation tier. Thus, it is important to take countermeasures such as implementing the components as *idempotent processors* (197). A similar problem may arise if the used storage offering is *eventually consistent* (126). This can be addressed by implementing the data access component as *idempotent processor* (197) detecting data inconsistencies or as *data abstractor* (194) hiding data inconsistencies.

Related Patterns

In addition to the patterns mentioned above that are used by the *three-tier cloud application*, it is related to the following pattern:
- *Two-tier cloud application* (290): the three-tier cloud application divides application functionality into three tiers that have different requirements on their hosting environment. If these requirements do not differ greatly, for example, if multiple application components need similar amounts of computation capability, they should be summarized in one application component. Especially, in usage scenarios where applications experience very small workloads, this summarization can lead to a more efficient use of resources as is possible in a *three-tier cloud application* that is deployed in a more distributed fashion. The separation of data from stateless application functionality is, however, still a good design decision leading to a *two-tier cloud application* (290).

- *Content distribution network* (300): if a globally distributed user group accesses the *three-tier cloud application,* application component instances and data can be replicated according to this pattern to exploit access locality in order to increase performance.
- Hybrid cloud application patterns (Sect. 6.3): the patterns of this section describe how the tiers of a *three-tier cloud application* can be hosted in different runtime environments forming a *hybrid cloud* (75). Following these patterns, different requirements of application components regarding elasticity, availability, privacy, security, and trust can be addressed and matched efficiently.
- *Hybrid development environment* (326): a *three-tier cloud application* can use different runtime environments during its development, test, and production phases, where requirements can differ greatly. How this can be realized is described by the *hybrid development environment* pattern.

Known Uses

Cloud providers such as Amazon AWS [138] and Microsoft Azure [52] offer all ingredients to build *three-tier cloud applications* and propose to build applications in the same or similar fashion: Varia [93, 154] suggests the same decomposition of application components into separate components and their *loose coupling* (156) via messages. Guest [206] discusses how to make the different tiers of applications using resources provided from Windows Azure [52] elastic.

When examining higher-load traditional Java EE [211] applications in an enterprise setting, you will often find these applications to be built using queued transaction processing as described by Bernstein and Newcomer [128] making them similar to the *three-tier cloud application* pattern. Message processors in these applications read messages from a *request queue,* process the message, and write the result as a message to a *reply queue* within the scope of one transaction. This ensures that request messages are not lost if their processing fails. This approach is also discussed in greater detail by the *transaction-based processor* (201) pattern in this book. Such Java EE applications implement similar mechanisms, for example, a data tier separated from individually scaling tiers for processing and the use of messaging between tiers.

The difference of a *three-tier cloud application* to a traditional Java EE three-tier application using, for example, Java Message Service (JMS)-based message queuing [145, 146] between presentation and business logic tier are the properties of the used messaging and storage offerings. Traditional application often assume and require that *message-oriented middleware* (136) provides *exactly-once-delivery* (141) and data stores provide *strict consistency* (123) many cloud-based messaging offerings do not assure this properties but display *at-least-once delivery* (144). Cloud-based storage offerings often assure *eventual consistency* (126). In Sect. 3.2 on Page 81, we cover this impact of cloud computing on offering properties in greater detail. In our experience, even for enterprise applications *at-least-once delivery* (144) and *eventual consistency* (126) may be sufficient – especially when business requirements are closely re-examined. Often, exact information handled by a data store is not required (i.e. when dealing with available seats or parking lots in a booking system), but only an estimation ("enough", "critical", "not enough"). Such data is often attainable with *at-least-once delivery* (144) messages from an *eventual consistent* (126) storage offering. The *data abstractor* (194) pattern covers different approaches to present and use eventual consistent date in greater detail. Under these conditions, what seems to be less-accurate can be accurate enough for a lot of business settings. Furthermore, many cloud storage offerings support different consistency behavior, a variation described by the *eventual consistency* (126) pattern. Thus, for a yearly inventory task the *strictly consistent* data retrieval can be used, whereas the *eventually consistent* but higher available or cheaper request can be used for the common requests, where availability of the system is valued higher than the consistency of returned data.

6.2.3   Content Distribution Network

> Application component instances and data handled by them are globally distributed to meet the access performance required by a global user group.

 How can timely access to an application be ensured for a globally distributed user group?

Context

The application components comprising a *distributed application* (160) are hosted in globally distributed environments. This application serves content and functionality to a user group of varying size, i.e., generating *periodic workload* (29), *once-in-a-lifetime workload* (33), *unpredictable workload* (36), or *continuously changing workload* (40). The served content shall be accessible in a timely manner. Especially, if the application provides multimedia content to users, for example, streamed videos and music the amount of data to be served increases drastically. This poses challenges for distribution networks. If such multimedia content is located too far from the user accessing it, the communication delay of the distribution network may hinder the timely access to data. Therefore, storing content in only one centralized location, i.e., one cloud or data center is unfeasible.

Solution

Content replicas are established in different physical locations of one or multiple clouds as depicted in Fig. 6.4. During this distribution of replicas, the topology of distribution networks is considered to ensure locality for all globally distributed user groups. Replicas are updated from a central location.

Result

Content accesses of users can be routed to replicas with the best connectivity to ensure performance. This connectivity may not be confused with geographical proximity. It only regards the connectivity and performance of the underlying connection network. A critical design decision in this scope is the number of replicates and their consistency assurances. A large number of replicas increases the access speed, because locality can be exploited more efficiently. However, it also increases the effort required to update replicas. Therefore, if content changes

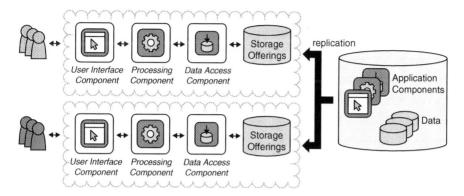

Fig. 6.4 Content distribution from a storage offering to two cloud environments

too frequently, updating the replicas may become a bottleneck. Replicas may be updated using two update distribution techniques.

Push replication of data: if a replica is accessible from a central location controlling the updates of replicas, content may be pushed to the replica. Therefore, changes of the main replica can be directly reflected to other replicas in the system leading to *strict consistency* (123) or updates can be pushed periodically leading to *eventual consistency* (126).

Pull replication of data: if the replica is not directly accessible from a central controlling location, the replica may pull updates. Therefore, after certain time intervals replicas check if the central data has been updated and updates itself accordingly. This results in *eventually consistent* (126) behavior by design.

Variations

Content may be replicated seamlessly through caching. In scope of the *content distribution network* pattern, replicas are explicitly managed by the application. Caches are replicas that are managed transparent to the application. They are distributed among the connection network and store accessed content seamlessly to reduce data access times. This approach, often, cannot be controlled by the application. Caches are kept up-to-date automatically, for example, by means of freshness control and validation used by Web caches, an approach described in the HTTP standard [212]. Freshness control refers to techniques to determine whether or not a cached data element is up-to-data or not. In contrast to caches, the *content distribution network* empowers the application to explicitly specify the location of replicas and influences the style in which they are updated.

Related Patterns

* *Strict consistency* (123): consistent updates to replicas are assured by handling updates to all replicas immediately, often, in one transaction. This, however,

makes the system vulnerable towards network partitioning and should, therefore, only be used if all users must be served with the same updated data instantly.

- *Eventually consistency* (126): if data and application component replicas are updated according to *eventual consistency*, updates propagate the global distribution network asynchronously. Therefore, different portions of the global user group may be served with different content or application functionality. As asynchronous changes make the application more resilient towards communication failures and partitions of the network, this approach should be chosen whenever the usage scenario allows it.

Known Uses

The video distribution product of Akamai [213] and also Akamai's overall network system architecture [214] are built similar to the content distribution pattern. Amazon's content delivery service, CloudFront [104] also provides a similar setup. Another content delivery network that may be integrated with existing websites is CloudFlare [215]. Dreibelbis et al. [216] describe more detailed patterns on how to manage different data sources spanning multiple regions an applications using so called *master data management*.

6.3   Hybrid Cloud Applications

A *hybrid cloud* (75) integrates multiple clouds and static data centers into a homogenous hosting environment. Often, *hybrid clouds* are used to address different requirements of applications and their components regarding three properties of the hosting environment: elasticity, accessibility, and the combined assurances for privacy, security, and trust.

Elasticity: resources available in different cloud environments can be provisioned and decommissioned at a different level of flexibility. Especially, application components experiencing *periodic workload* (29), *unpredictable workload* (36), *continuously changing workload* (40) can benefit from a more flexible environment, where no upfront investments in the infrastructure is necessary and the number or resources can be tightly adjusted to the current demand. Especially, in a *private cloud* (66) accessed by a small number of users, this property may be limited. Similar challenges may arise in small *community clouds* (71) as well.

Accessibility: resources in different environments are accessible through different means of communication. The infrastructure used within a company is usually accessible to employees only and is specifically guarded against access from the outside of the company. Applications used for collaboration with other companies, however, have to be made available to a much broader user group.

Privacy, security, and trust: this property is commonly determined by the importance of data handled by an application. If data contains business-critical information unwanted access to it can be damaging to a company. Even if the respective security mechanisms are supported by the cloud provider, it often remains an issue of trust in the provider and other cloud users whether or not a cloud environment is suitable to host an application or its components.

In the following, different composite patterns describe the distribution of application components among clouds and static data centers. The covered applications consist of *user-interface components* (175), *processing components* (180), and either *stateful components* (168) or *data access components* (188) relying on storage offerings (see Sect. 3.5 on Page 109). These components are distributed differently between cloud environments and static data centers forming a *hybrid cloud*. The patterns consider a *hybrid cloud* to be comprised of a static data center and an elastic cloud, for example, a *public cloud* (62) or *community cloud* (71). Because a static data center does not use cloud technologies and is considered the most secure environment while *public clouds* and *community clouds* commonly ensure the highest levels of accessibility and elasticity, these environments are most differential regarding the above mentioned environmental properties. We used this combination of clouds and static data centers to describe hybrid cloud applications, so that the requirements why applications components are assigned to an environment become as clear as possible. However, the hybrid cloud application patterns may also be used to integrate arbitrary clouds and static data centers to form a hybrid cloud, for example, a static data center and a *private cloud* (66), two *public clouds* (62) etc.

6.3.1 Hybrid User Interface

Varying workload from a user group interacting asynchronously with an
application is handled in an elastic environment while the remainder of an
application resides in a static environment.

 *How can a user interface for asynchronous interaction be hosted in a
cloud while being integrated with an application otherwise hosted in
a static data center?*

Context

An application serves user groups with different workload behavior. One user group
generates *static workload* (26), while another user group generates *periodic workload* (29), *once-in-a-lifetime workload* (33), *unpredictable workload* (36), or *continuously changing workload* (40). Therefore, the size of the first user group is
known during system design time, the number of other users may be unknown
beforehand or may change frequently over time. Furthermore, the user group
generating other workload than *static workload* (26) interacts with the application
in an asynchronous fashion, thus, users issue requests that do not generate any direct
feedback. They may, for example, issue orders to a shop, apply for a credit card, or
request that account information is sent to them via e-mail. Since the predictability
of the user group size and workload behavior differs, it shall be ensured that
unexpected peak workloads do not affect the performance of the application
while each user group is handled by the most suitable cloud environment.

Solution

The *user interface component* (175) serving users generating varying workload is
hosted in an elastic cloud environment as shown in Fig. 6.5. Other application
components that are more suited for an on-premise application due to the static
workload behavior of the other user group are hosted in a static environment. The
user interface deployed in the elastic cloud is integrated with the remainder of the
application in a decoupled fashion using messaging to ensure *loose coupling* (156)
between environments.

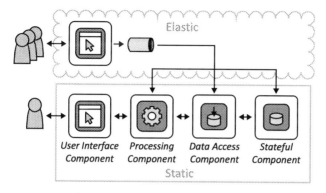

Fig. 6.5 Hybrid user interface in an elastic cloud and a static data center

Result

The *user interface component* (175) in the elastic cloud is decoupled from the application components in the static environment, as it can operate without any direct communication with application components hosted in the static environment. Due to this *loose coupling* (156) it is, thus, ensured that the elasticity provided by the cloud can be efficiently used to scale the elastic *user interface components* without being affected by the static performance of components that are hosted in the static environment. The cloud enables the *elastic user interface component* to scale out, in order to react to workload peaks of its user group. The underlying pay-per-use pricing model of the cloud ensures that costs are minimized. The user interface component in the elastic cloud provides asynchronous access to the application, because accessed functions do not directly give results that would require interaction with other application components. Provided functionality is, therefore, limited to data input and asynchronous data output. The data input functionality may only return the information that the inquiry or access performed by the user has been received and will be processed. Asynchronous data output may return information based on functionality and data provided in the static environment, but the users have to wait for results, which are provided asynchronously, for example, via e-mail.

Variations

The *hybrid user interface* pattern combines a *hybrid cloud* (75) formed by a static environment and an elastic cloud. The same approach can be used to integrate two elastic cloud environments and application components may also be distributed among more than two environments. If security is an issue, because the cloud environment is a *public cloud* (62) or *community cloud* (71), the data entered by the user can be encrypted in the *public cloud* by using an asymmetric encryption [217, 218], i.e., the data is encrypted in the public cloud by using a public key and after transmission to the *private cloud* (66) it is decrypted by using a private key.

Sensitive data that is sent from the user interface to the other application components in the *private cloud* are, thus, protected. However, data that is asynchronously sent from the private to the public cloud does not guarantee the same privacy and security, because it has to be decrypted by user interface components residing in the elastic cloud, thus, the key required for decryption has to be stored there as well.

Related Patterns

- *Idempotent processor* (197): if the *message-oriented middleware* (136) providing the message queue that is used for data transfer guarantees *at-least-once delivery* (144), the component receiving messages from the elastic user interface should implement the *idempotent processor* pattern to detect message duplicates.
- *Hybrid processing* (308) and *hybrid backend* (317): if the data obtained from the varying user group requires additional processing, one of these two patterns may be combined with the *hybrid user interface* to perform additional processing in the elastic cloud environment.
- *Hybrid application functions* (320): the *hybrid user interface* pattern distributes application components among different environments based on the different user groups accessing them. As an alternative, the user group can be homogeneous, but accesses application functionality differently, i.e., the application functions experience different workloads or have different security requirements. If this is the case, different environments may be used for different application functionality on all layers of the application stack, as described by the *hybrid application functions* pattern.
- *Stateless component* (171): the user interface provisioned in the elastic environment should be implemented as a *stateless component* to ease scaling it out among multiple cloud resources. This scaling can either be performed by a custom implementation provided by the application developer or through the use of existing scaling functionality of the used environment. In either case, the management patterns (Chap. 5) should be considered.
- *Three-tier cloud application* (294): the exemplary application shown in Fig. 6.5 considers three application tiers for user interfaces, processing, and data handling. The hybrid user interface could also be combined with other *distributed applications* (160) that do not use this decomposition of application functionality into three tiers, for example, a *two-tier cloud application* (290).

Known Uses

In the German city Friedrichshafen, different IT projects have been conducted to increase the quality of life of inhabitants, for example, by optimizing processes of the public administration and providing more user-friendly interfaces [219, 220]. One of the projects provided a Web interface through which parents can sign up their children for a kindergarten place via the Internet [30, 219]. The corresponding portal is made available at all times, but experiences *periodic workload* (29), because children are enrolled only during certain time periods each year. Parents can sign up their children until a certain deadline after which an internal process of the public administration office handles the assignment of children to available places. Since the parents do not get any direct feedback during the sign-up, the user interface used by them can be decoupled completely from the rest of the application. It is used only for asynchronous data input and is moved to an elastic cloud due to the inconsistent workload it experiences.

6.3.2 Hybrid Processing

Processing functionality that experiences varying workload is hosted in an elastic cloud while the remainder of an application resides in a static environment.

 How can processing components that experiences varying workload be hosted in an elastic cloud while the remainder of an application is hosted in a static data center?

Context

A *distributed application* (160) provides processing functionality that experience different workload behavior. The user group accessing the application is, thus, predictable in size, but accesses the functions provided by the application differently. While most of the functions are used equally over time and, therefore, experience *static workload* (26), some *processing components* (180) experience *periodic workload* (29), *unpredictable workload* (36), or *continuously changing workload* (40). While the *static workload* (26) can be handled efficiently in a static environment, investments in hardware and software required to handle the varying workload would be inefficient. Therefore, the processing functionality of the application for which access intensity varies shall be hosted in an elastic cloud.

Solution

The *processing components* (180) experiencing varying workloads are provisioned in an elastic cloud as shown in Fig. 6.6. To ease their provisioning and decommissioning and reduce the influence on components hosted in the static environment, *loose coupling* (156) is ensured by exchanging information between the hosting environments asynchronously via messages. Messages are handled by message queues provided by a *message-oriented middleware* (136). These messages contain all information required by the *processing components*, therefore, no data is stored in the cloud environment for longer periods of time.

Result

The *processing component* (180) experiencing varying workload is decoupled from the application through the use of messaging. It may be accessed directly

Fig. 6.6 Hybrid processing
in a static data center and
an elastic cloud

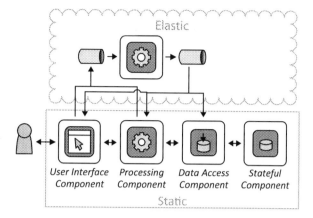

from other *user interface components* (175) or *processing components* (180) as
shown in Fig. 6.6. The results of this processing are either returned to the component that initiated the processing or to a different *user interface component*,
processing component or *data access component* (188).

The communication via messages ensures that the elastic processing component
can be provisioned flexibly. Multiple instances of this processing component are
coordinated by accessing the same queue, a concept introduced by Hohpe and
Woolf [1] as *competing consumer* and also covered in detail by the *processing
component* (180) pattern in Chap. 4. The asynchronous access, therefore, enables
the on-demand provisioning of elastic processing components only when they
are needed.

A critical design challenge is to determine when exactly to provision and
decommission the elastic processing components. The application can either rely
on scaling functionality of the cloud provider or implement custom management
components. In either case, the management patterns (Chap. 5) should be considered: an *elasticity manager* (250) can scale the processing component based on
the utilization of IT resources, such as virtual servers, on which the processing
component is hosted. An *elastic queue* (257) can additionally monitor the number
of messages in the message queue from which the processing component retrieves
requests to determine the required number of processing component instances.
Waiting for a certain number of requests in the input queue to process them as a
batch may also be an efficient approach as described by the *batch processing
component* (185) pattern in greater detail.

Variations

The *hybrid processing* pattern considers the *hybrid cloud* (75) to be comprised
of a static environment and an elastic environment. The same approach may be

applied to integrate different cloud environments. Especially, it can be used to integrate processing components from equal environments. When the processing functionality is then required, the application may identify the most suitable environment during runtime.

Related Patterns

- *Hybrid backend* (317): in case the processing components in the elastic cloud environment require access to larger amount of data than what can be transferred with each request, data exchange with the elastic cloud also has to be established, as described the *hybrid backend* pattern.
- *Idempotent processor* (197): if the *message-oriented middleware* (136) used to exchange messages assures *at-least-once delivery* (144) of messages, thus, if messages can be delivered more than once, the elastic processing components and its communication partners should implement the *idempotent processor* pattern in order to cope with such message duplicates.
- *Three-tier cloud application* (294): the exemplary application depicted in Fig. 6.6 divides application functionality among three components. The hybrid processing pattern could, however, also be combined with other *distributed applications* (160), for example, a *two-tier cloud application* (290).

Known Uses

Data format transformation is often performed using external cloud providers. For example, Ooyala.com [221] provides a cloud offering for video transformation. This task often requires specialized and expensive software. For many users, it is unprofitable to invest in such applications and the required infrastructure, if videos are only transformed occasionally. The digitalization of newspaper archives of the New York Times [31, 32] created an *once-in-a-lifetime workload* (33) for which a newspaper company could not provide the required resources. Scanned versions of newspapers were therefore transformed into PDF documents via external cloud resources obtained from Amazon EC2 [18]. Another example is the digitalization of Hillary Clinton's White House schedule [222]. If similar processing workload is required by an application on a more frequent basis relying on such large amounts of data, the *hybrid backend* (317) pattern should be used to integrate the corresponding processing components with the rest of the application in a coordinated fashion.

6.3.3   Hybrid Data

> Data of varying size is hosted in an elastic cloud while the remainder of an application resides in a static environment.

 How can a data handling functionality that experiences varying workload be hosted in an elastic cloud while the rest of the application is located in a static data center?

Context

A *distributed application* (160) handles data whose size varies drastically over time. Corresponding to the application workloads due to requests of users that can be characterized as *periodic workload* (29), *unpredictable workload* (36), or *continuously changing workload* (40), data handling components and storage offerings may experience varying workload leading to changes in the amount of handled data. Large amounts of data may, thus, be generated periodically and are then deleted again, may increase and decrease randomly, or may display a general increase or decrease over time. Especially, during these changes, the user number and their accesses to the application can be static resulting in *static workload* (26) on the remainder of the application components. Such a situation may, for example, arise if the processing components of an application generate large amounts of temporary data that is later consolidated. Archiving and backup applications display *continuously changing workload* (40) as data increases over time. Therefore, the main number of application components would be suitable for a static environment, but the size of handled data is a limiting factor.

Solution

Data whose varying size makes it unsuitable for hosting in a static environment is handled by storage offerings in an elastic cloud as depicted in Fig. 6.7. At this location data is either accessed by *data access components* (188) that are hosted in the static environment or by *data access components* hosted in the elastic environment. Some data that is static in size and possibly has higher requirements on privacy, security, and trust is handled by *stateful components* (168) hosted in the static data center. This distribution of application components enables the *distributed application* (160) to handle varying amounts of data even though it is mainly provisioned to a static environment.

Fig. 6.7 Hybrid data
residing in a static and
an elastic environment

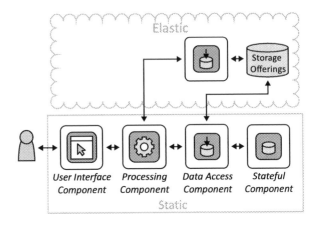

Result

The static application in Fig. 6.7 is decomposed into the three tiers, *user interface component* (175), *processing component* (180), and *data access component* (188). In the static environment a *stateful component* (168) is used for data storage. Alternatively, this could also be a different storage offering, for example, if a *private cloud* (66) is used. A critical design issue when integrating elastic data handling with a static application using this approach is the connection speed between the environments, which must be sufficient to guarantee timely data accesses. Data to which time-critical access must be ensured is often hosted close to the other application components in the static environment or is temporarily replicated when it is needed. Another issue may arise due to data transfer costs that should be revised carefully. To decrease these data transfer costs, some cloud providers offer customers to send in physical hard drives, which are then made accessible in the cloud environment. This is commonly used for initial data imports or large backup archives.

Variations

Multiple clouds may be used for data storage to increase the availability of stored data. A local cache can be used in the static environment to increase performance and decrease data transfer costs. Furthermore, the static data handling component may be configured to move data between the static and the elastic environment based on heuristics, such as the number of accesses. Therefore, if a data element is only accessed rarely, it is moved to the elastic cloud environment, where access speed may be reduced. Data that is accessed more often is moved to the static environment close to the remainder of the application. In such a setup, the data handling component may also reason about the amount of free space in the stateful application component and, thus, could only assign data to the elastic cloud environment when space is running low. However, during such optimization attempts data transfer costs billed by the cloud provider have to be considered carefully. This variation also reduces the dependency on the availability of the communication channel as the replication process can be delayed and, thus, executed in an *eventually consistent* (126) manner.

Related Patterns
- *Hybrid backend* (317): if data in the elastic environment is accessed often to perform complex processing on it, data transfer costs and access speed limitations may be reduced by also hosting *processing components* in the elastic environment. This is described by the *hybrid backend* pattern. To decide which pattern to use, the timeliness of data access and data transfer costs should be considered. However, this requires certain information about the behavior of the application, which may be unknown and hard to estimate.
- Storage offerings (Sect. 3.5 on Page 109): storage offering patterns describe the behavior of different storage options that may be used in the elastic environment to host data. Data may be accessed from the static environment similar virtual hard drives, as described by the *block storage* (110) pattern. A *blob storage* (112) offers remote data access similar to file systems. *Key-value storage* (119) and *relational databases* (115) offer table-centric data storage. These offerings may display *eventual consistency* (126) or *strict consistently* (123), meaning that data alterations become visible over time or immediately, respectively.
- *Content distribution network* (300): the variation of the *hybrid data* pattern distributing data among two environments based on heuristics is similar to a *content distribution network*. This pattern assures locality of data accessed by a globally distributed user group.

Known Uses

Cloud storage is offered by many providers, such as Amazon Simple Storage Service (S3) [132]. A provider offering automatic storage synchronization between multiple clients and their cloud offering is Dropbox [223]. StorSimple [224] offers cloud-based storage solutions that can be integrated with a company's Storage Area Network (SAN) [225] to seamlessly integrate enterprise storage with different cloud storage offerings [226]. Another provider offering data storage is Gladinet [227]. Varia [228] discusses different migration scenarios for existing applications to Amazon Web Services (AWS) [138]. One of the covered topics is the migration of large data objects to Amazon S3.

6.3.4 Hybrid Backup

> Data is periodically extracted from an application to be archived in an elastic cloud for disaster recovery purposes.

 How can data be archived in a remote environment while the remainder of the application is hosted in a static environment?

Context

Many applications are used by small and medium businesses which do not have the required IT skills to host and maintain their own highly available infrastructure. Especially, requirements regarding business resiliency – the ability to recover from an error – and business continuity – the ability to operate during an error – are challenging. Furthermore, there are laws and regulations making businesses liable to archive data and keep it accessible for audits, often over very long periods of time. In this scope, changes in the used hardware and software can be problematic, if data is only readable using specific applications and operating system versions that may become incompatible with newer hardware. Applications could be used according to *SaaS* (55) to address these challenges. This would, however, make the availability and user experience of the application dependent on the performance of communication channel. Also, applications may not be available as *SaaS* or a company may not be able to use them due to other restricting factors, such as laws and corporate regulations.

Solution

A *distributed application* (160) comprised of a *user interface component* (175), *processing component* (180), *data access component* (188), and a *stateful component* (168) is hosted in a local static environment of the company as seen in Fig. 6.8. Data handled by the *stateful component* is periodically extracted and replicated to a cloud storage offering.

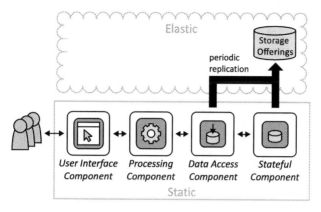

Fig. 6.8 Hybrid backup using an elastic cloud to archive data

Result

Instead of storing the data solely in the static environment, the data is archived and replicated in the cloud environment. Commonly, this process should be executed during times of low utilization, for example, overnight, to avoid an impact on the performance of the rest of the application. If the data throughput of the communication channel is insufficient for the amount of handled data, updates may be shipped on physical storage media to many cloud providers. Legal regulations may have to be considered when using a provider for data archiving purposes. To cope with this challenge, encryption may be used to enable some privacy for the remotely stored data, but this may decrease performance due to the additional encryption and decryption overhead. In addition to storing data in the cloud environment, the application required to access it may also be archived to ensure accessibility of data in the future. For example, an *IaaS* (45) provider could be used to archive an application hosted on a server in form of a virtual server image that can later be deployed on the provider's *elastic infrastructure* (87).

Variations

The decision how often data is replicated to the cloud environment is largely influenced by the requirement how much data may be lost in case of a disaster, i.e., if the backup process is executed nightly, data alterations performed during one day may be lost. If the requirement is that no data may be lost, data in the two environments must be kept in a consistent state. Therefore, the two replicas should be updated at the same time while the communication channel is available. The *hybrid backup* pattern considers the use of a *hybrid cloud* (75) comprised of a private static environment and an elastic cloud. However, the same approach can be followed to integrate two cloud environments. Especially, multiple cloud environments of different providers may be used to increase the availability of backed up data.

Related Patterns

- *Hybrid data* (311): the *hybrid backup* pattern replicates data between two environments. If data should also be hosted exclusively in a cloud environment or if it should be moved there when it is no longer accessed frequently, the *hybrid data* pattern should be considered and can possibly be combined with the *hybrid backup* pattern.
- *Compliant data replication* (231): if the data replica can be updated asynchronously, using messages, the *compliant data replication* pattern describes how these messages may be handled and can possibly be altered if not all of the data stored in the static environment may be replicated to the cloud provider or should be obfuscated during the process.

Known Uses

Archiving services complying with government regulations are a common example for the outsourcing of data. Often, the size of handled data is growing significantly over time and the stored information is accessed seldom. Another use case is the storage of backups in the cloud, for example, offered by Crashplan [229] and Acronis [230]. The above mentioned extraction of complete applications to virtual servers hosted in an *elastic infrastructure* (87) is supported by different *IaaS* (45) providers' import tools, such as the Amazon's VM Import/Export service [231] or the VMware vCenter Converter [232]. Backup and recovery of servers using Amazon AWS [138] is also covered by Elisha [233]. The backup of Oracle 11g databases is described in a separate Amazon report [234]. For file-based backups, Amazon offers a long-term data store called Amazon Glacier [235]. In contrast to its other *blob storage* (112), Amazon Simple Storage Service (S3) [132] storage costs are lower, but data retrieval times may be longer. Stored data may be listed and viewed instantaneously and data retrieval has to be notified in advance, thus, making the offering suitable for long-term backups.

6.3.5 Hybrid Backend

Backend functionality comprised of data-intensive processing and data storage is experiencing varying workloads and is hosted in an elastic cloud while the rest of an application is hosted in a static data center.

How can processing components that experience varying workload and need access to large amounts of data be hosted in an elastic environment while the remainder of the application is hosted in a static environment?

Context

A *distributed application* (160) provides processing functionality that experiences varying workload behavior. Mainly, *static workload* (26) has to be handled, but some processing components experience *periodic workload* (29), *unpredictable workload* (36), or *continuously changing workload* (40). Application components providing the respective processing functionality experiencing varying workload should, therefore, be hosted in an elastic environment. However, these components have to access large amounts of data during their execution making them highly dependent on the availability and the timely access to such data. During the operation of these processing components data, therefore, must be made available to them in an efficient manner. We call the set of data-intensive processing components and the data they rely upon *backend functionality*.

Solution

The processing components experiencing varying workloads are hosted in an elastic cloud together with the data accessed during their operation. Figure 6.9 depicts a *three-tier cloud application* (294) implementing the *hybrid backend* pattern. Processing components in the elastic cloud are triggered from the static environment through asynchronous messages exchanged via message queues provided by a *message-oriented middleware* (136). A *data access component* (188) in the static environment ensures that data required by elastic processing components is stored in storage offerings, commonly, a *relational database* (115), *key-value storage* (119), or *blob storage* (112). The location where this data is stored may then be passed to the elastic processing components during their enactment via messages. Data that is not required by the backend functionality may still be stored in *stateful components* (168) hosted in the static data center.

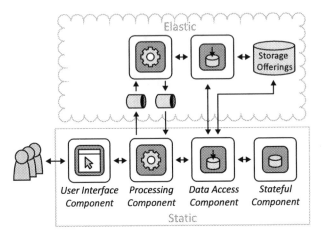

Fig. 6.9 Hybrid backend using a static data center and an elastic cloud

Result

Due to this provisioning of application components in separate environments, the processing component experiencing varying workload may benefit from the elasticity of the cloud. Data accessed by it is either hosted only in the cloud environment or replicated from the static environment. The style of replication used in this case depends on the duration for which the elastic processing components are active, how often they access the same data, and how much of that data is also accessed from the static environment.

If the elastic *processing components* (180) are accessed rarely, storing the data in the elastic environment at all times may be inefficient due to data storage costs. Similar, if the elastic *processing components* handle a specific data element only once, storing it in the elastic cloud may also be inefficient. The same is the case if other application components access large amounts of the processed data, which can results in high data transfer costs. Data transfer costs billed by the cloud providers also have to be considered when making data available to the elastic processing components. In this scope, some cloud providers allow customer to send in physical hard drives, which are then made available in the cloud and sent them back after the processing. In case the processing components are active for longer durations, data may be synchronized continuously between both environments (see related patterns).

Related Patterns
- *Compliant data replication* (231): the above mentioned replication of data between the two environments is described by this pattern with a special focus on automatic data alteration and obfuscation to respect possible legal or corporate regulations.

- *Hybrid processing* (308): if only a small amount of data has to be passed to the elastic *processing component*, it may be included in the message as described by the hybrid processing pattern. This may especially be the case, if the data on which the processing is conducted is offered and maintained by the cloud provider, i.e., a provider for stock market quotes.
- *Batch processing component* (185): .if the elastic processing component is seldom required and results do not have to be available immediately, it may additionally implement the *batch processing component* pattern to delay work-load until processing becomes feasible, for example, due to changing resource costs at a cloud provider.

Known Uses

An example for a *hybrid backend* implementation is the Automotive Simulation Center Stuttgart (ASC-S) [236]. In this use case, *processing components* are hosted on a *community cloud* (71) that is shared among multiple car manufacturers for simulation purposes. Since the simulation workload of a company tends to vary regarding the phase of car development projects, the use of elastic cloud environments is feasible.

Another prominent example for processing data intensively in an elastic cloud setting is the digitalization of the New York Times archives [31, 32] to make articles publicly searchable online [33]. We cover this example in greater in the section for *once-in-a-lifetime workload* (33) describing the workload it generated and the challenges arising from this. Varia [228] covers how applications may be migrated to Amazon Web Services (AWS) [138]. Especially, he points to detailed use cases on backend functionality [237] and data-intensive batch-processing [238].

6.3.6   Hybrid Application Functions

Some application functionality provided by user interfaces, processing, and data handling is experiencing varying workload and is hosted in an elastic cloud while other application functionality of the same type is hosted in a static environment.

 How can arbitrary functionality of an application be distributed among static data centers and elastic clouds best matching its requirements?

Context

Application components comprising a *distributed application* (160) experience varying workloads on all layers of the application *stack: user interface components* (175), *processing components* (180), and *data access components* (188). All of these components provide functionality to the user group of the application, but this user group accesses functionality differently. Some functions are accessed equally at all times resulting in *static workload* (26). Other functions may experience *periodic workload* (29), *unpredictable workload* (36), or *continuously changing workload* (40). While distribution of application components, which this functionality, among different runtime environments would be beneficial to best match workload requirements, components have to be integrated to provide a holistic and seamless user experience. In addition to the workload requirements other issues, such as legal and corporate regulations or requirements on security, privacy, and trust may limit the environments to which an application component may be provisioned.

Solution

Application components are grouped regarding similar requirements and are deployed into best fitting environments as shown in Fig. 6.10. Interdependencies between the components are reduced by exchanging data using asynchronous messaging to ensure *loose coupling* (156). Depending on the accessed function, a load balancer redirects user accesses to the different environments seamlessly.

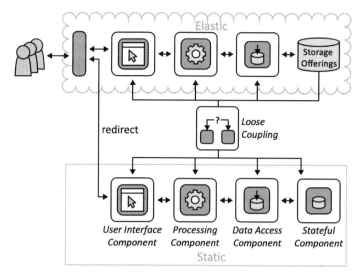

Fig. 6.10 Hybrid UI, processing, and data deployment

Result

Components with similar requirements on elasticity are assigned to the best fitting environments. Regulations and requirements regarding privacy, security, and trust are also considered in this decision. It has to be assured that the application components in the static environment do not influence the components in the elastic environment. This would reduce the beneficial effects of the elastic environments, because dependencies may reduce the ability of the elastic application components to scale out. Influences of application components hosted in different environments are reduced by using *loose coupling* (156) and *eventual consistency* (126) of data replicated between the environments. Therefore, communications between application components across environments boundaries are asynchronous and the state of the same data elements may differ in the environments. Replication of databases residing in different environments should either rely on messaging to propagate updates or should be handled by batch updates that are executed only at certain times. Especially, these concepts enable applications in different environments to be scaled independently. Synchronous access from static environments to the elastic environments may be acceptable, if the elastic environments can scale out to handle the possible workload that may be generated from the static environment. To provide a homogeneous user experience, user accesses are routed to different application components regarding the accessed function.

Variations

In Fig. 6.10, the load balancer handling the assignment of user accesses to different environments is hosted in the elastic environment. As a variation, it may also be hosted in the static environment. However, in this case it has to be ensured that it can scale well enough, i.e., that it can handle significantly large enough number of application component instances to which accesses are assigned. In the scope of multi-tenant applications, described by multi-tenancy patterns (see Sect. 4.4 on Page 208), the requirements of tenants may be different regarding the hosting of application components to different environments. If this is the case, application components may be provisioned in both environments to reflect the requirements of different tenants. Access to components may then be routed differently for every tenant.

Related Patterns
- *Message-oriented middleware* (136): the desired loose coupling between the environments is enabled by exchanging asynchronous messages through message queues. These are provided by an intermediary, the *message-oriented middleware* to make communication partners independent regarding each other's location, availability, and data format.
- *Hybrid processing* (308) and *hybrid data* (311): these patterns describe in detail how processing components and data components residing in different environments can be integrated.
- *Compliant data replication* (231): this pattern describes how data may be replicated between different environments while respecting different levels of privacy, security, and trust using data omission and obfuscation.

Known Uses

Online shops and travel booking sites use elastic environments to handle catalogs of items, fights, hotel info etc. These catalogs can be queried by many users and are scaled according to the current load. In case a booking or buy takes place, the user is redirected to a static environment or a specific cloud provider handling money transfers that also offers the required security.

6.3.7 Hybrid Multimedia Web Application

Website content is largely provided from a static environment. Multimedia files that cannot be cached efficiently are provided from a large distributed elastic environment for high-performance access.

How can non-cacheable content be integrated efficiently in a website that is accessed by a large globally distributed user group?

Context

A *distributed application* (160) provides a website accessed by a large globally distributed user group. While most of the website is comprised of static content, there is also a significant amount of multimedia content, such as videos or music that has to be streamed to users. The static textual content and images can be cached efficiently by cache servers on the Internet [239], the multimedia files are streamed directly to the clients and, thus, are provided from the application.

Solution

The cacheable website content is hosted in a static environment from where it is accessed by users as depicted in Fig. 6.11. It is cached by the users' browser software and by intermediary cache servers. The streaming content is provided by an elastic cloud environment where it is accessed from the application's *user interface component* (175). Effectively, the static content is provided to users' client software and in this static content, the multimedia content is referenced. Retrieval of this streaming content is often handled directly by the users' browser software. Therefore, many application scenarios do not require direct accesses between the application components hosted in the static environment and the streaming content hosted in the elastic environment as the retrieval of data is handled by the client application.

Result

The content that can be cached efficiently does not require the elasticity of a cloud environment as it can be cached elsewhere. It is, therefore, provided by a static infrastructure. The streaming content is only referenced in the cacheable content

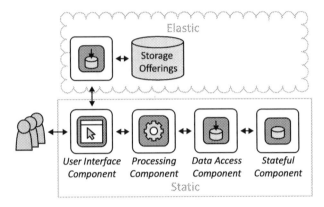

Fig. 6.11 Hybrid multimedia web application residing in an elastic cloud and a static data center

and can often be retrieved directly from client applications. For example, a Web browser of a user is provided with a cached Web site that references multimedia content hosted in the elastic cloud. This multimedia content may then be retrieved directly from the Web browser without any interaction with the *hybrid multimedia web application*. A data access component may be hosted in the elastic environment to encapsulate the data access and to provide an easier interface to the *user interface component* (175) than the storage offerings provide themselves. If the user group accessing the application is globally distributed, the content may further be replicated to various geographic regions using a *content distribution network* (300).

Variations

A *hybrid multimedia web application* may also use two elastic environments, for example, a *private cloud* (66) and a *public cloud* (62) specialized in streaming multimedia content. The decision to use a specific environment is, thus, largely based on its geographic location and its capabilities to stream content efficiently.

Related Patterns

- *Content distribution network* (300): as mentioned above, a content distribution network may be used to globally replicate streaming content in order to serve a globally distributed user group.
- *Hybrid application functions* (320): in case of a *hybrid multimedia web application*, content and application components are assigned to a hosting environment based on the type of data they handle and provide to users. The *hybrid application functions* (320) pattern on the other hand distributes application components based on the functionality they provide and the security assurances required by them as well as the handled data.

Known Uses

The separation of multimedia content from other website content is commonly used in website development. Baron et al. [240] cover different storage solutions based on Amazon storage offerings. One of them considers a web-based *SaaS* (55) application. The authors describe how such an application should use *key-value storage* (119) and *relational databases* (115) for table-centric data and *blob storage* (112) for the integration of large multimedia content. Varia [228] covers application migration to Amazon Web Services (AWS) [138]. Especially, he describes how a web application may be migrated fully or partially to Amazon's cloud [241].

6.3.8 Hybrid Development Environment

A production runtime environment is replicated and mocked in an elastic environment where new applications can be developed and tested.

 How can an application use different computing environments during its development, test, and production stages?

Context

Applications have very different requirements on the runtime environment during their development, test, and production phase. During development, hardware requirements are often uncertain, so hardware resources should be flexible to extend resources if necessary. During the test phase, diverse test systems may be needed to verify the proper functioning of the application on different operating systems or when being accessed using different client software, i.e., different browsers. Large numbers of resources may be required during development and test, for example, to build the application and to perform load tests. During the productive use other factors, such as security and availability may be of greater importance than resource flexibility. These requirements make it desirable to use an elastic environment, for example, a *public cloud* (62) for application development when requirements on availability, privacy, security, and trust are low, but resources are required dynamically. To use different environments and to move developed applications efficiently, multiple conditions should be met. First, *packaging formats* of migrated application components, for example, virtual servers have to be compatible or convertible. Second, an application should find similar *runtime conditions* in each environment to ensure that adjustments to the application are minimal upon transfer. Also, this similarity ensures that test results regarding the application behavior found in the development and test environments are likely to be similar in other environments.

Solution

The production environment of the application is simulated in the development and test environment through the use of equivalent addressing, similar mocking data, and equivalent functionality provided by the environment as shown in Fig. 6.12. An *elastic infrastructure* (87) or an *elastic platform* (91) may be used. Migration of

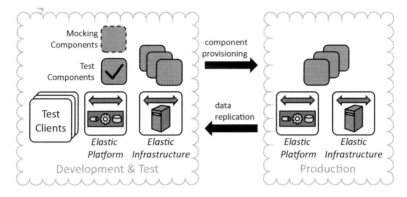

Fig. 6.12   Hybrid development environment and its integration with a production environment

developed applications is ensured through transformation of application components or compatibility of runtimes. In scope of an *elastic infrastructure*, this migration could happen on the level of virtual server images. In scope of an *elastic platform*, application component packages could be moved. Some testing resources are provided exclusively in the development environment to verify the application behavior under different circumstances. These could also be provided using an *elastic infrastructure* or *elastic platform*. For example, multiple virtual server images containing different operating systems and browser software could be provided to flexibly test a developed website.

Result

Hybrid development environments display three essential benefits. First, they can be easily provisioned initially. Second, resources used by the environment can be increased flexibly. And third, diverse test clients can be provided on-demand. Development, test, and production use of the application are performed in the most suitable environments as depicted in Fig. 6.12. Runtime functionality in the development environment should be based on the same implementation and middleware software that is used productively. This functionality subsumes, for example, domain name servers (DNS), message queuing systems, an enterprise service bus, authentication etc. These services may be scaled automatically by the development environment, for example, to ensure minimal influences on load tests. As *distributed applications* (160) are hard to debug, the development environment could offer special interfaces to the development platform services and could provide debug information to the developer [10, 146].

It is important, that the development environment offers similar functionality as the productive environment and also contains similar test data, such as user accounts, data that is queried by the application etc. A subset of productive data can either be replicated to achieve this or dummy data can used to mimics the behavior of the productive systems regarding the amount of data returned by services, the complexity of this data etc. The tests performed in the development environment are often influenced significantly by the sets of test data. Additional to a similar runtime environment, application components to be developed should be mimicked by specific test components as well. A developer may use this functionality to test an application even if certain parts are still being developed. This approach especially useful, if development of application components is distributed among several development teams.

The runtime behavior of the application can be estimated in the development environment by dynamically changing hardware specification and measuring performance. However, final knowledge about the required hardware capabilities may differ, because performance figures can be obfuscated by hardware virtualization and other development environment users sharing the environment. Especially, other virtual servers that share the same physical hardware as the tested application may influence the outcome of load tests.

Variations

There are two approaches to migrate a developed application to the runtime environments. In case an installable application is the desired outcome of the development process, it has to be built in the development environment and is then installed in the productive environment as any other application. However, if the application is developed to contain a certain state, it could be migrated completely to the productive environment. An example for the latter case is a content management systems (CMS) provisioned in the development environment. Different editors use this system to create a website. After development, this website needs to be migrated to a productive environment. In case of migration, the lowest layer of the application stack that is not available in the productive environment forms the migration point. If the website of the above example shall be migrated to a *PaaS* (49) production environment, only the created websites, configuration files, database tables etc. are migrated. If the productive environment is an *IaaS* (45) cloud, the complete CMS software and operating systems could be migrated as a virtual server.

Related Patterns
- *Two-tier cloud application* (290) and *three-tier cloud application* (294): the componentized architecture of these applications makes them very suitable to be created in a *hybrid development environment*.
- *Compliant data replication* (231) and *hybrid data* (311): these two patterns describe how data may be distributed and replicated between two hosting environments. Compliant data replication has an additional focus on the alteration of data during this replication to meet privacy, security, and trust regulations. The same approach may be employed in scope of the *hybrid*

development environment to replicate a smaller subset of productively used data to a *hybrid development environment*. During this replication, data may possibly be obfuscated.

- *Application component proxy* (228): under certain conditions, some productively used application components may be included in tests performed in the *hybrid development environment*. Since these application components are used productively, access to them is, however, likely to be restricted. The *application component proxy* pattern describes a solution to make them accessible in a different environment nevertheless.

Known Uses

Windows Azure [52] natively supports the integration of a development environment running locally on a developer's machine. Developed applications can be executed in this local environment and are afterwards deployed to Windows Azure. After this initial deployment, Windows Azure differentiates between a staging and production phase for deployed application components [242]. Adjustments to application components are made to their staging version, allowing them to be tested in the Azure environment. Then, an immediate switch can be initialized between the productively used application components and those in the staging phase.

CloudBees [46] is a product aiming at the easy development environment setup and flexible resource use. The provider offers ready-to-use development, build, and test environments to customers that can be reserved using a self-service portal. LoadUI [243] is a load test tool that can initiate various requests to an application. It integrates with Amazon EC2 [244] and other *elastic infrastructures* (87) to simulate a larger number of globally distributed clients. T-Systems provides virtual servers to company-internal website developers containing various browser and operating system configuration to test various clients.

Impact of Cloud Computing Properties

7

In Chap. 1, we introduced the basic principles of cloud computing, on-demand self-service, broad network access, pay-per-use, resource pooling and rapid elasticity. In Chaps. 2 and 3, we used a pattern format to describe workloads experienced by cloud applications, the hosting environments they use, and the cloud-specific properties of different cloud offerings in an abstract, vendor-neutral view. Chapter 4 covered patterns on how to deal with these properties in application architectures followed by best practices for managing cloud applications in Chap. 5. Chapter 6 covered compositions of the patterns described in previous chapters to create cloud applications.

Readers are now familiar with the principles and the properties of cloud offerings making cloud computing different from traditional computing. However, we have not explicitly reviewed how the cloud computing properties defined in Sect. 1.1 on Page 3 that are displayed cloud offerings influence the behavior of applications built on top of them on different levels of the application stack introduced in Sect. 2.3 on Page 42. Especially, we have not explicitly discussed how these properties of lower levels of the stack can be mitigated on higher levels so that an application can, for example, display required properties to its users and customers without necessarily requiring the same properties to be displayed at the middleware or infrastructure level. In this chapter, we discuss properties of cloud offerings that can be changed through application design and cloud-specific properties that cannot be mitigated within applications. As a result some properties can be changed and some propagate up to the business level where they have impact on how applications support the business processes and, thus, these properties have impact on the business itself. We will see that it is often unnecessary to mitigate cloud-specific properties on the application level. This is the case, as the impact on the business is less profound than it may seem at first glance.

In this chapter we examine more closely the impact that the cloud-specific properties of cloud offerings have on the levels of the application stack that build

---

All figures published with kind permission of © The Authors 2014. See list of figures.

C. Fehling et al., *Cloud Computing Patterns*,
DOI 10.1007/978-3-7091-1568-8_7, © Springer-Verlag Wien 2014

upon them. We do so by more closely inspecting the properties that are assumed and expressed by the patterns introduced in the chapters before.

Knowing the impacts of these properties and how to mitigate them is important for a range of scenarios:

- **Selecting the right cloud provider.** In this scenario, knowing the impacts of properties abstracted by the patterns enables customers to classify cloud providers and select the right one based on the business needs. Business needs can be mapped to cloud properties that cannot be changed and application architectural patterns can be evaluated to mitigate other properties to support the business needs.
- **Building a cloud infrastructure or platform.** In the *private cloud* (66) scenario knowing the impacts that are produced when selecting different implementation patterns will steer *private cloud* (66) providers to offer the right selection of infrastructures and platforms.
- **Rethink business requirements.** In case a cloud provider offers significantly lower prices while assuring only certain properties that do not directly meet business needs, it may be beneficial to rethink the impact these properties have on the business and if it is feasible to live with them.
- **Build cloud native applications.** Knowing the impact of properties on the infrastructure and platform levels and how to mitigate them on the application level enables application architects and developers to build cloud-native applications that make use of the full potential of the underlying cloud offerings by respecting offering properties in their architecture.

7.1 Cloud Computing Properties on Levels of the Application Stack

Having introduced patterns as a vehicle to describe the properties of cloud offerings and how to deal with them in application architectures, we can now use these patterns to deal with the cloud computing properties on all levels of the application stack. When using a cloud offering it important to understand the key properties that influence the upper levels of the application stack depending on the properties of the chosen lower level implementation. In software engineering for custom on-premise applications, requirements are traditionally propagated *top-down* the application stack as shown in Fig. 7.1.

During this propagation of requirements the requirements of a business usage scenario and its business processes are iteratively refined into application software requirements, middleware requirements and infrastructure requirements. In IT environments, where the whole application stack is fully controlled by the software architect and can, thus, be created in a custom fashion for each application, this approach leads to middleware and infrastructure layers that are very unique and diverse but well suited for the respective applications as they are optimized to meet the specific requirements of the business usage scenario.

In the cloud, however, when using existing *-as-a-Service* offerings this approach tends to be less successful, as the properties of the cloud offerings to be used can typically not be modified as freely as in an on-premise usage scenario.

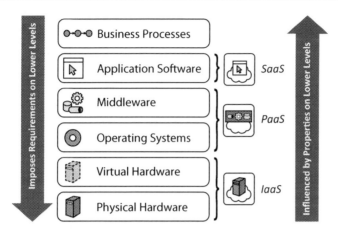

Fig. 7.1 Propagation of requirements in the application stack

This is the case as certain properties of a cloud offering are determined by the design of the offering by the provider. Thus, the homogenization of IT resources aspect of a cloud offering discussed on Page 4 in Sect. 1.1 comes into play here. The task of the software architect is now no longer to specify the requirements for a middleware or infrastructure top-down but to match the application requirements with the properties of the available cloud offerings.

Therefore, the force arises to take a more *bottom-up*-oriented approach into account, which includes identifying the cloud offerings to use that best fit the requirements imposed by the application. Following this approach, the application architecture may then compensate for cloud offerings not fulfilling the requirements. However, not all properties of cloud offerings may be compensated. We, therefore, differentiate between *compensatable* and *pass-through* properties and requirements.

Compensable Properties

Compensable properties are properties that can be mitigated on a given level by applying adequate counter-measures, such as designing the respective level to deal with the property. With compensable properties the cloud customer has to decide whether the required countermeasures, especially, their implementation complexity justify the benefits obtained through selecting the cloud provider. Compensable properties of lower-level cloud offerings may then be adjusted to requirements of the cloud application on higher levels of the application stack by following certain architectural styles that are captured in the patterns by previous chapters of this book. Examples for such compensable properties are:

- **Availability**: if single resources of a cloud provider do not assure an acceptable availability-level, the application can incorporate redundancies and failure-detection in its architecture to cope with this property.

- **Single-tenancy**: this property describes that a cloud middleware component is provided exclusively to one customer. However, despite this property, this component can still be used to build an application that is provided to multiple customers. The single-tenancy property can, therefore, be compensated for in the application by assuring appropriate isolation means between tenants in its architecture.
- **Privacy**: if a cloud resource can be accessed publicly or the cloud provider cannot be trusted to keep data save, encryption and data obfuscation can be used to meet higher-privacy requirements of applications.

Pass-Through Properties

Other properties, however, cannot be compensated in the application architecture and, therefore, pass-through the application stack unchanged. Thus, pass-through properties always "infect" all upper levels and trigger upwards all levels of the application. These properties subsume the following examples:
- **Location**: the physical location where a resource is hosted is restricted by the data centers maintained by a provider. While the customer may be able to choose to provision resources in certain number of geographic regions, these are always fixed by the provider.
- **Legal issues**: laws according to which the resources are offered often depend on the country in which a cloud provider resides and cannot be changed by the application.
- **Multi-tenancy**: if a resource is shared by multiple customers, they cannot provide functionality that guarantees a dedicated environment if this is required.

7.1.1   Downwards-Propagation of Requirements

Applications are built to support business functionality and capabilities that are used in business processes supporting the business model of an enterprise. The business model and subsequently the business processes impose requirements on the applications that implement them. Further requirements may be imposed by business ethics or regulatory bodies. Requirements imposed on an application traverse down through all the levels in the application stack of this application, from the application software level, through the middleware level down to the infrastructure, networks and datacenters. In a cloud usage scenario, i.e., when one or more of the levels in the application stack are obtained from a cloud provider, the offering of the cloud provider must comply with the necessary requirements imposed by the downward-propagation of the requirements on that particular level. For example, a regulatory requirement may be to disallow processing of customer-sensitive data outside of Europe. This requirement will traverse down to the infrastructure level and ultimately becomes a requirement for an *IaaS* (45) cloud provider, if application hosting is to be outsourced to such a provider.

In a traditional scenario using an on-premise data center where full control over the application stack is given, the requirements on a specific level translate into the selection criteria for the required components on that level that fulfill these requirements. In a cloud usage scenario, where control of a part of the application stack is outsourced to a cloud provider it is unfeasible to assume that all requirements on that level are always fulfilled by the cloud provider, because it would significantly limit the number of usable providers. Thus, it is important to check if the properties of the cloud provider fulfill the requirements directly or if they can be mitigated in the application architecture. To understand whether a lacking fulfillment of requirements automatically leads to a dismissal of a provider, we need to understand how properties of lower levels of the application stack propagate upwards.

7.1.2 Upwards-Propagation of Properties

Similar to the downward propagation of requirements from the business and regulatory levels down to the lower levels of the application stack, properties of the lower levels can propagate upwards. It is important for the application of the patterns discussed in this book to understand the implications of the upwards-propagation of properties in a cloud usage context. The cloud usage context in which we operate in this book implicitly assumes that some parts of the application are hosted by a cloud provider. As the cloud provider's business model is centered on resource sharing and, thus, homogenization of IT resources (see Page 4 in Sect. 1.1), the properties of the cloud provider and thus the supported requirements will be fixed or configurable in a very narrow means. Thus, in some cases upper levels in the application stack will be confronted by properties of lower levels that are non-compliant to the requirements imposed on them from their upper levels. In this case properties need to be compensated on that level.

7.1.3 Meet-in-the-Middle for Cloud Properties and Requirements

We argue that business requirements and cloud properties have to *meet in the middle* to obtain an optimal selection of cloud offerings. To meet requirements, pass-through properties should be mapped directly from the top down, while compensable properties have to be carefully considered in the architecture of the cloud application from the bottom up. In this chapter we use the cloud computing patterns to describe both, the properties of cloud offerings as well as requirements imposed by customers using these cloud offerings. We then also use the patterns to describe how to mitigate properties in upper levels of the application stack that are imposed on them by the lower levels when going bottom-up.

7.2   Impact of Core Cloud Properties

In the following we describe the impact of selected cloud properties on the different levels of the application stack and derive suitable mitigation strategies where required. We also describe how these cloud properties influence the application level and business process level when they are not mitigated.

7.2.1   Pay-Per-Use

Pay per use is one of the main requirements that is imposed by cloud consumers on cloud providers on all levels of the stack. From a cloud consumer's view the pay-per-use paradigm ensures that only those resources that are actually used result in costs. The importance of choosing the right granularity of payment units that correspond to a cloud offering is given by the fact that the implementation of that offering should be a black box to the cloud consumer. This is important for the cloud consumer and the cloud provider.

For the cloud consumer this gives an immediate control over the expected costs related to the business objects relevant on the respective level. Thus the cloud consumer does not need to be aware of details of the technical implementation to compute regardless of technical implementation.

For the cloud provider the right granularity of the payment unit and, thus, the black-box nature of the cloud offerings allows optimizing the offering internally without having to reveal details to the consumer and thus can benefit from economies of scale without having to reveal these economies to the cloud consumer.

Impact of Choosing the Right Payment Unit

Depending on the level of the stack, the units on which pay-per-use schemes are based are different. As a rule of thumb they should reflect the business objects processed on that level. Thus, on the business process level, the payment unit should be the number of process instances executed which corresponds for example to the core business object created during the business process. For example, if the business process supported by a cloud offering is a payroll processing process, the unit of payment should be the payroll and the payment scheme should be for example the number of payrolls processed. On the software application level, a suitable payment unit is the number of users of the application that concurrently use a certain functionality. On the middleware level, the payment unit depends on the platform service offered. In case of a processing platform the price model could be the amount of processed requests. In case of a messaging platform the number of messages exchanged and in a storage platform, the number of records stored. On the infrastructure level, the payment unit is the number of computing resources used (i.e. CPU time, bandwidth, or storage capacity).

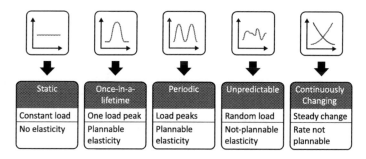

Fig. 7.2 Workloads and elasticity requirements

It is important that the unit of payment reflects the level on which the cloud offering is made. In the payroll example the "number of transactions" or "amount of CPU time used" are technical units that are at lower levels than the offering and, thus, are rather poor candidates for a payment unit as they violate the black box principle and reveal implementation details of the offering that the customer should not be concerned about.

The most important impact of pay-per-use on all levels of the stack is the requirement for rapid elasticity towards the cloud provider. Without elasticity pay per use models are not convenient to achieve by cloud providers. Elasticity enables the provider to adjust the consumed resources according to the load requested by the cloud consumer and assign unused resources to other consumers to improve utilization.

7.2.2 Rapid Elasticity

Elasticity is often provided by an *elastic infrastructure* (87) or an *elastic platform* (91). To be able to offer a pay-per-use pricing scheme, elasticity must be propagated by the cloud offerings to the application level and business process level. The level of required elasticity for an elastic infrastructure or elastic platform as shown in Fig. 7.2 is determined by the workload pattern experienced by an application or a business process. Thus, before defining the elasticity requirements for lower levels, it makes sense to capture the requirements for elasticity on the business level. Depending on the given workload for a business process or application the elasticity level can be determined. Taking this elasticity level into account requirements on the underlying platforms and infrastructures can be stated. Especially with *static workload* (26), elasticity of a cloud environment may not be needed at all.

Fig. 7.3 shows elasticity on the different levels of the application stack from a customer and a provider view. The customer requires the software, platform or infrastructure to behave in an elastic manner, providing exactly the number of resources required. The provider, on the other hand, seeks to balance the load of the

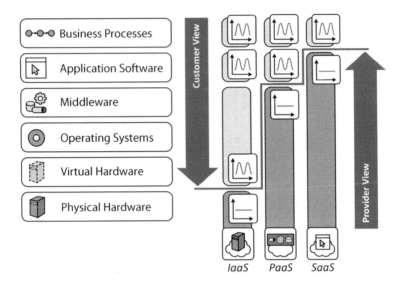

Fig. 7.3 Elasticity on different levels of the stack

different applications on a platform or infrastructure or the different tenants of a software, so that the whole system more or less experiences static workload that best utilizes the resources assigned to the customer(s) by the provider.

Impact of Elasticity on Infrastructure Level

On the infrastructure level, elasticity is achieved by adjusting the infrastructure resources, i.e., power of central processing units (CPU), memory, or hard drive storage to the requirements expressed by the customer. In cloud environments the granularity of adjustment is mostly the virtual server, i.e. to add more processing power or memory a customer has to start new virtual servers, to remove it, the customer has to shutdown virtual servers. In *private clouds* (66) build on common *hypervisors* (101) it is often possible to enlarge or shrink virtual servers to a certain extent, by assigning more or less CPU power or memory to them. However, eventually it will be necessary to start and stop whole machines to achieve elasticity on a large scale. Thus, infrastructure providers implement the *elastic platform* (91) pattern to cope with the required elasticity on the infrastructure level. The impact of building on top of an elastic infrastructure is that the upper levels (platform, application and business) must cope with horizontal scalability described on Page 6 in Sect. 1.2.

Impact of Elasticity on Platform Level

On the middleware level offered as *PaaS* (49), it should be transparent to the customer how elasticity is handled on the lower levels of the application stack.

To cope with this elasticity *PaaS* (49) providers implement the *elastic platform* (91) pattern. The difference between an *elastic platform* (91) and an *elastic infrastructure* (87) regarding the elasticity is that the *elastic platform* commonly shares resources on the middleware level whereas the *elastic infrastructure* only shares resources up to the physical hardware level.

The sharing of resources on the middleware level allows the applications built on the *elastic platform* to abstract from the virtual servers that are below it. This has two advantages: First, application developers do not have to deal with elastically by provisioning and decommissioning virtual servers and deploying their applications on top of them as well as balancing the load across these servers. Second, *PaaS* providers can host multiple applications from different customers on the same *elastic platform* and can dynamically assign processing power to these applications as requested. Providers, thus, balance the load of all applications hosted by the offering without having to start and stop servers when the load of one application changes. The elasticity is transparent to the customer, however to understand why *elastic platforms* of different types often have certain constraints compared to the middleware products found in on-premise usage scenarios it is beneficial to highlight how these platforms are implemented:

When realizing an elastic platform, two general implementation choices are possible:

- Elastic platform using non-elastic infrastructure
- Elastic platform using elastic infrastructure

Realizing an *elastic platform* on a non-elastic infrastructure essentially limits the elasticity of the platform to the use of the maximum resources provided by the infrastructure. However, in case of workload peaks extending the maximum resources that the elastic platform can use, additional resources cannot be assigned, thus, when it is required to deal with such peaks it is advisable to build the *elastic platform* (91) on top of an *elastic infrastructure* (87) where resources of the elastic infrastructure can be assigned to the elastic platform if needed.

Impact of Elastic Infrastructures and Platforms on the Application Level

The impact of an *elastic platform* (91) for application developers is that they have to design their application in a way that it can benefit from the elasticity of the platform. This is true regardless of the type of the platform. In essence this means that the application must be able to scale horizontally with the platform. The requirement to be able to scale horizontally is due to the fact that ultimately, the elastic platform will automatically distribute the application to multiple instances of the middleware installed on multiple virtual servers and will balance the load over these instances.

The same holds true for application components build on top of an *elastic infrastructure* (87) as the application components have to support the simultaneous deployment on multiple virtual servers and the balancing of load across these servers. Thus, applications built on top of *elastic platforms* (91) and *elastic infrastructures* have to be **built for horizontal scalability**: in case of a processing application component, the platform will dynamically distribute requests to multiple instances of the application components deployed on the underlying application servers. Thus, the application component on such a platform should implement the *stateless component* (171) pattern so that individual instances of the components are independent from each other and requests can dynamically be distributed to these instances. Therefore, elasticity and thus pay-per-use do not come for free. Application architectures must carefully manage state to benefit from horizontal up-scaling and down-scaling and, thus, efficient elasticity. In this scope, the *stateful component* (168) and *stateless component* (171) patterns discuss how *session state* – the state of client interaction with an application component and *application state* – the data handled by the application can be managed by application components or by storage offerings as discussed on Page 6 in Sect. 1.2.

Impact of Application Level Elasticity on the Business Level

Elasticity on the application level eventually impacts the business level. Similar to the infrastructure level where infrastructure resources are eventually limited, application resources on a higher level are eventually limited. This limitation can, especially, be present in *private cloud* (66) scenarios, if only a small number of applications share this environment. To realize maximum efficiency and minimal overprovisioning of resources, the elasticity of the underlying applications must be reflected in the business processes. Re-organization of business processes may provide more efficient balancing of load across different applications at different times. This leveling out of workload can prevent peak workloads on multiple applications at the same time, which would require overprovisioning on lower levels of the application stack. Cloud providers, therefore, often promote the execution of business process and, thus, applications during times of low overall demand by offering lower prices during those times while charging higher prices during workload peak times.

For example, a payroll processing business process is executed at fixed times before payrolls need to be sent out at the end of the month. During the rest of the month the resources for payroll processing can be used to drive inventory management. However, the inventory management business process is not available during payroll processing times as this would require overprovisioning of resources to accommodate simultaneous peak times.

7.2.3 Homogenization

Homogenization is one result of the resource pooling cloud property (see Page 4 in Sect. 1.1) that is essential to make any cloud environment economically feasible. Resources can only be shared across multiple applications or tenants if these applications or tenants require the same type of resource. Thus, homogenization of IT resources is of utmost importance and a side effect of the cloud computing properties. Depending on the level in the application stack different types of resources should be standardized for all users of the offering to ensure IT resource homogenization. These standardization efforts are not de jure industry standardization attempts undertaken by many companies, but are performed within one company establishing a *private cloud* (66), a limited number of companies sharing a *community cloud* (71), or by a *public cloud* (62) provider enforcing a certain standard on its customers.

Impact of Standardization on the Infrastructure Level (IaaS)

On the infrastructure level, the infrastructure, such as the type of (virtual) servers, routers, storage and network connections and the underlying hardware and datacenters are standardized. This enables hosted applications to share the hypervisor, networks, storage and all lower levels. Thus, the infrastructure components expose standardized interface in terms of their application programming interfaces (API) as well as in terms of the supported IT resource types they can host, i.e., virtual servers, storage, and networking that have to be used by the upper levels.

Impact of Standardization on the Platform Level (PaaS)

On the platform level, the platform also provides an API to provision and decommission hosted software artifacts depending to the type of runtimes (compute, storage, messaging etc.) supported by the platform. Additionally, the deployment artifacts (application components, record metadata, and queue definitions) must be standardized. This standardization limits the possibilities of how applications can be built compared to a non-standardized way of choosing middleware components. Thus when selecting a cloud platform provider (or building a private cloud platform), it is important to select a set of runtimes that are compliant with the existing and/or intended system architectures in the enterprise.

Impact of Standardization on the Application Level (SaaS)

On the application level, *SaaS* (55) applications have to standardize how new users and tenants are added, removed and how configuration data and content data can be deployed for the application. *SaaS* applications also implicitly standardize the functionality offered to their tenants. Common for all levels is that cloud providers have to provide standardized functionality that is feasible for their intended customers. From a customer's point-of-view, this enforced standardization must offer benefits (such as lower cost, faster time-to-market, managed maintenance...) that outweigh the flexibility disadvantages of using a standardized offering.

Impact of Standardization on the Business Level

Standardization on the lower levels (especially on the application level) ultimately affects the business level. Standardized cloud offerings on higher levels often are limited in customization and, thus, offer less flexibility than home-grown or specially-built applications. In case a standard on a certain level is unsuitable for a cloud customer, this customer can move one level lower in the application stack and implement the level that is not suitable him- or herself. For example, if a *SaaS* (55) customer relationship management (CRM) offering is not flexible enough to accommodate all the configuration requirements for a certain customer, this customer can build a custom CRM on a *PaaS* (49) offering either from scratch or by using COTS (commercial off the shelf) components. If the platform is unsuitable, the customer can use a cloud infrastructure provider to install suitable middleware on which he can build the CRM application. In this case standardization is pushed down the stack resulting in more flexibility but increased effort.

Standardization and Enterprise Architecture Management

When selecting a suitable cloud provider on any of the levels it is insufficient to only examine single applications. A detailed analysis of the application landscape of an enterprise will result in a better assessment on what are the standardized platform or infrastructure components that should be offered by an internal or external cloud provider to be shared within a company. Going up the application stack this assessment becomes more important as standardization higher up in the stack is most efficient as synergies between applications are increased.

7.2.4 Resource Sharing/Multi-Tenancy

One fundamental property of any cloud offering is the underlying principle of resource pooling or sharing as discussed on Page 4 in Sect. 1.1. Depending on the position of the offering in the application stack, different resources are shared. One property that enables resource sharing in commercial cloud offerings is multi-tenancy. Any cloud offering that is provided to multiple customers must ensure the isolation of these customers and, thus, implement multi-tenancy. In the (special) case of a *private cloud* (66) different tenants can be, for example, different departments of a company. Another special case are multiple components of the same tenant on the same underlying cloud offering. In this case two scenarios exist:

- Multiple components share one tenant, i.e., they can access resources of each other without being isolated.
- Multiple components of one tenant behave as if they were components of different tenants and, thus, are isolated against each other.

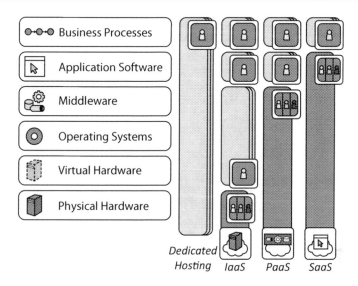

Fig. 7.4   Resource sharing/multi-tenancy on different levels in the stack

Impact of Resource Sharing on the Infrastructure Level

In case of *IaaS* (45) shared resources are the network, the datacenter, the physical hardware its host operating system and the *hypervisor* (101). Multi-tenancy is implemented in the hypervisor that must ensure that virtual servers of one tenant cannot access the virtual servers of another tenant unless explicitly authorized. The same must hold true for storage and network resources that must not be shared among different tenants to ensure isolation.

Everything above the infrastructure level is not explicitly shared and, thus, not isolated by the *IaaS* (45) offering. Fig. 7.4 shows that the levels up to the physical servers managed by a *hypervisor* (101) implement the *tenant-isolated component* (214) pattern, as they are shared among the different tenants but are multi-tenant aware and, thus, isolated. Everything above the hypervisor (starting from the virtual servers) then implements the *dedicated component* (218) pattern, i.e. each tenant gets its own instance of virtual servers, storage, network etc. that they can use.

Note that it is explicitly allowed for one tenant to build a multi-tenant aware platform or a multi-tenant aware application upon its resources obtained from an infrastructure provider. Thus one tenant on the infrastructure level can host multiple tenants again by applying isolation techniques on the upper levels.

Impact of Resource Sharing on the Platform Level

PaaS (49) takes resource sharing higher in the application stack than *IaaS* (45). In a *PaaS* offering the operating system and middleware components are shared among multiple tenants as shown in Fig. 7.4. Thus, they are implemented using the *tenant-*

isolated component (214) pattern. Everything above must then be implemented using the *dedicated component* (218) pattern.

Artifacts deployed on the platform are run in so-called *tenant-spaces* that ensure isolation of these artifacts against artifacts of other tenants. Tenant-spaces are a virtual space that contains all artifacts of one tenant. Isolation again must be on the access level as well as non-functional property level. That is if a provider ensures a certain amount of requests per hour for one application of a tenant, other tenants must not be able to reduce this number of requests by putting workload on their applications.

Depending on the type of runtimes offered in a platform different tenant-spaces that can host different artifacts have to exist:

- In a processing offering the underlying application server must ensure that application components deployed on it do not interfere with other application components of other tenants
- In a storage offering access to stored data must only be granted to the tenant to which the tenant-space in which this data is stored, is assigned.
- In a communication offering, for example, one providing messaging access to queues and topics can only be granted to authorized tenants.

Regarding load-balancing provided by the offering, rules must be separated and isolated among tenants. Again, it is explicitly possible to build multi-tenant aware applications in the tenant-space of one tenant on a platform. The application must then assure proper isolation of tenants on the application level, i.e., it must implement the *tenant-isolated component* (214) pattern.

Using the tenant isolation of the platform level to build *SaaS* (55) applications following the *dedicated component* (218) pattern is also possible. In this case multiple instances of the application level can co-exist in the different tenant spaces of the platform. On the one hand this behavior allows the *SaaS* application developer to reuse the tenant-isolation of the platform, on the other hand the components must be duplicated for each tenant with the known limitations such as higher resource consumption, higher update effort etc.

A mix-and-match of these two approaches, *tenant-isolated components* (214) in one tenant space and *dedicated components* (218) in multiple tenant spaces is also possible. An example for this approach is the common practice to run *processing components* (180) implementing the *dedicated component* (218) pattern on virtual servers and store their state on the storage offering implementing the *tenant-isolated component* (214) pattern.

Impact of Resource Sharing on the Application Level

Resource sharing on the application (component) level is the most efficient way of sharing resources, because it does not require the lower levels of the application stack to be duplicated for each tenant. Thus, all tenants can share the same physical hardware, hypervisor, virtual hardware (if existent), middleware and software components. The impact on resource sharing on the application (component) level is that the relevant application (components) must be developed in a multi-tenant enabled fashion, thus, they have to implement the *tenant-isolated component* (214) pattern.

How multi-tenancy is realized for different application components heavily depends on the type of application component. For databases, for example, different techniques exist. From pushing down isolation to the database platform level by setting up different database schemas or even databases for different tenants. Another technique, where multi-tenancy is realized on the application level, is to introduce a tenant-id field to tables and only allow tenants to create, retrieve, update or delete data that is associated with their tenant-id. The *tenant-isolated component* (214) pattern discusses these approaches in greater detail.

The required isolation for multi-tenancy on the application level can also be pushed down the stack in case it is unfeasible to enable multi-tenancy on the application level. The result is that the application level needs to be duplicated for each tenant. Again, mix-and-match approaches are possible under such conditions where some application components implement multi-tenancy themselves whereas others push it down to the lower (platform and infrastructure) levels.

Impact of Resource Sharing on the Business Level

On the business level the foundations for resource sharing often have to be laid. Whether resource sharing is possible on lower levels or not, heavily depends on the business requirements and accompanying regulations. The business level enables resource sharing on lower levels, by identifying business processes that are supported by the same common applications. On the business level it then has to be identified who is responsible for the shared application. Often, a suitable approach for resource sharing on the business process level is to share the processes (or parts thereof) between different local business units, as they often share the same supporting applications and the processes are implemented in a similar way. Under such conditions, it may make sense to explore if application supporting the business processes can be implemented using configurable *tenant-isolated components* (214).

7.3   Impact of Other Common Cloud Offering Properties

Similar to the cloud computing properties introduced in Sect. 1.1 on Page 3 other common properties of cloud offerings have impact on the levels of the application stack that build upon such cloud offerings. In the following, we examine these properties and their impact on levels building on top of them. These properties immediately originate from the common cloud properties. They are often a result of embracing cloud principles on provider side, however, they can also be found in large-scale systems outside of cloud environments.

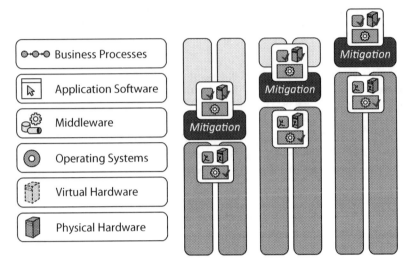

Fig. 7.5 Mitigation of environment-based availability on higher levels of the application stack

The properties we examine for their impact on higher levels are:

- *Environment-based availability* (98) commonly found in cloud computing infrastructure offerings.
- *Eventual consistency* (126) commonly found in cloud storage platforms.
- *At-least-once delivery* (144) of message queues commonly found in cloud communication offerings.

7.3.1   Environment-Based Availability

One success-factor of large-scale public *IaaS* clouds is often their reliance on standard commodity hardware. The result of using standard commodity hardware are lower infrastructure costs [64] but also lower service level agreements (SLA) for individual nodes, i.e., hosted servers than with the service level assured by expensive failsafe hardware that can guarantee availability of individual compute, storage or communication nodes. Therefore, if the availability assurance of a provider used on a lower level of the application stack is *environment-based availability* (98), measures can be taken on higher levels of the application stack to assure *node-based availability* (95) for IT resources hosted on that level. This mitigation of availability assurances on different levels of the application stack is depicted in Fig. 7.5.

Impact of Environment-Based Availability on the Infrastructure Level

As a result some cloud providers that rely on standard commodity hardware and, thus, implement the *environment-based availability* (98) pattern assure the availability of the whole environment and not individual (unreliable) nodes.

In the levels building on top of an infrastructure level with *environment-based availability* (98), precautions need to be taken to mitigate the properties in case low availability of individual nodes is not acceptable for the respective higher level. Such precautions are covered in greater detail by the *watchdog* (260) and the *resiliency management process* (283).

Impact of Environment-Based Availability on the Platform Level

Building an *elastic platform* (91) that guarantees *node-based availability* (95) for platform nodes represented by (virtual) middleware (clusters) that offer the platform runtimes requires intimate knowledge of the properties of the underlying infrastructure. Such a platform requires either an underlying infrastructure with node-based availability or the platform must ensure that the effects of the low availability nodes in an infrastructure with environment-based availability are mitigated in the platform.

Therefore, the platform has to monitor instances of provided middleware and replace failing ones by implementing the *watchdog* (260) pattern. The *resiliency management process* (283) handled by the *watchdog* is enabled by balancing workload among multiple redundant middleware instances of using an *elasticity manager* (250), *elastic load balancer* (254), or *elastic queue* (257). In case the watchdog observes the failure of a middleware instance caused by the lack of availability in one of the underlying infrastructure nodes it replaces the component and possibly notifies the *elastic load balancer* (254) to remove that instance from the balancing strategy.

Impact of Environment-Based Availability on the Application Level

When building a high-available application (component) on top of an offering assuring *environment-based availability* (98) and thus using possibly unreliable individual nodes as no *node-based availability* (95) is assured, the application (component) must be built following a set of guidelines to achieve higher availability in the upper levels of the application stack:

- **Design for failure**. Always assume that application components running on infrastructure nodes or platforms assuring *environment-based availability* (98) can fail at any time and will fail eventually. This can be handled by implementing a *watchdog* (260) on the application level monitoring and replacing application components.

- **Make use of elasticity**. When designing applications that should run on an infrastructure or platform assuring *environment-based availability*, incorporate *elasticity managers* (250), *elastic load balancers* (254), or *elastic queues* (257) in the design or follow the *two-tier cloud application* (290) or *three-tier cloud application* (294) pattern. This enables the application to handle replacements of failing application component more efficiently.
- **Deploy stateless application components on unreliable nodes if possible**. Only deploy application components that follow the *stateless component* (171) pattern on *elastic platforms* (91) or *elastic infrastructures* (87) with *environment-based availability*. This way you can use an *elasticity manager* (250), an *elastic load balancer* (254), or an *elastic queue* (257) easily together with a *watchdog* (260) to balance load over active instances of the application component and replace failing instances automatically. In case a node and the corresponding component fail, its work is lost and can be reassigned to another working node.
- **Use reliable means to store state**. When dealing with *stateless components* (171) hosted on unreliable infrastructure or platforms, the availability of state information becomes even more important than with reliable nodes. As state is completely held in the *stateful components* (168), these components must guarantee high availability. This can be achieved either by replicating state among *stateful components* (168). Challenges in this scope regarding the consistency of handled data are described by the *strict consistency* (123) and *eventual consistency* (126) patterns. Ideally, a cloud application using an environment-based *elastic infrastructure* (87) or *elastic platform* (91) use a provider-supplied storage offering or communication offerings to handle state. For these offerings, providers often assure a high availability for handled data, messages, etc.
- **Use reliable communication**. When distributing workload among unreliable application components use a *message-oriented middleware* (136) or a storage offering together with the *transaction-based processor* (201) or *timeout-based message processor* (204) pattern. These patterns ensure that data is exchanged and processed reliably through message queue or storage offerings, respectively. Data manipulations are only persisted in reliable storage, if the message or data element has been processed successfully. If a processor is unsuccessful, no data is lost, but the processing task is assigned to a replacement.

Impact of Low Availability Applications on the Business Level

In case an application (component) does not follow the guidelines above and, thus, fails this may have severe impact on the business processes using this application (component). In some usage scenarios, this may be acceptable as the overhead of producing a highly available application is not needed.

However, independently of the availability requirements for an application build upon an *elastic infrastructure* (87) or *elastic platform* (91) assuring *environment-based availability* (98) a provisioning of a replacement of the failed application components is necessary after the supporting infrastructure or platform nodes failed. Thus, the application must be designed in a way that a restart is possible which essentially means to sticking to all the guidelines above without the "make use of elasticity" guidelines.

In other usage scenarios, failure of applications can have severe and inacceptable impact on the business. Thus, from a business point of view it is important to mitigate the effects that availability assurances of a cloud provider on the upper levels of the application stack with regard to availability. As the guidelines for making use of elasticity are quite similar with the guidelines for mitigating low-availability, inherently elastic applications can deal with environment-based availability with unreliable nodes as long as they ensure that the state of the application is stored in highly-available storage offerings or communication offerings and separated from the unreliable nodes.

7.3.2 Eventual Consistency

In scope of a cloud offering that uses data replicas internally, *eventual consistency* (126) denotes that multiple reads of data held by the replica may return inconsistent data, i.e., multiple data may be returned even during the absence of intermediate writes between read operations. Eventual consistency is a result of prioritizing *availability* – the storage offering is reachable and functions as expected and *partition tolerance* – the storage offering is resilient towards failures of connection networks over *data consistency* – the data returned by the storage offering is consistent for read operations. The weighting of these properties and why all of them cannot be maximized at the same time is described in the CAP Theorem [67] and the *eventual consistency* (126) pattern. Some cloud providers offer *eventual consistency* for their highly available distributed data stores as they prioritize availability and partition tolerance higher than consistency.

Making data stores highly available is essential when application components deployed on unreliable nodes rely on the availability of the state at any time. In case data stores become very big, or they are built on unreliable nodes, they must be distributed to cope with the data volume or non-availability of individual nodes. Many cloud offerings additionally allow customers to adjust the desired consistency on a per-request basis.

Impact of Eventual Consistency on the Application Level

Application components that access *eventually consistent* (126) storage offerings must ensure that this eventual consistency is properly dealt with. If eventual consistency is not mitigated on the application level this has impact on the consistency of the results computed by the application. Multiple reads of data, for example, do not ensure that all obtained data was of the most up-to-date version. Thus, application components accessing *eventually consistent* data sources may retrieve obsolete data and, therefore, can only produce "eventually consistent" views and interpretations on that data. The *data abstractor* (194) pattern can be used in this scope to present abstracted views on inconsistent data to users of the application that hide data inconsistencies.

In cases, where inconsistent data cannot be passed-through to the business level, the *data access component* (188) pattern can be used with multiple strategies on how to mitigate eventual consistency, i.e., through version numbers. An introduction of *strict consistency* (123) on higher levels of the application stack may, however, reduce the ability of the application itself to assure the partition tolerance property, even though the storage offering assures it.

Impact of Eventual Consistency on the Business Level

If *eventual consistency* (126) cannot be mitigated on the application level, applications that build upon eventually consistent data stores will produce only eventually consistent views on that data for the business level. However, in many situations eventually consistent views are unproblematic as *strict consistency* (123) is not required by the business usage scenario anyways. Offering eventual consistency on the business level may require fundamental rethinking of how data is presented, but on the other hand is more often possible than one would initially think.

For example, if it is not essential for a Web shop to display the exact number of available items but only if items are available in general. A consistent view of the number of available items is not needed. Thus, using the *data abstractor* (194) pattern along with an eventual consistent data store backing the Web shop increases availability and still provides the necessary information. When using an eventually consistent data store, conditions can arise where a customer orders a product that is no longer available. In these cases compensation-based recovery of a purchase is needed and the customer must be notified that an error occurred. However, these are special cases and in summary occur less frequent than a large-scale Web shop would be unavailable due to the lack of availability by a strictly consistent data store. The *data abstractor* (194) pattern discusses data representations that inherently support eventual consistency in greater detail as well as gives more examples for business usage scenarios in which they may be applied.

In essence, eventual consistent data stores can impact the business level and require compensation-based recovery, however the gained availability may be beneficial and outweigh the problems arising due to eventual consistency. In the end it is a business-centric decision to balance the tradeoff between availability and consistent view on data.

7.3.3 At-Least-Once Messaging

Closely related to the discussion of *eventual consistency* (126) is the behavior that some cloud messaging offerings provide. As the cloud providers often built the *message-oriented middleware* (136) on a distributed eventually consistent data store to assure availability, the provided message queues do not guarantee *exactly-once–delivery* (141), but display *at-least-once delivery* (144).

Impact of At-Least-Once Delivery on the Application Level

At-least-once delivery (144) of messages has severe impacts on the application level messages may be delivered multiple times, a situation that has to be handled by the application. Thus, the message-processing application component must ensure that the fact that a message may be delivered multiple times does not affect application functionality or the state handled by the application. Two approaches to handle duplicate messages exist that are discussed in greater detail by the *idempotent processor* (197) pattern:

- **Use unique message identifiers.** When an application component receives a message it must check whether it has already received a message with the same identifier ID and discard it. However, when the consuming application component is distributed and, thus, instantiated multiple times, the overhead of coordinating the IDs in a distributed setting may be unfeasible.
- **Idempotent component.** The consuming application component retrieves messages and treats them as jobs handled with idempotent functionality, i.e. if a job is performed multiple times it will not lead to a different result as if it were performed only once. This requires messages to contain data that can be handled in an idempotent way. In a banking scenario it is beneficial to have a "modify balance" message to contain the new balance instead of the delta value, as this message can be executed multiple times without doing harm.

Impact of At-Least-Once Delivery on the Business Level

In case *at-least-once delivery* (144) cannot be mitigated on the application level it will have impact on the business level. This means that, for example, business processes that are triggered by a message that may appear multiple times will be executed multiple times. Under certain conditions, for example, if no additional cost occurs when executing a process multiple times or if actions can be easily undone this may be unproblematic. Therefore, it has to be specified on the business level if *at-least-once delivery* (144) of messages is acceptable or not. In some usage scenarios it may be more efficient, for example, due to reduced costs to accidentally execute certain activities twice once in a while, for example, sending duplicate letters to customers than to mitigate the effects of seldom occurring duplicate messages on the application level.

References

1. Hohpe, G., Woolf, B.: Enterprise Integration Patterns: Designing, Building, and Deploying Messaging Solutions. Addison-Wesley, Boston http://www.eaipatterns.com/ (2003)
2. Gamma, E., Helm, R., Johnson, R.: Design Patterns. Elements of Reusable Object-Oriented Software. Addison-Wesley, Boston (1994)
3. Mell, P., Grance, T.: The NIST definition of cloud computing. National Institute of Standards and Technology, Online http://csrc.nist.gov/publications/nistpubs/800-145/SP800-145.pdf (2011). Accessed June 2013
4. Hanmer, R.: Patterns for Fault Tolerant Software. Wiley, Chichester (2007)
5. Fehling, C., Leymann, F., Mietzner, R., Schupeck, W.: A collection of patterns for cloud types, cloud service models, and cloud-based application architectures. Technical report, University of Stuttgart (2011)
6. Smith, D.M.: Hype cycle for cloud computing. Technical report, Gartner (2012). http://www.gartner.com/id=2102116
7. Riempp, G., Gieffers-Ankel, S.: Application portfolio management: a decision-oriented view of enterprise architecture. Inf. Syst. E-Bus. Manag. 5, 359–378 (2007)
8. IBM Global Technology Services: Data center operational efficiency best practices. http://www.ibm.com/connect/ibm/attachments/N287879Q74060L27/IBM_DC_Study.pdf (2012)
9. Weerawarana, S., Curbera, F., Leymann, F., Storey, T., Ferguson, D.F.: Web Services Platform Architecture: SOAP, WSDL, WS-Policy, WS-Addressing, WS-BPEL, WS-Reliable Messaging, and More. Prentice Hall, Upper Saddle River (2005)
10. Krafzig, D., Banke, K., Slama, D.: Enterprise SOA. Prentice Hall, Indianapolis (2005)
11. Chappel, D.: Enterprise Service Bus. O'Reilly, Sebastopol (2004)
12. Alexander, C.: The Timeless Way of Building. Oxford University Press, New York (1980)
13. Alexander, C.: A Pattern Language: Towns, Buildings, Construction. Oxford University Press, New York (1978)
14. Buschmann, F., Meunier, R., Rohnert, H., Sommerlad, P., Stal, M.: Pattern-Oriented Software Architecture. Wiley, Chichester (1996)
15. Fowler, M.: Patterns of Enterprise Application Architecture. Addison-Wesley, Boston (2002)
16. Yahoo! Design Pattern Library:. http://developer.yahoo.com/ypatterns/
17. Petre, M.: Why looking isn't always seeing. Commun. ACM 38, 33–44 (1995)
18. Amazon.com: Elastic Compute Cloud (EC2). http://aws.amazon.com/ec2/. Accessed June 2013
19. Rackspace: Cloud servers. http://www.rackspace.com/cloud/public/servers/. Accessed June 2013
20. VMware: vCloud Suite. http://www.vmware.com/products/datacenter-virtualization/vcloud-suite/. Accessed June 2013
21. Google: Google App Engine. http://developers.google.com/appengine/. Accessed June 2013
22. Bauer, E., Adams, R.: Reliability and Availability of Cloud Computing. Wiley-IEEE Press, Hoboken (2012)
23. Allspaw, J.: The Art of Capacity Planning: Scaling Web Resources. O'Reilly, Sebastopol (2008)
24. Barroso, L.A., Hölzle, U.: The datacenter as a computer: an introduction to the design of warehouse-scale machines. Synth. Lect. Comput. Architect. 4, 1–45 (2009)

25. Fehling, C., Leymann, F., Rütschlin, J., Schumm, D.: Pattern-based development and management of cloud applications. Future Internet 4, 110–141 (2012). doi:10.3390/fi4010110
26. Fehling, C., Leymann, F., Retter, R., Schumm, D., Schupeck, W.: An architectural pattern language of cloud-based applications. In: Proceedings of the 18th Conference on Pattern Languages of Programs (PLoP), Portland, (2011)
27. Fehling, C., Ewald, T., Leymann, F., Pauly, M., Rütschlin, J., Schumm, D.: Capturing cloud computing knowledge and experience in patterns. In: Proceedings of the 5th IEEE International Conference on Cloud Computing (CLOUD), Honolulu, (2012)
28. Varia, J.: The total cost of (non) ownership of web applications in the cloud. Technical report, Amazon Web Services (2012)
29. Amazon.com: Amazon EC2 Reserved Instances. http://aws.amazon.com/ec2/reserved-instances/. Accessed June 2013
30. Belissent, J.: T-city provides valuable lessons for smart cities: which future is now?. http://blogs.forrester.com/jennifer_belissent_phd/12-03-10-t_city_provides_valuable_lessons_for_smart_cities_which_future_is_now (2012). Accessed June 2013
31. Gottfrid, D.: Self-service, prorated supercomputing fun!. http://open.blogs.nytimes.com/2007/11/01/self-service-prorated-super-computing-fun/ (2007). Accessed June 2013
32. Gottfrid, D.: The New York Times Archives + Amazon Web Services = TimesMachine. http://open.blogs.nytimes.com/2008/05/21/the-new-york-times-archives-amazon-web-services-timesmachine/ (2008). Accessed June 2013
33. The New York Times: Time machine. http://timesmachine.nytimes.com/
34. T-Systems: Resources delivered straight from the cloud dynamic services for infrastructure. http://www.t-systems.com/servlet/contentblob/t-systems-2012.de/en/umn/uti/803284_1/blobBinary/120224_DSI-ps.pdf (2012)
35. OpenStack: Open Stack open source cloud computing software. http://www.openstack.org/. Accessed June 2013
36. OpenNebula Project: Opennebula: the open source solution for data center virtualization. http://opennebula.org/. Accessed June 2013
37. Eucalyptus Systems: Cloud computing software from eucalyptus. http://www.eucalyptus.com/. Accessed June 2013
38. Amazon.com: Amazon Simple Queue Service (Amzon SQS). http://aws.amazon.com/sqs/. Accessed June 2013
39. WSO2: WSO2 Stratos Live. http://stratoslive.wso2.com/
40. Metasonic AG: http://www.metasonic.de/
41. RunMyProcess: http://www.runmyprocess.com/
42. Cordys: My business platform. http://www.cordys.com/. Accessed June 2013
43. T-Systems: Making SAP-supported business processes secure and flexible dynamic services for SAP® solutions.. http://www.t-systems.com/umn/uti/803272_1/blobBinary/120229_DS4SAPSol-ps.pdf (2012)
44. Salesforce: Force. http://www.force.com/. Accessed June 2013
45. Salesforce: CRM software & online CRM system. http://www.salesforce.com/. Accessed June 2013
46. CloudBees: How it works. http://www.cloudbees.com/platform-overview.cb. Accessed June 2013
47. Microsoft: Office Online Services – Microsoft Office 365. http://www.office365.com. Accessed June 2013
48. IBM: IBM SmartCloud for social business. http://www.lotuslive.com/. Accessed June 2013
49. Google: Google Apps for Business. http://apps.google.com. Accessed June 2013
50. Deutsche Telekom: Business marketplace. http://apps.telekomcloud.com/
51. National Institute of Standards and Technology (NIST): Cloud computing synopsis and recommendations. http://www.nist.gov/customcf/get_pdf.cfm?pub_id=911075 (2012). Accessed June 2013
52. Microsoft.: Windows Azure. http://www.windowsazure.com/
53. Amazon.com: Elastic Beanstalk. http://aws.amazon.com/elasticbeanstalk/. Accessed June 2013
54. VMware: ESXi and ESX info center. http://www.vmware.com/products/vsphere/esxi-and-esx/. Accessed June 2013

55. Amazon.com: Virtual Private Cloud (VPC). http://aws.amazon.com/vpc/. Accessed June 2013
56. Google: Apps for Government. http://www.google.com/enterprise/apps/government. Accessed June 2013
57. Apache Foundation: ServiceMix. http://servicemix.apache.org/. Accessed June 2013
58. IBM: WebSphere. http://www.ibm.com/software/websphere/. Accessed June 2013
59. T-Systems: Connecting virtualized it resources with the cloud. http://www.t-systems.com/solutions/uti/983844 (2012). Accessed June 2013
60. Apache Foundation: Deltacloud. http://deltacloud.apache.org/. Accessed June 2013
61. Apache Foundation: Apache libcloud. http://libcloud.apache.org/. Accessed June 2013
62. Jclouds: http://www.jclouds.org/
63. Barroso, L.A., Dean, J., Hölzle, U.: Web search for a planet: the Google cluster architecture. IEEE Micro. 23, 22–28 (2003)
64. Vishwanath, K.V., Greenberg, A., Reed, D.A.: Modular data centers: how to design them? In: Proceedings of the 1st ACM Workshop on Large-Scale System and Application Performance (LSAP), Indianapolis, (2009)
65. Vishwanath, K.V., Nagappan, N.: Characterizing cloud computing hardware reliability. In: Proceedings of the 1st ACM Symposium on Cloud Computing (2010)
66. Miller, R.: Failure rates in Google data centers. http://www.datacenterknowledge.com/archives/2008/05/30/failure-rates-in-google-data-centers/ (2008). Accessed June 2013
67. Gilbert, S., Lynch, N.: Brewer's conjecture and the feasibility of consistent, available, partition-tolerant web services. ACM SIGACT News 33, 51–59 (2002)
68. Brewer, E.: CAP twelve years later: how the "rules" have changed. IEEE Comput. Mag. 45, 23–28 (2012)
69. Ramakrishnan, R.: CAP and cloud data management. IEEE Comput. Mag. 45, 23–28 (2012)
70. Abadi, D.J.: Consistency tradeoffs in modern distributed database system design. IEEE Comput. Mag. 45, 23–28 (2012)
71. Baremetalcloud: Dedicated servers. http://www.baremetalcloud.com/. Accessed June 2013
72. Fielding, R.T., Taylor, R.N.: Principled design of the modern web architecture. ACM Trans. Internet Tech. 2(2), 115–150 (2002)
73. Apache Foundation: Apache Tomcat. http://tomcat.apache.org/. Accessed June 2013
74. WSO2: Stratos. http://wso2.com/cloud/stratos/
75. Wasson, C.S.: System Analysis, Design, and Development: Concepts, Principles, and Practices. Wiley, Hoboken (2005)
76. Leymann, F., Roller, D.: Production Workflow: Concepts and Techniques. Prentice Hall, Upper Saddle River (1999)
77. Amazon.com: Amazon EC2 Service Level Agreement. http://aws.amazon.com/ec2-sla/ (2008). Accessed June 2013
78. Goldberg, R.P.: Architecture of virtual machines. In: Proceedings of the Workshop on Virtual Computer Systems, New York, (1973)
79. Goldberg, R.P.: Architectural principles for virtual computer systems. Ph.D. thesis, Harvard University (1972)
80. Goldberg, R.P.: Virtual machines: semantics and examples. In: Proceedings IEEE International Computer Society Conference (1971)
81. IBM: System Z. http://www.ibm.com/systems/z/. Accessed June 2013
82. VMware: Workstation. http://www.vmware.com/products/workstation/. Accessed June 2013
83. VMware: Player. http://www.vmware.com/products/player/. Accessed June 2013
84. Citrix Systems: Xen. http://xen.org. Accessed June 2013
85. Microsoft: Hyper-V Server. http://www.microsoft.com/hyper-v-server/. Accessed June 2013
86. Red Hat: Kernel based virtual machine (KVM). http://www.linux-kvm.org/. Accessed June 2013
87. Oracle: VirtualBox. http://www.virtualbox.org/. Accessed June 2013
88. Oracle: JAVA. http://www.java.com/. Accessed June 2013
89. JBoss Community: JBoss ESB. http://www.jboss.org/jbossesb. Accessed June 2013
90. VMware: CloudFoundry. http://www.cloudfoundry.com/. Accessed June 2013
91. Cormen, T.H., Leiserson, C.E., Rivest, R.L., Stein, C.: Introduction to Algorithms. MIT Press, Cambridge (2009)

92. Dean, J., Ghemawat, S.: Mapreduce: simplified data processing on large clusters. Commun. ACM 51, 107–113 (2008)
93. Varia, J.: Cloud architectures. Technical report, Amazon Web Services, June 2008
94. Amazon.com: Amazon Elastic MapReduce (Amazon EMR). http://aws.amazon.com/elasticmapreduce/. Accessed June 2013
95. Apache Foundation: Apache Hadoop. http://hadoop.apache.org/
96. Microsoft: Windows Azure HDInsight. http://www.hadooponazure.com/
97. The application/json Media Type for JavaScript Object Notation (JSON). http://www.json.org/ (2006). Accessed June 2013
98. Apache Foundation: Couchdb. http://couchdb.apache.org/. Accessed June 2013
99. Internet Engineering Task Force (IETF), HTTP Extensions for Web Distributed Authoring and Versioning (WebDAV). http://www.webdav.org/specs/rfc4918.pdf (2007)
100. Microsoft: Common Internet File System (CIFS) Protocol Specification. http://download.microsoft.com/download/a/e/6/ae6e4142-aa58-45c6-8dcf-a657e5900cd3/[MS-BRWS].pdf June 2012
101. Microsoft: Windows Azure Drives. http://www.windowsazure.com/en-us/develop/net/fundamentals/cloud-storage/. Accessed June 2013
102. Amazon.com: Amazon Elastic Block Store (EBS). http://aws.amazon.com/ebs/. Accessed June 2013
103. Amazon.com: Amazon Simple Storage Service (S3). http://aws.amazon.com/s3/. Accessed June 2013
104. Amazon.com: Amazon CloudFront. http://aws.amazon.com/cloudfront/
105. Microsoft: Blob (Binary Large Object) Storage. http://www.windowsazure.com/en-us/home/features/data-management/
106. Codd, E.F.: A relational model of data for large shared data banks. Commun. ACM 13, 377–387 (1970)
107. Database language sql. ANSI/ISO/IEC, Database Language SQL, International Standard (IS) (1999)
108. Silberschatz, A., Korth, H.F., Sudarshan, S.: Database System Concepts. McGraw-Hill Professional, New York (2010)
109. Elmasri, R., Navathe, S.: Fundamentals of Database Systems. Addison Wesley, Upper Saddle River (2010)
110. IBM: DB2 database software. http://www.ibm.com/software/data/db2/. Accessed June 2013
111. Oracle: Database 11g. http://www.oracle.com/products/database/. Accessed June 2013
112. Oracle: MySQL. http://www.mysql.com/. Accessed June 2013
113. Microsoft: SQL Server. http://www.microsoft.com/sqlserver/. Accessed June 2013
114. Amazon.com: Amazon EC2 Running IBM. http://aws.amazon.com/ibm/. Accessed June 2013
115. Amazon.com: Oracle and AWS. http://aws.amazon.com/oracle/. Accessed June 2013
116. Amazon.com: Amazon Relational Database Service (Amazon RDS). http://aws.amazon.com/rds/. Accessed June 2013
117. Microsoft: SQL Azure. http://www.windowsazure.com/en-us/home/features/data-management/. Accessed June 2013
118. Jayasinghe, D., Malkowski, S., Wang, Q., Li, J., Xiong, P., Pu, C.: Variations in performance and scalability when migrating n-tier applications to different clouds. In: Proceedings of the IEEE International Conference on Cloud Computing (CLOUD), Washington DC, (2011)
119. Tiwari, S.: Professional NoSQL. Wrox, Hoboken (2011)
120. Sadalage, P.J., Fowler, M.: NoSQL Distilled: A Brief Guide to the Emerging World of Polyglot Persistence. Addison-Wesley, Upper Saddle River (2012)
121. Apache Foundation: Cassandra. http://cassandra.apache.org/. Accessed June 2013
122. 10gen: Mongodb. http://www.mongodb.org/. Accessed June 2013
123. Amazon.com: SimpleDB. http://aws.amazon.com/simpledb/. Accessed June 2013
124. Amazon.com: Dynamo. http://aws.amazon.com/dynamodb/. Accessed June 2013
125. Microsoft: Windows Azure Table. http://download.microsoft.com/download/3/B/1/3B170FF4-2354-4B2D-B4DC-8FED5F838F6A/Windows%20Azure%20Table%20-%20Dec%202008.docx (2008)

126. Chang, F., Dean, J., Ghemawat, S., Hsieh, W.C., Wallach, D.A., Burrows, M., Chandra, T., Fikes, A., Gruber, R.E.: Bigtable: a distributed storage system for structured data. Technical report, Google. http://research.google.com/archive/bigtable.html (2006)
127. Tanenbaum, A.S., van Steen, M.: Distributed Systems Principles and Paradigms, 2nd edn. Prentice Hall, Upper Saddle River (2006)
128. Bernstein, P.A., Newcomer, E.: Principles of Transaction Processing. Morgan Kaufmann, San Francisco (2009)
129. Gray, J., Reuter, A.: Transaction Processing – Concepts and Techniques. Morgan Kaufmann, San Francisco (1993)
130. Pritchett, D.: Base: an acid alternative. ACM Queue 6, 48–55 (2008)
131. Vogels, W.: Eventually consistent. Commun. ACM 52, 40–44 (2009)
132. Amazon.com: Amazon Simple Storage Service FAQs: what data consistency model does Amazon S3 employ? http://aws.amazon.com/s3/faqs/#What_data_consistency_model_does_Amazon_S3_employ
133. Shlomo Swidler: Read-after-write consistency in Amazon S3. Online, 10 2009. http://shlomoswidler.com/2009/12/read-after-write-consistency-in-amazon.html (2009). Accessed June 2013
134. Domain names – concepts and facilities. http://tools.ietf.org/html/rfc1034 (1987)
135. Hartpence, B.: Packet Guide to Routing and Switching. O'Reilly, Sebastopol (2011)
136. Odom, W.: CCNA INTRO Exam Certification Guide. Cisco Press (2003)
137. Deal, R.: Cisco Router Firewall Security. Cisco Press, Indianapolis (2004)
138. Amazon.com: Amazon Web Services (AWS). http://aws.amazon.com/
139. Amazon Web Services: Overview of Security Processes. Amazon.com. http://aws.amazon.com/articles/1697 (2008). Accessed June 2013
140. Microsoft: Windows Azure Messaging. http://www.windowsazure.com/en-us/home/features/messaging/
141. Apache Foundation: Apache camel. http://camel.apache.org/
142. IBM: WebSphere MQ. http://www.ibm.com/software/integration/wmq/
143. Apache Foundation: ActiveMQ. http://activemq.apache.org/
144. Web services reliable messaging (ws-reliablemessaging) version 1.2. http://docs.oasis-open.org/ws-rx/wsrm/v1.2/wsrm.html (2009). Accessed June 2013
145. Hapner, M., Burridge, R., Sharma, R., Fialli, J., Stout, K.: Java Message Service. Sun Microsystems, 901 San Antonio Road Palo Alto, CA 94303 U.S.A., 1.1 edition. http://download.oracle.com/otn-pub/jcp/7195-jms-1.1-fr-spec-oth-JSpec/jms-1_1-fr-spec.pdf (2002). Accessed June 2013
146. Chappell, D.A., Monson-Haefel, R.: Java Message Service. O'Reilly, Sebastopol (2000)
147. Amazon.com: Amazon Simple Notification Service FAQs: how many times will a subscriber receive each message? http://aws.amazon.com/sns/faqs/#44
148. Extensible markup language (xml) 1.0. http://www.w3.org/TR/xml/ (2006). Accessed June 2013
149. SOAP version 1.2. http://www.w3.org/TR/soap/ (2007). Accessed June 2013
150. Cheesman, J., Daniels, J.: UML Components: A Simple Process for Specifying Component-Based Software. Addison-Wesley, Boston (2001)
151. Eeles, P., Cripps, P.: The Process of Software Architecting. Addison-Wesley, Upper Saddle River (2009)
152. Daigneau, R.: Service Design Patterns: Fundamental Design Solutions for SOAP/WSDL and RESTful Web Services. Addison-Wesley, Upper Saddle River (2011)
153. Youngs, R., Redmond-Pyle, D., Spaas, P., Kahan, E.: A standard for architecture description. IBM Syst. J. 38, 32–50 (1999)
154. Varia J.: Architecting for the cloud: best practices. Technical report, Amazon Web Services, May 2010
155. Zimmermann, O., Milinski, S., Craes, M., Oellermann, F.: Second generation web services-oriented architecture in production in the finance industry. In: Companion to the 19th annual ACM SIGPLAN Conference on Object-oriented Programming Systems, Languages, and Applications (OOPSLA), Vancouver, (2004)

156. Zimmermann, O., Doubrovski, V., Grundler, J., Hogg, K.: Service-oriented architecture and business process choreography in an order management scenario: rationale, concepts, lessons learned. In: Companion to the 20th Annual ACM SIGPLAN Conference on Object-oriented Programming, Systems, Languages, and Applications (OOPSLA), San Diego, (2005)

157. T-Systems: Process & service platform flexible business processes from the cloud. http://www.t-systems.com/innovations/uti/824042 (2012)

158. Web services business process execution language version 2.0. http://docs.oasis-open.org/wsbpel/2.0/OS/wsbpel-v2.0-OS.html (2007). Accessed June 2013

159. Business process model and notation (BPMN) version 2.0. http://www.omg.org/spec/BPMN/2.0/ (2011)

160. Web services description language (WSDL) version 2.0. http://www.w3.org/TR/wsdl20/ (2007)

161. Fielding, R.T.: Architectural styles and the design of network-based software architectures. Ph.D. thesis, University of California (2000)

162. Rodriguez, A.: Restful web services: the basics. Technical report, IBM developerWorks. https://www.ibm.com/developerworks/webservices/library/ws-restful/ (2008). Accessed June 2013

163. Tatnall, A. (ed.): Web Portals: The New Gateways to Internet Information and Services. IGI Publishing, Hershey (2005)

164. Google: Google Web Toolkit. http://developers.google.com/web-toolkit/. Accessed June 2013

165. Garrett, J.J.: Ajax: a new approach to web applications. http://www.adaptivepath.com/ideas/ajax-new-approach-web-applications (2005). Accessed June 2013

166. Yahoo!: Yahoo pipes. http://pipes.yahoo.com/pipes/

167. Yahoo!: Yahoo widgets. http://widgets.yahoo.com/

168. Mahemoff, M.: Ajax Design Patterns. O'Reilly, Sebastopol (2006)

169. Gross, C.: Ajax Patterns and Best Practices. Apress, Berkeley (2006)

170. Chappell, D.: The windows azure programming model. http://www.windowsazure.com/en-us/develop/net/other-resources/white-papers/ (2010). Accessed June 2013

171. Amazon.com: Amazon EC2 spot instances. http://aws.amazon.com/ec2/spot-instances/

172. Henderson, C.: Building Scalable Web Sites: Building, Scaling, and Optimizing the Next Generation of Web Applications. O'Reilly, Sebastopol (2006)

173. Fowler, M.: Data access routines. IEEE Software 20, 96–98 (2003)

174. Chong, F., Carraro, G.: Architecture strategies for catching the long tail. Technical report, Microsoft. http://msdn.microsoft.com/en-us/library/aa479069.aspx (2006)

175. San Francisco Municipal Transportation Agency (SFMTA): SFpark. http://sfpark.org. Accessed June 2013

176. Mizonov, V., Manheim, S.: Windows azure queues and windows azure service bus queues – compared and contrasted. http://msdn.microsoft.com/en-us/library/windowsazure/hh767287.aspx. Accessed June 2013

177. Perry, M., Balachandran, M., Plata, J., Solano, P., Thomas, P.: MQSeries Programming Patterns. IBM Redbook. http://www.redbooks.ibm.com/redbooks/pdfs/sg246506.pdf

178. Abbott, M.L., Fisher, M.T.: The Art of Scalability: Scalable Web Architecture, Processes and Organizations for the Modern Enterprise. Addison-Wesley, Upper Saddle River (2009)

179. Leymann, F., Fehling, C., Mietzner, R., Nowak, A., Dustdar, S.: Moving applications to the cloud: An approach based on application model enrichment. Int. J. Cooperative Info. Syst. 20(3), 307–356 (2011). doi:10.1142/S0218843011002250

180. National Oceanic and Atmospheric Administration: National digital forecast database (NDFD) simple object access protocol (SOAP) web service. http://graphical.weather.gov/xml/. Accessed June 2013

181. Jacobs, D., Aulbach, S.: Ruminations on multi-tenant databases. In: Proceedings of the Conference on Business, Technology, and Web, Aachen, (2007)

182. Guo, C.J., Sun, W., Huang, Y., Wang, Z.H., Gao, B.: A framework for native multi-tenancy application development and management. In: The 9th IEEE International Conference on

E-Commerce Technology and the 4th IEEE International Conference on Enterprise Computing, E-Commerce, and E-Services, Tokyo, (2007)

183. WSO2: WSO2 Cloud Services Gateway. http://wso2.com/cloud/connectors/services-gateway/. Accessed June 2013

184. Chappell, D.A.: Introducing OData: Data Access for the Web, the cloud, mobile devices, and more. Microsoft Whitepaper, May 2011

185. Microsoft: How to use the service bus relay service. http://www.windowsazure.com/en-us/develop/net/how-to-guides/service-bus-relay/. Accessed June 2013

186. Topology and orchestration specification for cloud applications version 1.0. http://docs.oasis-open.org/tosca/TOSCA/v1.0/csd04/TOSCA-v1.0-csd04.html (2012). Accessed June 2013

187. DMTF Cloud Management Working Group: Cloud Infrastructure Management Interface (CIMI) Model and RESTful HTTP-based Protocol. http://dmtf.org/sites/default/files/standards/documents/DSP0263_1.0.1.pdf (2012). Accessed June 2013

188. IEEE: Cloud profiles working group (CPWG). http://standards.ieee.org/develop/wg/CPWG-2301_WG.html. Accessed June 2013

189. IEEE: Intercloud working group (ICWG). http://standards.ieee.org/develop/wg/ICWG-2302_WG.html. Accessed June 2013

190. Opscode: Chef. http://www.opscode.com/chef/

191. Puppet Labs: It automation software for system administrators. http://puppetlabs.com/

192. RightScale: Cloud management. http://www.rightscale.com/products/cloud-management.php

193. Scalr: Features. http://scalr.net/features/

194. Amazon.com: Auto Scaling. http://aws.amazon.com/autoscaling/

195. Microsoft: The autoscaling application block. http://msdn.microsoft.com/en-us/library/hh680892.aspx (2012)

196. Menasce, D.A., Almeida, V.A.F.: Capacity Planning for Web Services: Metrics, Models, and Methods. Prentice Hall, Upper Saddle River (2001)

197. Microsoft: Overview of Windows Azure traffic manager. http://msdn.microsoft.com/en-us/library/windowsazure/hh744833.aspx. Accessed June 2013

198. Amazon.com: Amazon CloudWatch. http://aws.amazon.com/cloudwatch/. Accessed June 2013

199. Douglass, B.P.: Real-Time Design Patterns: Robust Scalable Architecture for Real-Time Systems. Addison-Wesley, Boston (2002)

200. Murch, R.: Autonomic Computing. IBM Press/Prentice Hall, Upper Saddle River (2004)

201. Hill, Z., Li, J., Mao, M., Ruiz-Alvarez, A., Humphrey, M.: Early observations on the performance of windows azure. In: Proceedings of the 19th ACM International Symposium on High Performance Distributed Computing, Chicago, (2010)

202. ParaleapTechnologies: Elasticity-as-a-service for Windows Azure. http://www.paraleap.com/

203. Hull, S.: 5 things toxic to scalability. http://www.iheavy.com/2011/08/26/5-things-are-toxic-to-scalability/ (2011). Accessed June 2013

204. Hoff, T.: Strategy: guaranteed availability requires reserving instances in specific zones. http://highscalability.com/blog/2011/12/28/strategy-guaranteed-availability-requires-reserving-instance.html (2011). Accessed June 2013

205. Humble, J., Farley, D.: Continuous Delivery: Reliable Software Releases Through Build, Test, and Deployment Automation. Addison-Wesley, Upper Saddle River (2010)

206. Guest S.: Patterns for cloud computing. slideshare.net/simonguest/patterns-for-cloud-computing (2009)

207. The PHP Group: PHP: Hypertext preprocessor. http://www.php.net/. Accessed June 2013

208. Microsoft: Active Server Pages (ASP). http://msdn.microsoft.com/en-us/library/aa286483.aspx

209. Apache Foundation: Http server project. http://httpd.apache.org/. Accessed June 2013

210. Microsoft: Internet information services (IIS). http://www.iis.net

211. Oracle: Java EE reference at a glance. http://www.oracle.com/technetwork/java/javaee/documentation/. Accessed June 2013

212. Hypertext transfer protocol – HTTP/1.1. http://tools.ietf.org/pdf/rfc2616.pdf (1999)

213. Akamai: HD network. http://www.akamai.com/html/solutions/hdnetwork.html. Accessed June 2013
214. Nygren, E., Sitaraman, R.K., Sun, J.: The Akamai network: a platform for high-performance internet applications. ACM SIGOPS Oper. Syst. Rev. 44, 2–19 (2010)
215. CloudFlare: CloudFlare is the next-generation CDN. http://www.cloudflare.com/features-cdn. Accessed June 2013
216. Dreibelbis, A., Hechler, E., Mathews, Bill., Oberhofer, M., Sauter, G.: Information service patterns, part 4: Master data management architecture patterns. Technical report, IBM developerWorks. http://www.ibm.com/developerworks/data/library/techarticle/dm-0703sauter/ (2007)
217. Ferguson, N., Schneier, B.: Practical Cryptography. Wiley, New York (2003)
218. Kahate, A.: Cryptography and Network Security. Tata McGraw-Hill, New Delhi (2003)
219. Hatzelhoffer, L., Humboldt, K., Lobeck, M., Wiegandt, C.-C.: Smart City in Practice: Innovation Lab Between Vision and Reality. Jovis Verlag, Berlin (2012)
220. Hatzelhoffer, L., Humboldt, K., Lobeck, M., Wiegandt, C.-C.: Smart City konkret – Eine Zukunftswerkstatt in Deutschland zwischen Idee und Praxis. Jovis Verlag, Berlin (2012)
221. Amazon.com: AWS Case Study: Ooyala. http://aws.amazon.com/de/solutions/case-studies/ooyala/ (2011). Accessed June 2013
222. Amazon.com: AWS case study: Washington Post. http://aws.amazon.com/solutions/case-studies/washington-post/. Accessed June 2013
223. Dropbox: http://www.dropbox.com
224. StorSimple: http://www.storsimple.com/
225. Tate, J., Lucchese, F., Moore, R.: Introduction to Storage Area Networks. IBM, red book edition, Online (2006)
226. Farley, M.: StorSimple solution for cloud-integrated enterprise storage. StorSimple Whitepaper. http://www.storsimple.com/Portals/65157/docs/StorSimple_CES_%20White_Paper_Rev1_3.pdf (2012)
227. Gladinet: http://gladinet.com/
228. Varia, J.: Migrating your existing applications to the cloud – a phase-driven approach to cloud migration. Technical report, Amazon Web Services (2010)
229. Crashplan: Online backup and storage. http://www.crashplan.com/. Accessed June 2013
230. Acronis: Acronis online backup. http://www.acronis.com/homecomputing/products/online-backup/index.html. Accessed June 2013
231. Amazon.com: VM import/export. http://aws.amazon.com/ec2/vmimport/. Accessed June 2013
232. VMware: vCenter Converter. http://www.vmware.com/products/datacenter-virtualization/converter/. Accessed June 2013
233. Elisha, S.: Backup and recovery approaches using Amazon web services. Technical report, Amazon Web Services. http://media.amazonwebservices.com/AWS_Backup_Recovery.pdf (2012). Accessed June 2012
234. Amazon Corporate IT Team: Amazon.com leverages the AWS cloud for database backups. Technical report, Amazon. http://media.amazonwebservices.com/AWS_Amazon_Oracle_Backups.pdf (2012)
235. Amazon.com: Amazon Glacier. http://aws.amazon.com/glacier/
236. Automotive Simulation Center Stuttgart (ASC-S): http://www.asc-s.de/
237. Amazon Web Services: Migration scenario: Migrating backend processing pipeline to the aws cloud. http://media.amazonwebservices.com/CloudMigration-scenario-backend-processing.pdf (2010)
238. Amazon Web Services: Migration scenarios: Batch processing. http://media.amazonwebservices.com/CloudMigration-scenario-batch-apps.pdf (2010)
239. Wessels, D.: Web Caching. O'Reilly, Sebastopol (2001)
240. Baron, J., Schneider, R.: Storage options in the AWS cloud: use cases. Technical report, Amazon Web Services (2010)
241. Amazon Web Services: Migration scenarios: Web application architecture. http://media.amazonwebservices.com/CloudMigration-scenario-wep-app.pdf (2010)

242. Chappell, D.A.: Introducing Windows Azure. http://www.windowsazure.com/en-us/develop/net/other-resources/white-papers/ (2010). Accessed June 2013
243. SmartBear: loadUI. http://www.loadui.org/
244. SmartBear: Testing in the cloud. http://www.loadui.org/Distribution/load-testing-in-amazon-cloud.html (2012). Accessed June 2013

Index

A

Abstraction, 195
Access isolation, 208
ACID, 124, 146, 202
Acknowledgement, 145, 149, 204
Activity, 265
AJAX. *See* Asynchronous Java Script
    and XML (AJAX)
Application component, 228. *See also*
    Component
Application state, 172
Approximation, 195
As a service
    infrastructure, 45
    platform, 49
    software, 55
Asynchronous communication, 136, 175, 235
Asynchronous Java Script and XML
    (AJAX), 178
At-least-once delivery, 144, 354
Atomicity, 124
Automated management, 7
Availability, 82, 194
    environment-based, 98, 349
    node-based, 95

B

Backup, 111
Batch processing, 185
Binary large object (BLOB), 112
Blob storage, 112
Block device, 110
Block storage, 110
BPMN. *See* Business Process Model and
    Notation (BPMN)
Business continuity, 314
Business logic tier, 291, 295

Business Process Model and Notation
    (BPMN), 165, 183, 264
Business resiliency, 314

C

Caches, 173, 301, 312, 323
CAP. *See* Consistency, availability, and
    partitioning tolerance (CAP)
Capital expenditures (CAPEX), 4, 23
Change tendency, 195
Client-side consistency, 200
Cloud
    customer, 3
    hybrid, 75
    -native application, 5
    offering, 3
    outsourced private, 67
    private, 66
    properties, 3
    provider, 3
    public, 62
    resource, 3
    virtual private, 67, 69
Cloud application
    properties, 5
    three-tier, 294
    two-tier, 290
Cloud computing properties, 3
Cloud offering
    communication, 131
    processing, 100
    storage, 109
Cloud properties, 3
    compensable, 333
    pass-through, 334
    upwards-propagation, 336
Cluster, 170

Collapsed sub process, 265
Communication
    asynchronous, 136, 175, 235
    overhead, 181
    synchronous, 236
Compensable properties, 333
Competing consumer, 108
Compliance, 231
Component
    batch processing, 185
    data access, 188
    dedicated, 218
    health, 283
    processing, 180
    proxy, 228
    shared, 210
    stateful, 168
    stateless, 171
    tenant-isolated, 208, 214
    user interface, 175
Component version, 275
Configurability, 177, 182
Configuration, 175, 247
    managed, 247
Consistency, 83, 194
    client-side, 200
    eventual, 126, 352
    strict, 123
Consistency, availability, and partitioning
    tolerance (CAP), 83, 194
Content distribution network, 300
Continuously changing workload, 40
Coupling
    loose, 156
    tight, 136, 155

D
Data abstraction, 194
Data access, 188
Database, 115
Data replication, 231
Data store, 266
Data tier, 291, 295
Data volume isolation, 208
Decommission, 4
Dedicated component, 218
Degradation, 272
Delivery
    at-least-once, 144, 354
    exactly-once, 141
    guaranteed, 138
    timeout-based, 149
    transaction-based, 146

Distributed application, 160
Distributed systems, 155
Distribution, 6
Divide and conquer, 108
Domain model, 120
Duplicate reads, 292
Durability, 125

E
Economies of scale, 5
Elastic infrastructure, 87
Elasticity, 5, 6, 267, 275, 339
    load balancer, 254
    management, 240, 267
    manager, 250
    queue, 257
Elastic platform, 91
Elastic scaling, 25
Encrypted channel, 134
Encryption, 305
End event, 265
Enterprise service bus (ESB), 157
Environment-based availability, 98, 346
ESB. *See* Enterprise service bus (ESB)
Event
    end, 265
    message, 264
    start, 264
    timer, 264
Eventual consistency, 126, 349
Exactly-once delivery, 141
Exclusive event-based gateway, 264
Exclusive gateway, 265
Execution environment, 104
Experienced workload, 24

F
Failure, 260, 283
Failure resiliency, 240
Feature, 271
Feature flag, 271
File system, 112
File transfer, 138
Firewall, 133
Folder, 112
Freshness control, 301

G
Gateway
    exclusive, 265
    exclusive event-based, 264
    parallel, 266

Growing workload, 40
Guaranteed delivery, 141

H
Hard drive, 110
Health, 283
Heartbeat, 96, 261, 283
High availability, 260
Homogenization, 340
Horizontal scalability, 6, 155
Hot pool, 97, 263
Hybrid
    application functions, 320
    backend, 317
    backup, 314
    cloud, 75
    data, 311
    development environment, 326
    multimedia web application, 323
    processing, 308
    user interface, 304
Hypervisor, 101
    type 1, 101
    type 2, 101

I
IaaS. *See* Infrastructure as a Service (IaaS)
Idempotent semantic, 198
Inconsistency detection, 198
Inconsistent view, 292
Infrastructure as a Service (IaaS), 45
Integration, 75, 234
Isolated state, 6
Isolation, 125
    access, 208
    data volume, 208
    performance, 208
IT resources, 3

K
Key-value storage, 119

L
Lane, 266
Law, 217, 218
Layer, 161
Lazy loading, 274
Load balancer, 11, 254
Loose coupling, 7, 156

M
Managed configuration, 247
Management processes, 240, 264
    elasticity, 267
    feature flag, 271
    resiliency, 283
    standby pooling, 279
    update transition, 275
MAPE, 270
Map reduce, 106
Mean time between failures (MTBF), 97
Mean time to recovery (MTTR), 97
Measured service, 4
Message, 136
    duplicity, 141, 142
    event, 264
    filter, 199
    queue, 137
    sequence, 138
    start event, 264
Message mover, 225
Message-oriented middleware, 136
Middleware, 43, 49, 104
Middleware version, 275
MTBF. *See* Mean time between failures
        (MTBF)
MTTR. *See* Mean time to recovery (MTTR)
Multi-component image, 206
Multimedia, 323
Multi-tenancy, 208, 345

N
Networking, 132
Network partition, 83, 123, 127
NIST, 3
Node-based availability, 95
None start event, 264
NoSQL, 121

O
Obfuscation, 222
Offering, 3
    communication, 131
    processing, 100
    storage, 109
Once-in-a-lifetime workload, 33
On-demand, 4
Operating system, 43, 49
Operational expenditures (OPEX), 4, 23
Outsourced private cloud, 66
Overprovisioning, 24

P

PaaS. *See* Platform as a Service (PaaS)
Parallel gateway, 266
Paravirtualization, 102
Partitioning tolerance, 194
Pass-through properties, 334
Pattern, 9, 10
Pay-per-use, 4, 336
Performance isolation, 208
Periodic workload, 29
Pipes-and-filters, 138, 162, 182, 183
Platform as a Service (PaaS), 49
Polling, 248
Pool, 266
Portal, 177
Portlets, 177
Predicted workload, 24
Presentation tier, 291
Privacy, 66
Private cloud, 66
Processing
    component, 180
    timeout-based, 204
    transaction-based, 201
Production, 329
Progress bar, 195
Propagation of properties
    upward, 336
Propagation of requirements
    downward, 335
Properties
    compensable, 333
    pass-through, 334
    upwards-propagation, 336
Provider adapter, 243
Provision, 4
Provisioning
    over, 24
    under, 24
Proxy, 228
Public cloud, 62
Pub-sub, 137
Pushing, 248

Q

Queue, 137, 257

R

Rapid elasticity, 5, 337
Regulation, 217, 218

Relational database, 115
Replica, 123, 126
Requirements, downward propagation, 335
Resiliency, 11, 275, 283
Resource pool(ing), 4
REST, 172, 174
Restricted data access, 222
Robust, 161
Router, 132, 133
Row-based tenant isolation, 215

S

SaaS. *See* Software as a Service (SaaS)
SAN. *See* Storage area network (SAN)
Scalability, 6
    horizontal, 6, 155
Scaling
    elastic, 25
    horizontal, 6
    out, 6, 106, 250, 254, 257
    static, 24
    up, 6
    vertical, 6
Scatter–gather, 108
Security, 66
Security regulations, 66
Self-
    configuration, 269
    healing, 269
    management, 269
    service, 4
Sequence flow, 265
Service level agreements (SLA), 56
Session state, 6, 172
Shared component, 210
Shrinking workload, 40
SLA. *See* Service level agreements (SLA)
Software as a Service (SaaS), 55
Spill-over, 76
Staging, 329
Standby, 279
    list, 279
Start event
    message, 264
    none, 264
    timer, 264
State
    application, 6, 172
    session, 6, 172
Stateful, 6, 168
Stateful component, 168

Stateless, 6, 166, 171, 190
Stateless component, 171,
Static scaling, 24
Static workload, 26
Storage
    blob, 112
    block, 110
    key-value, 119
Storage area network (SAN), 313
Strict consistency, 123
Sub-process, 265
    collapsed, 265
Summarization, 195
Switch, 133
Synchronous communication, 175, 236

T
Table-based tenant isolation, 215
Tenant-isolated component, 214
Tenant isolation, 208
    row-based, 215
    table-based, 215
Tier, 161
    business logic, 291, 295
    data, 291, 295
    presentation, 291, 294
Tight coupling, 136
Timeout-based delivery, 149
Timeout-based message processor, 204
Timer, 264
Time-slot, 279
Traffic light, 195
Transaction, 124, 125
Transaction-based delivery, 146
Transaction-based processor, 201
Trust, 66

U
Underprovisioning, 24
Unpredictable workload, 36
Update, 275
    transition, 275
Upwards-propagation of properties, 335
User interface, 175

Utilization, 23, 267
    continuously changing, 40
    equal, 26
    grow, 40
    once-in-a-lifetime, 33
    peak, 29
    periodic, 29
    shrink, 40
    static, 26
    unpredictable, 36

V
Version, 275
    application component, 275
    middleware, 275
    update, 240
Vertical scaling, 6
Virtualization, 102
    para-, 102
Virtual local area networks (VLAN), 132, 133
Virtual networking, 132
Virtual private cloud, 66, 69
Virtual private networks (VPN), 68, 132, 134
Visibility
    timeout, 149, 204
    window, 149, 204
VLAN. *See* Virtual local area networks
    (VLAN)
VPN. *See* Virtual private networks (VPN)

W
Watchdog, 260
Web role, 184
Worker role, 184
Workload, 3, 5, 23
    continuously changing, 40
    experienced, 24
    growing, 40
    once-in-a-lifetime, 33
    periodic, 29
    predicted, 24
    shrinking, 40
    static, 26
    unpredictable, 36

Printed in the United States
By Bookmasters